THE LANGUAGE OF CANAAN

THE LANGUAGE OF CANAAN.

Metaphor and Symbol in New England
from the Puritans to the Transcendentalists

Mason I. Lowance, Jr.

HARVARD UNIVERSITY PRESS
Cambridge, Massachusetts
and London, England
1980

Publication of this book has been aided by a grant from the
Andrew W. Mellon Foundation.

Library of Congress Cataloging in Publication Data

Lowance, Mason I.   1938-
  The language of Canaan.

  Includes bibliographical references and index.
  1. American literature — New England — History and
criticism. 2. Puritans — New England.
3. Transcendentalism (New England) 4. Bible —
Language, Style. 5. Christian art and symbolism.
I. Title.
PS243.L6   810'.9'15   79-21179
ISBN 0-674-50949-8

For Susan,
Susan Radcliffe, and Margaret Elizabeth
and
dedicated to the memory
of
Lawrance Thompson

Preface

The "language of Canaan" is a phrase that refers to the prophetic and metaphorical language used by God's chosen people when they talk of the kingdom of God and its realization in the last days. It was employed by the Puritans in the sixteenth and seventeenth centuries to describe the language the saints will use when the kingdom has been established. The phrase thus refers at once to a prophetic vocabulary available to contemporary saints as they speak of the future and to the mode of discourse to be enjoyed by those saints when the Scripture promises are fulfilled. The language of Canaan is specifically identified with the Protestant exegetical tradition but did not always enjoy the conventional and valued associations that its prominent use in this book would suggest. Biblical figures were a source of prophetic enthusiasm for the nonconformist saints, whose interpretation of Scripture as a major source of God's revealed will added complexity to their plain and direct way of expressing holy truth.

It is important to understand that history for the New England Puritans was believed to be a related series of divinely inspired events, so that the guiding hand of Providence might be perceived in the drama of human experience. The record of these historical events—the Bible—and the language employed in its composition became for the Puritans a rich source for describing their own contemporary history. The Bible became the most prominent source of literal and metaphorical examples to illustrate providential intervention in human affairs, and its prophetic language became a primary vehicle through which later events of contemporary history might be comprehended and explained. The expression of historical developments in the language of the Bible became a means of associating the experience of New England with literal, historical movements in the past record of ancient Israel. Moreover, it provided the Puritans with a method for predicting future historical events, since all human history was ultimately contained between the creation in Genesis and the judgment in Revelation. The prophetic language of Canaan was essentially the language of biblical revelation and eschatology, to which the events of all human history might be related through proper exegesis of scriptural metaphor and symbol. In this book I will attempt an explanation of this complex process and will examine its development over time in New England from the Puritan uses of biblical "types" and "figures" through the eighteenth century and on to the work of the transcendentalists.

The English background for American symbolic expression is especially important in this context, since two fundamental traditions arise as dominant patterns of symbolism in New England writing of the seventeenth century and each had its origin in Continental and English Protestantism. First, eschatological and prophetic symbolism found throughout religious writings in seventeenth-century New England, from the prophetic proclamations of John Cotton to the chiliasm of Increase Mather, had originals in the Scripture commentary of millennial theologians like Joseph Mede and Thomas Brightman, English writers whose works were well known to the New England Puritans.

A second prominent pattern emerging from an examination of symbolic writing among the Puritans is the influence of a single book of Scripture on exegesis in old and New England. The Canticles, or Song of Solomon, became the point of dispute among Protestant theologians who were attempting to determine the correct way in which the promises of Scripture might be understood by those citizens of the elect nation who had inherited the blessing of ancient Israel. The imagery of Canticles, however, was sensual and erotic; how could the content of this work in any way be understood literally and still have meaning for the holy mission of New England's providential "errand into the wilderness"? John Cotton tried to answer this question in *A Briefe Exposition of the Whole Book of Canticles* (London, 1642) by arguing that the Canticles were not only acceptable in the traditional context of Protestant interpretation, which had emphasized a literal rather than an allegorical reading of the Bible, but that they were indeed the central way God had found to reveal to man's understanding the complexities of his love. However, Cotton argued, in order to comprehend the mysteries of divine love, we must be willing to allow God to accommodate himself to our understanding allegorically or spiritually. Although Cotton was himself following the example of earlier and contemporary English Protestant writers like Mede and Brightman, he effectively opened the floodgates for American symbolic expression and made available to the poet Edward Taylor an imaginative concept around which he would organize the sermon sequence known as *Christographia*. Many of Taylor's highly symbolic meditative poems use the Canticles as a Scripture text from which arguments assuming the extensive use of metaphor and prophetic typology in the conversion experience are advanced by the poet.

As a prophetic language, the language of Canaan is closely associated with eschatology and millennialism. Samuel Mather demonstrated the systematic ordering of God's principles of revelation in his *Figures or Types of the Old Testament* (1683), a book that had demonstrable influence on Taylor and Cotton Mather. Much of this study is concerned with symbolic expression in its peculiarly prophetic role, with particular emphasis placed on the development of millennial and eschatological symbols derived from the biblical process of typological foreshadowing and antitypical fulfillment. Scriptural and traditional foundations were amplified in the writings of Increase and Cotton Mather, Thomas Shepard, Samuel Sewall, and Jonathan Edwards. The prophetic expression of the Great Awakening was in turn modified by the epic poet Joel Barlow, who provided a transition to the nineteenth-century writers of the American Renaissance. By the 1840s, eschatological and prophetic images were found throughout nature so that one was able to understand figural expression not only through the words and word pictures that appear in the Bible but also through the seemingly more direct revelation of the divine principle in the activities of the natural world. The epistemological continuities between Edwards, Emerson, and Thoreau make their association in the history of American ideas more plausible than their philosophical differences might at first suggest. The utopian design of much nineteenth- and twentieth-century American writing owes a great debt to the symbolic language of New England Puritanism, and the present study focuses on the continuity of millennial expression from the late sixteenth century to the American Civil War.

For permission to use previously published materials in a substantially altered form, I am grateful to the Johnson Reprint Corporation for portions of chapter 4, which were adapted from the introduction to Samuel Mather's *Figures or Types of the Old Testament* (New York, 1969); to the Princeton University Press for sections of chapter 6, originally published in Earl Miner's *Literary Uses of Typology from the Late Middle Ages to the Present* (Princeton, 1977); to the University of Massachusetts Press for permission to use portions of essays on Cotton Mather and Jonathan Edwards that were published in Sacvan Bercovitch's *Typology and Early American Literature* (Amherst, 1972); and to Sanford Marovitz, who edited a special issue of the *American Transcendental Quarterly* in which portions of chapter 11 appear. To Charles Mignon of the University of Nebraska I owe a special debt for permitting me to publish portions of the Edward Taylor sermon notebook that he is currently editing and for generously giving time and advice in the correction of my transcripts from that important recent discovery.

I am indebted to the National Endowment for the Humanities for a fellowship during the spring of 1977 and to the director and staff of the American Antiquarian Society in Worcester, Massachusetts, where for several years I have enjoyed privacy, courtesy, and the free use of early American resources. The Huntington Library in San Marino, California, provided two summers of excellent research opportunities and generous support. To the American Philosophical Society I owe thanks for a grant during the summer of 1977, when I traveled to the British Museum to investigate the Canticles tradition and its place in English Protestant writing of the seventeenth century. The librarians at the Bodleian, Oxford University, and the British Museum were extremely helpful when time ran short. Similarly, Marjorie Wynne and the staff of the Beinecke Library, Yale University, have offered me every possible assistance. The Research Council of the University of Massachusetts has provided several kinds of aid, from xerography and typing grants to microfilm funding, and the National Humanities Institute of Yale University gave me time and space for bringing it all together during 1977-78. Terry Rumble, Kim Kwaak, and Susan Proctor turned clutter into clarity.

Finally, I should like to thank my colleagues Thomas Davis, Sacvan Bercovitch, Everett Emerson, Barbara Lewalski, Milton Stern, Christopher Jedrey, Charles Mignon, Kenneth Silverman, Alan Heimert, and Jules Chametzky, all of whom have either listened patiently, read portions of the book in various stages of draft, or both. To David Watters, I owe special thanks for editing with me Increase Mather's *The New Jerusalem* for the *Proceedings of the American Antiquarian Society* and for intelligent and perceptive criticism throughout. William Goodman's courtesy and understanding are equaled by his perception and skill as an editor. Lawrance Thompson, a gifted teacher, provocative scholar, and devoted friend, aroused and nurtured my longstanding interest in literary and religious symbolism. To Susan, Margaret Elizabeth, and Susan Radcliffe, the simplicity of a dedication is hardly enough to repay the many personal sacrifices that accompany the writing of a book, from time not spent together to toleration of bad moods and moments of enthusiasm when they had no reason to feel either. But the meaning is there all the same, the "spirit" behind the "letter," a loving appreciation for understanding as *The Language of Canaan* moved from initial conception to final form.

Contents

THE LANGUAGE OF CANAAN

INTRODUCTION

The iconoclasm of the New Model Army was not vandalism, it was artistic criticism; neither Cromwell's soldiers nor the New England
ministers could perceive anything beautiful in the sermons of John
Donne or the stained glass which they tossed upon rubbish heaps; both
alike kept out the light . . . The supreme criterion of the style was, in-
escapably, the doctrine of means; metaphors were more prized than
antitheses, similes more admired than assonances, because they were
better instruments for convincing the mind and moving the passions.
Scripture itself used earthly similitudes, comparisons and parables, "to
convey truth to us under sensible things, things that wee can feele,
because that we are led with senses in this life."

> —Perry Miller, *The New England Mind:*
> *The Seventeenth Century*

T HE PURPOSE of this book is to explore modes of metaphorical
        expression in New England literature from the Puritan
        settlements of early seventeenth century to the later symbolic
writings of the "American Renaissance," particularly the literature of the
transcendentalists Ralph Waldo Emerson and Henry David Thoreau.
My method is historical and analytical, and the structure of the book's
argument is chronological. The examination of symbolic habits of mind
among New England Puritans suggest a continuity of thinking with
earlier English Puritanism and illustrates the influence of Puritanism on
later American writing. The final chapters are designed to explore the
extensions of Puritan figuralism into nineteenth-century forms as they
demonstrate a clear continuity in the American understanding of
language. Everett Emerson reminds us, "Like it or not, Americans have
a Puritan heritage, and to cope with it requires an understanding of it."[1]

One of the most neglected aspects of that heritage has been the influence of the Puritan way of reading Scripture and the Book of Nature
upon later New England writers like Thoreau and Robert Frost. Only
recently, in studies like Sacvan Bercovitch's *The Puritan Origins of the
American Self* (New Haven: Yale University Press, 1975) and Lawrance
Thompson's *Robert Frost: Years of Triumph* (New York: Holt, Rinehart,
and Winston, 1973) have we come to understand the complexities of
metaphorical writing in New England and the continuities of this process from the earliest American literature to the poetry and fiction of the
nineteenth and twentieth centuries, though we have long assumed the

1

connections between the "elect nation," the "city upon a hill," the "errand into the wilderness," and the imperial designs of "manifest destiny." This study explores the rhetorical strategies and historical transformations of language linking these important ideological abstractions to the writers who conceived them and to scripture origins.

The book's title suggests a particular aspect of exegesis and rhetoric among the New England Puritans. However, the literary problem out of which the topic grew involves much broader concerns. The examination of the role of typology and figuralism of a few selected theologians in the seventeenth and eighteenth centuries is only a fragment of the larger investigation of the role of metaphor and symbol in American literature from the Puritans to the American Renaissance. This book has been designed to establish the foundations of the Puritan understanding of prophetic biblical figures and types and to relate that understanding to American metaphorical writing from the Puritans to the transcendentalists. From such a reconstructed foundation, it has been possible to infer how Puritan epistemology influenced symbolic modes in American literature during the nineteenth century and to issue some corrective notions about the role of Puritanism in determining the epistemology of nineteenth-century American writers.

It has commonly been assumed that the Puritan habit of finding "remarkable Providences" in the daily life of New England was responsible for the modes of symbolism adopted by writers during the American Renaissance. Moreover, the Puritans have been blamed for the sparse imagistic quality of colonial literature, and for the castigation of the artist in American society. In his book, *Symbolism in American Literature,* Charles Feidelson says:

> The intellectual stance of the conscious artist in American literature has been determined very largely by problems inherent in the method of the Puritans. The isolation of the American artist in sociey, so often lamented, is actually parallel to the furtive and unacknowledged role of the artistic method in the American mind; both factors began in the seventeenth century with the establishment of Puritan philosophy and of a society that tried to live by it. Hence, the crudity or conventionality of a great part of American literature from 1620 through the third quarter of the nineteenth century may be no more surely attributed to frontier conditions, provinciality, and industrialism than to inherited mental habits which proscribed a funcitional artistic form ... And the symbolism of Emerson, Thoreau, Melville, Hawthorne, and Whitman was an attempt to hew out such a form in defiance of intellectual methods that denied its validity.[2]

The Puritan attempt to establish a literature that should instruct, while not pleasing, doubtless had a considerable influence on the artistic development of the generations that followed the last resurgence of a dying faith, the Great Awakening of the 1740s. However, it is misleading to argue the emergence of nineteenth-century American literature as if the writers of the American Renaissance had achieved the status of artists by rejecting the heritage of Puritanism. Some habits of mind were continous from the sermons of John Cotton to the lectures of Ralph Waldo Emerson, and the Puritan's use of the typology of nature as a source of revelation had much to do with the kind of symbolism evolved during the American Renaissance.

It is equally misleading to denigrate the Puritan aesthetic, as though there had been only a few writers who employed rhetorical and stylistic methods with a consciousness of their value in pleasing the listener or reader. Though Puritan literature had a functional value, most Puritans had highly sophisticated intellectual capabilities that were accustomed to strenuous exercise through reading and participation in the Sunday morning services. Perry Miller wrote, "By temperament and by deliberate intention the Puritan was less of an 'imagist' and more of an 'allegorist.' He was not insensible to beauty or sublimity, but in the face of every experience he was obliged to ask himself, what does this signify? What is God saying to me at this moment?"[3]

This allegorical habit of mind is clearly present in Hawthorne's writing, and the "remarkable Providence" in the appearance of a scarlet A in the sky while Hester, Dimmesdale, and Pearl are standing on the scaffold has numerous analogues recorded in Puritan diaries and chronicles. However, Miller underestimated the sophistication of the Puritan mind when he suggested that sermons were created for the common man whose imagination was "homely." "The Puritan stylist studiously held his fancy in check, sought his metaphors and similes in the commonplace, and remorselessly extracted the last ounce of meaning by a direct translation of the trope into moral so that nothing would be left to the imagination of the reader. He sought communication, not expression."[4] The accommodation of Christian doctrine was clearly the purpose behind every piece of Puritan writing, but the modes of this accommodation and the complexity of stylistic problems posed by Puritan literature suggest that the Puritan intellectuals were common people of uncommon abilities. Many of the first generation, after all, had been educated in England, and some held degrees from Cambridge University. The primers and hornbooks reveal that their children were given a classical education, and the sermons are evidence that the Puritans were scholarly in their understanding of the Bible.

It is the Puritan use of the Bible as a means of understanding both nature and history that defines the academic boundaries of this study. Feidelson cites the Puritan habit of mind by which the Book of Nature became a source of revelation, and he shows how this influenced the nineteenth-century artist's penchant for discovering in nature a realm of the spirit. This comparison mitigates Feidelson's castigation of the Puritans as the source of the alienation of the American artist, but it is an oversimplification. Although the Puritan habit of reading nature as a supplementary source of revelation for Scripture has had a considerable influence on American writers since the seventeenth century, it is an overemphasis of this aspect of the Puritan heritage to assert that the symbolic modes of the American Renaissance were derived principally from the "remarkable Providences." Puritan epistemology was a much more complex affair than a reading of the Book of Nature or an assessment of remarkable providences might make it seem, and numerous qualifications and exceptions to these general assumptions indicate the necessity of defining clearly the exact influences of New England Puritanism on the literature of the nineteenth century in America. Puritan epistemology relied on the revelation of God in Scripture and in nature, but an understanding of each was the result of knowing figural writing and typology.

Basically, there are two kinds of "types" in literature. The first is a simple representative figure. In the rhetorical tradition of synecdoche, this type stands for the whole, or for an abstract idea. Thus Adam is a type of mankind, who represents the process through which all men eventually go in falling from divine grace. His value in this classification is entirely symbolic; historical authenticity is of no relevance, though he may have coincidentally been historically real. Primarily, however, these types represent abstractions, so that the essential relation between the type and that which is represents involves no historical continuity. Many notable fictional characters fit this classification, such as Bunyan's Christian, Milton's Comus, Marlowe's Faustus, and the medieval everyman.

The second type is the more important for New England Puritanism, and it is the one with which this study is almost exclusively concerned. Biblical or exegetical typology is derived from the practices of the early fathers and medieval theologians, who attempted to give continuity to the canon of Holy Scripture by demonstrating how the Old Testament prefigured the New through types and figures of which the New Testament persons and events were the antitype, or fulfillment. Thus, the historical Abraham became a type of God the Father in the sacrifice of his only son, Issac. In contrast to the purely representative type, the exegetical type exists in the historical context of time, and its relation to the substance it represents is that of foreshadowing, or adumbration. The substance foreshadowed is denoted the antitype and it usually exists in time, fulfilling the type.

Rules distinguishing the biblical figures—which are prophetic of Christ and His Kingdom—from the Platonic, more allegorical symbolic mode were written for each succeeding generation of Puritanism in

England and New England. Although typology permeates earlier theological treatises by Reformers, Protestant and Puritan works devoted solely to the identification of typological parallels first appear in 1620 with William Guild's *Moses Unvailed: or, those Figures which Served unto the patterne and shaddow of heavenly things.* Following Guild's example, theologians published typological guides throughout the seventeenth century, including Thomas Taylor's *Moses and Aaron, or the Types and Shadows ... Opened and Explained* (1635), Samuel Mather's *The Figures or Types of the Old Testament by which Christ and the Heavenly Things of the Gospel were Preached and Shadowed to the People of God of Old* (1683; second edition 1705), and Benjamin Keach's *Tropologia: A Key to Open Scripture Metaphors and Types* (1681).

These crucial Puritan handbooks of exegesis have minor disagreements, but all concur on one central point: the most crucial distinction between the type and trope involved a concept of linear time. The trope was a Platonic representation of one thing by another, but the type by definition preceded the antitype in the context of time, one element being instituted by the same author to foreshadow the other. Perry Miller has noted that:

> Types were not allegories or emblems or fictitious narratives, the spirit of which might be that of Christ, but they were preliminary, factual prefigurations of what Christ finally did. Typology repeatedly gave rise to a host of extravagances, but even at its most fantastic it strove to distinguish between the type, which was true, and the trope, which was merely invention and therefore suspect. In the type there must be evidence of the one eternal intention of one writer. The type exists in history and is factual ... By contrast, the allegory, the simile, and the metaphor have been made according to the fancy of men, and they mean whatever the brain of the begetter is pleased they should mean. In the type there is a rigorous correspondence, which is not a chance resemblance, between the representation and the antitype; in the trope there is a correspondence only between the thing and the associations it happens to excite in the impressionable but treacherous senses of men.[5]

Of course, there were many shades of grey between these two extremes. Some exegetes would regard as types only those Old Testament events and figures that are specifically instituted in the New Testament; others would be more liberal in their judgements, allowing such figures as Jacob's Ladder to adumbrate Christ's union of heaven and earth. Some go so far as to include the red cord of Rahab, the prostitute of Jericho, as a type of the saving blood of Jesus. From the beginning, there have been schools among the typologists that reflect conservative or traditional tendencies, and these place great emphasis on the historical veracity of the type and the specific institution of the type and its antitype in Scripture. More liberal typologists sometimes border on using the Platonic, ahistorical symbol, and these exegetes are called spiritual-izers or allegorizers.

The essential characteristic of typological exegesis—historical adumbration and fulfillment—was lost during the Middle Ages when typology became a department of allegory under the fourfold method of exegesis. It was only natural that the more literal-minded Puritans would return to the simpler exegetical practices of the early church in preference to the fourfold method, and during the sixteenth and seven-teenth centuries a virtual renaissance of typological exegesis was found among reformed theologians. Luther and Calvin abandoned medieval exegetical practices in adopting the less elaborate twofold reading of Scripture for its literal and spiritual significance. In the best tradition of typological conservatism, that of the fourth-century Antioch school, the early Puritans approached the Old Testament as a figural adumbration of the New.

The uses to which this exegetical practice was put vary in kind, but from 1580 to 1800 eschatological typology and biblical figuralism in-fluenced the writing of history and of literature both in Europe and in America. A major portion of this study is given to an examination of typology as it was used by Puritan theologians and writers in New England during the seventeenth century and the early decades of the eighteenth century when these influences were extremely powerful. Although there were strong influences toward a transformation of the types into Platonic symbols and allegorical configurations, a mainstream of conservative typological exegesis persisted in New England even into the second half of the eighteenth century. Typology as a way of reading history and an instrument for examining the Book of Nature presented serious challenges to those theologians who would preserve the types in their biblical and historial contexts. These tensions were never suc-cessfully resolved, although Jonathan Edwards attempted a reconcilia-tion of typology and natural empiricism in his transformation of the epistemology of John Locke.

Typology provided a method of reading history and Scripture as well as nature for the early New England Puritan, but this attitude was very different from that of the Lockean Puritan, Edwards, who read nature more like his empiricist successors than his Puritan predecessors. The vast distinctions between Edwards and Emerson in matters of salva-tion and damnation are a poor guide for measuring their proximity in the area of epistemology. Of course, Edwards confined the ability to perceive the spiritual through the natural to those who were elect, while for Emerson, "Nature [was] a symbol of Spirit," and the understanding of this relationship was available to anyone of sensitivity, most par-ticularly to the poet-prophet-seer. But for the Puritan, nature and history were to be read in terms of God's Providence and His design for mankind. If in natural events man could perceive the "remarkable Providences" of God, he was also obligated to turn to his Bible in an attempt to establish a relationship between the actual events of history and the revelation he found in Scripture.

It is this attempted reconciliation between Scripture and history that lingered after Edwards despite assumptions posited by rationalism and Lockean epistemology. Edwards himself did much to unite the revelations of nature to those of Scripture. In his *Images or Shadows of Divine Things,* Edwards attempted to show that for the elect, divine agency may be perceived through natural sources. Locke's *Essay Concerning Human Understanding* may have had a considerable influence on the young Edwards, but the epistemological position of *Images or Shadows* provided a reconciliation of rationalist empiricism with the nomenclature of Christian theology.

Edwards' Calvinism and his rejection of the Puritan Federal, or Covenant theology, separated him from the seventeenth century, and his epistemology was in some respects also distant from that of the earlier Puritans. The most obvious example of this disparity is to be found by examining Edwards' use of the word "type" as it is employed in the *Images or Shadows of Divine Things.* Here, Edwards employed the term to mean a natural object through which the elect might perceive the spiritual. This could be misconstrued as corresponding to the medieval use of emblems and natural symbols. Natural objects, such as stones, became for Edwards types or figures embodying spiritual value, and though this habit of mind is similar in method to the Puritan penchant for finding remarkable providences in natural events, it is certainly not what the early Puritans meant when they talked of history or nature in terms of exegetical typology, though for Jonathan Edwards, even natural symbols always had some prophetic and eschatological value. The historical or biblical type, moreover, was also a vital part of Edwards' eschatological doctrine. In his *History of the Work of Redemption,* which treats the history of the church from the fall of man through the mid-eighteenth century, Edwards devoted a section to the period from the "Fall to the Incarnation," in which he discussed the traditional typology of the Old Testament in specific detail. Nevertheless, his employment of the biblical figures and types in the *Images or Shadows of Divine Things* is a use of instituted figures taken from Scripture in the new context of Lockean epistemology and natural empiricism, so that some distinctions need to be drawn concerning Edwards' modification of the language of Canaan as he had inherited it.

With Edwards' vital and important synthesis of Calvinism and Lockean psychology, the symbolic movement in New England was significantly advanced because now writers were able to explore the world of spirit that lay around them throughout all nature rather than in the

sanctioned confines of biblical expression, eschatological symbol, and
divine event. In a radical reordering of typological reasoning, Edwards
posited new conclusions about the divine source and its manifestation to
the elect perception. Emerson and Thoreau owe much to this transformation, though many of their own beliefs came from Edwards through
Scotland and from Germany, where Enlightenment idealism was an
avenue for Emerson's understanding of the English poets Coleridge and
Wordsworth. But the "oversoul" had been released to the regenerate
perception in Edwards' *A Divine and Supernatural Light* and *A Treatise Concerning Religious Affections,* so that the influence of Puritan symbolism,
with its unique fusion of regeneration and eschatological promise,
became a fundamental thematic principle in *Walden,* Thoreau's carefully crafted study of renewal. Although the influences of Coleridge, Kant,
and European transcendentalism are indicated were appropriate, the
primary emphasis of the concluding chapter is on the continuity of the
American metaphorical tradition from Edwards, the last significant Puritan thinker in America, to Emerson and Thoreau. Their development,
in turn, released for Robert Frost the tradition of Puritan symbolism,
the language of Canaan, which he found so compatible. This language is
an undeniable influence in American expression, particularly in that
rich tradition of New England writing which has always balanced an understanding of the past with a vibrant vision of future fulfillment.

Finding evidence of these influences in later American writing,
even in mid-twentieth-century literature, is not difficult. Robert Frost's
poetry and letters are filled with obvious echoes of the Puritan past.
Frost declared, for example, "If I must be classified as a poet, I might be
called a synecdochist, for I prefer the synecdoche in poetry — the figure
of speech in which we use a part for the whole." He once said that the
poetic use of synecdoche was the figurative act of touching the hem of the
garment, a reference to Matthew 14:36, where the story is told of those
diseased persons who came to Jesus "and besought him that they might
only touch the hem of his garment: and as many as touched were made
perfectly whole." Clearly Robert Frost shared the Puritan penchant for
regarding nature to be a veil of spirit, as his narrative poem "After Apple
Picking" suggests. A restructuring of the Pauline doctrine (I Corinthians
13) that now we know "in part" but "then, face to face," this poem echoes
Frost's sentiment governing imagery in poetry: "Imagery and after-
imagery are about all there is to poetry. Synecdoche and synecdoche.
My motto is that something has to be left to God."

Like many modern writers, Frost was not a Puritan typologist in
the strict sense. He is coy and timid in some of his own spiritualizing of
nature, and he shies away from doctrinal allegorizing. But his writing is
all metaphorial and "analogical" and it is clear from the Thompson
biographies that Frost's early years were spent being saturated with

Scotch-Presbyterian theology, which was closely related to the Puritan habits of mind that appear in his poetry. Obviously, it would be extremely dangerous to infer too much about the influences of Puritan doctrine on Frost; however, the elements of the Puritan imagination that are discernible in his work have much to do with the biblical and figural ways of understanding divine revelation in nature that were commonplaces in early New England theology. Thus the language of Canaan perseveres and though the literature of postwar America owes little to the Protestant poetics of the Puritan past, a Calvinist theology of history is clearly present in the novels of William Faulkner, and the symbolic language of Frost's poetry is saturated with biblical figures as they were understood by the New England Puritans. The language of Canaan lives on in the rhetorical strategies of speakers and in literary continuities of writers, though its prophetic importance has been lost and it now recalls the visionary power of a past era.

I

The Beginnings of Figural Expression

1
MEDIEVAL AND REFORMATION BACKGROUNDS

Seeing that all things which the Scripture noteth as characters, whereby the true Messiah is described, are found only in this Jesus, of whom we speak; in him the Types (both reall and personall) of the Messiah are verified, in him the Prophesies concerning the Messiah are accomplished, and ended; in him all the Genealogies that lead unto the Messiah cease; by him all the Miracles were wrought, which were foretold as proper to the Messiah; in him are fully found all things that were foretold concerning the Life, Death, Buriall, Resurrection, Ascension, and Session at the Right Hand of God the Father, and Judging Power of the Messiah. And lastly, the Mediatoriall Office of the Messiah, in the three Functions of it, Prophetically, Priestly, and Kingly, is fully committed to him, and executed by him for his people.

—John Davenport, *The Knowledge of Christ,* 1653

Figural interpretation establishes a connection between two events or persons [or ceremonies], the first of which signifies not only itself but also the second, while the second encompasses or fulfills the first. The two poles of the figure are separate in time, but both, being real events or figures, are within time, within the stream of historical life. Only the understanding of the two persons or events is a spiritual act, but this spiritual act deals with concrete events whether past, present, or future . . . since promise and fulfillment are real historical events, which have either happened in the incarnation of the Word, or will happen in the second coming.

—Eric Auerbach, *Scenes from the Drama of European Literature*

THE EXEGESIS OF SCRIPTURE according to the historical principles of typology and prophetic figuralism was a practice that originated with the early Christian church. The Fathers had relied on precedents, and prophetic figures abound in the exegetical writings of ancient Israel, including those that were eventually canonized as Scripture and many that were not. The application of prophetic scriptural figures to contemporary history was also practiced by the early

13

church, so that the New England Puritans inherited a number of alternative modes for examining the Bible and its vital relation to their own times. As original as Puritanism proved to be in its development of new doctrine and in its rejection of aspects of medieval and Anglican habits of mind, there is much in the language of Canaan that can be traced to medieval and Reformation backgrounds. This chapter explores the specific exegetical practices out of which the New England Puritans developed their own modes of metaphorical expression.

It is well known that the Protestant theologians deplored the tropological and allegorical developments of the late Middle Ages; however, they evolved their own forms of "letter" and "spirit" in the reading of Scripture, and the language of Canaan was one means by which the Bible came to have prophetic as well as literal value. This language was the focus of attacks from the opposition, and Samuel Parker, in *A Discourse of Ecclesiastical Polity,* alleged that the "phantastick Phrases" that abuse "Scripture-Expressions" manifest themselves in "fulsom and luscious Metaphors," the use of which should be abridged by an Act of Parliament.[1] Similarly, William Sherlock (*A Discourse Concerning the Knowledge of Jesus Christ*) accused John Owen and Thomas Watson for "jumbling metaphors, and Allegories, and Types, and Figures, altogether, and proving one thing from another in a most wonderful manner."[2] The Puritans employed Scripture phrasing as a corollary to their belief that they were the people of God acting out His will in contemporary history. Viewed from their own perspective, this sanctioned their activity in a divine dispensation writ large; however, the opposition always regarded their treatment of biblical language to be distorted and perverse. According to Symon Patrick, they applied "all that concerned *Israel,* to Themselves; and all that concern'd the *seven accursed Nations,* or *Aegypt* and *Babylon,* to their Neighbors."[3] And Samuel Butler, in *Hudibras,* accused the Presbyterians and the Independents of trying to "Outcant the Baylonian Labourers, / At all their Dialects and Jabberers."[4]

From the perspective of Anglican, Elizabethan England, the nonconformist preaching was a particularly offensive form of unconventional cant. To audiences saturated with Shakespeare, Sir Andrew Aguecheek must have stated the case very clearly when he argued that he'd "as soon be a Brownist as a Politician."[5] Indeed, the phrase "language of Canaan" was employed pejoratively to indicate the unconventional nature of non-conformist preaching, although the original meaning referred to Hebrew, the holy tongue of the Old Testament. For example, the "Mad Zealot" admits that

> In the holy tongue of *Canaan,*
> I plac'd my chiefest pleasure,

> Til I prickt my foot
> With a *Hebrew* root,
> That I bled beyond all measure.[6]

The language of Canaan came to be associated with the peculiar religious jargon, or cant, coined by the saints, and Symon Patrick has his conformist ask the nonconformist: "Is it a commendable thing to be *Singular* without any need? and to separate from us even in your words and forms of speech? Or is this a part of the *Language of Canaan* (so much talk't in late times) to be learnt of all those that will be accounted the *People of God?*"[7]

But among New England Puritans, the language of Canaan did not suffer disrepute. John Cotton used the phrase to describe that language that the saints will speak when the kingdom of God is realized on earth, and his New England emphasis is reinforced by Patrick's distinctions, which merely identify the tongue with nonconformist dialogue. But the predominant view of Puritan speaking and exegesis in early seventeenth-century England was expressed in the *Alchemist* by Ben Jonson's Ananias, who—though we may suspect his judgment—tells Tribulation Wholesome: "I do not like the man: He is a *heathen.*/ And speakes the language of *Canaan,* truely."[8] Symon Patrick rightly perceived the Puritan habit of mind by which the "new English Israel" was associated with the persons and events of the Old Testament dispensation when he alleged that

> The whole gang [of Nonconformist *Phrasemongers*] thought God was fulfilling Phrophesies, and making good the Revelation, and they must help and be instrumental to him in this *Generation-work*: Else they might be shut out of the *land of Promise,* and not enter into the *New Jerusalem* . . . Nay, those whom you count the soberest persons were so drunk with this conceit, that they fancied themselves or their Friends to be *Angels powring out Vials,* or some such thing.[9]

Patrick and the other critics of Puritan preaching were correct in isolating the dissenters' coining of biblical phrases as part of the nonconformist contemporary mode of discourse. But the hostile tone of the passage above clearly shows that Patrick and his colleagues had missed the point. For the Puritan exegete, God was indeed fulfilling prophecies in modern history, and the recapitulation of biblical patterns that they perceived in the world around them convinced them of their own divine election and role in realizing the long-awaited New Jerusalem. The locus of this climactic, historical event was perceived first to be England, and the concept of an elect nation, sanctioned by Scripture to carry forward the promises originally given to ancient Israel, had strong support among millennialists like Joseph Mede and Thomas Brightman, whose contributions to New England eschatology are examined in Chapter 6.

The extraordinary and prophetic power of figural language to be used by the saints was also understood by the English Puritan Richard Baxter, who had a profound influence on writers in New England. Baxter observed that "surely, if we can get into the Holy of Holies, and bring thence the Name and Image of God and get it closed up in our hearts, this would enable us to work wonders; every duty we performed would be a wonder; and they that heard, would be ready to say, never man spake as this man speaketh. The spirit would possess us, as those flaming tongues, and *make us every one to speak not in the variety of the confounded Languages, but in the Primitive pure Language of Canaan,* the wonderful works of God" (italics mine).[10]

But it was to be New England that would allow the appropriate conflation of historical and geographical forces to give rise to speculation about a literal and historical fulfillment of those metaphorical and figural revelations provided by the divine author through the scriptural language of Canaan. In America—first in New England and later in the American Revolution—the historical cycles of secular development could be fused with the biblical pattern of prophecy and fulfillment, so that the paradigm of Armageddon followed by a pastoral paradise could be demonstrated not only in contemporary events but also in the language of Scripture revelation. Both secular and sacred Americans were able to view their history and the events of their times in the traditional and orderly context of Jonathan Edwards' *A History of the Work of Redemption* (1774), which identifies the cycles of historical revolution with the inevitable patterns of regenerative progress.

This conflation of sacred and secular images of historical progress constituted an important achievement for the Puritans and their followers. By providing adherents of the revolutionary psychology with a traditional authority and a rational view of progress in comtemporary times, such divergent writers as John Cotton and Philip Freneau or Joel Barlow advanced a historiography that was rooted in the exegesis of biblical figures, and all heralded a restoration of the grand design for America that the original settlers had deduced from their reading of Scripture and from their nurture in the English protestant tradition. The literal cycles of historical recapitulation were made analogous to biblical patterns of divine dispensation by the writers of eighteenth-century New England, and one purpose of this book is to establish the foundations of the language through which these richly metaphorical associations were made.

Until very recently, when studies by critics of language and literature like Sacvan Bercovitch, Barbara Lewalski, and William Madsen appeared, interpretation of the Puritan use of language has focused on its continuity with the medieval traditions of allegory and typology.[11] Indeed, there is much in the language of Scripture exegesis during the Middle Ages and Renaissance to suggest a close association between the language of Canaan and the methodology of the past. As Barbara Lewalski suggests, one of the most important historical approaches to Scripture during the Middle Ages was the sense of its allegorical and symbolic character. The basic medieval formula, first articulated by Augustine and modified by subsequent writers, recognized a literal or historical meaning of Scripture contained in the words themselves and, in addition, a spiritual meaning whereby the things or events signified by the words point beyond themselves to other things or events. For Augustine and his followers, the poetic character of the Bible was its unique fusion of truth and art.[12]

The meanings were expanded by Thomas Aquinas in four ways. The first, according to the *sensus historicus* or *literalis*, was a simple explanation of the words. Second, the sense was altered according to the *sensus tropologicus,* which is concerned with instruction or the correction and teaching of morals, and the progress of the individual soul toward salvation. Third, the meaning of a text could be allegorical, or interpreted according to the *sensus allegoricus.* This is perhaps the broadest category established by Aquinas, and exposition by this sense is exposition by a sense other than the literal. "David rules in Jerusalem," which according to the literal sense is to be interpreted exactly as the words sound, by the allegorical sense signifies that "Christ reigns in the Church Militant." The *sensus allegoricus* uses exemplification by simile, as when the life of Christ, or lives of the saints, are introduced, with an injunction that the hearer follow in their footsteps. It has historically been associated with the progress of the church. The fourth sense was the *sensus anagogicus,* used mystically or openly, by which the minds of the listeners or readers would be exhorted to the contemplation of heavenly things, and this has always been associated with eschatological figures, those images of the last days and the nature of heaven. The single word "Jerusalem" is instructive here. Literally, it is the city of that name; allegorically, it represents holy church; tropologically, it signifies the faithful soul whoever aspires to the vision of eternal peace: anagogically, it denotes the life of the dwellers in heaven who see God revealed in Zion.[13]

Similarly, Dante followed the Augustinian formula in his discussion of the literal and figurative levels of meaning to include four ways of expanding the meaning of any written expression; in short, he allows at least three levels of spiritual meaning:

If we consider the *letter* alone, the departure of the children of Israel from Egypt in the time of Moses is signified; if the *allegory,* our redemption accomplished by Christ is signified; if the moral meaning, the conversion of the soul from the sorrow and misery of sin to a state of grace is signified; if the *anagogical,* the departure of the sanctified soul from the slavery of this corruption to the liberty of everlasting glory.[14]

It is well known that the Puritans rejected the extravagances of the fourfold method and that they stressed a literal and historical interpretation of scriptural revelation. However, in many respects, the Puritan exegetical method is an echo of the Augustinian division of Scripture meaning into literal and spiritual forms of the same revelation. The reformers, however, personalized Augustine's abstract method and incorporated elements of it into their own correlation of Scripture dispensation with contemporary historical events.[15] For the New England Puritan, and for Reformation theologians generally, all literary genres were forms through which the language of Canaan might associate contemporary history with the original biblical dispensation. The Augustinian principle reappears in New England, particularly in the sermons and histories of Massachusetts Bay Colony.

In a sermon Cotton Mather preached in 1689, this Augustinian echo is clear. Preaching on the Old Testament subject of Noah and the ark, Mather shows that the ark was not only intended to be a literal vehicle for the salvation of Noah and his family but a prophetic symbol of the restorative salvation that Christ makes available for his saints and his church. Mather's interpretation of the ark is a recapitulation of the exegesis provided in *The City of God* by Augustine. This interpretation is a good example of Augustine's sense of the literal and figurative dimensions of Scripture, and Noah's ark, like all Scripture elements, is to be studied for its historical *and* allegorical truths: "Yet no one ought to suppose either that these things were written for no purpose, or that we should study only the historical truth, apart from any allegorical meanings; or, on the contrary, that they are only allegories, and that there were no such at all, or that, whether it be so or no, there is here no prophecy of the church."[16] The literal accuracy with which Augustine read the Genesis account is evidenced in his continuing commentary. He proceeds to give the exact measurements of the ark, an explanation of how insects were preserved in the ark, what exactly was meant by "male" and "female," and how God provided food for so many of his creatures in so small a place for so long a time.

However, Augustine's literal reading of Scripture did not preclude a figurative meaning. If he endorsed the historical authenticity of the Old Testament, persons and events, he also saw the possibility of finding in the types a spiritual value. He continues: "Not even the most audacious will presume to assert that these things were written without a purpose, or that though the events really happened they mean nothing, or that at all events they are far from having any figurative reference to the Church."[17] But the sense in which Augustine intended the figurative is ambiguous. He does not endorse the purely literal reading of Scripture; but he implies that it is also improper to read only the figurative meaning. However, allegorical or figurative meanings that concur with the literal sense are acceptable and should be read alongside the literal exposition of Scripture. In his essay, "Figura," Eric Auerbach makes the following assessment of Augustine's double sense of Scripture:

> It is clear that Augustine has in mind two promises, one concealed and seemingly temporal in the old Testament, the other clearly expressed and supratemporal in the gospel. This gives the doctrine of the fourfold meaning of Scripture a far more realistic, historical, and concrete character, for three of the four meanings [literal, tropological, anagogical] become concrete, historical, and interrelated, while only one remains purely ethical and allegorical.[18]

Auerbach argues that Augustine explicity adopted the figural, or typological, interpretation of the Old Testament, and he provides numerous examples from Augustine's works to reinforce his point.[19] Yet Augustine was able to maintain a balance between the figurative, or allegorical as he called it, and the literal sense of Scripture. By insisting on the dual sense of a text, he was able to refute those allegorists who would read the Old Testament only in metaphorical terms, and he dispensed with the literal minded who would only accept historical truths. However, because Augustine insisted on labeling the figurative interpretation "allegory," he allowed possibilities for spiritualization of the types he interpreted that he may not have intended. Later Puritan adaptations of the Augustinian principle depend heavily on this distinction,[20] and viewed from this perspective, the language of Canaan was an extension of Augustinian exegesis.

Since the middle ages, typology, or figural interpretation, with its emphasis on prophecy and fulfillment has existed in tension with the allegorical reading of Scripture, which emphasized correspondences between the literal or historical and the spiritual or mystical. It has not always been easy for exegetical commentators to keep these distinctions clear when interpreting biblical figures and it has been characteristically even more difficult for religious poets who employ biblical images to adhere strictly to a prophetic or a Platonic reading. Edward Taylor, for example, draws heavily on a broadened view of the prefigurative biblical type when he uses the verses of Canticles as scriptural texts for some of his meditations. Indeed, Taylor frequently personalized the biblical figures in a way that is more eternal and timeless than it is historical and prophetic. Therefore these distinctions must be viewed in the context of historical development and transitions in rhetorical strategy. The Puritans were exceedingly faithful to a literal and figurative directness in reading the Bible; but they stood at the end of a long tradition of biblical exegesis, which included modes of rhetorical discourse that sometimes influenced their own "plaine stile" and pure sense of God's revealed truth. Their powerful and prophetic symbolic mode was derived from the exegetical practice of typology, the foundation of their self-proclaimed analogy to biblical revelation.

William G. Madsen has recently provided a concise account of the most prominent and essential features of typological exegesis. In defining a "type," Madsen says:

1.   A type is a historical person or event, not a mythical person or a recurrent event like the rising and setting of the sun.

2.   A type looks forward in time, not upward through the scale of being. The theory of typology is thus firmly grounded in the Judeo-Christian world of existences and is fundamentally alien to the Greek world of essences.

3.   Natural objects may be types, but they are usually such only in special historical circumstances. St. Paul tells us that the rock that Moses struck was Christ (the water that issued forth was regarded as a type of the blood and water that flowed from the side of Christ when it was pierced by the spear); this does not mean that every rock is a type of Christ.

4.   There must be differences as well as similarities between a type and its antitype.

5.   Neither the actors of a typical event nor the authors of their history understand the typological significance of what they are doing or writing. The Jews wandering did not know that manna prefigured the Eucharist, nor did Joshua know that in leading the people of Israel into the Promised Land he was a type of Jesus leading his people to heaven.[21]

This definition is helpful, and its examples are accurate applications of the early church practices in conservative typological exegesis which the Puritans later resurrected. But the emphasis of the medieval exegete varied tremendously. Not only was typology challenged by the adherents of the allegorical school; there were variant readings among the exponents of a literal and figural reading of Scripture. The pure allegorists, however, were easy to distinguish from the typologists. K. J. Woollcombe says, "There is no theological similarity whatever between the typology of Philo and that of St. Paul. The only point of contact between the two writers is their common use of the typological vocabulary. But whereas in St. Paul the vocabulary is harnessed to the exposition of God's redemption work in history, in Philo it is harnessed to allegorism. It is in fact hardly possible to separate typology from allegorism in Philo, and if the word typology must be used of certain aspects of Philonic exegesis, it should always be qualified by the adjective *symbolic,* in contradistinction to the *historical* typology of the New Testament."[22] Conditioned by the presuppositions of Platonism, Philo believed that ideas were hidden within the Old Testament types, which in and for themselves had no value. Therefore, his exegetical method consisted largely in finding a way of stripping away the literal fact to get at the spiritual truth hidden beneath. He was vigorously opposed by the most ardent early typologist, Tertullian. Tertullian understood the figurative interpretation of the Old Testament to mean the spiritual prefiguration of Christ in the New. He opposed those allegorists who regarded a literal reading of the text as a denial of its figurative meaning and value.[23]

Tertullian and Augustine may have shared a sense of the literal veracity of the Old Testament, but Tertullian differed from Augustine in distinguishing the allegorical from the typological method of approaching Scripture. Typology emphasizes the historical and the concrete and is set within a linear scheme of time; allegory is abstract and nonhistorical, and the allegorist places little value on typology's scheme of prophecy and fulfillment. "Figural interpretation [typology] established a connection between two events or persons, the first of which signifies not only itself but the second, while the second encompasses or fulfills the first. The two poles of the figure are separate in time, but both being real events or figures, are within time, within the stream of historical life."[24]

In the context of these distinctions, it is useful to examine one or two examples of the medieval tendency to add spiritualized dimensions to the biblical types through a system of purely allegorical correspondences that were not constituted under typological parallels. A clear and legitimate typological correspondence would be the association between Adam, the "Old Man," and Christ, the "New Man"; nothing more than Scripture is needed to develop this relationship. Both Adam the type and Christ the antitype are clearly marked as having meaning in terms of each other:

For as in Adam all die, so also in Christ shall all be made alive. (I Corinthians 15:22)

And so it is written, the first man Adam was made a living soul; the last Adam was made a quickening spirit. (I Corinthians 15:45)

The first man is of the earth, earthy: The second man is the Lord from heaven. (I Corinthians 15:47)

Nevertheless, death reigned from Adam to Moses, even over them that had not sinned after the similitude of Adam's transgression, who is the figure of him that was to come.

> But not as the offence, so also is the free gift. For if through the offence of one many be dead, much more the grace of God, and the gift of grace, which is by one man, Jesus Christ, hath abounded unto many.
>
> For if by one man's offence death reigned by one; much more they which receive abundance of grace and of the gift of righteousness shall reign in life by one, Jesus Christ. (Romans 5:17)[25]

Now if by types we mean only those elements of the Old Testament which are designated as being fulfilled by the New, then we shall confine legitimate typological correspondences to only a handful of references in the New Testament where Old Testament events or persons are considered specifically in relation to their antitypes.

Christ himself makes such an allusion to Jonah, in Matthew 12:40, when he remarks, "For as Jonah was three days and three nights in the whale's belly, so shall the Son of Man be three days and three nights in the heart of the earth." Restricting typology to references such as this would eliminate all correspondences that were not specified in the New Testament, and it would have inhibited the Church Fathers from accommodating the new Christian faith to an essentially Jewish world through continuous reference to the Old Testament. Typology was no accident; it grew out of the necessity of the early church to adapt itself to the heritage of Judaism and the rich cultural tradition out of which Christianity developed. And still, the exegetes of Antioch attempted to remain faithful to correspondences that were at least present and identifiable in Scripture if not specifically mentioned as "type" and "antitype." What they sought to avoid was the kind of allegorizing that led to the fourfold method. For example, several references to the Virgin Mary came to be endowed with antitypical significance: "Eve, being a virgin and undefiled, conceiving the word which was from the serpent, brought forth disobedience and death; but the Virgin Mary, taking faith and joy, when the Angel Gabriel told her the good things, answered: Be it unto me according to thy word."[26] This allusion, found in the *Trypho* of Justin Martyr, was common and a similar correspondence was established by Irenaeus: "The knot of Eve's disobedience was loosed by the obedience of Mary. For what the virgin Eve has bound fast through unbelief, this did the Virgin Mary set free through faith . . . And thus, as the human race fell into bondage to death by means of a virgin, so it is rescued by a virgin."[27] These correspondences, though derived from evidence found in Scripture, are not legitimate typological relationships culminating in an antitypical fulfillment by the new dispensation in Christ. They are simply correspondences between the Old and New Testaments and cannot be considered instituted types and antitypes.

However, because this kind of typological extension was wrought within the framework of faith, it was often difficult for the Fathers to control their colleagues who found numerous resemblances between the Old and New Testaments which were not authentic typological prefigurations but were, instead, allegorial parallels. Allegorical typology is deceptive, because it may resemble the historical figure. "It tries to find correspondences between the Old Testament and the New, but, unlike the typology which depends upon the Biblical view of history, the methods of this form of typology are wholly unhistorical. The corresondence which it seeks to establish is not so much a relation between the past and the future, between the foreshadowing and the fulfillment, as between earthly and the heavenly, the shadow and the reality."[28] This kind of typology, similar in so may ways to the instituted resemblances, owes much of its philosophical foundations to Platonism.[29] Thus a spectrum of symbolic value came to be understood, ranging from the historical typology of Augustine and Tertullian to the Platonic allegorizing of the fourfold method.

The difficulty with these distinctions is that for many interpreters, biblical figures appeared to be both allegorical and typological. The Puritans were always careful to anchor their interpretations in Scripture and to view biblical figures in the context of history; moreover, in exalting their rhetorical strategies of interpretation for Canticles, even their use of allegory had a historical and prophetic character. The language of Canaan denoted metaphorical discourse with historical and prophetic value, where biblical figures gave promise and hope to God's "New English Israel." However, once allowed outside the straightjacket of legitimate, instituted typological correspondences, the exegete was free to construct allegorical parallels between Scripture and almost anything else. With the fourfold method, for example, Abraham became a type — in this case, a representative type — of the Good Man, an example of the kind of person the Christian life sought to develop through faith. But his value in metaphorical terms came to be unlimited. Soon, the Good Man was used in many unscriptural contexts, and he was signified by the good ship sailing across the sea of life, a *perigrinus* seeking the way from Babylon to Jerusalem. For example, a late medieval English sermon recorded by S.P. Bromyard contains metaphorical extension of this parallel to include England in its journey toward heaven:

Therefore the master mariner, *Oure Sovereyn Lord* . . . desiring from his heart the *wele* and *honour* of us all, *besied him* by great means to repair the *reekes of oure ship*, and *rere up agen our spirit onto God*, that hath *stalkid fro him mony day* through vices and sins . . . Our ship, *ful repaired* through virtue, according to its own desire can *crosse sail* when it pleases, and savelich take the sea . . . God, *sovereyn Lord of Lordes, spede him in his Iourne,* preserve him from perils and *Increase* his honor, and give us glory so to repair oure ship by increase of virtue that *we now passe* the perils of the sea and *saile* a true course to the port of Heaven.[30]

The theologians of the Reformation were quick to seize these distinctions, and to use them in their rejection of the scholastic methods of fourfold exegesis.

The late Middle Ages had found the decoding of types so congenial that they had turned interpretation of the Bible into a fabulous game. By the fifteenth century, scholastic nominalists had worked out a nine-fold scheme which was so complicated that even they could not keep the levels distinct; to the eyes of the reformers the mixture of literal, grammatical, allegorical, moral, anagogical, and tropological readings by which the types were supposedly being expounded had become something far more impious than anything a pagan rhetorician had ever imagined.[31]

The classic arguments for the rejection of scholastic nominalism and the fourfold method and for the adoption of the simple literal and figurative method of exegesis were provided by Luther and Calvin during the sixteenth century, as they set out principles of biblical interpretation based on Augustine's understanding of the literal and the figurative sense of Scripture. The typological systems the Puritans ultimately followed were developed by Luther and Calvin, and it is to their commentaries that we must now turn for a clearer understanding of the twofold method the New England Puritans inherited from William Perkins and the English and Continental Reformation.

The Puritans of the seventeenth century inherited the attitudes and values of the sixteenth-century reformers. Scholastic nominalism fell into disrepute under the savage attacks of Peter Ramus, and the whole question of exegesis was challenged by a return to the testimony of Scripture, in an effort to establish through the sanctions of the Word an approach to exegesis that would at once illuminate the reader while maintaining fidelity to the revelation of truth. Martin Luther insisted that Scripture should be interpreted by Scripture and in accordance with the rule of faith. The fourfold method must be discarded, he argued, because it was an attempt to go beyond the Word and substitute man's rational perceptions for God's revealed will. In his early exegesis, Luther followed the fourfold method, but later abandoned the *quadriga* as an empty and unsatisfactory way of getting at the core of the Scriptures. Luther's own concern was that the truths of Scripture should be accommodated to every reader, whether or not he was blessed with an education in the rules of exegesis. But his comprehension of the Scriptures as a body of writing instituted by a single author and pervaded by a unified spirit led him to espouse historical typological exegesis, which became for him a satisfactory solution to the problem of exegeting the Old Testament within the larger scheme of accommodation. He writes: "Holy Scripture handles its expressions in the same way as God handles His works. Now God always works so that the figure or type appears first, and the true reality and filfillment of the type follows. So the Old Testament first comes forth as a type, and the New Testament follows as the true reality. So too when Scripture makes new tropes . . . It takes the old work, which is the likeness, and gives it new meaning, which is the true reality."[32] The concluding suggestion that typology works to foreshadow the "true reality," which is only partially present in the type, and that tropology operates in much the same manner should not be taken as an indication that Luther's understanding of typology digressed into spiritualizing along typological lines. Luther's typology complicates the historical emphasis of orthodox typology, but his actual reading of the biblical types was wholly acceptable within the framework of orthodox exegesis in the Antioch tradition, because he insisted on the prefiguration of Christ in linear time through the adumbration provided in types. Luther's particular difficulty in establishing an orthodox typology was that he found it necessary to emphasize the role of the mystical presence of Christ in the sacrament, thereby begging the question of a mystical presence in the ceremonies and sacraments of the Old Testament which prefigured the Lord's Supper.

In his later arguments disclaiming transubstantiation and asserting the doctrine of consubstantiation, Luther emphasized Christ's mystical presence in a way that would suggest his sense of a mystical continuity from the Old Testament ceremonies to the New Testament sacrament. However, in his *Lectures on the Psalms*, he is more explicit in describing the reality of Christ in the Old Testament rites: "The ceremonies were intended to be understood as pictures or symbols, to remind those of the promise of Christ until He came to establish the right service of worship . . . This does not consist in external conduct or in lifeless types; instead, it lives in the heart and produces a genuinely new being."[33] This seeming irreverence for typology was characteristic of the reformed attitude toward the types as they have been incorporated into the medieval fourfold method. However, Luther was attempting to distinguish between types that have only historical value, types that were spiritualized under the fourfold method, and a proper typology, as he conceived it, whereby the type had historical and prefigurative value and contained a moral or ethical purpose. Lifeless and static symbolism had little meaning for the sixteenth-century reformers, and Luther's allusion here is to the highly elaborate symbolic methods employed by the medieval church to unfold the mysteries hidden in Scripture. Luther and the reformers sought to simplify the reading of Scripture, and he employed the typological correspondences sanctioned in the New Testament as an instrument for interpreting the Old: "Luther's concept of Christ's historical presence in both sign and rite means that his typology becomes very different from medieval exegesis which considered the types as mere shadows of things to come. For Luther, the Old Testament events have taken place; they are confirmations within temporal history of the Messiah. The types and figures are to be accepted literally and not searched for abstract, eternal verities."[34]

The emphasis in Luther's approach to Scripture on the mystery of Christ confirms that the Old Testament signs and ceremonies needed no further allegorizing to prove a mystical relation to the New Dispensation. The typologial prefiguration of Christ contained in them, which was part of a larger scheme of redemption in Christ accommodated by the Word but which was not Christ's essence, was sufficient evidence of the continuing ministry of God's Providence. Regardless of the ironies in Aaron's failure to realize his role as a prefiguration of Christ's priesthood, and despite the many differences in Aaron's moral example and the example provided by Christ at a later time, there could be no doubt that God had intended the correspondences that were implicit in Luther's reading of the Old Testament account.

Like Luther, Calvin rejected the allegorical method of the medieval church because it permitted a variety of interpretations under the allegorical or figurative sense — interpretations that were usually the products of man's ingenuity rather than of God's institutions. Like his Puritan followers on both sides of the Atlantic, he sought to distinguish a simple twofold reading of Scripture: "Thus, through the centuries, it has been commonly accepted and passed around that here Paul has provided us with a key for the allegorical interpretation of Scripture. But nothing was further from his mind. In the word *letter* Paul means preaching which is external and does not reach the heart . . . *Spirit* on the other hand, means spiritual teaching, which is not merely a matter of mouthing words, but rather has the power to penetrate the soul and bring it to life."[35] Like Milton and Roger Williams, Calvin insisted that the types had been fulfilled in Christ, but he regarded both the Old and New Testaments as a prefiguration of the spiritual kingdom that was to come and thus released to Puritanism a view of the Bible filled with prophetic and eschatological symbols. Calvin distinguished between the abrogation of a ceremony when it ceased to be used in church practice, and the abrogation of the spiritual effects of that same Old Testament rite. In the institution of the Old Testament types, there would therefore have been a purpose that extends beyond the fulfillment of the figure in the flesh. Luther had confined his typology to Scripture itself and to the refutation of the fourfold method by an adoption of the "letter" and the "spirit," or the "literal" and the "figurative" senses of Scripture, but Calvin saw in the types not only an adumbration of the New Testament; he regarded the New Testament to be a foreshadowing of the spiritual kingdom also shadowed in the old dispensation.

This distinction was crucial. Had the Puritans followed Luther's exegetical practices and sanctioned only a typology that was allowable through Scripture, they might have evolved no sense of continuity between their own mission and the Old Israel's Exodus from Egypt. But they did formulate such an analogy, confidently following the more loosely stipulated proscriptions of William Perkins' rejection of the fourfold method, and deriving a rationale from Calvin's insistence that the Church and the Kingdom of God were prefigured in the New Testament as well as the Old. The "errand into the wilderness" needed justification; an extension of the kingdom of God to the American stand seemed to be ample for John Cotton and the early settlers of New England, who found in their Old Testaments an analogy for the journey westward. Herman Melville would later write, "Escaped from the house of bondage, Israel of old did not follow after the ways of the Egyptians. To her was given an express dispensation; to her were given new things under the sun. And we Americans are the peculiar, chosen people — the Israel of our time; we bear the ark of the liberties of the world."[36]

2

THE PURITAN FIGURAL IMAGINATION AND THE LANGUAGE OF CANAAN

Now as the people of God in old time, were called out of Babylon civil, the place of their bodily bondage; and were to come to Jerusalem, and there to build the Lord's temple, or tabernacle, leaving Babylon to that destruction, which the Lord by his servants, the prophets, had denounced against it . . . so are the people of God, now to go out of Babylon spiritual to Jerusalem . . . and to build up themselves as lively stones into a spiritual house, or temple for the Lord to dwell in, leaving Babylon to that destruction and desolation, yea, furthering the same, to which she is devoted by the Lord.

—John Robinson, *A Justification of Separation from the Church of England*

THE LOUDEST CRITICS of the fourfold method were the early Puritan reformers, and through their exegetical commentaries the language of Canaan was given preliminary definition. In *The Arte of Prophesying*, William Perkins declared:

The Church of Rome maketh 4. Senses of the Scripture, the literall, allegoricall, tropologicall, & anagogicall, as in this her example. *Melchisedek offered bred & wine.* The literall sense is, that the King of Salem with meate which he brought, refreshed the souldiers of *Abraham* being tyred with trauell. The allegoricall is, that the Priest doth offer vp Christ in ye Masse. The tropologicall is therefore something is to be given to the poore. The Anagogicall is, that Christ in like manner being in heauen, shall be the bread of life to the faithful. But this here deuice of the fourfold meaning must be exploded and rejected. THERE IS ONE ONELIE SENSE, AND THE SAME IS THE LITERALL. An Allegorie is onely a certaine manner of vttering the same sense. The Analogue and Tropologie are waies, whereby the sense may be applied. The Principall interpreter of the Scripture is the Holy Ghost.[1]

The difficulty with this declaration is that it fails to accomplish its stated purpose. Instead of rejecting the multiple levels of interpretation, Perkins has actually affirmed them by redefining the limits of exegetical possibility. He continued by dividing the narrative elements of Scripture into two kinds, the "analogical and plaine" and the "crypticall and darke." The plain places yield their meaning "without any delay" in accordance with the "analogy of faith," but the cryptic places have to be interpreted by the following "Rule and Leader": "If the natiue (or natural)

28

signification of the words doe manifestly disagree with, either the analogy of faith, or very perspicuous places of the Scripture; then the other meaning which is given of the place propounded, is natural and proper, if it agree with contrarie and like places, with the circumstances and words of the place, and with the nature of that thing which is intreated of" (p. 33).

Although Perkins' *Arte of Prophesying* was a popular handbook for preachers and for lay exegetes, his ambiguous assertions concerning the two senses of Scripture were not wholly representative of reformed exegesis. Despite Perkins' habit of linking types, antitypes, tropes, and Old Testament figures together, his assumption of a double "literal" method was a step toward formulating the Puritan conception of a simple and direct revelation in Scripture.

Perkins provided an example of this double meaning in Scripture: I Corinthians 11:24, "This is my body, which is broken for you," which he calls a "cryptical place" where the natural signification is at odds with the article of faith professing Christ's ascension to heaven. In this "cryptical place," Perkins argues, exegetical interpretation is necessary, and the proper meaning is the *"newe or second sense,"* which interprets bread as a "signe of my bodie: by a Metonymie of the subject for the adjunct" (p. 48). Perkins was extremely cautious, however, about allowing a multitude of interpretations to intrude on the one true meaning of any Scripture text. "The principall Interpreter of the Scripture is the holy Ghost," he argued, "so that ye first know this, that no prophecie in the Scripture is of any private Interpretation. Moreover, He that makes the law, is the best and highest interpreter of the law" (p. 51). But Perkins insisted on a mysterious dimension in Scripture, explicable only through the "analogy of faith," and in so asserting he established the foundation for subsequent Puritan interpretation of Scripture and history in a double sense:

The manner or waies of interpreting, are according to the places of Scripture which are to be handled. Places are either Analogicall and plaine, or Crypticall and Darke. Analogicall places are such as have an apparent meaning agreeable to the analogy of faith, and that is the first view. Concerning these places, observe this rule: *If the naturall signification of the words of the place propounded doe agree with the circumstances of the same place, it is the proper meaning of the place* (p. 38).

But this ease of understanding is not always available, even to the regenerate perception, and for the "crypticall and darke" places it is necessary to employ some simple guidelines for exegesis, or interpretation: the "native or natural" signification is not always the only signification of a word or words.

It is, of course, the faith of the believer that makes the "crypticall and darke" places clear, rather than some sophisticated, multilevel schema for interpreting any and all passages of Scripture. In *A Cloud of Faithfull Witnesses, Leading to the Heavenly Kingdom,* Perkins again declared how Scripture is subject to the natural and spiritual exegetical rule, applying his views to the very heart of the controversy between Protestant and Catholic interpretation of the sacrament of the Lord's supper:

> Here they are confuted, that teach the Lords Supper is no Sacrament, unlesse the body and bloud of Christ be either truly turned into the bread and wine, or at least bee in or about the bread; and that so he is locally present, and must be locally and substantially received; . . . but these men know not this notable prerogative of true faith, *faith* which gives being to things which are not, and makes things present which are absent . . . We need not goe in this Sacrament to require a corporall presence; it is sufficient if wee have true faith; for that makes him present much more comfortably, than it might be his bodily presence would make unto us.[2]

This reasoning was later to appear in Edward Taylor's *Christographia,* those fourteen sermons concerning the personal meaning of biblical figures, and in the *Treatise Concerning the Lord's Supper,* where Taylor argued for a spiritual (though not a literal and personal) presence of Christ in the sacrament. While it is tempting to infer a direct borrowing, it is more likely that Taylor and Perkins shared the common source of the Puritan-Protestant aesthetic and theory of language.

Perkins' position on the biblical figures and types is straight-forward. Biblical figures are to be employed morally, as examples, but not as having a spiritual presence in themselves. In *A Reformed Catholike: or, a Declaration Shewing How Neere we may Come to the Present Church of Rome in Sundry Points of Religion, and Wherein We must Forever Depart from Them,* he provided some categorical rules concerning images and worship:

> I.   We acknowledge the civill use of images are freely and truly as the Church of Rome doth . . . And this to be lawfull, it appeareth; because the arts of painting and graving are the ordinance of God; and to be skilfull in them is the gift of God . . .

> II.   We hold the historicall use of images to bee good and lawfull; and that is, to represent to the eye the actes of histories whether they be humane, or divine. And thus we thinke the Histories of the Bible may be painted in private places . . .

> III. In one case it is lawfull to make an image to testifie the presence or the effects of the maiestie of God, namely, when God himself giues any speciall commandment so to doe. In this case Moses made and erected a brazen serpent, to be a type, signe, or image to represent Christ crucified.[3]

Here Perkins was criticizing the imagistic manner in which Puritanism
had imitated the medieval tradition, a process that his protestations
would not be able to contain entirely. But he simultaneously allowed the
"literal and spiritual" meanings for Scripture interpretation, which he
checked carefully by disallowing a purely allegorical or figural reading of
any passage. A superb example is his interpretation of the episode in
Genesis 22, where the sacrifice of Isaac calls into question the moral im-
peratives of God and the symbolic significance of this Old Testament
figure. In *A Cloud of Faithfull Witnesses* Perkins examined this trope closely and concluded, "Now whereas *Abraham* offered *Isaac* in sacrifice to
God, and yet *Isaac* liveth, and the Ram is slaine in his stead; Hence,
some gather this use, and we may profitably consider of the same; to wit,
that the sacrifices which we offer unto God, now under the Gospel, must
bee living sacrifices; for *Isaac* he was offered in sacrifice to God, and yet
he lived, and died not, but the Ram is slaine for him" (pp. 121-122).
Perkins was careful to keep his literal and spiritual significances
separated and he goes on the draw a "moral" conclusion from this Old
Testament figure: "So must we offer ourselves in [spiritual] sacrifice unto God, not dead in sinne, but living unto God in righteousnesse and
true holinesse. And thus shall wee offer up ourselves living sacrifices
unto God, as when we consecrate ourselves unto Gods service, and obey
him in our lives and callings" (p. 122). But Perkins was hostile to the
typological interpretation of this passage and warned his readers to
beware of reading too much into those figural passages of the Old Testament that tempt the fancy: "Hence also some gather, that this sacrificing
of *Isaac* was a signe and type of Christs sacrifice upon the Crosse. For as
Isaac was sacrificed and lived, so did Christ; though he died, yet rose
againe, and now liveth forever; *but because it hath no ground in this place,
though it be true which is said of both therefore I will not stand to urge the same*" (p.
122).

However, Henry Ainsworth, the separatist, argued for the figural
reading of Scripture in his *Booke of the Psalmes, and the Song of Songs, or
Canticles.* In *Annotations Upon the Five Bookes of Moses,* Ainsworth im-
aginatively expanded the Old Testament figures to foreshadow, more
allegorically than typologically, the progress of the individual soul.

> In Genesis, (which history endeth with the going down of Israel into Egypt)
> we have the Image of a naturall man, fallen from God into the bondage of
> sinne. In Exodus, is the type of our regeneration, and state renewed by Jesus
> Christ. In Leviticus, the shadow of our mortification, whiles we are made
> sacrifices unto God. In Numbers, the figure of our spiritual warfare;
> whereunto we are mustered and armed to fight the good fight of faith. In
> Deuteronomie, the doctrine of our sanctification, and preparation to enter in-
> to our heavenly Canaan (after Moses death) by the conduct of Jesus the sonne
> of God.[4]

And if this highly figural interpretation were not suggestive enough of the method he would endorse for associating the letter with the spirit of Scripture, Ainsworth states the doctrine unmistakably: "The literall sense of Moses's Hebrew . . . is the ground of all interpretation" (Preface). Like William Perkins' declaration that the literal is the only sense of Scripture, this declaration was almost immediately qualified: Moses' Hebrew was found to have "figures and properties of speech, different from ours" and, if the exegete were careful, to provide a "true and sound literal explication, the spiritual meaning may the better be discerned" (Preface). Consequently, Ainsworth's writings on Canticles and the Books of Moses are filled with typological correspondences. His use of the Old Testament was clearly an attempt to amplify and clarify the greater dispensation of the New but unlike his successors John Cotton, Samuel Mather, and Edward Taylor, he did not make significant distinctions among the kinds of figures found in the Old Testament. "Typology was not sharply distinguished from other kinds of allegorical or symbolic interpretation by Ainsworth. He used interchangably various forms of the words 'type,' 'figure,' 'pattern,' 'shadow,' and even 'similitude' and 'example.' But his typology was not merely undisciplined allegorizing. In his exegesis both terms of the figurative relationship remained within the Bible, and almost always it was the standard form of an Old Testament type foreshadowing a New Testament antitype."[5]

As with many of his contemporaries, figural typology for Ainsworth added eternal dimensions to the literal reading of a Scripture text. The figurative reading did not replace or invalidate the literal but enriched and amplified it. As figural exegesis gained in prominence among the Puritans, some commentators realized the need to clarify terms and the distinguish trope for type, *allegoria* from synecdoche. As swiftly as Perkins had produced *The Arte of Prophesying* to distinguish Puritan from medieval rhetorical practices, several handbooks of exegesis appeared which provided these important definitions.

Early in the seventeenth century, English Puritanism was directed in these interpretative matters by two prominent and influential handbooks of exegesis, William Guild's *Moses Unvailed, or, those figures which Served unto the Patterne and Shaddow of Heavenly Things* (1626) and Thomas Taylor's *Christ Revealed: or the Old Testament Explained* (1635). With intense interest among Puritans in figural exegesis, these commentators attempted a reading of the Bible that would establish the prophetic parallels between the Old and New Testaments in the context of static parallels associated with "correlative" typology.

The role of Christ as antitype in these diverse connections lends itself to various applications — related to though distinguishable from Christology and soteriology — particularly in the context of Reformation thought. Two of these applications may be singled out as having direct bearing upon American Puritan thought: *developmental typology* and *correlative typology*. The former related Old Testament figures not only to the Incarnation but to the Second Coming. Thus typical objects, institutions, and events (e.g., Noah's Ark and the flood, the wilderness trials, and the Sabbath, the Babylonian captivity and the Promised Land) come to pre-figure end-time events as well as aspects of the story of Christ. This historiographic view is complemented by the static biographical parallellism offered by correlative typology, in which the focus is not primarily upon Christ but upon certain Old Testament heroes.[6]

Bercovitch's distinctions are crucial for an understanding of English Puritan commentators like Mede, Perkins, and Ames. The Puritan vision of covenant theology was the theological foundation for this exegesis, and "both of these uses of typology rely in different ways on covenant theology, especially as this develops through Cocceius and the federalist school. Thus typology may be seen as a link between the concept of a recurrent national covenant and the concept of an unchanging covenant of grace manifest in succeeding stages of the history of redemption. It should be noted, too, that the New Englanders always retained the traditional figural mode of joining the Old and New Testaments by spiritual-literal exegesis."[7]

William Guild expressed the doctrine of correlative typology when he structured out the simple parallels between the Testaments in *Moses Unvailed*. The book is brief and printed in double columns, so that those Old Testament figures may be viewed in direct correlation to the New Testament parallels. In his "Epistle Dedicatorie," the fundamental doctrine of correlative typology is articulated:

> As in the Creation darkness went before light, or as the dawning precedes the brightnesse of the day, & as Joseph obscurely at first behaved himselfe unto his Brethren, and Moses covered with a vaile stood before the people; Even so, in the detection of the glorious worke of man's redemption, mysticall promises went before mercifull performance, darke shadowes were the forerunners of that bright substance, obscure types were harbingers to the glorious anti-type, the Messiah, who coming after Levi's law with its figurative and vailed ceremonies, was the resemblance, painting and pointing out that cleere Lampe and Lambe of God, the express Image and ingraven Character of the Father.[8]

Similarly, Thomas Taylor turned to Hebrews for this text to argue that "the *Law had but a Shadow of Good Things to Come*" and not the image and truth itself; that is, it had a rude and darke delineation of good things to come, as a draught made by a painter with a coale, but the Gospel exhibits the picture itself in the flourish and beauty, that is, in the truth and being of it."[9] He continued by denouncing the imitation of Hebrew ceremonies in Puritan worship, showing that "those Ceremonies were not given to merit remission of sinnes by them, nor to appease God's anger, nor to bee an acceptable worship by the worth of the worke done, nor to justifie the observer; but to shew justification by Jesus Christ, the truth and substance of them; to bee *types* of him, pointing at him in whom the Father is pleased; to bee *Allegories* and resemblances of the benefits of Christ, exhibited in the New Testament . . . and seales of faith on the part of the beleeving Jew, exciting and confirming his faith in the Messiah" (pp. 4-5). The Christological focus is stronger in Taylor than in Guild, but the correlative typological scheme is clear: "The same Testator made both Testaments, and these differ not really, but accidentally, the Old infolding the New with some Darknesse, . . . through such shadows and figures, to the true image of the thing signified, who, in our Text, calleth himselfe TRUTH, in opposition to all those shadowes" (pp. 4-15).

As these passages make clear, figural and prophetic images were very carefully analyzed by the English Puritans of the early seventeenth century, many of whom held Anglican and Catholic symbolism in hostile contempt. Typology and figural prophecy were often drawn into arguments condemning allegory, and frequently, the Old Testament prefigurative types were denigrated as having too close an association with the "humane ingenuity" of medieval tropology. The English Puritans were superb scholars of the Bible, and their commitment to the "plaine stile" and to a literal and historical reading of Scripture embraced a carefully wrought exegesis that would render a "historical" and a "prefigurative" meaning in the biblical passages. A central concern in figural interpretation was the meaning of the Lord's Supper, and Perkins' contemporary, William Ames, also had difficulty bringing the Old Testament ceremonies into focus with sacraments instituted in the new dispensation. In *A Fresh Suit Against Human Ceremonies in God's Worship* (1633), Ames used typology to argue that the New English Israel should not import those practices of ancient Israel into their own time because the prefigurative types had been established only to lead the Jews to God before the coming of Christ in the incarnation. "All interpreters terme the types of the ould law ceremonies," Ames argued, "for that spiritual disposition they have, and typicalnes which the Lord set upon them . . . These which were properly types, were properly ceremonies."[10]

Although Ames admitted the prefigurative value of the types for the Old Testament Jews, he was quite clear in declaring the abrogation of such figures in contemporary forms of worship. "Now all the outward types appointed thus by God, which foretold Christ to come, and those other rites which by way of signification taught our mynds and so helped

and stirred our hearts to grace or duty, all these are ceremonies," and as
such, they are very different from those moral ordinances of the Old
Testament, such as the ten commandments, which "carry a constant and
perpetual equity and necessity of our honouring the Lord."[11] This
typological argument against the Anglican ceremonies would be echoed
later by Samuel Mather, and Ames sounded the characteristic Puritan
call to arms in announcing that, by analogy to the abrogation of Jewish
rites and rituals, all Anglican and Catholic figures should also be
abolished: "If the ceremonies of Moses were removed because they were
typicall, why should not the Popish Ceremonies be removeed which are
not lesse typicall?"[12]

The Old Testament ceremonies, however, were only one aspect of
the Puritan argument regarding biblical types. While professing the
abrogation of Jewish ceremonies and practices for modern Christians,
the Puritans paradoxically declared the extreme relevance of the Old
Testament for their contemporary Christian experience by showing,
through figural typology, how prefigurative images were partial and incomplete manifestations of Christ's kindgom.

We must, however, be careful to make the same distinctions among
the biblical figures that Ames, Perkins, and the early seventeenth-
century writers would have made. Ames's uneasiness with the Old
Testament ceremonies was no measure of his acceptance of the biblical
types and figures as prophetic images relevant to his own time. Indeed,
his anti-ceremonial argument was a rational use of the prefigurative
system to indicate which elements in the Old Testament were intended
to foreshadow Christ's first coming and which were instituted to
prefigure the remainder of Christian history until the end of the world.
In this way, Ames set the pattern that later Puritans, including John
Cotton and the New England communities, would follow. All regarded
the Bible to be saturated with types and figures of God's divine dispensation; however, there were certain interpretations allowable under the
"literal" and "spiritual" methodology, and others that violated the
abrogation of Old Testament rites and ceremonies in the coming of the
flesh.

Ames made all this very clear in his immensely valuable book, *The
Marrow of Sacred Divinity,* first published in Latin as *Medulla Sacrae
Theologiae* in 1612. This very straightforward statement organized
Puritan thought topically, and it echoed the Augustinian-Calvinistic
model allowing a literal and spiritual meaning to each passage of Scripture, to be interpreted by the rational but metaphorical mind of man on
the analogy of faith. As Puritans all believed, the covenant of God's
grace and His continuous relationship with fallen man in history lay at
the bottom of instituted figural dispensations (as contrasted with the fanciful creations of human ingenuity), so that each historical person or

event might not only exist really, at a particular moment in human time but might also contain divinely instituted elements of a future manifestation of God's grace through an eternal and continuous covenant relationship. Therefore, in a chapter in the *Medulla* called "The Administration of the Covenant of Grace before the Coming of Christ," Ames allowed a prefigurative value to the abrogated Jewish ceremonies by declaring that "sanctification was expressly taught by the prophets and foreshadowed by typical oblations and rites of sacrifice." He even asserted that "sanctification was prefigured by circumcision," thus providing a figural reading that borders on allegory and spiritualizing rather than the linear constructs of conservative typologizing. But Ames's intentions are articulated well. He would bring the Old and New Testaments together in one eternal dispensation, commencing with creation and ending with the last days prophesied in Daniel and Revelation. Metaphorically, the progress of the individual soul parallels the historical moments in God's dramatic dispensations, so that episodes in the Bible, both Old and New Testaments, may be correlated with stages in the individual's movement toward salvation, as well as later historical episodes in the continuing history of the work of redemption. "Redemption and its application were extraordinary," Ames asserted.

> They were signified, first, in the deliverance from Egypt through the ministry of Moses, who was a type of Christ, and by the entrance into the land of Canaan through the ministry of Joshua, another type of Christ. Second, in the brass serpent, by looking at which men who were about to die were restored to health ... Third, in the cloud which shielded the Israelites from all injuries from enemies and from the sky ... Fourth, in the passing through the Red Sea where a way was opened to the land of promise, their enemies being overwhelmed and destroyed ... Fifth, in the manna from heaven and the water from the rock whence they received continual nourishment, so to speak, out of God's hand ... In the *ordinary* sense, Christ and redemption were foreshadowed by the high priest, the altars, and sacrifices for sins.[13]

It is the distinction between ordinary and extraordinary that is critical in Ames's typology. Both readings are figural, and both differ from Platonic allegory because they exist in a historical continuum; that is, each presupposes a historical and literal meaning, which is attended by a deeper, prefigurative, spiritual sense. But the ordinary ceremonies of the Jewish nation were abrogated by the coming of the flesh, and the extraordinary figures continue to have equity for subsequent history, since they correspond to those spiraling patterns of the redemptive process, from lapses into sin, through regeneration by grace, to sanctification. Thus, in the pattern of "developmental" typology, the Old Testament prefigures the New, as well as the unwritten historical process that

lies between the epistles of Paul and the eschatology of John's vision of
the apocalypse. For example, in a chapter entitled "The Administration
of the Covenant from the Coming of Christ to the end of the World"
(Chapter 39), Ames stated clearly that "the testament is new in relation
to what existed from the time of Moses and in relation to the promise
made to the fathers. *But it is new not in essence but in form.* In the former circumstances, the form for administration gave some evidence of the covenant of works, from which this testament is essentially different. Since
the complete difference between the new covenant and the old appeared
only in the administration which came after Christ, this administration
is properly termed the covenant and testament which is new." When
analyzing "Baptism and the Lord's Supper" (Chapter 40), Ames again
distinguished between those Old Testament ceremonies that were "supplanted" by the incarnation, and those figural elements that prefigure
good things to come. "The sacraments are baptism and the Lord's Supper," he asserted, "no other sacraments or sacramental signs were
delivered to the church by Christ or his apostles, nor can others be appointed by men in the church." Water is to be used in the sacrament
because of its figural value: "Nothing in common use more fitly
represents the spiritual washing performed by the blood or the death of
Christ, nor is the sprinkling or application of the blood of Christ more
fitly expressed by anything. For since Christ's death there should be no
use of natural blood in holy things."

The reasoning present in the *Medulla* posited a serious problem for
the Puritan imagination, namely, how types and figures from the Old
Testament that were obrogated in the first coming of Christ could have
relevance for the Puritan movement. Figuralism was already
distinguished from allegory (as the medieval church had practiced it) by
its historical, linear, and prefigurative role in exegesis of biblical texts.
But what about post-biblical history? Or, more specifically, what about
the history of the visible church from the concluding lines of the Epistle
of Jude to those dramatic moments foretold in the Book of Revelation?
How could seventeenth-century Christians identify themselves with the
abrogated figures and types of the Old Testament while simultaneously
acknowledging Christ's incarnation, the supplanting of the old law by
the new?

Fortunately, these questions were to be answered fully by John Cotton, Thomas Shepard, Samuel Mather, and Jonathan Edwards, as they
successively approached the problems, building upon the inherited history
of exegesis to establish principles on which Scripture might be interpreted figurally as having meaning and relevance beyond the incarnation. The common element governing the Puritan response to these problems was that God's dispensations and institutions are eternal, not
temporal, and that the Jewish ceremonies, figures, and types were

relatively significant in preparing the way for the historical work of redemption, that is, whereas the ceremonies as rites were to be abolished in worship among the Puritans because they had been abrogated by the coming of the flesh, their figural significance might be viewed differently if they were also regarded to be metaphors of the process of salvation, abrogated temporally but verifiable eternally. The fundamental assumption was that Christ's spiritual presence was an eternal not a temporal phenomenon, and that the vision of John related to a continuous spiritual process as well as providing an eschatological vision of a temporal end to human history and time. Ames, too, noted this distinction in Chapter 41 of the *Marrow,* "The End of the World," when he said "the second coming of Christ will be like the first in that it shall be real, visible, and apparent . . . But it will be dissimilar in that first, it will be attended with the greatest glory and power, and . . . second, it will dispense the greatest terror among the ungodly and the greatest joy among the godly."

These distinctions were absolutely essential to an understanding of the language of Canaan, and the Puritans on both sides of the Atlantic shared a penchant for metaphorical expression that has sometimes obscured modern interpretation of their writings and habits of mind. Language and interpretation are historically relative phenomena, and the modern reader's task is compounded because Puritans believed in the eternal veracity of Scripture revelation, despite their scholarly awareness of ambiguity in translation from the original Hebrew and Greek. It was their function in history, they argued, to establish the language of Canaan as the only true language for understanding God's revealed will, which was unchanging and eternal. It was man's understanding that was thought to be imperfect, not the language of divine revelation, and the Scriptures were searched for hidden expressions which man's fallen capacities might have overlooked. This belief, and its application to Scripture rhetoric, was well expressed by the Biblical critic Joseph Galloway, in his *Brief Commentaries on Revelation,* where he attempted to clarify the problem of temporal and eternal value in Scripture language and to indicate the prophetic importance of the Bible.

And as, in all other languages, each word has a certain meaning affixed to it by human compact; so in this, each figure has a literal and moral sense annexed to it, and to which it refers with the nicest accuracy, and indeed with absolute certainty. Other languages being founded in human agreement may be changed according to the caprice of men; hence, the great variety of them in the world. But the language of *Prophecy* is derived from the symbols of things in the natural world, and its meaning established in moral objects, and bears a proper similitude and representation of their respective symbols; neither of which admitting of change, the language itself must be unchangeable and must continue as long as those objects shall endure. And as, in all probability, it was the primeval language, perhaps that of Paradise itself, so it will continue until the end of time; the more especially as it has pleased God, in his wisdom, to deliver the *Prophecies* in it, which are, from the tenor of his holy word, to be useful and necessary to the salvation of man, down to the awful consummation of all things.

Prophecy was indeed the central question, as the language of Canaan evolved from the revealed words of Scripture to a sophisticated and systematic means of understanding the ways of God to man.

The prophetic and figural value of Scripture is easily seen in Canticles and Revelation, two books richly endowed with prophetic value, both providing the Puritan imagination with fertile ground for nurturing metaphorical habits of mind and for extending typological interpretation into histories of Old and New England. For example, Puritans on both sides of the Atlantic were very concerned to interpret those prophetic images of John's vision correctly, for to do so would insure their right understanding of God's historical intentions for their own times. They were equally concerned to know the meaning of the most figural book of the Old Testament, the Canticles or Song of Solomon. If Revelation could be assessed in terms of typological and historical processes that would give meaning and sanction to the "errand into the wilderness," the figural reading of Canticles provided a model for understanding the more intimate relationship of Christ to the church, and the progress of the individual soul through the stages leading to redemption. Most Puritan commentators wrote about both these books (though it is interesting that John Calvin was unable to cope with the mysteries of the apocalypse, by his own admission), and the significance of these two texts is seen in the abundance of interpretive materials written on them by Puritans in London and Boston during the seventeenth century. The language of Canaan, after all, is that universal tongue that will be understood and spoken by all the elect saints at the time of the resurrection and millennium, and it was revealed to the regenerate saints in the complex imagery of Scripture, particularly in such figural works as Canticles. The following chapter examines seventeenth-century interpretations of Canticles, and these rhetorical developments are applied to the poetry of Edward Taylor, whose use of the Old Testament is almost wholly figural. Samuel Mather, a contemporary of Taylor, whose *Figures or Types of the Old Testament Opened and Explained* (1683) may be used as a gloss on Taylor's *Meditations*, provides a historical context for assessing the status of the language of Canaan at the close of the seventeenth century, when shifting perspectives on Scripture were yielding new eschatological interpretations of Canticles and Revelation. Samuel Mather codified the Puritan understanding of figural writing in his sermon-sequence and drew crucial distinctions between figural and allegorical expression which summarize the clarifications begun on the Continent and in England and suggest ways of understanding the chiliasm of writers like Increase and Cotton Mather. Ultimately, the prophetic power of the language of Canaan found its most obvious expression in Revelation and the eschatological interpretations Puritans gave that work. However, among the Old Testament typological documents, Canticles afforded the Puritan writer with a rich source of sustained analogy, one that had powerful meaning for a gathering of visible saints whose historical purpose could be explained through the metaphorical union of Christ and his church.

3
THE CANTICLES TRADITION

If God be the only Teacher of his Church to instruct it by Word and
Sign, then no Ceremonies significant may be admitted into the solemn
Worship of God for doctrine and instruction, but such as bear his
stamp, are marked with his Seal, are warranted by holy Scripture; For
the chaste Spouse of Christ, who knowes the voyce of her Beloved, will
not acknowledg unwritten Traditions for the Word of God; but God is
the only Teacher of his Church both by Word and Sign.

—John Cotton, *Some Treasure Fetched
Out of Rubbish*, 1650

There is a great difference betwixt an Allegorick Exposition of Scripture, and an Exposition of Allegorick Scripture; The first is that, which
many Fathers and School-men fail in, that is, when they Allegorize
plain Scriptures and Histories, seeking to draw out some secret meaning, other than appeareth in the words, and so will fasten many senses
upon one Scripture . . . An exposition of an Allegorick Scripture is, the
opening and expounding of some dark Scripture wherein the mind of
the Spirit is couched and hid under Figures and Allegories, making it
plain and edifying, by bringing out the sense according to the meaning
of the Spirit in the place.

—James Durham, *Clavis Cantici,*
1669

IT IS SIGNIFICANT that John Cotton and Thomas Brightman, Mede's contemporaries, both read Canticles typologically
and prophetically, giving the book a historical emphasis it
had not previously enjoyed. In Cotton's interpretations of Daniel,
Revelation, and Canticles, we find an imaginative and ingenious
conflation of allegorical interpretation and typological historicity. John Cotton was clearly the avenue through which the distinctions
originally drawn by Perkins and Ames, and the figural reading of
Revelation advanced by Joseph Mede would enter the theological world
of New England Puritanism. For the purposes of examining Cotton's influence in the literature of New England figuralism, we must turn to his
Treatise on the Canticles (1642), which exerted a profound influence on the
sermons and meditations of Edward Taylor, whose poems often took as
a text a passage from the Song of Solomon. A figural reading of the

eschatological and prophetic books of Daniel and Revelation had made
available to the New England Puritan a new way of assessing his relationship to God's historical work of redemption and to the errand into
the wilderness. The allegorical and figural reading of Canticles would
show him new ways of examining the progress of his individual soul. "In
such a manner did John Cotton knit the covenanted church to the
catholic church, knit New England to England. In so doing he helped
keep Massachusetts Bay in the mainstream of modern life rather than
allowing it to become, as did other exiled religious groups, an enclave of
contentious sectaries who alone were right and who, in isolation, were
therefore dead to the larger human commmunity."[1] Cotton was indeed
the eschatological and figural link between Old England and New
England, and his reading of Canticles shows conclusively that the traditions of exegesis refined in the early stages of English Puritanism were
alive and well among the "New English Israel" and those settlers on the
"American Strand."

John Cotton's essential conservatism in Scripture interpretation is
clearly seen in his reading of Canticles. With Thomas Brightman, he
argued against the purely allegorical interpretation, although this view
of the Song of Solomon had long been the conventional way of understanding the pagan love song both in the medieval and the reformed
tradition. Essentially, what Brightman and Cotton sought to do was to
restore to the Canticles a historical and prophetic value that they found
in the other books of the Old Testament when they were considered as
figural documents. Moreover, Cotton was always concerned to establish
the abrogation of Old Testament forms of worship, indicating their
moral equity for contemporary times but clearly distinguishing this from
the prefigurative value they had in foreshadowing the Lord's Supper and
incarnation. Characteristically, Cotton argued this conservative position
by using a homely metaphor:

> When the Church was an Infant, kept under the Rudiments of the Law, she
> was to be taught onely by those shadows and figures that God prescribed;
> And now, in the brightness of the Gospel when all figures, shadows, vails,
> adumbrations; whether signifying things present or to come, be done away:
> Shall we think the light of reason sufficient to direct, without the guidance of
> Scripture in matters of Rites and Ceremonies, appropriated to the solemn
> worship of God for the Instruction of his People?[2]

The imitation of Old Testament ceremonies had been a long-
standing issue between Anglicans and Puritans, and for John Cotton, it
was moral equity, and not prophetic and typological value, that endowed the ceremonies of the first dispensation with importance for modern church worship. As if to confirm Thomas Shepard's arguments in the

Theses Sabbaticae, Cotton wrote to Shepard that the typical value of the sabbath as an instituted prefiguration of Christ's rest was abrogated in the incarnation:

> And seeing after our Fallen estate, sanctification is an Effect of our Redemp-
> tion, the Sabbath being now given for a signe of our sanctification by God, It
> is Argued, that it had now a Typicall use putt upon it of our Redemption, &
> so of our sanctification by Christ. If it be actuel, wherein stood ye
> Resemblance of that Type? As ye mysticall Body of Christ (ye Church of
> Israel) Rested on the 7th day from Labor; so ye naturall Body of Christ
> Rested in ye grave, ye whole 7th Day, night & day, from All Actions of
> Humane Life; and by that Rest Procured our Rest from sinne unto himself in
> Peace, as being the Accomplishment of his Death and Humiliation. Here is
> the Application: the Sabbath is firstly called ye Type, a shadow of Christ to
> wit, his Body resting in ye Grave, Collos. 2.16, 17. (This I learned from
> Brightman, whose letter I send you to peruse.)[3]

Although Cotton's use of the sabbath is both metaphorical and spiritual, reflecting those aspects of the progress of the soul from sin to redemption, he is very careful to isolate the typological mode and dissociate the abrogated value of the sabbath from its perpetual equity:

> Now because this shadowy use of ye sabbath (for a Type of our Redemption
> and sanctification) was unto man fallen, so some greater Consideration then
> the first morall use of it (as it was a monument of the Creation) Therefore, ye
> Body of this shadow being come, It was meete, ye shadow of ye Sabbath of ye
> 7th day, should be Abolished. And yet because ye morall use of it (as a monu-
> ment of ye Creation) has still been preserved, Therefore Christ Appointed the
> First Day of ye weeke, to be kept in ye stead of it, which was ye First Day of
> ye Breaking forth both of our Redemption & Creation.[4]

The moral equity which Cotton found in the Sabbath and in other elements of the Old Testament that had been abolished in the first com-ing of Christ, seemed to suggest an allegorical rather than a figural or typological understanding of Scripture, because the clear linear and historical paradigm that was urged by conservative commentators in the reformed tradition lost emphasis in this view. It is in this tension be-tween allegory and typology, between the spiritual meaning and the pro-phetic value of the imagery of Canticles, that John Cotton's most impor-tant contributions to the use of metaphor may be found. Canticles had always been a disburbing book of Scripture; how could faithful Chris-tians who believed both the literal and the spiritual interpretations of the Holy Canon take seriously and the erotic and sensual passages of Can-ticles on a literal level? Did not Canticles demand a wholly figurative or allegorical reading, so that the imagery would become spiritual rather than literal and possibly erotic?

From the time of the Church Fathers, the book had been read allegorically, so that the bridegroom represented Christ, and the bride, His Church. The allegorical reading, moreover, permitted a more personal, mystical, and individual interpretation of the lovesong than did the prophetic imagery of a typological reading. John Cotton and Thomas Brightman both attempted to reconcile the prophetic and personal modes in their reading of Canticles, but for most commentators, the exegetical pattern would be either allegory or typology. Thus Theodore Beza, in his 1587 sermons on Canticles, argued that the 45th Psalm, like the Song of Solomon, was "an excellent and most divine treatise touching the most strait and spirituall bonde and alliance which is between Jesus Christ and his church, every point thereof being prosecuted and continued under such formes and phrases of speech as are customarily used in the treaty of the conditions of a naturall marriage."[5] The defense of an allegorical interpretation of Canticles rested on the necessity of perceiving the work as metaphor, which has a very limited literal value (as Solomon's behavior would thereby become suspect even in the most liberal of Christian traditions); and on the fact that the book was written in poetry rather than prose. For example, William Gouge, in his *Exposition of the Song of Solomon* (1615), assessed the song to be "a kind of Poesie, and Poesies are commonly adorned with allegories and figures."[6]

The Separatist Puritan Henry Ainsworth also commented on Canticles, calling it an allegory and defending the spiritual rather than the literal interpretation: "As the Scripture mentioneth, *the Bride, the Bridegroom* and the friends of them both, *the Children of the Bride Chamber* . . . so in this song all these are brought in as speakers . . . The Bride is the Church espoused to Christ and called the wife of the Lamb . . . to whom she is to be presented as a chast virgin . . . and this Church Christ loved."[7] And Joseph Hall, a prominent Anglican of the seventeenth century, distinguished prophecy from allegory in scriptural interpretation, and labeled the Song of Solomon a clear allegory: "Two things make the Scriptures hard: Prophecies, Allegories. Both are met in this, but the latter so sensibly to the weakest eyes, that this whole Pastoral-marriage song (for such it is) is no other than one allegory sweetly contrived."[8]

If analogies were often drawn between the matchless love shown the bridegroom for the bride and the divine love of Christ for his church, the allegorical tradition rejected a prophetic or figural reading of the book and declared the specific parallels that should be drawn with the figures appearing in the erotic song. Thus William Guild, in *Love's Entercours between the Lamb and his Bride, Christ and His Church* (1658), rhapsodized that God used Canticles to accommodate his divine mysteries to the common reason of man: "He unfolds to us the highest mysteries that may be . . . in the lowest termes and resemblances, that can be, for our instruction,

stooping downe for us that we may step up to him . . . and that conjugal
chaste love that is between the bridegroome and bride, or the loving
spouse and his dearly beloved" is analogous to "that cordiall and
matchless affection" that "without measure Christ carries to his
Church."[9] According to Guild, God accommodates himself to man, or
"admits himselfe to our capacities" (p. 7). Similarly, Arthur Hildersham
argued that "the Song in respect both of the matter of it, is a declamation
of the holy espousals, and sweet communion, between Christ and His
Church, and the mutual love and affection they bear to each other."[10]
Ecclesiastes was joined to Canticles in a spiritual, allegorical progression
by Symon Patrick, the Dean of Peterborough, who said that "the mind
not being filled for such sublime thoughts, as lye hid under the Figures,
in the book of Canticles, till it hath learned by Ecclesiastes the Vanity of
all earthy enjoyments,"[11] thus demonstrating that the long tradition was
sustained well into the eighteenth century and beyond. Christopher Jellinger, in *The Excellency of Christ* (1641) proved the value of Canticles in
the canon of holy Scripture by arguing that God utilized this allegory to
bring his divinity to the level of man's reason:

> The whole son, is transcendentall and mysticall, composed by Salomon the
> wisest King . . . that the matter of contemplation therein contained is con-
> nubial, touching the mysticall union and communion between Christ the
> celestial bridegrome and the Church his Spouse, set forth in a dramaticall
> stile, so sublime and elegant, that the whole treatise might well be stiled, THE
> SONG OF SONGS WHICH IS SALOMONS WHO WAS KING OF KINGS.[12]

But the love song was easily adapted to the union of Christ to His
church at the end of time, and some commentators, while arguing the
allegorical reading of Canticles, would interpret the allegory as having a
fixed time in the future, usually at the end of the world, providing a conflation of eschatology and allegory.

It is the mixed reading of the book, a seeming reconciliation of two
contrary modes, the typological and the allegorical, that often confused
contemporary critics and interpreters. For example, in 1598, George
Gyfford, in *Fifteene Sermons Upon the Song of Songs of Solomon,* said, "Jesus
Christ, the King of Kings, betrothed himself to his church of olden time,
she is become his spouse whom he loveth deerly,"[13] but he quickly urged
that "*the marriage shall be at the generall judgement in the end of this world,* when
it shall be solemnized with great joy and triumph, as it is written, Rev.
19.6,7."[14] Gyfford was careful to declare that "*All things in this Song be
Mysticall,*" which would mean Platonic or allegorical, and even though he
envisioned the marriage to be solemnized "*at the day of Judgment*" (p. 16),
he affirmed the allegorical reading while acknowledging that the opposite historical view represents an alternative reading. Gyfford's reading

is eschatological and mystical or allegorical but not figural and typological.

Nathanael Homes, however, argued the other side. In his *A Commentary Literal or Historical, and Mystical or Spiritual, on the Book of Canticles,* Homes saw the Canticles as "a Prophetical History, or Historical Prophesie (after the manner of Daniel's Prophesying), applying the several parts and passages thereof, to several times and states in succeeding generations, from *Solomon's* time, down to the second coming of Christ."[15]

But Homes, like many of his contemporaries, tries to have it both ways and draws little distinction between the allegorical and figural. Judging the "whole book," he argues that it "is Mysticall signifying that *spiritual love* which is between Christ and His Church."[16] The typological mode is conflated with the allegorical throughout Home's treatise, and we find such confusions as "Mystical" associated with the historical pattern in his declaration that "Solomon made affinity with Pharoah, King of Egypt, and Solomon loved the Lord; and therein was a Type of Christ's Call of the Gentiles" (p. 18). The Song itself contained many types, according to Homes, who saw the church "now contented with Types, Ceremonies and miracular Providences . . . For the *mysticall* and *spirituall Sence* of the text in relation to Christ and his Church in all ages . . . is briefly this: By *Beloved* is meant the Lord Christ, of whom the High-Priesthood was a Type" (p. 255). Homes goes on to argue some loose associations between the Canticles, Solomon, and Christ's offices, none of which are very convincing because Homes himself appears to be confused about the historical and mystical modes of interpretation.

A more definite position is assumed by Henoch Clapham, an early seventeenth-century Anglican commentator, who saw in the book essentially a typological and figural foreshadowing of historical union between Christ and the church. He saw "Salomon [as] a figure of Christ, in respect of his continuing plenty and peace in the midst of Israel his Church," and he brought together the allegorical and figural by showing how the narrative of Canticles had been a representation of "Salomon, the Churches amiable Spouse, and passionate lover" with the historical congregation of saints.[17] Clapham's exposition, like Home's, is unsophisticated and primitive; he was obviously attempting to explain the numerous narrative elements by showing how they had prefigurative value in terms of Christ incarnation. But he interpreted the whole song allegorically, or spiritually, and never lost sight of the importance of reading the work mystically.

Many early commentators reflect efforts by English reformers to incorporate a complex allegory into the literal and figural frames of reference. Arthur Jackson, for example, in his *Annotations Upon Jobe and the Song of Solomon* (1658), suggested that, though Canticles could be read allegorically, in any age, as a representation of Solomon and his bride the Shulamite, we must understand Solomon to be a "most excellent *type* and *figure* of Christ, admitting the church of the Gentiles, as his spouse, into the nearest fellowship and communion with himself."[18] Having established the representative qualities of Solomon and the Shulamite, he then provides an exact statement of that which is mystically represented: "And indeed, the Bridegroome is here described to be a King of transcendent majesty and glory, as is proper to none but onely to Christ, and the Bride is set forth by such rare beauty and glory, as can belong to none but the Church, the *Lamb's wife,* Revel. 19.7."[19] Jackson everywhere conflates the allegorical and typological, though he attempts to keep the distinctions clear. He concludes finally that "the Scripture doth frequently elsewhere speake of Christ in these *figurative expressions*" (p. 121), thus drawing the allegorical and figural together in one descriptive term.

It was a commonplace to separate Solomon, the author, from his creation, and to see Solomon as typological while regarding the book as an allegory. Thus John Robotham, in *An Exposition of the Whole Booke of Solomon's Song* (1651), developed a whole section of his work on Solomon as a "figure and type of Christ," while emphatically declaring that

> because this song speaketh of Christ's love to his Church, and the churches love to Christ more largely, sweetly, and comfortably than any other song in the Scripture, and by such allegories and amiable resemblances, taken from the most beautiful and stateliest things under heaven . . . these with the like set forth and expresse the spirituall and heavenly ornaments which Christ bestoweth upon his Church, with the fruits of her love to him again.[20]

So also argued Thomas Ager, in *Paraphrase on the Canticles or Song of Solomon,* when he said that the book was "a *spiritual communion* between Christ and his Church . . . even this song setteth out unto her the love and tender compassion of Christ, her bridegroom" (p. 4).

The allegorical mode was easily adaptable to the personalizing of biblical figures, a common practice among seventeenth-century poets of Catholic and Reformed persuasion. Figurative language allowed the creative writer a flexible a range that was not as readily available under the most conservative strictures of typological exegetical practices. John Gill wrote:

> The whole [of *Canticles*] is figurative and allegorical, abounding with a variety of lively metaphors . . . This divine poem sets forth in the most striking manner the mutual love, union, and communion, which are between Christ and his church; also expresses the several different frames, cases, and circumstances, which attend the beleevers in this life; so that they can come into no state or condition, but here is something in this song suited to their experience which serves to recommend it to believers, and discovers the excellency of it.[21]

Gill's impression is almost romantic in its impulse; the allegory is so rich
and varied that in it there is something for everyone, where the historical
figural reading demanded a more precise association between in-
individual, historical movement, and the sequential dispensation of
God's grace through Providence. Even when Thomas Draxe, in *The
Lambe's Spouse, or, the Heavenly Bride* (1608), argued that the marriage of
Canticles was "meritorious and a *Type* of the perfection of eternal life,"
he more intelligently and sensibly argued that the Song of Solomon "is
mysticall and spirituall, because the persons between whom it is made,
viz., CHRIST (as man) and the Church Militant, are farre distant in
place, and therefore it cannot be any NATURALL or CARNALL conjunction."[22] Draxe, who had also allegorized the Book of Revelation, here
has adopted the nomenclature of the prophetic reading in labeling the
marriage a type of heavenly perfection; however, his method is clear.
The entire document is ahistorical and mystical, with no literal level
either now or in the future.

Among these early reformed Christians, few clearly understood the
prophetic and figural importance of the Canticles. Thomas Brightman
demonstrated that Canticles prophesied the state of the church from the
time of David to the second coming of Christ, and John Cotton showed
how Canticles was a prophetic history of the church from Solomon's time
until the end of the world. Even Henry Ainsworth, the Separatist, had
shown how Canticles was a prophecy of the church, but he extended it
from the time of Solomon indefinitely, giving it an eternal or perpetual,
moral significance. In the seventeenth century, one English commmen-
tary appeared that clarified, better than all others, the allegorical and
figural reading of Canticles. Its author, James Durham, had written
Clavis Cantici: or, an Exposition of the Song of Solomon (1669), in order to
show how incorrect the typologists were and how correct the allegorical
reading of Canticles was; however, his treatise provided the clearest
statement of these different modes of interpretation that would come out
of the period. When Edward Taylor, who used figural readings of Scripture throughout the early poems in his Second Series of *Meditations*,
sought a commentary to gloss his own interpretation of Canticles for
those poems which specifically treat Canticles themes, it was to Durham
that he turned, and it was essentially Durham's allegorical reading of
Canticles that he adopted. It was Durham's distinctions—though drawn
after John Cotton had penned his two interpretations of the Canticles—that best interpret Cotton's allegorical and typological reading of
the book.

John Owen prefaces the *Clavis Cantici* by clearly stating that "the
book of the Canticles is not in any part of it, much less in the whole, a
meet subject for every ordinary undertaker to exercise upon. The Matter of it is totally Sublime, Spirituall, and Mysticall; and the Manner of

it's handling universally Allegorical. So did God think meet in his manifold Wisdom to instruct his Church of old."[23] Both Owen and Durham were well aware of the value of "types and allegories" in the interpretation of Scripture; their ultimate aim, therefore, was to use the Canticles as a way of showing the important distinctions between these mutually supportive modes of interpretation and to indicate how God has used both in his effort to accommodate divine mystery to the mind of man. Somewhat critical of those who would incorrectly read the Canticles historically Owen argued that

> they plainly acknowledge the mystery and allegory of the whole, ascribing the things mentioned to the Transactors between God and the Church, partly Historically, partly Prophetically, with such a respect unto the Messiah . . . from them, have some Learned Persons of late taken occasion to wrest the whole Allegory into an History and a Prophesy, but with more sobriety then they, and with more respect unto the Analogy of faith . . . The more general persuasion of Learned men is, that the whole is one holy Declaration of that Mystically Spiritual Commmunion, that is between the great Bridegroom and his Spouse, the Lord Christ and his Church, and every believing Soul that belongs thereunto (Preface).

This broad definition enabled the Christian reader to read himself into the narrative of Canticles (to "personalize" its imagery) in two ways: first, as a member of the historical church referred to in the allegorical correspondence between spouse and church; and second, as a personal and individual soul who would be, in those last days, literally and really married to Christ in the way that is only represented allegorically in the Canticles. No wonder that this reading was prominent among Reformed interpreters.

It is because such confusion as this existed that Durham's *Clavis Cantici* exerted so important an influence at the time it first appeared in clarifying the interpretive alternatives for Canticles. Numerous handbooks of exegesis were already available, such as William Guild's *Moses Unvailed* and Thomas Taylor's *Christ Revealed,* both of which had been published in the first half of the century. However, Durham's essential contribution was that he applied these doctrinal and rhetorical distinctions to the one book with which his treatise was concerned: the Song of Solomon. The work was published posthumously; however, its own preface and narrative, both authored by Durham, were among the most important critical statments issued during the seventeenth century. We could, of course, dwell on the minute detail and numerous examples provided in the *Clavis Cantici*, through which Durham exerted this astonishing influence on later writers like Edward Taylor, who relied almost exclusively on the *Clavis* in his arrangement of those *Meditations* (115-165, Second Series), many of which treat Canticles texts and the.

theme of marriage. But Durham's method is so clear that a brief examination of his initial doctrinal positions will show the essential meaning and will provide a backdrop for discussing John Cotton's dual interpretations of this troublesome Old Testament book.

Durham goes right to the heard of the matter: "This Song is not to be taken properly, or literally, that is, as the words do at first sound; but it is to be taken and understood spiritually, figuratively and allegorically, as having some spiritual meaning contained under these figurative expressions."[24] But he must clarify, in good Protestant fashion, this disruption of the literal meaning of a scripture text:

> I grant it hath a literal meaning, but I say, that literal meaning is not immediate, and that which first looketh out as in Historical Scriptures, or others which are not figurative, but that which is spiritually and especially meant by these Allegorick and Figurative speeches, is the Literal meaning of this Song; . . . a Literal sense is that which floweth from such a place of Scripture as intended by the Spirit in the words, whether properly or figuratively used, and is to be gathered from the whole complex expression together, applyed thereunto, as in the Exposition of Parables, Allegories, and Figurative Scriptures is clear; and it were as improper and absurd to deny a Figurative Sense to these, as it were to fix Figurative Expositions upon plain Scriptures, which are properly to be taken (p. 6).

Durham's sleight of hand with distinctions between the literal meaning of Scripture an the figurative meaning of a literal text is clear; like Perkins, he insisted on the literal veracity of God's word, but would also argue that God used figurative expressions to accommodate divine meaning to man's reason. His distinctions are unmistakable: allegorical figures differ from typological figures and the Song of Solomon is an allegory.

> First, Types suppose still the verity of some History . . . Allegories have no such necessary supposition, but are as Parables proposed for some mystical end . . .
>
> 2. Types look only to matters of Fact, and compare one fact with another . . . Allegories take in Words, Sentences, Doctrines both of Faith and manners . . .
>
> 3. Types compare Persons, and Facts, under the Old Testament, with Persons, and Facts, under the New, and is made up of something that is present; prefiguring another to come; Allegories look especially to matters in hand and intend the putting of some high spiritual sense upon words, which at first they seem not to bear, whether the Allegorie be only in the Old Testament, or only in the New, or in both, it looks to the sense, and meaning, being so considered in itself, as the words may best serve the scope, and teach or manifest the thing the Spirit intends, without any comparison betwixt this, and that of the Old Testament and the new . . .

4. Types are only Historical as such, and the truth of Fact agreeing in Anti-type, make them up, it being clear in Scripture that such things are Types; for we must not forge Types without Scripture-warrant: But allegories are principally Doctrinal, and in their scope intend not to clear, or compare Facts, but to hold forth and explain Doctrines, or by such similitudes to make them better understood . . .

5. Types in the Old Testament respect only some things, persons, and events, as Christ, the Gospel, and its Spreading, and *cannot be extended beyond these* [italics mine] . . . but Allegories take in every thing, that belong either to Doctrine, or Instuction in Faith, or to practise for ordering one's life. Hence, we may see that Allegories are much more extensive, and comprehensive in their meaning and application, then Types (which cannot be extended further then some one thing) (pp. 9-10).

For these very sound reasons, all argued from a conservative understanding of the Protestant habit of mind by which the Bible was to be interpreted figurally and historically or typologically, Durham was able to conclude that "this Song is not Typical, a being made up of two Histories, to wit, Solomon's Marriage, and Christ's . . . but it is Allegorick, not respecting Solomon or his Marriage, but aiming to set out spiritual Mysteries in figurative expressions, in such a manner as may most effectuate that end, for inlightening the judgement, and moving of the affections without any respect to that Story or Fact of Solomon's" (p. 10).

John Cotton's exegesis of Canticles exhibits a similar understanding of these distinctions, but the two versions also indicate his penchant for prophetic and eschatological figuralism. Cotton's figural language was pervasive and natural to his theology of prophecy and fulfillment. About ten years after his arrival in America, he gave a series of lectures on Revelation, Chapter 13, in which he set 1655 as the date for Christ's arrival in New England and His establishment of the long-awaited kingdom, which would include the final, ultimate fulfillment of all types (both Old and New Testament, correlative and developmental) and in another series of sermons called *The Powring Out of the Seven Vials* (1645) Cotton exhorted his congregation to provide for the spiritual rivers flowing from the rock of Christ, an obvious figural association.[25] And in some early sermons on I John (*Commentary upon First John Generall* [1656]) Cotton argued that the Old Testament types could have a perpetual equity, and like Ames, showed that Noah was a type of the renewal of all creation. These early examples indicate the figural habit of mind ever present in Cotton's exegesis, and one has only to examine the voluminous dissertation evidence that has recently been produced on the subject of Cotton's typology to understand how important figural expression was not only to his writing and preaching but also to the foundations of his theology.[26]

It should not be surprising that we find Cotton espousing the typological and figural reading of Canticles in his 1642 version of *A Brief Exposition of the Whole Book of Canticles, or Song of Solomon.* In the 1642 edition, he had begun a figural reading of the work, and had shown how the book was not a mere allegory of "the gloriousnesse of the restored Estate of the Church of the Jewes, and the happy accesse of the Gentiles, in the approaching days of Reformation, when the wall of Partition shall be taken away."[27] Throughout the exposition, Cotton shows his conviction that the language of Canticles is prophetic rather than pure allegory:

> ...this song admitteth more varietie of interpretation then any other, and also of singular use: some have applied it to expresse the mutuall affection and fellowship between Christ and every Christian soule; some betweene Christ and the Catholick church; some to particular churches, from Solomons time to the last Judgment; and there is an holy and usefull truth in each one of these interpretations; but the last doth exceedingly magnifie the wonderfull excellency of this Song, making it a divine abridgement of the Acts and Monuments of the Church ... *This booke was chiefly penned to bee such an historical prophecie or propheticall history.* [28]

Throughout the document, eschatological and prophetic interpretation dominate. Cotton follows the conventional wisdom in designating Solomon as a type of Christ: "But consider further that Solomon, when hee is here set forth as the desire, praise, and blessednesse of all his people, hee is then a type of Christ, greater than Solomon, whose heavenly fellowship and instruction the Church desires above wine" (Preface). But it is in the 1655 edition, which clearly modifies the influence of Thomas Brightman's interpretation of Canticles, that Cotton amplifies the figural reading and sets the typological interpretation in its larger context.

Anthony Tuckney, in his preface to that edition, said "there is a threefold meaning of this Book; as expressing 1. The affection and relation between Christ and his Church in General. 2. The affection and relation between Christ and every sincere soul. 3. The estate and condition of every Church from Solomon's time to the last judgement. In the former Exposition, or copy [e.g., the 1642 edition], the last sense was chiefly intended, and not the two former, which yet ought not to lie hid."[29]

It was as though Cotton had been challenged on his figural reading of Canticles and forced to recant. Tuckney almost chides him for having given so much emphasis to the typological reading in 1642 and criticizes his prophetic reading, again with Brightman, of Revelation: "As for his way of expounding this Scripture, as a *Propheticall History* of the Church, he for the most part treadeth in the steps of a very godly Learned Divine ... Sometime I knew him of another judgement, when much approved of Master Brightman's Exposition of the *Revelation,* but thought somewhat strange of this his way of Expounding the *Canticles*"(Tuckney's Preface).

Tuckney's apology for Cotton's ambivalence in his interpretation of Canticles, stressing allegory and figural typology, did not vitiate the significance of Cotton's figural reading. He and Brightman had both issued typological readings almost simultaneously, and Cotton did not simply assign typological value to the author, Solomon, who was conventionally seen as a type of Christ. Rather he interpreted the allegory typologically, as in this powerful passage concerning the roe image:

> First, this teacheth us that in all the instruments of the Churches deliverance, we should see and discerne Christ speaking and working in them . . . *Untill the day breake, and the shadowes flee away.* That is, till Christ come, and the Ceremoniall shadowes vanish . . . Doe they heare a rumour of a deliverance? It is the voyce of Christ, and it must needs by a strong voyce which Christ is the author of . . . Secondly, this teacheth us, that when the time of the Churches deliverance is come, Christ will come quickly and speedily for her deliverance, leaping and skipping as a Roe or a Hart.[30]

This figural reading, while not unique to John Cotton, was an important achievement among Reformed theologians, who were resisting the purely fanciful and allegorical interpretations of Canticles set forth by the medieval church. Since Origen had formulated the allegorical view that Canticles was a celebration of the passion between the individual soul and Christ, the Church fathers and medieval exegetes had established a variety of interpretations of the book that invoked the ingenuity of personal and individual interpretation. John Cotton sought a prophetic understanding of the clearly symbolic poem, and his figural reading made possible a conflation of allegory and typology that endowed the erotic images with the significance of prophecy and fulfillment. But it remained for Edward Taylor, the New England Puritan poet of the late seventeenth century, to use the Canticles texts in a unified series of *Preparatory Mediations* that would establish the eternal and personal presence of Christ in the Old Testament types and figures. Taylor followed James Durham in acknowledging the differences between typological and allegorical readings of Scripture; however, he would show how both forms of God's word set forth Christ's nature and his achievements.[31] In the *Christographia* sermons, Taylor argued that the Old Testament believers

> Had Christ dispensed in Promises and Types, as a Mediator to come. We have him dispensed in a Cleare, and Manifest way as come already. But the different manner of dispensing of the Messiah, doth not produce, a Different Christ, nor a different Faith in Christ. Sometimes the Church sets forth

Christ as an obscure person standing behinde the Wall, peeping in at the Window, and making a flowrish thro' the lattice as Can. 2.9. Sometimes she setts him out in orientall Colours and in most Allegorical accomplishments as Cant. 5.10-16. Yet this differing way of Setting him out, makes not any Personall difference. Its the same Person, and Beloved in the one description, as it is described in the other.[32]

The poetry of Edward Taylor is a suitable subject for examining the evolution of figural writing in seventeenth-century New England, for his *Meditations* were based on scriptural texts which he read in a variety of ways, that is, allegorically and typologically. Until very recently, we have had only a few of the sermons long believed to accompany the scriptural texts and *Meditations*, for example, the *Christographia* and the *Treatise Concerning the Lord's Supper*; both groups were edited by Norman Grabo during the last fifteen years. In 1977 Charles Mignon discovered yet another series of sermons by Edward Taylor, a group that corresponds to the first thirty-six *Meditations* of the Second Series, the group in which Taylor specifically talked of Old Testament typological figures and related them to his personal experience of Christ. We do not have the sermons that correspond to the Canticles meditations of the same series, but it is clear that, like John Cotton, Edward Taylor was attempting to personalize the metaphors of the Bible throughout his writing, and that in some instances he relied on allegory for a sustained personal metaphor and in others his personal experience was caught up in the providential scheme of historical prophecy and fulfillment, type and antitype. The distinctions Taylor drew between figural writing and allegory were traditional ones, and though his conceits and images reflect a highly sophisticated employment of rhetorical strategies and baroque metaphors, his doctrinal statements exhibit a conservative exegesis of the biblical types. In his treatment of Canticles, Taylor found eschatological and prophetic meaning in the analogy of the bridegroom and his beloved, and in the Old Testament types, he found a vehicle for expressing his belief in the continuity of God's Providence throughout human time.

Both these developments in Taylor's writing mirror larger patterns discernible in the evolving theology of late seventeenth-century New England. Perry Miller's declension thesis has its counterpart in the transformation of orthodox typological figures into allegorical symbols in the late writings of Jonathan Edwards and in some of the metaphorical habits of mind exhibited by Cotton Mather. The tensions between allegory and typology as ways of comprehending the ways of God to man reached a high point in the late seventeenth century, and Taylor's poetry and sermons are best understood in the context exegetical manuals published during this time, like Benjamin Keach's *Tropologia* and Samuel Mather's *Figures or Types of the Old Testament*.

II
Figuralism in Late Seventeenth Century New England

4

SAMUEL MATHER: FIGURES, TYPES, AND ALLEGORIES

1. *That all this typical Dispensation is expired and abolished by the exhibition of Jesus Christ the Truth and Substance and Scope of all:* These shadows are vanished away by the rising of that Sun of Righteousness . . .

2. *The Gospel-Dispensation doth succeed, and is substituted* . . . Instead of the Law and Prophets, we have the Gospel and Evangelists, who give us an History instead of Prophecy . . .

3. *This Gospel-Dispensation is far more glorious then the old Legal Dispensation.* For is not the Substance better then the Shadows . . . The spirit is better then the Letter. The Letter there is not the *written Word,* and the Spirit the *Enthusiasms* of a deluded Fancy, (as some have understood it); but the Letter is the *Law,* and the Spirit is the *Gospel,* as the whole context shows.

And the Apostle hath some Expressions looking that way in other Scriptures; as when he saith, that *here we see but in a Glass darkly,* that is, the Glass of Gospel-Administrations . . . He is there comparing the Law and the Gospel, *But in Heaven we shall see Face to Face* . . . Under the Law they had no more but the Shadow; but now, under the Gospel, we have the very Image, we see things as in a Glass; but in Heaven, we have *the Things Themselves.*

— Samuel Mather, *Figures or Types of the
Old Testament,* 1683

WITH THE PASSING of John Cotton, in 1655, Puritanism in New England entered a second major phase. It was no longer easy to read the history of the times as an antitypical fulfillment of the Old Testament types, and it was more difficult to anticipate a literal millennium and the establishment of Christ's kingdom in Massachusetts Bay. In England, the failure of the Commonwealth seemed to echo this general disillusion, and in 1660 a new wave of immigrants came to the shores of Massachusetts seeking asylum from the reprisals of Charles II and the Restoration. John Milton had gone blind, but he did not need his eyes to see that his long awaited utopian commonwealth would never be realized on earth. In New England, the "errand into the wilderness" was assessed by Samuel Danforth, who delivered the election sermon to the Massachusetts Bay Colony on May 11, 1670. He chose for his text Matthew 11:7-9, and for his title, *A Briefe Recognition of New England's Errand Into the Wilderness.*

Danforth's exegesis of the text was standard, if a little elaborate and somewhat detailed. However, his abstracting of a doctrine, and the application of that doctrine, could be understood in only one sense: the New Israel had fallen into a period of apostasy and would soon be punished for her sins. Danforth declared: "DOCT: *Such as have sometime left their pleasant cities and Habitations to enjoy the Pure Worship of God in a Wilderness, are apt in time abate and cool in their affection thereunto.*" [1] And how did they spend their time in the Wilderness," Danforth says, "but in tempting God, and in murmuring against their godly and faithful teachers and rulers?"

Danforth's analogizing of New England and ancient Israel includes a harsh admonition to New England that she remember her providential role and return from her apostasy:

USE I. Of solemn and serious inquiry to us all in this general Assembly, Whether we have not in a great measure forgotten our Errand into the Wilderness . . . Now let us sadly consider whether our ancient and primitive affections to the Lord Jesus, his glorious gospel, his pure and spiritual worship and the Order of His House, remain, abide, and continue firm, constant, entire, and inviolate (pp. 9-10).

This warning is but a prelude for the judgment that follows. New England's apostasy from her original mission has been marked by "Pride, Contention, Worldliness, Covetousness, Luxury, Drunkenness, and Uncleanness," Danforth asserts, all of which "break in like a flood upon us," so that "good men grow cold in their love to God and to one another" (p. 13). The rhetoric of the jeremiad was denunciatory, but the language of Canaan was employed to show how a potential realization of Christ's kingdom was all but lost.

The sermon continues with the development of several specific parallels between Israel and New England drawn from relevant scriptural passages. Danforth announces clearly the theme of the errand into the wilderness and states its peculiar importance for God's chosen people:

To what Purpose then Came we into this Wilderness? And What Expectation Drew us Thither? Was it not the expectation of the *Pure and Faithful Dispensation* of the Gospel and the Kingdom of God? The times were such that we could not enjoy it in our own land; and therefore having obtained *Liberty* and a *Gracious Patent* from our *Soveraign,* we left our Country, Kindred, and Father's Houses, and came into these wilde Woods and Deserts, where the Lord hath planted us, and made us *Dwell in a Place of Our Own, that we Might Move No More, and That the Children of Wickedness Might not Afflict us Any More (II Sam. 7.10)* (p. 18).

The text, interestingly enough, is the same one that John Cotton had used in 1630, forty years earlier, in his sermon to the Winthrop fleet. *God's Promise to His Plantations* had presented the idea that God originally covenanted with His chosen people, the New England Israel, to fulfill His spiritual promises made in the Old Testament and embodied in the types. During the forty years separating John Cotton's sermon from Danforth's jeremiad, attitudes among the Puritans shifted away from a conviction that God's mission was somehow organically planted in Massachusetts Bay, and it is important to measure the differences between John Cotton and Samuel Danforth as writers and preachers of the language of Canaan, just as it is illuminating to compare their uses of the errand theme. For each succeeding generation of New England Puritanism, the language of Canaan was employed with slight differences. The allegory/typology tension present from earliest times became increasingly significant as biblical figures were endowed with value by the exegetical practices of ministers over the centuries.

When John Cotton used II Samuel 7:10 as a text for his earlier sermon, "planting" was a metaphor for the spiritual kingdom, and he had firmly believed that the kingdom would be a literal event in the future history of New England. The rhetorical metaphor was not to be dissociated from God's historical promises to His chosen people. However, in Danforth's sermon, it is clear that the metaphor has been confined to its scriptural context and that the eschatological anticipation of Christ's kingdom, so prominent in Cotton's understanding of the errand, has been transformed into an apprehension of God's judgment of New England. Danforth's sermon contains some brilliant examples of this shift in emphasis, one of which presents logical arguments for New England's uniqueness among the colonies:

> *What* is it that *Distinguisheth New England* from Other Colonies and Plantations in *America?* Not our transportation over the *Atlantick* ocean, but the *Ministry* of God's Faithful Prophets and the fruition of *His Holy Ordinances.* Did not the Lord bring the *Philistines* from *Caphtor,* and the *Assyrians from Kir,* as well as *Israel from Egypt?* Amos. 9.7. But by a *Prophet* the *Lord Brought Israel Out of Egypt* and by a *Prophet was he preserved,* Hos. 12.13. What is the Price of Esteem of God's prophet and their faithful dispensations, now fallen in our hearts? (p. 18).

The distinguishing mark of the New English Israel has been exchanged for a nostalgic lamentation of her apostasy from the errand. We find, at the close of the sermon, a lament modeled on the Old Testament lament over the loss of God's love, in a moving passage of exhortation:

> Hath the Lord been wanting to us, or failed our expectations? . . . How sadly hath the Lord testified against us, because of our loss of our first love, and our remissness and negligence in his Work? Why hath the Lord smitten us with

Blasting and Mildew now seven years together, superadding sometimes severe Drought, sometimes great Tempests, Floods, and sweeping rains, that leave no food behind them? Is it not because the *House of the Lord Lyeth Waste?* Temple-Work in our Hearts, Families, Churches, is shamefully neglected (pp. 18-19).

Finally, Danforth reaches the climax and pleads with the people to return to God:

It is High Time for us to Remember Whence We are Fallen, and Repent, and Do Our First Works. Wherefore Let us lift up the hands that hang down, and strengthen the feeble knees, and make straight paths for our feet lest that which is lame be turned out of the way, but let it rather be healed. (Heb. 12:12, 13) (p. 19).

It was too late. The apostasy of New England might have been corrected had moral behavior and the fiber of a theocracy at Massachusetts Bay been the only factors involved, but there were more. The collapse of the Puritan Commonwealth in England, while not directly affecting affairs in Massachusetts, brought to the colony larger numbers of disillusioned Puritans who sought a new life in ways other than through the fulfillment of an utopian dream. Meanwhile, immigrants from the old world who did not share the original sense of mission had reached the colonial shores, and many of these regarded the wilderness to be an unharnessed, unspoiled land needing civilization's progress and cultivation. The merchants of the colonies, even in Massachusetts Bay, had much to do with the dissolution of the theocracy and the turning of the people from their original mission. However, a most serious result of the apostasy occured in the gradual transformation of leadership among the New England Puritans.

No longer did the theologian combine his reading of Scripture with the activity of his mission in the wilderness; no longer did a John Cotton provide a theological justification for the errand into the wilderness and then the leadership to carry out that mission. Rather, the theologian and secular leader began to separate (although from the beginning, in Massachusetts Bay, the ministers had not been the magistrates). Theologians and intellectuals like Increase Mather and John Davenport kept alive an idea by condemning contemporary events in terms of that original idea. For this new rhetoric of eschatology and judgment, they employed a sermon form harsh in its criticism, the jeremiad, through which the New English Israel was compared to the Israel of old and then warned of the impending dangers in further apostasy from God's providential calling. Criticism of the people by the leaders who exhorted them to return to God's guidance was an old as the period of the Judges; however, the voluminous flow of sermons during the last half of the seventeenth century allows the second and third generations of New

England Puritanism to claim the jeremiad as their own contribution to evolving rhetorical strategies. Through the jeremiads, the biblical types were revived to show the continuity of God's historical concern for his chosen people, and in many of these sermons, the design of Providence was extended beyond Scripture to incorporate the early history of New England. Few ministers, however, were bold enough to assert that the contemporary history of New England reflected progress toward Christ's kingdom on earth, which has been an earlier eschatological emphasis. Most were too busy warning their congregations of the last judgment, which was sure to arrive as a reproof of apostasy from the original errand.

Meanwhile, writers and thinkers like Samuel Mather, Increase Mather, Benjamin Keach, and John Davenport attempted to hold together a world view, a method of exegesis, a way of reading history, and an epistemology in their monumental efforts to assert the efficacy of typology and biblical figuralism in a period that was falling away from a belief in the active relevance of Scripture for its own historical circumstances. The literature of the period, much of it ignored until the twentieth century, has revealed significant changes in the uses of biblical types. Edward Taylor, for example, preached numerous sermons on the efficacy of biblical types in the Old Testament in addition to his *Christographia* sequence and *Treatise Concerning the Lord's Supper*. However, he also penned over two hundred meditations, poems based on selected scriptural texts, and in many of these, he spiritualized and allegorized the biblical types out of their purely historical and typological contexts. Michael Wigglesworth published his popular *Day of Doom,* an eschatological poem that became one of the most important jeremiads in all the warnings that appeared during the late seventeenth century. John Flavel's *Husbandry Spiritualized,* an adaptation of the allegorical method of the medieval exegetes, took its text from nature, rather than from Scripture.

In all of these, the biblical and figural language of Canaan had an important place. It was not the place it had enjoyed during its prominence as a method for reading Puritan history; however, its role in that exegetical context was not abandoned overnight. Nevertheless, typology gradually became a function of epistemology, because the Puritan continued to ask himself, "How may I know the truth about God?" In seeking an answer, he turned to typology as a means of reading not only the Scripture and his own history, but also as a way of reading the Book of Nature.

Meanwhile, the conservative exegetes—the Mathers, Keach, Thomas Taylor, and Davenport—upheld the sanctity of Scripture and its instituted typological correspondences with little departure into spiritualizing. However, the theological typologists were now in competition with secular typologists and with theological spiritualizers, of whom John Flavel was the most prominent representative. As in most periods of extreme uncertainty, each group produced a literature that characterized its theology, exhibiting orthodox tendencies in some areas and serious departures from biblical contexts in others. Although the Bible continued to provide the Puritans with a thorough mythology on which to base their sermons and from which to take their sermon illustrations, there were some serious alternations in the original intentions of the conservative typologist that led to what Paul Hunter has called a "broadened typology": "Typology had never been a very exact science, and the seventeenth century, with great ease, broadened typology's scope beyond the confines of the Old and New Testaments, for its rules were loosely formulated; typology had remained more of a useful tool of interpretation than a distinct discipline. The broadened typology simply extended to contemporary history the principle of reading one time in terms of another: biblical objects or events now might not only prefigure other biblical events or concepts but also the events of later history."[2] It is a version of this broadened typology that John Cotton employed to declare New England the "antitypical fulfillment" of the Old Testament types. Altough he abandoned this emphasis and later regarded the types to be relevant for New England by a moral equity that transcended their typical and prefigurative institution, he had utilized the broadened developmental typology in order to demonstrate the continuity of God's Providence from biblical times to the seventeenth century. Contemporary Puritans found various uses for the types that had not been instituted in Scripture and had not been sanctioned by the typologists of the early church.

> The broadened typology offered contemporary history an extended mythic dimension based upon past history frozen into static form. Different interpreters might choose to emphasize different segments of the biblical myth, but nearly all Puritan thinkers represented contemporary times as reflections (sometimes distorted, often blurred) of the Judeo-Christian experience recorded by inspired writers who understood divine purposes, and as part of the continuing movement of earthly history toward an inevitable climax. The broadened typology, violating the aims but not the methods of the traditional typology, thus relieved biblical history of primary interpretive attention and instead made this history the ultimate symbolic referent of contemporary events.[3]

It is this broadened typology that became the foundation of epistemology among theologians, poets, and historians of the second and third generations, and it is this kind of typology that is found later in the writing of Cotton Mather, whose *Magnalia Christi Americana* (1702) incorporated aspects of the myth into a narration of the ecclesiastical history of New England. These expansive tendencies are also to be found in the poetry and theology of Edward Taylor and John Milton, and yet, loosely formulated approaches to typology were always kept in check by the more traditional and conservative opinions of Thomas Taylor, Samuel Mather, Benjamin Keach, and John Davenport. The polarity between these two groups of thinkers, writers, and poets and more traditionally oriented theologians was widened by the gaps that appeared between the epistemology of nature in the form of "spiritualizing," and the resurgence of orthodox exegesis that appeared in many forms during the second half of the seventeenth century. It is nowhere more clearly demonstrated than in the adaptations of typology by the writers and spiritualizers as distinguished from the systematic assessments of typology provided by several prominent convervative theologians. It will be useful to examine those differences in some detail, since the role of typology as an exegetical method became gradually distinct from the epistemological function of types in the reading of history and in the explanation of the nature universe. These distinctions are crucial for an understanding of Edward Taylor's sermons and poetry, which exhibit a tension between the allegorical and typological uses of Scripture texts.

TYPOLOGY AND THE NEW ENGLAND WAY

It is a commonplace that the Puritans were fond of discovering evidence of God's Providence in their daily lives. Sermon and essay titles from the late seventeenth century, such as Increase Mather's *Essay for the Recording of Illustrious Providences* (1684), are but one measure of the widespread tendency to prove God's concern for His chosen people. This habit of mind, however, was a corollary of the reading of history in terms of God's providential dispensations, and it was only indirectly related to typological exegesis of Scripture. If God had elected his New English Israel for an errand into the wilderness, then it made sense to search through the events of contemporary life for indications and affirmations of this election. This, in turn, might provide assurance that the Puritans were indeed the chosen of God, but it did not demonstrate that New England was the antitypical fulfillment of the biblical types, "Remarkable Providences" were little more than sermon illustrations for the second and third generations, who had lost faith in the idea of Christ's kingdom on earth being established in Massachusetts Bay. However, the metaphorical and illustrative value of the providences came to rival the authority of Scripture itself in proving to New England that they were in the hands of the Almighty.

Basically, there were two distinct kinds of providences, the general providences, by which God continued his divine supervision of human activity begun at the creation, usually assumed to correspond to the law of nature and operations of the natural world, and special providences, those miraculous intrusions into the natural order, explicable only through reference to God's election of His saints and concern for their welfare. Through the medium of special providence, God could punish as well as reward, and the New England Puritans were extremely sensitive to an evolving pattern of disapprobation that they were able to discern in the special providential treatment of their elect group. Special providence relieved them of concluding that misfortune was a general sign that their enterprise was misguided and not predestined to usher in the kingdom of God. Although the "remarkable providences" needed no scriptural analogues, and although they rarely had a resemblance to a biblical type, they were a persistent means of assuring the Puritans that they had been chosen by God for a special purpose.

In William Bradford's *History of Plimouth Plantation*, we find an early example of this habit of mind:

> And I may not omite a spetiall worke of Godes Providence. Ther was a proud and very profane younge man, one of the sea-men, of a lustie, able body, which made him the more hauty; he would allway be contemning the poore people in their sicknes, and cursing them dayly with greevous execrations, and did not let to tell them, that he hoped to help to cast halfe of them over board before they came to their jurneys end, and to make mery with what they had; and if he were by any gently reproved, he would curse and swear most bitterly. But it pleased God before they came halfe seas over, to smite this yong man with a greevous disease, of which he dyed in a desperate maner, and so was him selfe the first that was throwne overbord. Thus his curses light on his owne head; and it was an astonishmente to all his fellows, for they noted it to be the just hand of God upon him.[4]

Similar "remarkable providences" appear throughout the Puritan diaries, and frequently they are used by preachers as sermon illustrations. As Puritan rhetoric developed more sophisticated tendencies, the "Providence" was sometimes employed in the same manner that a medieval preacher would have used an "emblem," or contemporary *exemplum*. Since history was no more than the gradual unfolding of God's divine will, the specific events of history, and the affairs of daily life, would obviously be manifestations of that will revealed.

In the late seventeenth century, this tendency to find providences throughout nature and history emerged as an opposing force to the conservative tradition of typological exegesis. Just as the medieval writers has "allegorized" nature and had even spiritualized the biblical types in some of the mystery plays, for example the Brome Cycle version of *Abraham and Isaac,* the Puritans turned to nature to find types of God's Providence. Interestingly enough, a particularly good example of the varying applications of typology is found in another saga of the sea:

On the 16th of October, 1634, Mr. Shepard and his friends sailed from Harwich, a seaport in Essex, at the mouth of the river Stour. They had proceeded but a few leagues, when, the wind suddenly changing, they were obliged to cast anchor in a very dangerous place. The wind continued to blow all night, and, in the morning of the 17th, became so violent that the ship dragged her anchors, and was driven upon the sands near the harbor of Harwich, where she was for some time in the most imminent peril. To add to their distress, one of the sailors, in endeavoring to execute some order, fell overboard, and was carried a mile or so out to sea, apparently beyond the reach of any human aid. The ship and crew were at that moment in so much danger, that no one could be spared to go in search of him, if indeed, the boat could have lived a moment in the sea that was breaking around them; and when the immediate danger to the ship was over, no one on board supposed that the poor man was alive. He was, however, discovered floating upon the waves at a great distance though it was known that he was not able to swim; and three seamen put off in the boat at the hazard of their lives, to save him. When they reached him, though he was floating, — supported, as it were, by a divine hand, — he exhibited no signs of life; and having taken him on board, they laid him in the bottom of the boat, supposing him to be dead. One of the men, however, was unwilling to give up his shipmate without using all the means in their power for his resuscitation. Upon turning his head downward, in order to let the water run out, he began to breathe; in a few moments, under such good treatment as their good sense suggested, he was able to move and to speak, and by the time they had reached the ship, he had recovered the use of his limbs, having been in the water more than an hour.[5]

This incident is not in itself unusual; many providential rescues appear throughout Puritan chronicles. What is significant about it is the use it was given by either Dr. Norton or Thomas Shepard, both fellow passengers on the voyage, as a type or example of God's Providence: "This man's danger and deliverance is a *type* of ours. We are in great danger, and yet the Lord's power will be shown in saving us."[6] We have already seen how exegetes used typology and typological systems anywhere they desired to show how one event prefigured another in the providentially guided history of the universe. Now we find the preacher using the "representative type" anywhere there is evidence of God's handiwork in earthly affairs, to prefigure the salvation of mankind.

This penchant for discovering providences was as old as Puritanism itself. Edward Johnson's *Wonder-Working Providence of Sions Saviour in New England, 1628-1651* presented the major events of the errand into the wilderness as part of the grand providential design. But the habit of mind engendered by early Puritan attempts to record and illustrate God's activity in this world resulted in a wholesale spiritualization of nature and Scripture by the late seventeenth century. Perry Miller has said that "Puritans had always dwelt with particular fondness upon those events that could be explained only as contrivances of the divine intelligence. They seem to have been temperamentally uncomfortable at the thought of miracles, and rather relieved that the era of violent exceptions to the law of nature was finished; but they took particular comfort in moralizing over oddities which seemed to be produced by natural causes, but in which the pious investigator could perceive the finger of God."[7] Through the discovery of remarkable providences, the Puritan exegete might not only perceive the handiwork of God in His operation of the natural universe; he might also understand some of the remarkable deliverances of Israel in the Old Testament, through a comparison of his own situation with that of the early analogue.

This departure from the historically verified and divinely instituted typological correspondences was a prominent feature of developments in Puritan rhetoric during the latter part of the seventeenth century. Although the discerning of analogies between Israel, or even the New Testament, and New England was a commonly accepted practice among the Puritans from the beginning, it was another matter altogether to include New England in a typological scheme by which natural occurrences had typical significance similar to the events of the Old Testament, all prefiguring the long-awaited kingdom of God on earth. Moreover, the word "type" was sometimes used to mean no more than representative figure, just as the medieval exegete would have pointed to Everyman as a moral exemplum for his congregations. Therefore, the crucial distinction between those types that had relevance for the New English Israel and those that belonged to another era came to be measured in the moral equity or exemplary value the type possessed, as Thomas Shepard and Samuel Mather were to show. Not only was it important to provide historical veracity when exegeting a type; it was also necessary to assess the moral authority of the figure, by which it spoke directly to New England, even though as a typical prefiguration of Christ it may have been fulfilled in the coming of the flesh. The place of the types in the historical scheme of prefiguration and abrogation proved a difficult problem for the Puritan ministers, and, in some cases no distinction was made between the typical role and the moral value of an Old Testament figure.

By the middle of the seventeenth century, therefore, the Puritan was provided with a number of epistemological alternatives. He could turn to his Bible for the most authoritative revelation of truth; but he might also use the powers of right reason guided by an informed conscience to discern theological truth through revelation in the created universe. More important, perhaps, he was endowed with powers of interpretation so that he no longer needed the ministrations of institutional exegesis, as the medieval layman had. Although these alternatives were much to the same as those available to the lay exegete during any century since the Reformation, the New England Puritan in the seventeenth century found his reliance on the authority of Scripture—paricularly his literal-minded approach to the interpretation of Scripture—challenged on all sides by new kinds of epistemology. Nature and reason came to the assistance of Scripture in revealing the will of God.

NATURE METHODIZED

Exegesis during the seventeenth century differed primarily in emphasis from the reading of Scripture in any other post-Reformation period. Basically, the theologian and the layman were concerned to understand God, and both sought new ways to comprehend His revelation. As in any other century, conservative theologians were challenged by innovative thinkers who would seek revelation outside the limits of Scripture. What distinguished the tensions of the seventeenth century was the concomitant transformation of the world order that had dominated intellectual progress for over five hundred years by a *weltanschauung* founded on the emerging scientific and rationalistic empiricism. Among the Puritans, the conservative exegetes like Keach, Samuel Mather, Thomas Taylor, and Davenport reinforced the authority of Scripture in their reassertions of the tenets of traditional typological exegesis; others, like John Flavel, saw in nature not only analogies for the truths revealed in Scripture but a new source of revelation. The tension, therefore, was almost wholly epistemological; one was constantly faced with the probing question of theodicy, and the answers did not come easily. The epistemology of the Hebrews could hardly keep pace with Baconian innovations; but it held the key to salvation for large numbers of Puritan ministers and their congregations. The Puritan's literal and figural commitment to Scripture was continuously assailed by contemporary discoveries and revelations, so that he was forced to accommodate his understanding of the mysteries of Scripture through a reading of nature. The book of nature was no longer a simple reflection of the divine order, made imperfect by man's fall from grace; rather, it was now a new source of revealed truth, a direct line of communication to the divine intelligence, if only the elect saint could understand the "language of Canaan," by which God would speak to his earthly creatures. Thus contemporary science and epistemology came to rival theology not only in those areas of secular development generally hostile to religion but also in areas theology had always governed, for example, revelation of the Divine Will, and the interpretation of Scripture. Nature was now viewed emblematically and allegorically as a source of divine revelation that could lead, as easily as Scripture, to understanding and truth. Writers like Samuel Mather and poets like Edward Taylor evolved a methodology for approaching these alternative modes of spiritual fulfillment through nature and through Scripture. It was not an amicable reconciliation and would finally be accomplished by Jonathan

Edwards; however, the problems began to emerge in the form-
ulations of Benjamin Keach and Samuel Mather in the late seventeenth
century.

As the book of nature became a source of truth requiring explanation and interpretation, the Puritan developed methods of exegesis that
allowed him to read nature as a complement to the revealed truths of
Scripture. His conservatism or liberalism might depend entirely on his
emphasis; a conservative would be receptive to the evidences of natural
revelation, but his untilmate authority would reside on Scripture alone.
For him, the rock that Moses struck would retain mystical and
typological significances beyond its natural qualities, and the parting of
the Red Sea would signify the future avenues to the heavenly kingdom
as much as it would be regarded as a marvelous natural phenomenon.

In the end, however, the accommodation of theological truth
through revelation in nature gained prominence among the Puritans,
and an epistemological doctrine developed to explain the use of nature as
a source for truth. The conception of nature as a vast book revealing the
will of God was inherited from medieval exegesis, but the Puritans
evolved a new role for human reason in the process of accommodation,
and their immense synthesis of reason, Scripture, nature, and revelation
was known as *technologia*. Perry Miller has summarized the major tenets
of the doctrine in this way:

> When God created the world, He formed a plan or scheme of it in His mind,
> of which the universe is the embodiment; in His mind the plan is single, but
> in the universe, it is reflected through concrete objects and so seems diverse to
> the eyes of human reason; these apparently diverse and temporal segments
> of the single and timeless divine order are the various arts; the principles of
> them are gathered from things by men through the use of their inherent
> capacities, their natural powers; once assembled, the principles are arranged
> into series of axiomatical propositions according to sequences determined by
> the laws of method. It must be obvious to begin with that God sent forth His
> wisdom to an end, and so each of the arts, being a part of that wisdom, tends
> toward the end; God created the arts by the method of exegesis, combining
> arguments into the patterns of His intention, but man must find the prin-
> ciples of the arts by the method of analysis, discriminating the particulars
> within the synthesis; however, once man has formulated the rules of the arts,
> he should imitate God by using them, according to the method of genesis, to
> achieve the results for which they were predestined. In other words,
> *Technologia* was an assertion that the arts direct conduct to ends enunciated by
> God; it was itself a science of distinguishing and defining both their contents
> and relations—in reality the wisdom of God—and their purpose which was
> identical with the will of God.[8]

Technologia, therefore, formed the basis for a new system of metaphorical
interpretation among the Puritans, and the liberal exegetes during the

seventeenth century were not alone in their insistence that nature might contain theological truth. However, by deciding where he would place his emphasis, on nature as a supplement to the revealed truths of Scripture, or on nature as a primary avenue for man's understanding of God, the exegete would declare his purposes.

Two documents from the mid-seventeenth century provide good examples of this tension in exegesis. John Davenport's sermon, *The Knowledge of Christ,* is an epistemological treatise preached in New Haven in 1652, and its author is clearly a conservative exegete who relies entirely on Scripture for revealed truth and on nature for illustrations and analogies or parallels. On the other hand, John Flavel's *Husbandry Spiritualized* (1669) was one of a series of similar documents prepared by Flavel, whose purpose was to endow nature with moral authority and exemplary value in the guidance of human activity and to indicate ways through which nature could become the source of theological truth.

"The irrational and inanimate, as well as rational creatures have a language," says Flavel, *"and though not by articulate speech, yet in a metaphorical sense, they preach unto man the wisdom, power, and goodness of God."*[9] Even the title of Flavel's account indicates the author's method: *"Husbandry Spiritualized: or, The Heavenly Use of Earthly Things . . ."* But it would be misleading to assume that Flavel joined those Puritans who discovered in "earthly things" simple analogies which they used as evidence to support the truths revealed in Scripture. Although a suitable text is taken from the Bible, I Corinthians 3:9, "Ye are God's Husbandry," Flavel's Epistle Dedicatory and other introductory remarks indicate clearly that his method is the inverse of scriptural exegesis: he has turned to nature for his text, and it is the relation between nature and spirituality that is at the bottom of his concern. For example, he begins by comparing the "uses" of natural elements with the "uses" of doctrines that are abstracted by the conservative exegete from Scripture texts: "As Man is compounding of fleshly & spiritual substance, so God hath endowed the Creatures with a spiritual as well as fleshly usefulness; they have not only a natural use in Alimental and Physical respects, but also a spiritual use, as they bear the figures and similitudes of many sublime and heavenly Mysteries" (sig. A2). Nature is more than metaphorical illustration of Scripture truth; its "similitudes" and "figures" teach and reveal the heavenly mysteries just as effectively as Scripture. But the lessons of nature are not immediately apparent to the unregenerate, although they are available to anyone who sets out methodically to discover theological and moral truth through God's creation:

And as the creatures teach divine and excellent things; so they teach them in a perspicuous and talking manner . . . They teach us, though not formally, yet virtually, they answer and resolve the Question put to them, though not explicitly to the ear, yet convincingly to the Conscience. So then, we ask the Creatures, when we diligently consider them, when we search out the Perfections and virtues that God hath put into or stampt upon them. To set our mind thus upon the Creature, is to discourse with the Creature; the questions which man asks of a Beast, are only his own Meditations. Again, the Creatures teach us, when we in Meditation make our Collections, and draw down a demonstration of the Power, Wisdome, and Goodness of God in making them or of the frailty of Man in needing them. Such Conclusions and Inferences are the teachings of the Creatures (sig. A3).

The most revealing concession to the doctrine of accommodation, however, comes in Flavel's admission that even poetry, often castigated by the Puritans, may contain spiritual insight for the layman who is not moved by preaching of the word: "That of *Herbert* is experimentally true: 'A Verse May Find Him That a Sermon Flies, and Turn Delight into a Sacrifice' "(sig. A4).

Husbandry Spiritualized is a systematic meditative exercise, but it differs markedly from the meditative poetry of the seventeenth century in which scriptural subjects were chosen as the objects for contemplation. Although Flavel's text is technically derived from Scripture, his doctrine is taken from the law of nature. In the orderly processes of nature he has perceived the will of God and wishes to "open" this text to every "reader":

Many plow and sow, dig and delve in the Earth, till about the Beasts of the Field, till themselves became even beastive. Is it not then a blessed design which this author aims and desires at, so to spiritualize all sorts of the whole compass of earthly Husbandry, that all sorts of Husbandmen may become Spiritual and Heavenly? (sig. A4).

Despite its lucidity, Joseph Caryl's preface is but mild preparation for the wholesale spiritualizing provided by Flavel. The author intends no exegesis of Scripture. "Husbandry," he says, "runs to this: That the Life and Imployment of an Husbandman, excellently shadows forth the relation betwixt God & His Church, and the relative Duties betwixt its Ministers and Members. Or more briefly thus: The Church is God's Husbandry, about which his Ministers are employed."[10] Flavel's casual invocation of typology's "shadow" and method of analogy is nowhere developed as a system of one thing adumbrating another. Rather, the life of the Husbandman, somewhat romantically described, is metaphorically associated with the relationship between Christ, his ministers, and the church. This is the real business of *Husbandry Spiritualized*, and the biblical types where they appear, are entirely subordinated to natural revelation.

Flavel's account of the husbandman's routine is so exaggerated that it could never be accorded historical or literal veracity; and even if that were possible, it would hardly matter, since husbandry as a subject is merely the vehicle for the spiritualization of nature. The rejection of typological schemes of adumbration and fulfillment, and the adoption of an approach to nature by which the object is endowed with a spiritual or allegorical dimension independent of historical time is clearly seen when Flavel sets out, in the *Proem,* his "Twenty Propositions":

> I.   Prop. Thus the Husbandman purchases his *Fields,* and gives a valuable consideration for them, *Job.* 32.9.10. Ref. So God hath purchased his Church with a full valuable Prince, even the precious Blood of his own Son, *Acts* 20.28. *Feed the Church of God, which he hath purchased, or acquired with his own blood*
> . . .
> II.   Prop. *Husbandmen* divide and separate their lands from other mens, they have their Landmarks and Boundaries by which property is preserved. So are the People of God wonderfully separated, and distinguisht from the People of the earth. It is a special act of Grace, to be inclosed by God out of the Waste Howling Wilderness of the World (Deut. 33.16).[11]

Although Flavel intends an identification of New England with Israel and though he uses the wilderness of the Old Testament as a metaphor for the historical circumstances of New England, his starting point has been the activity of husbandmen, from which he has derived both the doctrine and the application of his natural text. Each of the twenty propositions is treated in the same manner; first, details from the activity of husbandmen are presented straightforwardly. Then the activity is romanticized and spiritualized, after which it is endowed with allegorical significance and enriched through scriptural allusions.

Following the twenty propositions, Flavel introduces "Five Corollaries," each of which extends the analogies developed in the earlier parts. The underlying motif of the entire piece, the comparison of husbandry to the church of Christ, is developed in detail in the Fifth Corollary:

> To conclude, If the church be Gods Husbandry, that is, if Husbandry have so many resemblances of God's Work about the Church in it; then how inexcusable is the Ignorance of Husbandmen in the things of God, who besides the Word of the Gospel, have the teaching of the Creatures; and can hardly turn their hand to any part of their work, but the Spirit hints one Spiritual use or other from it to their Souls? How do the Scriptures abound with Parables, & Lively Similitudes taken from Husbandry? From the Field, the Seed, the Plow, the Barn, from the threshing and winnowing, similitudes also from planting, grassing, and pruning of trees, and not a few from the ordering of Cattel. So that to what business soever you turn your hands, in any part of our calling, still God meets you with one Heavenly Instruction or other.[12]

The lengthy *Proem* is followed by numerous examples of "husbandry spiritualized," each of which is given a topical introduction, for example,

"Upon the Industry of the Husbandman," and a brief verse introducing
the idea that is subsequently allegorized. These examples are repetitious
and tedious in the extreme, since all are echoes of the central theme.

However, the declared intention of *Husbandry Spiritualized* is meditation, and the "reflections" that follow these introductory procedures indicate how closely Flavel is following the three-part Puritan sermon
form. The meditative "reflections" are organized according to kind, and
they represent attempts to accommodate spiritual truth to the unin-
formed reader. Flavel has spiritualized natural things from which he has
developed theological doctrines and through which he has arrived at
spiritual analogues. In *Husbandry Spiritualized,* the application of each
observation becomes a spiritual lesson for the reader, and the reflection
is actually a meditation on the doctrine abstracted from the observation
of nature.

The result of this transformed epistemology was that exegetes were
provided with a three-stage method for reading nature that closely
paralleled the Puritan explication of Scripture passages through the exegesis of the text, the extraction of a doctrine, and the application of that
doctrine. Although Flavel's emphasis was clearly on the employment of
natural metaphors in the illumination of spiritual truth rather than on
seeking out natural examples to reinforce scriptural revelation, his
method of exegesis was not unique to spiritualizing during the latter part
of the seventeenth century, and it is interesting to find Cotton Mather
experimenting with the same kind of innovative, "spiritualizing"
epistemology in his imitation of *Husbandry Spiritualized,* which he called
Agricola, or the Religious Husbandman, published in 1727.

THE MAINSTREAM OF CONSERVATISM

Flavel's husbandry has taken us a long way from the conservative
forces of the period that were his perpetual rivals. His spiritualization of
nature, and his allegorizing of a few biblical types were crucial, however,
because they paved the way for the attempted reconciliation between
natural revelation and scriptural authority that would take place later in
the transformed typology of Jonathan Edwards. Nevertheless, typological exegesis in the framework of the biblical dispensations continued to
be employed by the Puritans, and one of the most striking mid-century
examples of a sermon reinforcing this orthodoxy was John Davenport's
1652 document called *The Knowledge of Christ.*

Basically, Davenport is concerned about the ways of knowing God,
but his primary authority and foundation for epistemology is Scripture
alone. The structure of his sermon, subtitled "The True Messiah," is
logical and clear, reflecting the influence of Peter Ramus, the sixteenth-
century anti-Scholastic logician, in the rhetoric of the Puritan theology.
The arguments indicating the ways by which we "know" Christ are

many, including: the revelation of Christ in the types; the foreshadowing of His coming in prophecy; and the miracles He performed in His
earthly ministry. The conservative epistemological focus of the piece is
never abandoned; *The Knowledge of Christ* is nowhere transformed into a
treatise accommodating spiritual truth through elements of the natural
universe. The revelation of God through the types, moreover, is structured along extremely traditional lines.

Like Samuel Mather, Davenport's contemporary, the author
distinguished "personal types" from "real types":

> The Types of the Only True Messiah are vertified in this Jesus alone. The
> Scripture expresseth to sorts of Types of the Messiah. 1. Reall 2. Personall
> . . . The Reall Types, which I shall take notice of, are ten: 1. Jacob's Ladder,
> 2. Circumcision, 3. The Pass-over, 4. The Pillar of Cloud and Fire. 5. Their
> passing through the Red Sea. 6. Manna. 7. Water out of the Rock. 8. The
> Brazen Serpent. 9. The Jubilee. 10. The Temple.[13]

The types are each reviewed and examined for their relation to Christ of
the Gospels, and the usual juxtaposition of Old Testament text with
New Testament reference is found throughout, indicating how Davenport allowed Scripture to interpret Scripture in the Lutheran fashion.

The logical and meticulous manner of Davenport's exegesis is
reflected in his transition from the "reall" to the "personall" types:

> I have done with the Real Types, and shall now proceed to the Personall
> Types; in the choice of whom I shall wholly insist upon the clearest, as I finde
> them owned by Christ and his Apostles in the New Testament, pretermitting
> sundry, who yet may bee looked at, as Types of Christ, in sundry respects.
>   Personall Types of Christ, of whom I shall take notice, are these: 1.
> *Adam.* 2. *Noah.* 3. *Melchisedeck.* 4. Isaack. 5. Moses. 6. Joshua. 7. Sampson. 8.
> *David.* 9. *Solomon.* 10. *Jonah* (p. 22).

None of the parallels cited by Davenport are original; all but a few appear in the *Moses and Aaron* of Thomas Taylor, which was first published
in 1635 in London, and many appear in the *Philologia Sacra* of Solomon
Glassius, published in Jena from 1623 to 1626. Both of these documents
were reprinted several times during Davenport's ministry, and they were
imitated by ministers who sought to preserve conservative typology during the waning of the Puritan errand in the later seventeenth century.

However, the significance of *The Knowledge of Christ* is not that it
broadens the horizons of exegesis, but that it narrows them. Davenport's
conclusion of the matter of typology is as pedestrian a statement as his
explication of each succesive type: "So much may serve to have been
spoken to prove that this Jesus is the truth of the Types of the Messiah,
both Reall and Personall. Whence, I thus argue, He that is the only

truth of all the Scripture-Types of the Messiah, is the onely true Messiah. But this Jesus who was crucified, is the onely truth of all the Scripture-Types of the Messiah. Therefore, he is the onely true Messiah" (p. 33).

In an age that as gradually turning toward natural revelation for the understanding of spiritual truth, this kind of conservative assertion reaffirmed the traditional methods of knowing God. The tension between the authority of Scripture and the revealed truth of reason applied to nature was to continue for some time to come.

Examples of the polarity like Flavel's *Husbandry Spiritualized* and Davenport's *The Knowledge of Christ* continue to appear well into the eighteenth century. Cotton Mather may have worked many years preparing the *Magnalia Christi Americana* (1702) and even longer in writing his unpublished biblical commentary, "Biblia Americana," but he also penned the imitation of Flavel called *Agricola, or the Religious Husbandman* (1727) together with other books of spiritualized instruction, such as *The Religious Mariner* (1700). The focus of his epistemology never wholly shifted from Scripture to nature, but it is significant that *Agricola* came late in Cotton Mather's career, after he had been made a Fellow of the Royal Society and following his period of deepest interest in natural science.

Even after Jonathan Edwards had pieced together his *Images or Shadows of Divine Things,* an epistemological treatise which inverts traditional typology and employs spiritualized natural types as new or revived figures that shadow forth spiritual truth, conservative exegesis persisted in contrast to spiritualizing and allegorizing. By the eighteenth century, however, the rhetoric of the typologists shows that figuralism and typology were being turned to rational and even secular purposes, such as a vindication of the role of magistrates in the theocracy of Massachusetts Bay. As always, the Puritans felt they should examine Scripture to discover the authority by which they should govern their lives, and increasingly, typology provided the obvious key for understanding the Old Testament dispensation and its immediate relevance for New England.

THE CONSERVATIVE SYMBOLISM OF SAMUEL MATHER

The spiritualization of the types and the broadening of figural exegesis continued throughout the late seventeenth century, and the extension of typology beyond biblical boundaries developed new eschatological frameworks such as the jeremiad and Michael Wigglesworth's *Day of Doom* (1662). However, conservative exegesis persisted in the face of a variety of new influences, not so much as a reaction against innovation as a steady and continuous reaffirmation of orthodoxy. As the conservative theology of the New England Way became sharply distinguished from liberal movements during the second and third generations, it became synonymous, to a large extent, with the name of a single New England family: Mather.

Richard Mather, the patriarch, had been born in Lancashire, England, in 1596. His education at Royalist Oxford did not prevent his becoming one of the foremost English Puritans, and his beliefs later led him to emigrate to Massachusetts, where he accepted a pulpit at Dorchester and continued to minister until his death in 1669. As author of the Cambridge Platform, which reasserted the principles of the Westminster Confession and established the mold for the New England Way, Richard Mather (with John Cotton) also penned the renowed introduction to the *Bay Psalm Book,* so frequently used by modern critics as an example of the Puritan disdain for the fine arts.

Samuel Mather, one of his sons and brother to Increase, had a more exciting, international career. He was born before Richard had departed England, and in 1635 his father took him to New England, where he was educated at Harvard College and graduated as a Master of Arts in 1643. He became the first fellow of Harvard to have received a degree there. Samuel preached for some time in New England, but in 1650 returned to England, where he was made one of the chaplains of Magdalen College, Oxford, and eventually settled in Ireland.

On December 5, 1656, Samuel Mather was ordained in St. Nicholas' Church, Dublin. A more appropriate symbol of his success as an Irish Protestant could not have been obtained, and his ordination was attended by a number of prominent Congregationalists. His duties included the morning services at St. Nicholas' Church, and a sermon before the Lord Deputy Cromwell every six weeks. His relations with the Anglican Divines, during the period of the Protectorate, were cordial, but after the Restoration he grew impatient with the Anglican ceremonies and in 1662 preached two important sermons against the idolatry and superstitions contained in the Episcopal rites. For this affront to the Establishment he was temporarily restrained from his pulpit. These sermons are of tremendous importance to an understanding of Samuel Mather's typology and theory of figural expression, as the language of Canaan once again assumed a crucial political role.

The two sermons were collectively called *A Testimony from the Scripture Against Idolatry & Superstition*, and the text for both was taken from II Kings 18:4, where the author applauds the actions of "that great King Hezekiah," who "removed the High places, and broke the Images, and cut down the Groves, and brake in pieces the brazen Serpent, that Moses had made, for unto those dayes, the Children of Israel did burn Incense to it." The first of these sermons considered "Witnessing in generall against all the Idols and Inventions of men in the Worship of God," while the second was directed "more particularly against the Ceremonies, and some other corruptions of the Church of *England.*" [14]

Mather also attacked rites and ceremonies in *A Defense of the Protestant Religion Against Popery, in Answer to a Discourse of a Roman Catholick* (1672), but in the *Testimony from Scripture,* he spelled out his objections to the reinstitution of ceremonies that accompanied the Restoration of Charles II. Extracting a doctrine from the text, he asserts, *"It is a Thing very Right, and Pleasing in the Sight of God, when the Sin of Idolary and all the Monuments of it, All the Remembrances and Remainders of It, are Quite Destroyed and Rooted out From Among His People"* (p. 31). From this general assertion, which serves as the Doctrine of both sermons, Mather deduces, in the second sermon, that

> This Doctrine Condemns at once all the Ceremonies, and other corruptions, and Inventions of men which were introduced and brought into the worship of God by the Pope, in the time of Anti-Christian bondage and darkness, but they had been continued by some reforming Magistrates, who have made incompleat and imperfect Reformations. They are commonly known, and recommended by this name, *The Ceremonies of the Church of England,* the doctrine whereof in the *Nine and Thirty Articles,* is generally owned by good men as sound and good, but the worship hath much of the old leaven of popish corruptions unpurged out (p. 31).

Two sections of argument follow, "General Arguments against the Ceremonies" and "A More Particular Examination of the Principal Ceremonies of the Church of England." The importance of these logically developed sections is that they utilize the types to show how God had designed the Old Testament rites and ceremonies for specific purposes, which were abrogated and abolished in Christ. Mather is quite specific in his accusations against the Anglican ceremonies: "They are a means of worship which the Lord never appointed; there is no stamp of God upon them, no stamp of Institution" (p. 32).

But these general arguments are reinforced by a "more particular tryal" in the second section. Mather objects to the idolatry and superstition of the Anglican ceremonies, and he is especially critical of the resurrection of types that were abrogated in Christ. Like Thomas Shepard, he was troubled by the resemblance of ceremonies and types and indicated that ceremonies were really "particular kinds of Types."[15] The underlying motif of the entire document is that all types were abolished in Christ, so that the efficacy of a ceremony ceased in His fulfillment of the old dispensation.

This central attitude is made abundantly clear in the second section of the *Testimony from Scripture,* where all the principal ceremonies are examined separately. The attack is commenced with a vitriolic accusation indicting the Anglican church for practicing illegitimate ceremonies and using garments that were not instituted by God: "The *Surplice* with all the rest of that Popish Wardrobe of Superstitious garments, *Hoods, Tippetts,*

Rochets, &c . . . there is the same reason of them all, they are all Popish idols and ancient wayes of Superstition."[16] But the detailed examination of each ceremony is presented with more academic skill and reflects a consistently conservative typology that reappears throughout Mather's career. About the priestly robes, he says

> Those garments of *Aaron,* are said to be for glory, *Exod.* 28.2. (a) Because they typified and shadowed out the beauty of Christ, our true high Priest, in all those glorious graces of the Spirit of holiness in him. But when the Sun ariseth, the shadows fly away, and therefore now that Christ the body is come, and that Sun of Righteousness arisen upon the world, those legal shadows are done away: and to retain them in these times of the New Testament, doth interpretively deny that Christ is come in the flesh, and therefore there should be no difference between the garments of Ministers and their holy ministrations, and the garments of other persons, or of themselves at other times, but they should go in their habit according to the grave and comely manner of those among whom they live (p. 36).

The abrogation of the priestly garments does not stand alone in Mather's denunciation of the Anglican practices; he also judges the holy places and the use of music in the church, both arguments being founded on his conviction that the types of the Old Testament were wholly abrogated in the new dispensation.

> The Temple itself was a Sign of His Presence, and the Altar, the Ark, the Mercy-Seat, were affixed by Gods appointment into those places to be observed and celebrated there, viz., in the *Temple,* and in *Jerusalem,* but there is no place that is now privileged with this *Symbolical Presence.* There are no such standings signs and tokens of his Presence annexed unto any place. God hath given his *Ordinances,* to his Church, but he hath not tyed them to any place, *He Dwells Not in Temples made with Hands,* Acts 17.24 (*Testimony,* p. 61).

If the holy places of the Old Testament received the sanction of providential appointment, the contemporary world could not participate in that dispensation, since all these were abolished in Christ. Mather does not dispute the value of the holy places as they were designated under the old dispensation, but he was unwilling to extend this typological correspondence to New England, or any other time in history. "The temple was more holy, because it typified the Body of Christ, in whom the Godhead dwelt bodily, Coloss. 2.9. But Christ the Substance being come, all the *Types* and *Shadows* therefore done away, there are not, there cannot be typical Places, or typical Holiness in Places in these times" (*Testimony,* p. 61).

Samuel Mather specifically prohibits his contemporaries from considering their churches, or meetinghouses, in purely typological terms. They are moral but not antitypical.

Our Publick Meeting Places for worship in these gospel times, do not suceed in the stead of the Jewish Tabernacle or Temple, because they are not priviledged with that extraordinary visible Presence of God in them, which was in the Temple at some times, neither have they that Symbolical Presence, and residence of God in them, which was in the Temple at all times, neither have they that typical respect to Christ, neither hath God sanctified them, and set them apart to himself as his own peculiar (*Testimony*, p. 62).

The churches of the New English Israel "are of the Same Nature with the Jewish Synagogue, which were the places of the publick Moral Worship of God in those times, and were without question every whit as holy as our Churches" (*Testimony*, pp. 62-63). But they were in no way to be considered as the antitypical fulfillment of the original dispensation.

Mather is able, however, to retain a sense of Israel's moral example for New England by distinguishing between "temple worship," which was only ceremonial and was therefore abrogated in Christ, and "synagogue worship," which was moral and might provide an example, through analogy, for worship in New England. In this reasoning he was close to Thomas Shepard's arguments concerning the "moral equity" of the Sabbath.[17] In "A Testimony from Scripture against Cathedral Musick," this distinction is applied directly to the use of music and instruments in public worship: *"I do not finde in the Scripture, that these Musical Instruments were a part of their Synagogue-Worship, which was moral, but rather of their Temple-Worship, which was Ceremonial.* In their synagogues they had the publick Moral Worship of God, reading and expounding the Law, &c. Acts. 13.15" (*Testimony*, p. 66). Having shown how the "Musical instruments were appointed to be used continually before the Ark," Mather insists that "seeing Christ is come, and hath caused the Sacrifice and the Oblation to cease, and the city and the Sanctuary being both destroyed, as Dan. 9.26, 27, all the Worship that was affixed thereto is ceased with it" (*Testimony*, pp. 66-67).

The signigicant role of typology in determining Samuel Mather's objections to the ceremonies and sacraments of the Anglican church has not always been understood. The loss of his pulpit after the Restoration, and following the preaching of these two sermons, is only evidence that his views of the ceremonies were unacceptable to the Establishment. Many Puritans, moreover, had objected to the Anglican and "popish" use of "idolatrous ceremonies," but few had worked out their arguments almost exclusively in terms of Christ's abrogation of the Old Testament ceremonial types. Mather's unusual insight is reflected in the distinctions between synagogue-worship and temple worship, which were later to be echoed in his *Figures or Types of the Old Testament,* so that the declarations of the *Testimony from Scripture against Idolatry and Superstition* reflect a theology that Mather continued to preach to the end of his ministry. If the two sermons were prompted by the immediate circumstances of the

Restoration, and the return of falsely grounded ceremonies after the interregnum of Cromwell's Commonwealth, Mather's life-long defense of
the Puritan abstinence from ceremonial worship was argued almost exclusively by his insistence that the ceremonies were a "species of type"
that had been abrogated in Christ.

In 1666, having already suffered at the hands of the government for
his two sermons, Mather set to work on a series of elaborate sermons for
his Dublin congregation, in which he sought to accommodate the full
doctrine of typology. Cotton Mather, in his biographical sketch of his
uncle Samuel, says this about the typology sermons in Dublin:

> Our Mr. Mather . . . [wrote] unto one of his brothers, the *Types and Shadows of
> the Old Testament, if but a little understood, how full they are of gospel light and glory!
> Having Gone Through Diverse of them, I must Acknowledge with Thankfulness to the
> Praise of the Freeness of the Grace of the Lord Jesus Christ that I have seen more of him,
> then I saw before.*[18]

The text of the *Figures or Types* is a clear testimony to this early enthusiasm.

"A type," writes Samuel Mather, "is some outward or sensible thing
ordained of God under the Old Testament, to represent and hold forth
something of Christ in the New."[19] But in the same chapter, we also find
this: "There is in a *type*, some *outward* or *sensible* thing, that represents an
higher spiritual thing, which may be called a sign or an *resemblance*, a *patterne* or *figure*, or the like" (p. 72). By leaving the definition of "type" in
this way, Mather would have unwittingly opened the floodgates for
spiritualization and allegorizing because he is saying that the "representation" by an "outward of sensible thing," in the Platonic sense, is more
important than the historical scheme by which the types prefigure the
antitypes. Fortunately, his discussion is long and his examples of the
types are many, so that his distinction between types, parables,
allegories, and other rhetorical figures is sufficient to clarify the Puritan
doctrine of typology as it was later to be understood and practiced during the second and third generations in New England.

Samuel Mather's typology provided that regardless of other kinds of
significations for Christ that appear in the Old Testament, the type must
be historically verifiable. If a ceremony could be regarded as a type of
Christ, it must nevertheless be historically real and true:

> What is the Difference between a *Type* and a *Ceremony?* This is only that which
> is between the Genus and the Species. For all the *Ceremonies* were *Types,* but
> all the *Types* were not *Ceremonies*; the Pillar of Cloud and fire was a type, but
> not a Ceremony . . . A Ceremony was some law, or external observation pre-
> scribed unto them, to teach and shadow forth some Gospel-Mystery; so that
> a *Type* is more Generall, a Ceremony is one particular kind of *Type* (pp.
> 75-76).

This represents a crucial distinction, in Mather's view, between the spiritualized or allegorized forms and historically oriented typology: the types were verifiable and real. "They (the real types) are not bare *Allegories,* or parabolical poems, such as the *Song of Solomon,* or *Jotham's* parable, Judg. 9.7. or *Nathan's* Parable to *David,* 2 Sam. 12, but they are a true Narration of Things really existent and acted in the world, and are literally and historically understood" (p. 57).

The Puritan sense of the literal historicity of Scripture was nowhere more vigorously manifested than in Mather's defense of typological correspondences, which were based on literal events in the Old Testament and were in no way allegorical fictions.

The allegorizing of nature, and the multifaceted reading of Scripture on a variety of interpretative levels, as the medieval exegetes had done, was for Samuel Mather as unscriptural as the Catholic ceremonies. "For Men to set their *Fancies* at work to extract *Allegories* out of every *Scripture-History,* as the Popish Interpreters used to do, is not safe nor becomeing a *Judicious Interpreter*" (p. 55), Mather declares, and in an effort to be as through as possible in his definition of a type, he continues by distinguishing typology from all other forms of rhetoric. But he is careful to show the correspondences between typology and the sacraments:

> What is the difference between a *Type* and a *Sacrament;* I answer, they differ in the number and multitude of them, that they had many *Types,* we have but two *Sacraments.* But there was no difference in the nature of them, further than this, that our Sacraments are signs of Christ already come; but their *types* were signs of Christ that was for to come; our Sacraments are signs *Christi exhibiti;* their *Types Christi exhibendi* (pp. 56-57).

If the type was mystically associated with Christ through the ceremony and sacraments of the Old and New Testaments, it needed to be dissociated from the rhetorical devices used by the biblical writers:

> A *Parable* is nothing else but a sacred similitude; we commonly take it as the Scripture doth, for such a similitude wherein not only the Truth and Mind of God is the scope and matter of it; but whereof God himself is the author . . . But in a *Type* the Lord doth not occasionally use such or such a similitude; but sets such a thing apart, sets a stamp or Institution upon it, and so makes it an ordinance to hold forth Christ and His Benefits (p. 57).

The crucial significance, however, of the *Figures or Types* of Samuel Mather, was that it systematized typological exegesis for the New England Puritans in a new way. Although it served the same purposes that Thomas Taylor's *Moses and Aaron* had served at the time of George Herbert in England, the *Figures or Types* afforded a systematic view of the science in a period when the efficacy of typology as a way of understanding history was being seriously challenged by alternative ways of comprehending God's revealed will. Moreover, Mather approached his subject logically and methodically, so that the understanding of the types would be made available to many kinds of readers. The influence and popularity of this work is indicated by the three reprintings of the first edition and by the demand for a second edition in 1705.

The structure of the book is simple and informative. Mather has left nothing to guesswork. His first two sermons provide us with a rationale for the reading of Scripture typologically, and the first section of the group of sermons discusses in detail the causes and efficacy of typological exegesis. The distinctions between the revelation of the Old Testament and the dispensation of the New are made by comparing the law and the Gospel, and there is never any doubt about the superiority of the Gospel dispensation:

> We must distinguish between the *Thing* preached and the Manner of preaching, between the *Shell,* and the *Kernel,* the Shadow, and the Substance. Now the *Thing* preached was the *Gospel;* tho' manner of preaching it was *Legal:* The Kernal was Gospel, tho' the shell was Law: the Spirit and Substance, and mystery of that Dispensation was evangelical, tho' it was involved in a legal Shell and outside, and overshadowed with the Shades and Figures of the Law. *God Never Had But One Way only to Save Men By:* but it had divers fashions and forms, divers outward discoveries and manifestations; in those times a more legal manner, but afterwards, more like itself, in a more Evangelical Manner (p. 12).

He then indicates how typology fits into the general pattern of revelation contained in the two Testaments, which, in his view are inextricably linked by Christ, rather than divided by the law and the Gospel accounts:

> That the Gospel was preached unto them under the Old Testament, as well as to us under the New, hath been cleared from *Heb.* 4.2, where the Apostle saith *Unto Us Was the Gospel Preached, as Well as Unto Them.* We are next to consider, *How* it was preached unto them. Now to this the text answers that it was done in *Divers Manners* and at *Sundry Times* . . . These divers manners therefore of Gods speaking, or revealing his mind of Old, may be referred chiefly to these seven heads:
> 1. By Visions
> 2. By Dreams
> 3. By Voices
> 4. By Inward Inspirations and Impulses of his Spirit
> 5. By legal Types and Shadows
> 6. By Signs and Wonders
> 7. By a special and peculiar kind of Intimacy and Familiarity (pp. 12-14).

The general classification of modes of revelation prepares us for the detailed account of the "*legal Types and Shadows,*" of which Mather's sermons were a thorough exposition. Christ was partially, though not fully, revealed in these "speaking things," which "spake forth the Gospel in *Types and Shadows.* Heb. 10.1 *The Law Having a Shadow of Good Things to Come.* A *Type* is a legal shadow of Gospel Truths and Mysteries" (p. 17).

Mather has successfully answered those commentators who would dismiss the Old Testament with a rigid discrimination against the law in their preference for the Gospel revelation. His systematic approach to Scripture not only provides an analytical methodology, but it also links the two Testaments together under the unified dispensation of God's redeeming grace. However, he repeatedly insists on the superiority of the new dispensation and the abrogation of the old:

> The text is plain enough: that instead of all those divers manners used by God of Old, he hath now substituted instead thereof this *One* and *Onely* way of revealing himself, viz., in and by his Son. And his Son speaks by his *Word* and *Ordinances;* as also by the works of *His Providence;* in all which his spirit breaths: Therefore, there we are to meet with God, and to hear his voice, and there only to expect it. *These Old Things are Vanished Away* (p. 20).

It is important that Mather felt compelled to justify the types as a way of perceiving God's revelation. His *Figures or Types of the Old Testament* represents the Puritan's attempt to hold together an important method of reading both history and Scripture in an age that was losing sight of the value of typology for either. Mather's introductory explanation of typology's significance and value is one of the most important sections of his sermonbook, since it provides an apologetic examination of exegetical typology in the light of other methods of reading Scripture. Although the book is not conceived in a defensive posture, the occasion of Mather's defense of typology enriches his text with allusions throughout to other methods of exegesis and interpretation.

In the body of the work, Mather divides the Old Testament types into two main classifications, the "personal types," and the "real types." The personal types include such figures as Adam, with whom the first covenant was formed, Noah, Melchisedek, Abraham, with whom the second covenant was formed, Isaac, Jacob, and Joseph. Mather has also distinguished certain groups of types through linkages of roles in prefiguring Christ: Moses with Joshua, Samson with David and Solomon, Elisha and Jonah. Finally, we find the "collective types," which he calls the "*Typical Orders and Ranks of Men*: 1. The whole Nation and people of *Israel.* 2. The First-Born of that Nation. 3. Their Nazarites. 4. Their Prophets. 5. Their Priests. 6. Their Kings" (p. 118). Mather sees the nation of Israel as a "typical People," and their church-state as "being very ceremonial and Peculiar to those legal times," but he is always insistent that they are "now ceased and abolished" (p. 119). Never far away is the sense that the New English Israel is typical in her analogous relation to the Israel of old, but Mather is too convinced that the types, particularly the ceremonial types, were abrogated and abolished in Christ to make this anachronistic claim.

Under the "real types," Mather distinguished the "occasional types" and "perpetual types." Among the occasionial types, there are two general sorts: those which derive out of things, hence, "typical things," and those which derive out of actions, or "typical actions." Occasional things include the ark of Noah, Jacob's ladder, the burning bush, and bread and manna, which become the bread of life under the new dispensation. Occasional typical actions include the exodus, the trip across the Red Sea, the journey in the wilderness, the crossing of the river during the entry into Canaan, and the experience at Babylon during the captivity. The perpetual types, on the other hand, had a more lasting value and were epitomized by the Old Testament ceremonies. "By the *Perpetual Types*," Mather declares, "we intend *such as God by Institution settled and stated in that Church, to the End of that Age, of that Whole Old Testament Dispensation, till the Coming of Christ, the Truth Substance, and Scope of them*" (p. 166). But "perpetual" came to mean more.

Mather's whole aim in the *Figures or Types* is to demonstrate that the Bible is one book written by the same spirit, and this is nowhere more easily seen than in his use of the word "Gospel" as a title for each section in which typology is discussed. However, the unity of the Scriptures under Mather's scheme is deceiving; if the Bible is one book instituted by a single spirit, the Old Testament contains a dispensation that is only a shadow of the revelation contained in the New. It is true that Mather, like Thomas Shepard, has done much to minimize the differences between the dispensations, but he has also raised some serious questions that were treated more thoroughly in the *Theses Sabbaticae* a generation earlier. For example, the classifications of the types as "personal" and "real," and the subdivision of the real types into "occasional" and "perpetual" beg the question of moral and exemplary value instituted in the types. Mather attempts to answer this indicating that certain types possess a permanent value for Christian society while others have only occasional value: "For some Types were transient, and some Permanent: some were *Extraordinary* and *Occasional,* as *Manna,* the *Brazen Serpent,* and some were Perpetual, viz., the whole *Ceremonial Law;* the ordinances whereof are frequently called *Everlasting Statutes;* so that this Distinction is founded both in the Nature of the Things, and in the Scripture Expressions about them" (pp. 127-129). The assertion that some types were perpetual and permanent while others were only transient and therefore abrogated in Christ differs greatly from Thomas Shepard's efforts to align those types endowed with moral and perpetual equity with the law of nature, which was also divine and stood above the

instituted typological correspondences. While Shepard's position is defended by his constant invocation of the law of nature, Samuel Mather
schematized the Old Testament types so that none were left in the valley
of doubt. He skirted the problem posed by his notion concerning the
abrogation of the types by insisting that all types, whether or not they
had been fulfilled in Christ, possessed a moral equity sufficient for them
to be regarded by future times as exemplary of a covenant society.

To Insist upon the general *Ends of All the Types* . . . there were three great
ends.
    1. *For Outward and Temporal Good.* They had by these outward Supply and
Deliverance: So the passing thro' the Red Sea, the Manna, the Water out of
the Rock were outward mercies; So the brazen Serpent gave outward and
bodily Healing to them, beside that spiritual and sacramental Use it had to
adumbrate Jesus Christ.
    2. *They Were Instructions in Moral Duties, as indeed all Providences Are.* The
Lord's giving them Water out of the Rock, and Bread from Heaven, were instructing Providences to depend upon God in Straits, and to trust in Him at
all Times.
    3. The Third End was the *Typical Adumbration of Christ and Gospel
Mysteries.* Besides all other ends and Uses of them; besides outward and temporal good, and moral instruction; they did, by the positive Intention of the
Spirit of God, point at Christ, and lead to Him. For this the text is the express, *All These Things Happened Unto Them in Types,* and ver. 4. *That Rock Was
Christ* (p. 129).

    Throughout his *Figures or Types,* Samuel Mather declared that
although the types were ordained by God they were concluded in Christ.
If he allowed a moral of perpetual equity to linger after the abrogation in
Christ, he maintained a conservative approach to the systematic dispensation that was offered first in the types and finally in Christ. He
nowhere distinguished the several kinds of law, which Thomas Shepard
used to endow his types with moral equity, but he asserted throughout
that that legal shadows of the Old Testament were only a figure of the
new dispensation.

The Law Came By Moses, that is, the Law as opposed to Grace and Truth, *Jesus
Christ.* Truth here is not opposed to Falsehood, for *Moses* spake no lies; but to
Shadows and shadowy *Promises,* and so the *Truth* of them is the *Performance* and
Accomplishment of them, in opposition to the bare *Shadow* and *Typical* promise
of them . . . So the sense amounts to thus much: that *Moses* delivered the *Law,*
that is, *Shadows* and *Ceremonies,* which were but legal, and dark and rigorous;
but *Christ* brought *Grace* and *Truth ,* that is, the real and sweet *Accomplishment*
and *Performance,* of all the Good that *Moses* had promised in that dark and low
and legal way, which is to that we have here in the text, that *The Law hath the
Shadow, but not the Very Image of the Things Themselves* (pp. 167-168).

If the ceremonial law contained images and shadows of the true substance, it was superseded by the greater law dispensed in the Gospel. The abrogation of Old Testament types exceeded their value as moral authority for post-New Testament times, and the only relationship with the Old Testament ceremonies that New England might have would be that of analogy and imitation, by which the type was revived in the context of seventeenth-century New England. The abrogation of the old law would therefore prohibit any ceremonial extension of the types into New England's history, so that the colonies would not consider themselves the antitypical fulfillment of the scriptural types.

There is absolutely no doubt that Edward Taylor, Increase Mather, Cotton Mather, and their contemporaries were familiar with Samuel Mather's *Figures or Types of the Old Testament*. Originally written as a series of sermons, the first edition had been edited by Nathaniel Mather, Samuel's younger brother, and was published posthumously in Dublin in 1683. Distribution was widespread, both in England and in America, and the sheets that were printed in 1683 were apparently stored and reissued with a new title page in 1685. Fortunately, the same sheets were transferred to London, and in 1695 a third issue of the first edition appeared with no significant variants. In 1705, the type was reset and the second major edition of this popular work appeared in London. This edition was reprinted in 1969, and an abridgement by Caroline Fry Wilson appeared in 1833.[20]

Because Samuel Mather was so important in the development of the language of Canaan, it is useful to compare his judgments about the types with contemporary Puritan documents on the same subject which were being issued in England and America, and to evolve a sense of how the second generation Puritans must have regarded the types of which they heard so much. One of the most influential documents in the explication of biblical rhetoric was not a product of New England at all, though it had a considerable influence among the immigrant Puritans. In 1681, the English Puritan Benjamin Keach published the *Tropologia: a Key to Open Scripture Metaphors . . . Together with Types of the Old Testament*. While this document was little more than a redaction of the *Philologia Sacra* of Solomon Glassius, it was extremely significant in the English version because so many New England divines derived their distinctions between allegory and type from the definitions it contained and from Samuel Mather's *Figures or Types*, which it influenced. Keach's distinctions are echoed in Cotton Mather's prefatory remarks to his *Work Upon the Ark* (1689), and they are useful for measuring the conservative approach to typological exegesis during the latter part of the seventeenth century. Keach declares, following Glassius: "Similitudes or Metaphors are borrowing from visible things, to display and illustrate the excellent Nature of Invisible things. Yea, heavenly Things are often called by the

very names, that material or earthly things are; which is not to obscure
or hide the meaning from us, but to accommodate them to our understandings.[21] Keach is careful to distinguish similitudes and metaphors,
which are founded on Platonic correspondences between things material
and things immaterial, from biblical types, and Keach's distinctions,
cited here, were echoed by Samuel Mather in his own manual of figural
expression:

> I believe there is a great difference between metaphorical and typical Scrip-
> tures . . .
>
> 1. *Types* suppose the Verity of some history, such as *Jonah's* being three
> days and three nights in the Whale's belly. When it is applied to Christ in the
> New Testament, it supposeth such a thing was once done. Allegories have no
> such supposition, but are as Parables, propounded for some Mystical End.
>
> 2. *Types* look only to matters of fact, and compare one fact with another,
> as Christ's being slain and lying three days in the Grave, to Jonah's lying so
> long in the whale's belly. But Allegories take in words, Sentences, and Doc-
> trines, both of Faith and Manners . . .
>
> 3. *Types* compare persons and facts under the Old Testaments, with Per-
> sons and facts under the New, thus prefiguring another to come. Allegories
> regard matters in Hand, and intend the explaining some mystical sense
> upon the word, which at present they do not seem to bear.
>
> 4. *Types* are only Historical and the Truth of fact agreeing in the An-
> titype, makes them up. But allegories are not intended to clear Facts, but to
> explain doctrines, affect the heart, and convince Conscience . . . Hence,
> many learned and judicious Persons are of Opinion, that allegories and
> Metaphors are more extensive and comprehensive in their meaning, and ap-
> plications then *types:* though Care ought to be had that they are not taken
> beyond the analogy of faith (p. *1v*).

In echoing Glassius, Keach has provided an extremely conservative
rule for interpreting the types. If "types are only Historical and the truth
of fact agreeing in the Antitype makes them up," then we are prohibited
from using the types as models or examples for moral and ethical
behavior. The king of Israel is a historical prefiguration of Christ, and
more. This is essentially the argument that Roger Williams used against
John Cotton, and while Williams was anything but an orthodox typologist when his overall exegesis is considered, he did stand up for the abrogation of types in Christ as He is presented in the Gospel accounts.

It is ironic in the extreme, therefore, that the handbooks provided
by Glassius, Keach, and Samuel Mather were utilized by ministers and
writers of the second generation to provide sermon illustrations and
moral examples for poetry. Basing the power of the illustration or image
on the contemporary understanding of typology and its relevance for
biblical exegesis, the writers of the second and third generations used
types and figures from the Old Testament in much the same way that
the Greeks came to use the gods and mythological figures as moral ex-

amples in their literature. This spiritualizing of the types, the endowing of the type with moral and ethical value outside its Old Testament context, was not unique to the second and third generations of Puritanism in New England. We have already seen how Calvin allowed a type to be moral and ethical as well as historical and how Augustine had used the types in two senses. But Luther had objected to this extension of typology, and kept his exegesis within the bounds of orthodox correspondences established in the New Testament. His penchant for allowing "Scripture to interpret Scripture" was a popular approach to exegesis during the sixteenth and early seventeenth centuries, and yet it developed simultaneously with a more sophisticated exegesis through which the types might also be considered a moral example for contemporary times. John Cotton's changing typology moved in this direction from an earlier conviction that New England was indeed the antitypical fulfillment of both the Old and the New Testament types.

It is obvious from the frantic outpouring of evidence that the conservative figural writers in Europe, England, and New England during the seventeenth century were united in an effort to define their terms. This necessary task was greatly assisted by the tensions that naturally developed among the Puritans between the spiritualizers and the typologists, and throughout the century, several important handbooks of typology appeared, the first being Thomas Taylor's *Moses and Aaron* (1635), which had a significant influence on the Anglican typology of George Herbert. Taylor's typology was the most conservative assessment of typological exegesis available to the seventeenth-century reader. However, the strong conservative influences of Keach, Mather, and Davenport must not underestimated although their works came to be used, in some instances, as handbooks of Puritan mythology. Although Keach and Samuel Mather had difficulty keeping their typology within the bounds of historically oriented exegesis, they nevertheless represented an effort toward the clarification of theological types in an age when typology was being abused and spiritualized out of recognition.

From a trained, contemporary perspective, some of Keach's parallels appear a bit fantastic, and although he was more liberal in his exegesis than either Samuel Mather or Thomas Taylor, his *Tropologia* stands with Taylor's *Moses and Aaron* and with Mather's *Figures or Types* as a monument to biblical typology in a period which was losing sight of the relevance of typology for the reading of history and for the interpretation of Scripture.

It remained for Increase and Cotton Mather to employ typology systematically as a way of reading both history as providential revelation, and Scripture as the revealed will of God, and for the poet Edward Taylor to distinguish between allegory and typology in selecting biblical

images for his verse. Although Cotton Mather was thoroughly immersed
in the scientific and philosophical developments of his time, he was successful in maintaining a balance between his indulgence of contemporary habits of mind, and his reassertion of conservative Puritan orthodoxy. An examination of the Mather understanding of scriptural
typology provides one of the most interesting chapters in the history of
Puritan eschatology, and is the subject of Part III. Increase and Cotton
Mather stood at the close of the seventeenth century as figures of transition. Both were men of public affairs, sharing the pulpit of the Old
North Church in Boston, even while Increase Mather was president of
Harvard, a position Cotton was never to hold. It would be unwise to
associate their thinking in all matters too closely, although together they
represent an attempt at the turn of the century to restore to New
England that sense of purpose with which it had been founded. Biblical
figuralism and the language of Canaan played a crucial role in determining the parameters of that teleology for the Mathers, and their relative,
Samuel Mather, provided guidelines for interpreting the metaphors of
the Old Testament dispensation. Mather's *Figures or Types* had also exerted a considerable influence on Edward Taylor of Westfield, the
reclusive poet-minister whose work is progressively discovered by succeeding generations of scholars of Puritanism. The following chapter
demonstrates this influence in Taylor's sermons and poems, contrasting
Taylor's Canticles allegory with his typology sequence in the Second
Series of sermons and *Meditations*. Edward Taylor shared with Increase
Mather a doctrinal conservatism during the transitions that characterized the late seventeenth century, but he composed poetry that extended
the language of Canaan into the eighteenth century by reasserting the
prophetic force of the biblical metaphor and scriptural figures on which
his meditations were based. In his prose and poetry, Taylor shows
clearly the influences of the Puritan exegesis of types and the preceding
figural tradition.

5

TAYLOR'S MEDITATIONS AND SERMONS AND THE PERSONALIZING OF THE BIBLICAL FIGURES

Might but my pen in natures Inventory
   Its progress make, 't might make such things to jump,
All which are but Inventions Vents or glory
   Wits Wantonings, and Fancies frollicks plump:
   Within whose maws lies buried Times, and Treasures
   Embalmed up in thick dawbd sinfull pleasures.

Nature doth better work than Art: yet thine
   Out vie both works of nature and of Art.
Natures Perfection and the perfect shine
   Of Grace attend thy deed in ev'ry part.
   A Thought, a Word, and Worke of thine, will kill
   Sin, Satan, and the Curse: and Law fulfill.

Thou art the Tree of Life in Paradise,
   Whose lively branches are with Clusters hung
Of Lovely fruits, and Flowers more sweet than spice.
   Bende down to us: and doe outshine the sun.
   Delightful unto God, doe man rejoyce
   The pleasant'st fruits in all Gods Paradise.
                — Edward Taylor, *Meditation*
                Fifty-Six, Second Series

LIKE JOHN COTTON, Edward Taylor provides a most important link between rhetorical practices in old and New England, because his poetry and sermons reveal not only a use of both the allegorical and figural readings for Old Testament books but because Taylor also exhibits a scholarly knowledge of the important distinctions between the two. Unlike John Cotton's or Samuel Mather's ministry, Taylor's Westfield ministry was relatively quiet and withdrawn from public view; his meditations were discovered in 1937, and only a few of his sermons — forty-nine of which are extant — were known until very recently.

Taylor's importance in the continuity of figural interpretation cannot be overestimated. It is clear from what he wrote that he was throughly familiar with James Durham's *Clavis Cantici,* which influenced the poet's interpretation of Canticles and inspired his use of texts from that book for the long sequence of poems in the *Meditations,* Second Series (115-153), that treat the relationship of Christ to the church allegorically. It is equally clear that Taylor was as thoroughly familiar with Samuel Mather's *Figures or Types of the Old Testament,* (1683) and that he based his interpretation of Old Testament typology and figural expression on Mather's well-ordered approach to the language of Canaan. Finally, it is clear that Taylor attempted to personalize the types and to give immediate, personal value to allegorical symbols as he would interpret Scripture, so that in the complex rhetorical design of the *Christographia* sermons and their accompanying meditations, modern readers can discern a scholar's awareness of typology and allegory together with a poet's attempt to use the meditative process to make both rhetorical forms imminent and personal. This chapter introduces Taylor's rhetorical strategies in the Canticles allegory and in the typology poems, both found in the Second Series, and examines closely several of the prophetic and figural poems in the typology group, correlating the principles Taylor expresses in verse with figural doctrine found in the recently discovered typology sermons. The *Christographia* sequence is examined as a paradigm of Taylor's supreme rhetorical development — where scriptural foundation and prophetic language are fused in a moment of spiritual fulfillment that is personal, metaphysical, and perhaps mystical.

> That the Faith of the Old Testament Church, and of the Church of the New Testament is set on the Same Object: that Christ was as truely the Object of old testament faith as [The Ancient Israelites had Christ dispensed] of the New. in Promises and Types, as a Mediator to Come. We have him dispensed in a Cleare, and Manifest way as Come already. But the different manner of dispensing of the Messiah, doth not produce, a Different Christ, nor a different Faith on Christ. Sometimes the Church sets forth Christ as an Obscure person standing behinde the Wall, peeping in at the Window, and making a flowrish thro' the lattice as Cant. 2.9. Sometimes she setts him out in orientall Colours and in most Allegorical accomplishments as Cant. 5.10-16. Yet this differing way of Setting him out, makes not any Personall Difference. Its the same Person, and Beloved in the one description, as it described in the other.[1]

Here, in the ninth sermon of the fourteen that comprise the *Christographia,* Taylor articulates a doctrine of prophetic language that had long governed his approach to typology and allegory. For Taylor, both the allegorical and typological modes were ways of expressing the personal significance of Christ, but he is careful, following the distinctions established by Samuel Mather, to maintain allegory and figural typology as different vehicles for expressing the same essential substance. For example, the Second Series of *Meditations* is thematically

divided to exhibit the different rhetorical techniques in separate sequences of poetry. *Meditations* 1-30 specifically treat Old Testament
typology, and it is this group with which this chapter is particularly concerned. Texts from the Canticles, and poems treating the subject of
Christ as bridegroom and the church as bride, are found throughout
Meditations II, 115-153, the forty-nine poems specifically designed to exhibit the allegorical significance of that Old Testament dispensation of
Christ. The meditations in between these two specific groups, II,
31-114, are essentially the central panel in a triptych, and in this
group—which is flanked on one side by typology and on the other by
allegory—Taylor concentrates on themes expressing Christ's superiority
to the types and the salvational value of the believer's identification with
the savior's personal presence. It is the most mystical segment of the
three groups and relies more on the metaphysical mode of *discordia concors*
than either of the Canticles allegory or typological group. In this center
panel, the spiritual and corporeal elements seem mystically fused, but it
is important to understand how Taylor has made an effort to avoid the
wholesale spiritualization of nature as medieval allegorizers had done.
Like Samuel Mather, he was sensitive to the prophetic value of figural
associations, and he drew upon his sophisticated understanding of
biblical metaphor to develop parallels between his own experience and
the saving power of Christ. It is important to remember that Taylor did
not publish the poems, and, indeed, that most of the meditations remained unpublished until 1960. The verse seems to express deep
religious feeling governed by intellectual control, and it is this element of
metaphorical control that concerns us in this chapter.

The Canticles Allegory

Since the publication of thirty-five meditations in 1939, scholars
have debated whether Taylor's allegorizing and use of conceit made him
more metaphysical than Puritan. Recent scholarship has laid to rest this
false argument and currently attention has been properly focused on his
imagery and more particularly, on his use of biblical metaphor.[2] Barbara Lewalski argues that the Canticles allegory provided Taylor with a
concrete image of Christ and His kingdom:

At times Taylor relates himself to the spousal metaphor by begging association with and incorporation within the Spouse; at other times he does so by
exploring whether the Bridegroom's words to the Spouse apply in the particular sense to himself as an elect soul. He reads the other primary metaphor
of *Canticles,* the Garden, in terms of the same conventional allegorical symbolism: "This Garden, Lord (is) thy Church:" "The Garden too's the Soule, of
thye Redeem'd" (II. 83; 19, 25). The speaker's stance in such poems is to
seek plantation and cultivation within the Garden-Church, e.g., to be a

flower-bed, vine, or lilly in the Garden, and sometimes to ask the Garden to be planted and tilled within him. In most of these poems, Taylor probes intensively the metaphors and emblems of *Canticles* to produce praises for the Bridegroom and Spouse, and to clarify the theological basis of the speaker's relation to both. The few poems in which the speaker relates his own experience of Christ's love to that of the Spouse, or takes on her persona to describe such experiences are not mystical in any precise sense, but display the spiritual affections often treated at length in the Protestant allegory of *Canticles*.[3]

Moreover, Louis Martz has established the Taylor *Meditations* in the tradition of Ignatian meditation in his foreword to the Stanford edition of *The Poems of Edward Taylor,* published by the Yale University Press in 1960. Since Martz and Ursula Brumm first examined Taylor's meditations as part of traditional religious expression, Martz establishing Taylor in the context of sixteenth- and seventeenth-century meditative poetry and Brumm briefly examining the imagery, there has been no doubt that Taylor borrowed heavily from conventional religious rhetorical modes. Brumm is well aware of the problem of allegorizing of spiritualizing the types and concedes that "while we are, in this simplified manner, distinguishing the symbol from allegory, we must not neglect to add that these two literary devices for reproducing the world frequently occur in mixed versions."[4]

Edward Taylor, however, was very clear in his distinctions, as his separation of the typological and figural meditations from those associated with Canticles would indicate. Taylor follows James Durham in allegorizing the Canticles texts, and it is misleading to state, as does Brumm, that "Taylor's fantasy . . . succumbs to the charm of biblico-Oriental word pictures . . . [which] would surely have aroused the ire of his fellow theologians, who would have condemned his rich, sensual imagery and his radical spiritualizations as the latest form in idolatry."[5] Taylor's erotic imagery, as seen in *Meditation* II, 116, is allegorically associated with divine love, as the final stanza makes perfectly clear. The poem reads:

> I sent mine Eye, love's Pursevant, to seek
>   This Object out, the which to naturall
> I found it mixt with White and Red most sweet.
>   On which love naturall doth sweetly fall.
>   But if its spirituall, then Orient Grace
>   Imbellisheth th' object in this Case (7-12).

As Karen Rowe suggests, the object here is Christ, although the poet dresses his subject with those attributes usually associated with conventional love poetry of the seventeenth century. Later, the lines state the association of physical and natural beauty with spiritual qualities in a direct and unmistakable way:

> Hence purest White and red in Spirituall Sense
>   Make up thy Beauty to the Spirituall Eye.
> Thus thou art object to love Spirituall. Hence
> The Purest Spirituall Love doth to thee high (19-28).

The poem explicitly associates natural beauty and natural love with spiritual beauty and divine love, so that the metaphorical associations throughout reinforce Taylor's use of natural and physical qualities to preach the attributes of Christ.[6]

Taylor's recognition of the figurative (as contrasted with the literal) value of Canticles clearly follows those patterns established by the English Puritans and by John Cotton's allegorical and figural reading of the book. Moreover, it is clear that Taylor's method was significantly fluenced by the emblem writers like George Wither (*A Collection of Emblemes, Ancient and Moderne,* 1635) and Francis Quarles (*Divine Fancies, Digested, into Epigrams, Meditations, and Observations,* 1632). Donald Stanford, editor of *The Poems of Edward Taylor,* has shown that George Herbert was a significant influence on the American poet, and Barbara Lewalski argues that

> There are several more or less obvious allusions and echos: Herbert's phrase, "crumb of dust" from "The Temple I" occurs five times in Taylor's "Prologue," and the opening lines "Lord, Can a Crumb of Dust the Earth outweigh,/Outmatch all mountains, nay the Chrystall Sky?" especially recall the Herbert poem. Taylor's refrain "Was ever Heart like mine?" (I.40) seems to echo Herbert's refrain from "The Sacrifice," "Was ever Grief like mine?" The few titled poems in Taylor's meditative sequences—"The Experience," "The Return," and "The Reflexion"—recall Herbert's titles, and Taylor's stanza form throughout is that of Herbert's "Church-Porch" . . . Taylor analyzes the manifold properties of the Rose of Sharon (I.4) and his witty figure of the Church as Rose seated at the banquet table ("The Reflexion") strongly recall very similar metaphoric procedures in Herbert's "The Rose" and "Churchrents and Schisms."[7]

But the language of Canaan appears most specifically in Taylor's verse in those early poems of the Second Series, the sermons for which were only very recently discovered. We have long known the *Christographia,* that cycle of fourteen sermons which serves as a gloss on the meditations that accompany them, and because the additional thirty-six sermons relate to meditations that specifically treat figural and typological language in Taylor's writing, we have new and valuable insight into the poet's doctrine of prophetic language and new understanding of these specific poems to which the sermons relate.

Scholars have long recognized that Taylor's *Meditations* were most likely associated with sermons preached on the same subject, and that the meditations generated out of common biblical texts, were probably composed sometime during the night preceding or early in the morning on the day of the sermon delivery. Moreover, the common themes of clusters of meditations have led to the conclusion that Taylor must have preached series of sermons along lines reflected in the meditation clusters. Norman Grabo said,

> Taylor's *Meditations*, 115-153, which cite texts from Canticles 5:10 to 7:6, cover a span of six years. Because they were based upon his sermons, we know that he must have been preaching a series of sermons based on Canticles over the same length of time. Whether in the case of these poems, or in the twenty-odd poems on typology that begin the second series, or the interlocking images, or the image clusters, each of the poems is separately conceived and developed. Their sequential relationship is an accident of the sermon sequence, and not a poetic invention, though certainly Prof. Martz is correct in concluding that individual poems gain in strength and richness, and are, in a very real way, sustained by the sequence in which they occur.[8]

Taylor's poems stand on their own as original and superbly crafted examples of seventeenth-century religious poetry, so that the association of an individual poem with a sequence of meditations all relating to a single spiritual idea does not detract from the poet's artistic achievements. Herbert's poem sequences, after all, had both individual and collective merit. The difference is that Taylor's poems also have a clear association with sequential sermons that address a specific doctrinal theme. For example, the Canticles poems should be associated with broader, doctrinal statements in prose that would gloss or corroborate the allegorical movement the *Meditations* advance.[9]

The allegorical reading of Canticles so clearly found in Taylor's exegesis and expressed in his imagery in the *Meditations* does, however, tempt one to a mystical interpretation. Throughout the Canticles poems, the allegorical mode dominates the figural or typological, and the metaphorical love union with Christ has misguided readers through the centuries to understand the image in the purely Platonic, mystical sense advanced by medieval scholars. But Taylor was suggesting the conflation of spiritual and literal meaning that is best represented in figural writing, that language of Canaan by which images are endowed with a prophetic power of Christ's second coming. The allegorical love union of Canticles was for Taylor not inconsistent with a prophetic image of the kingdom to come; like John Cotton, Taylor read the love song allegorically in a way that did not deny its figural or prophetic value. For Taylor, the mystical response was an invalid reading of the biblical document; moreover, Taylor's poetry, and probably the accompanying sermons, are exegetical, not mystical, and the allegorical reading is conventional and traditional, derived largely from James Durham's *Clavis Cantici*. The bridegroom is Christ, and the spouse is the church considered to be the gathered body of visible saints, the entire company of the elect. Taylor set up the association himself: "thy Spouse . . . doth consist of all/God's blesst Elect regenerate within/The tract of time from first to last" (II. 136, 31-33).

In another passage, Taylor's use of allegory to illuminate figural reading and employment of typology to explain allegory is more straightforward. In Sermon 4, Second Series, which was preached on the Pauline text, Galatians 4:24, "Which things are in allegory: For these are the two Covenants," Taylor argues that Abraham and his spouses may be read both allegorically and prophetically, and says that both interpretive modes may be maintained simmultaneously, but that they should illumine each other rather than restrict interpretive freedom.

They are an Allegory, αλληγορούμενι, that is to say they are to be treated as Containing a Speciall meaning in them of some Spirituall Mystery, as Figures, Tropes, Types, &c ever do For an Allegory . . . For these . . . are the two Covenants, i.e., the Covenant given at Mount Sinai, & that to be given on Mount Zion . . . For this Hagar is Mount Sinai in Arabia. Sinai was a mountain in Arabia Deserta on which Moses received the Law. The Apostle asserts this Hagar to be this Sinai, not as if its Signification was the Same with that of Sina as Chrysostom labours to bring about. for the Apostles Speech is Allegoricall & Sinai Signifies a Bush . . . but Hagar Signifies a Stranger Such as Hagar was in Abrams family, Gen. 16.1 . . . But she may be said to be Sinai mount by a Metonomy of the subject for the Adjunct . . . (Nebraska manuscript Sermon 4, typescript pp. 3-4).

Taylor then clearly defines the allegorical significance in the more conservative terms by which he reads Genesis according to instituted scheme and prophetic symbol.

But the Apostle respects not this as their Countrey, but doth explain the Allegory thus, & saith, this is the meaning of the Allegory. Hagar, Abrahams bond woman is first to be taken as an Emblem of Mount Sinai in Arabia. Mount Sinai is to be taken for the Law, or Testament there given as she was not free but a Bond Servant so she speakes of the Law or Testament given at Mount Sinai . . . Then he turns to Sarah implicitly the Free woman to whom the promise was made & makes her to Carry a type of the Church of the Elect saying, v. 26, Jerusalem which is above is free which is the Mother of us all . . . Hence the Allegory holds out this Doctrinall Conclusion.

Taylor continues the sermon with elaborate "proofs," which include quotations from Origen, who "makes Abraham in his faith a Form or Type & image of the Gospell Mystery," and from Calvin, who argues that "the house of Abraham was then a true Church, so its not to be doubted but the Chiefe & most memorable Events therein, are so many types to us: as therefore in Circumcision, in Sacrifices, in all the Leviticall [lacuna] there was an Allegory" (Nebraska manuscript Sermon 4, typescript p. 16).

Thus the allegorical reading carries prophetic or figural significance even though modes of interpretation remain distinct. The sermon's purpose is like the objective implicit in the entire sequence of meditations and sermons: to show how language reveals the personal relationship of Christ to the true believer and, in this specific case, to show that "Abraham, & that in relation to Hager, & Sarah, & their two Sons, is a Type of the Lord, & that in his relation to his Mystical Visible Body & Church, we may be hence informed." In Sermon 6 of the Second Series, preached on Isaiah 49:3, "And said unto me. Thou art my sergant, Oh Israel, in whom I will be glorified" (1694), Taylor again argued the doctrine that "Jacob was a Famous Type of Christ" with elaborate proofs that border on allegorical reading while retaining the prophetic force of each parallel developed. Linear typology is thus preserved, and the allegorical readings are consistent with conservative Protestant exegesis that sought to avoid the fanciful Platonic excesses of the Middle Ages.

The point is that the *Meditations* cannot be fully and completely understood in *vacuo,* nor should we assume that Taylor has represented an entire doctrinal position through the metaphysical language of his poems that commence with consideration of a particular verse of Scripture. Moreover, it is clear that some of the poems and sermons were associated with each other in sequences deliberately designed to develop an idea more comprehensively than would be possible through the exegesis of a single poem or sermon, or combination of the two. Students of Taylor have long advanced this argument when discussing the *Christographia* sermons, those fourteen sermons that are associated with meditations belonging to the Second Series. However, the sequence of poems on typology, that commence the Second Series, are clearly another intentional doctrinal sequence, which, until recently, we have only been able to splice together by associating the doctrine contained in the verses themselves. This has been relatively easy to do because the typology *Meditations* are clear examples of Taylor's theories concerning figural and prophetic imagery. However, the Nebraska discovery now makes it possible to gloss those typology *Meditations* with prose statements of doctrine from sermons that were designed to accompany the poems. We may also formulate assumptions about figural writing in Taylor's work that more clearly show the enormous influence of this habit of mind in the Westfield poet's thinking.

THE TYPOLOGY MEDITATIONS

The Nebraska volume is a holograph manuscript consisting of 36 sermons on 905 folio sheets that resemble the *Christographia* group and the *Treatise on the Lord's Supper* in that it is organized around a central theme, in this case, the types of the Old Testament. The volume is crudely bound in vellum which is stitched and glued to paperboard made from discarded gatherings of manuscript materials, suggesting that the binding is Taylor's. The book consists of two groups of sermons: twenty-nine sermons dating from 28/3m/1693 to 5/12m/1698 almost parallel to some Second Series *Preparatory Meditations,* 2.1 through 2.29; and seven sermons dating from 5/10m/1703 to 20/8m/1706, the first five of which are parallel to some Second Series *Preparatory Meditations,* for example, 2.58 through 2.61; the last of these sermons corresponds to *Meditation* 2.71. The title at the top of the first leaf makes the subject clear: "Upon ye Types of ye old Testament." On a half-sheet before the first page, Taylor, in an aged but discernible hand, has written the following notes:

Types are either { Personall
                   Not Personall

following distinctions drawn also by Samuel Mather in the *Figures or Types of the Old Testament* (1683). He then instructs the reader in his methodology:

> Touching the Personall. I have followed other learned men & Some of them have very lean Scripture proof confirming their typicall Relation: and in that I have laid down reasons to proove the Same. I would not Belabor as accounting the reasons sufficient to Evince their being types: But rather to bee demonstrations of matter upon them rendering the Suitable to stand in a typicall Relation: & accepted for [lacuna] thereby, as other are that have their Typehood affirmed by the holy Scriptures.

The general plan of these sermons is consistent with the development of theme in the series of *Meditations.* It will be useful and important to the continued examination of the language of Canaan to examine selected sermons and meditations from this intriguing series. The dates and texts of the sermons (with pagination) as they appear in the manuscript are in the notes to this chapter.[10] The numbers of the sermons correspond to the meditations in the Second Series with which they are associated.

Figural and prophetic language is critical to Taylor's poetry and to the interpretation modern critics have given to his role as a minister in Westfield. It is well known that he was a conservative in theology, aligned with Increase Mather against Solomon Stoddard, the "bastard of the valley," who liberalized admission to the Lord's Supper and extended church membership more freely than the Half-Way Covenant of 1662 had provided. The typology *Meditations* and sermons are consistent with Taylor's conservatism and reflect the general theology of his *Treatise Concerning the Lord's Supper* (1693-94), in which the poet challenges Stoddard's claims for the efficacy of the sacrament as a converting ordinance.

Scholars have also long recognized the extraordinary genius of Taylor's poetry, which exhibits sophistication and ingenuity usually associated with the metaphysical school or the theological complexities of a scholar-poet like John Milton. That Taylor should have achieved such a level of development while ministering to the frontier community of Westfield, Massachusetts, is indeed remarkable; however, the doctrinal sources Taylor used are clearly reflected in his typology *Meditations* and sermons, so that his very consistency with earlier thinkers and with contemporary theologians helps explain the sophistication of his unpublished writing, which was composed under primitive conditions without access to the resources one might enjoy in London or Boston. The major traditional influences, however, are straightforward and easily discernible.

The Beinecke Library of Yale University holds Taylor's annotated copy of Thomas Taylor's *Christ Revealed,* a significant treatise on the relationship between Old Testament prophetic typology and New Testament fulfillment. Even without this confirmation, we already know that in Ezra Stiles' catalog of his library holding in "Itineraries and Memoirs, 1760," this volume of "Taylor's Types" appears. It is marked "Grandfather's Book apprized in Father's Lib.," and no doubt came to Yale through Isaac Stiles, Edward Taylor's son-in-law. Taylor inherited the whole tradition of Puritan figuralism, and the clearest evidence of this influence is his annotated copy of Samuel Mather's *Figures or Types of the Old Testament,* which is also housed in the Beinecke. Modern scholarship is gradually demonstrating the specific sources in Samuel Mather's work for Edward Taylor's design in the *Meditations,* and it is clear that the poet borrowed heavily from thematic and organizational paradigms in the typological system of Samuel Mather.

There are two central places in Taylor's writing that set forth his own understanding of this tradition, and provide a coherent typological doctrine. The first sermon and meditation of the Second Series argue the Pauline-Augustinian thesis found in Colossians 2:17, that the Old Testament figures are "shaddows of things to come and the body is Christs." Then in the *Christographia,* where Taylor internalizes and personalizes biblical figures as part of the sacramental process, the ninth sermon and meditation are a central statement of the poet's conservative exegetical practice. Both of these are prominent *loci* and are corroborated by passages found elsewhere in Taylor's work. For example, in the two "sequences," to which each belongs—the typology sermons and meditations and the *Christographia* cycle—these central statements are reinforced and extensively developed. Finally, Taylor has advanced a conservative figural reading of Scripture in his long statement on the day of judgment that appears in the "Profession of Faith" in the Westfield Church Records.

In the day of judgment statement, Taylor follows the premillennial view of Joseph Mede and Increase Mather, predicting that Christ's throne will be "high and lifted up with Shining Angels attending on it."[11] Moreover, he follows this assertion with a declaration concerning the efficacy of Christ's fulfillment of prophetic figures and types:

> Solomons was a yellow throne but Christs a White Throne. as Rev. 20.12. Solomons was a glorious throne. But Christs a Throne of Glory, Mat. 25.31. Oh what glory is here? Christs Throne then doth so far Shine the glory of Solomons Throne, that the glory of Solomons Throne is onely darksome in Comparison unto the glory of Christs Throne. & thus much for the glory of the throne (Davis, p. 536).

And in discussing the resurrection of the body—which is literal and real both for saints and sinners, so that Taylor is able to describe the torments of the damned in graphic detail—he advances the argument by showing that Christ's glory will "outshine" that of the sun and other prophetic figures that point to the fulfillment of types in the second coming.

> He shall now come in trandscendent Glory, for he shall come to be admired ... Then he shall come in his glory, Mat. 25.31. If the bodies of the Saints shall at the Resurrection Shine like the body of the Sun, what shall the body of Christ the Son of God shine like. It is called a body of glory now, Phil. 3.21. If he appeared so glorious in the Vision among his churches, Rev. 1.12—what shall his glory be now he comes to appear in his glory? (p. 535).

Then, utilizing the figural value of Canticles, Taylor turns to that book for an image of Christ's transcendent glory in the last judgment: "If his description, Cant. 5.10—shows his glory to be so transcendent; what shall he show himselfe to be when he shall appeare in a more transcendent Glory then there is in that?" (p. 535).

This relativity of glorification is echoed in Taylor's opening meditation of the Second Series:

> The glory of the world slickt up in types
>   In all Choise things chosen to typify,
> His glory upon whom the worke doth light,
>   To thine's a Shaddow, or a butterfly.
>   How glorious then, my Lord, art thou to mee
>   Seing to cleanse me, 's worke alone for thee (II.1.13-18).[12]

The evanescence of the butterfly, nonetheless a reminder of extraordinary natural and temporal beauty, is contrasted with the greater beauty of Christ, who is only foreshadowed, not fulfilled, in the types. But the antitypical fulfillment in Christ's glory is also stated:

> The glory of all Types doth meet in thee.
>   Thy glory doth their glory quite excell:

> More than the Sun excells in its bright glee
> A nat, an Earewig, Weevill, Snaile, or Shell (II.19-22).

The transience of the type and the permanence of the antitype become a central theme for the accompanying sermon, and the butterfly and shadows images are not far away in Taylor's explanation of the term "shadowy darkness."

> Now a Sparkling Pearle Coming between the Sun, and any thing Objected to the Sun gives a glorious Shade upon the Objected body. So here the Types are Shadows of Christ as he is this precious Orient Pearle: therefore Carry an Excellent light with them, and yet their Excellency is but a Shadowy darkness Compared to the Excellency of Christ. & so the term Shadow imports. Some take the Word Shadow, to be an allusion to the first draught of a Picture which is pensild out with a Coale, or black Lead, & as such is calld the Shadow; but after its compleated with fair Colours . . . Its a transient, and fleeting Excellency. Shadows fly away: Can. 2.17 . . . But Christs is perminent (Nebraska manuscript Sermon I, typescript p. 1).

Taylor continues the association between earthly glory and that made available through Christ's grace. The hierarchical pattern of relative glory reflected through images of light and darkness create a *chiaroscuro* that will reappear in Jonathan Edwards' epistemological treatise, *A Divine and Supernatural Light.* (1734). Taylor works up through the order of creation, which only reflects Christ's glory, to the final excellency of Christ's revelation in the second coming:

> Here is the highest of[fice] & higher than merely Created excellency at Worke to redeem thee. Here was, during the Umbratick State of the Church, the Chiefe Excellency of all the World Singled out one way, or other to be a Type respecting mans Recovery. & hence the Shoulders of all this Excellency was, & hath been, at the Worke. But yet all this Excellency is but a Shadow to the Excellency that did the work: the Excellency, that is typified by it. Now if the Excellency of the type which is so unspeakable is but a Shadow to the Excellency of Christ which hath done the worke, & is still at the work of mans Redemption; then what? What unconceivable Excellency is it, that is at work to bring about thy Salvation . . . For all this Excellencie that is at work, is at worke in the person of the Redeemer (Nebraska manuscript Sermon I, typescript p. 33).

The final line here is crucial to an understanding of Taylor's personalizing or spiritualizing of the types, which can be fully demonstrated through an examination of the *Christographia* sequence. Taylor understands the systematic structures of typical foreshadowing and antitypical fulfillment and follows Samuel Mather closely in arguing the linear fulfillment scheme; however, he exceeds Mather in applying the types to the process of his personal redemption and to the larger redemptive history of mankind, which he implies here by associating the excellency of Christ's glory, foreshadowed in the types and fully reflected in the antitype of Christ's person, with the "glorious" work of individual redemption.

This process of personalizing, or spiritualizing, the type-antitype association is critical for Taylor's theology, for he otherwise argues the abrogation of types and their conclusion in Christ's first coming, the incarnation. The opening of this sermon's text, (Col. 2:17, "Which are a Shadow of things to Come, but the Body is of Christ"), shows that Taylor is primarily concerned to demonstrate that "the Greate worke of Divine Grace in the Dispensation of the Gospell is to bring persons out of a State of Sin, unto Christ Jesus" but that he soon moves into the area of rhetorical strategies by demonstrating the principles of progressive revelation "in Prophecies variously Shining with his Excellencie, and in Types most Gorgeously laid down before us The Glory of all which is but a darke Shadow of his Excellency. Now that this glory of Christ might Smite its enamoring Rayes upon our Affections to draw us thereby to Christ, I am now come to lay open Somewhat the Excellency of the Type & that in General from this text read" (Nebraska manuscript Sermon I, typescript p. 2). In the most conservative exegetical Reformed tradition, Taylor states that the Jewish Ceremonies, for example, are "Shadows of things to Come, but the body is Christs and therefore now Christ is Come they must cease" (Nebraska manuscript Sermon I, typescript p. 3). The uncompromising phrasing, and the seeming rigidity of this position is the conventional Puritan opposition to the Anglican justification for continuation of ceremonies in worship that the Puritans had abolished. Taylor emphatically states:

> All the Ceremonies of the Law were Shadows of Good things to come: Of things to come that should bee. Whether Person, Qualification of the Person, or Performance & action all belonging to the said person of the Messiah. All this is granted by the Apostle & therefore that it had been more than lawfull: it was a positive Duty to observe them. But herein there was indeed an argument against the Constant use of them: they were but Shadows, & therefore not Durable. They were but Shadows, & therefore not Substantiall to rest on. They were but Shadows, & therefore not to be imbraced when the Substance outed them, for when the body giving the Shadow possesseth the Subject place of the Shadow, the Shadowe is outed thereby: they cannot both be in the same place *Ubi umbra definit, ibi Corpus incipit*. Hence the Types being but Shadows they must Cease, when Christ the Substance of them is come (Nebraska manuscript Sermon I, typescript p. 5).

The moral or perpetual equity of the Old Testament figures for Puritan theology is not the question here; rather, Taylor follows Samuel Mather in distinguishing between prophetic figure and fulfilling incarnation. In a passage that takes as its text the same biblical verse from Colossians, Samuel Mather says that

> There is the *thing shadowed* or represented by the *Type,* And what is that? *Things to come,* saith the Apostle, *Col.* 2.17. and *good things to come,* Heb. 10.1. The good things of the Gospel, *Christ and his Benefits; but the Body is of Christ,* as Col. 2.17. This we call the *Correlate,* or the *Antitype;* the other is the *Shadow,* this the *Substance:* The *Type* is the Shell; this the Kernel; the *Type* is the Letter, this the Spirit and Mystery of the *Type.* This we are still to look at, and to search into in every *Type;* we must look beyond the Shadow, to the Substance, to the Truth and Mystery of it: And this is Christ and the Gospel, was future, and hereafter to be exhibited.[13]

How, then, does the regenerate believer enter into association with Christ through a reading and understanding of the prophetic figures of the Old Testament, the language of Canaan, through which Christ was revealed in shadows to those who had preceded the incarnation? Taylor's doctrinal concerns were with contemporary Christians, not with the saving of the Jews before Christ. So he continually stresses that Christ was the true end and object of all Testament figures and that this essential truth will render all typological foreshadowings spiritually, not just morally and perpetually, valid for all human time. Believers have only to distinguish between those ceremonies and laws of the Old Testament that were abrogated in Christ and those qualifications of Christ that are eternally valid to comprehend the supreme glory of God's redemptive power. Christ may be prefigured in the Old Testament, but He is eternal and perpetual in His Glorious majesty, one substance, in different forms. Taylor's imaginative understanding of the process of doctrinal dispensation looks forward itself to Jonathan Edwards' assertion concerning Christ's eternal antitype, and backward to figural writers like Thomas Taylor, who also declared that "by the Gospel the Lord hath revealed the Covenant of Grace, which is in substance but one, as God is but one, and Christ is but one, who is the substance of it . . . Christ, and his doctrine, and Covenant, being *the same yesterday, and today, and forever,* Heb. 13.8. for substance, altereth and differeth onely in the forme an manner of dispensation; according to which, it is diversely propounded in the old Testament and the New."[14]

> That the old Testament believer did as truelie believe in Christ, as the New doth. Christ is the Same Christ to both: that the faith in Christ was the Same faith to both: that they are both Saved by the Same Faith, as the means: by the Same Christ, as the Cause of Salvation, the one as the other. For in that the one Was under Christ in the Promise, Prophecy and Type, and the other under Christ dispensed in the Substance, Spirit, and Power of the Gospell:

they both Sit under the Exhibition of the Same Christ, of the Same Grace, and in the Exercise of the Same faith; onely there is a difference as to the manner of the Dispensing the Same. They had Christ dispensed in Promises and Types, as a Mediator to Come. We have him dispensed in a Cleare, and Manifest way as Come already. But the different manner of dispensing of the Messiah, doth not produce, a different Christ, nor a different Faith on Christ . . . Now to use the type is to say, the Shadow is better than the Substance, and to denie that the thing typified is come (*Christographia,* IX, pp. 287-288).

Here, as elsewhere in the *Meditations,* Taylor employs typology as a vehicle for minimizing the differences between the two dispensations. Scripture becomes part of the historical record of God's continuous revelation of the Messiah, and the process by which Christ is accommodated to mankind involves prophetic prefiguration and antitypical fulfillment. Still, at the incarnation the types were fulfilled by the coming of the flesh, so that in modern times, recapitulative and correlative typology are necessary to the believer's understanding of those promises that await fulfillment at the end of human time. Taylor said in the ninth *Meditation* of the *Christographia, Meditation* 50 of the Second Series:

> The Artist puts his glorious hand again
>   Out to the Worke: His Skill out flames more bright
> Now than before. The worke he goes to gain,
>   He did portray in flaming Rayes of light.
>   A Box of Pearle shall from this Sory, pass
>   More rich than that Smaragdine Truth-Box was.
>
> Which Box, four thousand yeares, o'r ere 'twas made,
>   In golden Scutchons lay'd in inke Divine
> Of Promises, of a Prophetick Shade,
>   And in embellishments of Types that Shine,
>   Whose Beames in this Choice pearle-made-Box all meet
>   And bedded in't their glorious Truth to keep.

The image described here of the jeweled box, covered with pearl and gold, suggests the elaborately decorated embossed covers for Bibles that were common in medieval churches and would have been well known to Taylor by way of the disdain for them prominent in Puritan doctrine. However, he has here transformed the literal jewels and pearl into figural metaphors of Christ, which, in turn, are prophetic of his own, personal relationship to messianic salvation:

> But now, my Lord, thy Humane Nature, I
>   Doe by the Rayes this Scutcheon sends out, finde
> In this Smaragdine Box where Truth doth ly

> Of Types, and Promises, that thee out lin'de.
> Their Truth they finde in thee: this makes them shine.
> Their Shine on thee makes thee appeare Divine.
>
> Thou givst thy Truth to them, thus true they bee.
> They bring their Witness out for thee. Hereby
> Their Truth appears emboxt indeed in thee,
>   And thou the true Messiah shin'st thereby.
>   Hence Thou, and They make One another true
>   And They, and Thou each others Glory Shew.

This mutual dependence of the types and Christ in a process of revealed glory extended the efficacy of the types for Taylor beyond the boundaries set by Samuel Mather and the Scripture confines without designating "moral" or "perpetual" equity for the types as Thomas Shepard had done in the *Theses Sabbaticae* (1649). Taylor acknowledges the important differences the prefigural efficacy of Old Testament ceremonies that were abrogated in Christ's incarnation, but he identifies with the types through correlation and recapitulation to give spiritual meaning to those metaphors from the Bible that speak of Christ's personal importance for the poet in his own time. The process appears to be mystical — even transcendent — and some modern critics have labeled Taylor a mystic for this apparent trace of timeless union with Christ's person. But the process is not timeless; rather, it is consummating, fulfilling, and firmly anchored in a moment through which Christ's personal qualities, as exhaustively delineated in the entire *Christographia* sequence, are fused in a synthesis of the divine and human, the *theanthropy* which has long been argued as the focal point of the *Christographia* cycle. The two final stanzas of *Meditation* 50 exhibit this transformation from intellectual abstraction to personal identification with the prophetic and figural power of the Old Testament figures:

> Hence thou art full of Truth, and full dost stand,
>   Of Promises, of Prophesies, and Types.
> But that's not all: All truth is in thy hand,
>   Thy lips drop onely Truth, give Falshood gripes.
>   Leade through the World to glory, that ne'er ends,
>   By Truth's bright Hand all Such as Grace befriends.
>
> O! Box of Truth! tenent my Credence in
>   The mortase of thy Truth; and Thou in Mee.
> These Mortases, and Tenents make so trim.
>   That They and Thou and I ne'er severed bee.
>   Embox my faith, Lord, in thy Truth a part
>   And I'st by Faith embox thee in my heart (II.50, 15-50).

By turning to the immediate and literal image of box construction in the final stanza, Taylor makes the process of identification with Christ both personal and imminent; no longer is the type a jeweled figure reminding us of the transcendent value of messianic glory; nor is the allusion to irradiated glory and its connection to truth lost in the abstract theory of typological prefiguration and antitypical fulfillment. Rather, for a moment that is immediate and real, Taylor assumes the burden and the joy of "joining" with Christ, a moment that is made possible by his understanding of recapitulative typology and the prophetic value of those figures around which he has developed his highly imagistic poem.[15]

The overall design of the *Christographia* supports this claim. Sermons I and II develop the nature of Christ and Sermons III, IV, and V move toward the hypostatical union of divine and human in *theanthropy* through contemplations of Christ's true nature and an examination of the person of Christ as eternally incarnate, much as Taylor argued in the long passage from Sermon IX quoted above. Sermons IV-XIII display Christ's various properties and examine his "qualifications" as Messiah. The "personal" and "relative" qualities are set forth, and throughout, especially in the harmony of sermon and poem, Taylor shows how personal, figural, and historical theology can come together in an aesthetically satisfying, doctrinally sound statement of individual spiritual fulfillment. For example, the ark of the covenant, so obvious an allusion in the "Smaragdine Box" (smaragdine is a kind of emerald) invokes all the historical value of God's providential guidance of ancient Israel through his divine presence among them in the ark, which was carried with the nomadic Israelites, but it is through Christ's humanity that ultimately we are able to partake of the hypostatic union that has occurred between His human and divine natures. The scheme of mutual dependence between Christ and the types for the revelation of truth makes possible the full participation of man's understanding and belief in the efficacy of Christ's truth; that is, Christ not only relies on the figural and typological foreshadowings of His incarnation that reveal Him to man, He also associates with man through human understanding of the process of prophecy and fulfillment. Arminian though this may appear to be, it is conventional covenant theology, where God and man were mutually engaged in a mandatory scheme of contractual obligation.

It is important that Taylor has not advanced the notion of "moral" or "perpetual" equity to replace the figural value of the Old Testament types. As the following chapter will make clear, Thomas Shepard followed earlier English Puritans in advancing this notion when, according to their interpretations, it was clear that the Old Testament figures and types were abrogated in the incarnation. To have argued otherwise would have allowed the imitation of ancient ceremonies in worship, as the Anglicans reasoned. Rather, Taylor has set in motion a process by which the recapitulations of the typological scheme of prophecy and fulfillment will create a new personal identification with Christ through assumption of His glory as it revealed in the prophetic types, which, after all, were once instituted to show forth His glory that was to come. No one understood the importance of abrogation more than Taylor. "All those that He instituted Whether of a Morall, or Ceremoniall Significancy, are abolished," he argued in the ninth *Christographia* sermon: "Seeing those Ceremonies that God instituted for religious worship are laid aside, Humane Ceremonies of a Significant nature are utterly unlawful." But Taylor efectively argues here, and elsewhere, that the "truth" with which the types are endowed is eternal, not temporal, though our understanding of that truth will take place in a transcendent moment:

> Because he is the Truth of all the Prophesies, and Types of the Old Testament, Now he in whom lies the Truth of all the Old Testament Prophesies, and Types, aboute the Messiah, and his Kingdom, must needs be full of Truth, For the truth of all these lies in him. They are given out by the God of Truth, and therefore must needs be true, or what becomes of the truth of God? They are not untrue before they are fulfilld: nor are they true before they are accomplished. The accomplishment of them is necessary in order to their truth ... Yet if these Promises and Types should never be fulfilld; they would be false; and assert untruth. Hence, in respect unto their being true, there must be the fulfilling of them. The Supposition of their not being at all fulfilld, doth not onely yield Such an inference as striketh down their truth, but also, that Strikes against the Deity of their author ... & They derive their Truth from him in whom they are fulfilld, and therefore their truth is all Stored up in him ... He is the end of the Law ... The types, and Ceremonies were shadows of Good things to come, but the body is of Christ, Col. 2.17 ... Now then seing the truth of these things lies in their fulfilling, and their fulfilling lies in Christ, its plain that their truth is in Christ, and hence Christ is full of Truth (*Christographia*, IX, pp. 276-277).

Christ, of course, is eternal not temporal. To argue that the types are therefore temporal and abrogated is to deny their essential truth. Taylor finds the types "full of truth," and clearly reflective of Christ's eternal — not "perpetual" — glory, which he argued was available to the regenerate perception. The question becomes one of epistemology as much as theology, and for Taylor, the process of personal indentification was historical in origin, continuous in nature, and eternally valid. Kathleen Blake wrote,

> Taylor devoted one series of sermons, the *Christographia*, to the Incarnation. Its subject is spirit made flesh through the hypostatical union of God and

man in Christ. There is, in a sense, a reverse version of this union when flesh is made spirit, which is what happens when bread and wine "become" Christ's body and blood in the sacrament. This is the subject of Taylor's *Treatise Concerning the Lord's Supper,* as well as the most pervasive theme in his *Meditations.*

Thus the sacrament of Holy Communion can be said to provide a fundamental Christian model or emblem of the relationship between man and God, a relationship which is also a communication. For the English and American Protestants, it was closely analogous to that between the terms of a metaphor, an analogy which works for all it is worth.[16]

This argument is supported not only by the evidence of Taylor's transformation of recapitulated Old Testament figure into a personal identification with Christ; it is also shown clearly in the full title of the book of his meditations, which were designed to accompany sermons that were preached at the celebration of the Lord's Supper, *Preparatory Meditations: Before My Approach to the Lords Supper. Chiefly Upon the Doctrin preached upon the Day of Administration.*

This close association between the sermon, the meditation, and the doctrine of personal identification with the biblical figure is best revealed in one of the groupings made possible by the new Taylor sermon manuscript. The fifth *Meditation* in the Second Series addresses a well-known typological figure from the Old Testament. Although its text is taken from Galatians, 3:16, "And to thy Seed Which is Christ" it refers to God's covenant with Abraham and his seed, Isaac, a type of Christ. The figure is the sacrifice of Isaac, a trope around which much doctrinal discussion has centered, and to which Cotton Mather also addresses himself in the "Biblia Americana" (see Chapter 7 of this study). In this meditation, Christ is compared to a pearl once again, just as in the sixth *Meditation* of this series, he is made analogous to the jeweled Bible cover: "I spy thyselfe, as Golden Bosses fixt/On Bible Covers, shine in Types out bright,/Of Abraham, Isaac, Jacob, where's immixt/Their streaming Beames of Christ displaying Light." But in the fifth *Meditation,* Taylor is deeply concerned with the problem of hypostatic union, and he argues his case in terms of the Old Testament prefiguration of God's sacrifice of His Son, the passage in Genesis 22, where Abraham is asked to sacrifice Isaac. The doctrinal lines are not always clear in this poem, and it is very important to use the sermon as a gloss on the poem now that it is available. The essential stanzas in the meditation are:

> Christ's Antitype Isaac his Type up spires
> In many things, but Chiefly this because
> This Isaac, and the Ram caught in the briars
> One Sacrifice, fore shew by typick laws
> Christs Person, all Divine, joynd whereto's made
> Unperson'd Manhood, on the Altar's laid.

> The full grown Ram, provided none knows how,
>   Typing Christ's Manhood, made by God alone
> Caught in the brambles by the horns, must bow,
>   Under the Knife: The manhoods Death, and Groan.
>   Yet Isaac's leaping from the Altar's bed,
>   Foretold its glorious rising from the Dead (II.5, 7-19).

These two stanzas identify the typological association; however, the subject and theme of the meditation are Christ's person. Taylor will conclude his poem with an impassioned appeal to have the sacrifice of Christ made personally meaningful to his own salvation; but not before he has clearly established the terms of the arrangment. Christ is a consummate example of partial revelations of this sacrifice and promises that have been made throughout history. Moreover, he is a fulfillment of all "emblems" and "types" that have shadowed out the process of salvation in the history of redemption. Taylor stated in the sermon,

> 1.   Isaac is a Type of Christs Person in generall in this Sacrifice. Isaac is a Type of our Saviour the Lord, saith Augustin and he typifies Christs person in Severall things belonging to it, as they were accomplisht in Christs Sacrifice, as viz., 1. As to Time, which was on the third day. Gen. 22. 4. Some take it to be a token of the Trinity. & its Sure that frequently in Scripture we have things to be done on the third day where no reason is given of the Same. & hence Some have said that the third day is fitted for a Mystery. Some make these three days an Emblem of the three years of Christs Ministry before his Suffering. Others of Christs lying in the grave. But why may it not note those three last dayes that went before Christs Suffering, whereof Christ is so express? (Nebraska manuscript Sermon 5, typescript p. 5).

Indeed, the whole of this sermon is given over to providing the efficacy of Isaac as a type of Christ, so that the sacrifice motif continuous from the initial establishing of the covenant of grace will be meaningful in the redemptive process. "The Blessing promised lying in a Promised Seed, doth implicitly contain a Promise made unto that Seed by whom this Promised Blessing is Effected, & this was Individually [78] Isaac, as a Type, & so Containd in him Christ in his own Person as the Very Kirnell, and Marrow of the Promise & this Brings me unto the Matter before us: that Isaac is a Type of Christ" (Nebraska manuscript Sermon 5, typescript p. 2). Using the kirnell/shell analogy found also in Samuel Mather's *Figures or Types,* Taylor goes on to argue that "it must be granted that, as Isaac was a Promised Seed, he was wholy typicall & so not the Onely promised Seed, but given in the Promise wholy with respect unto the Lord Christ the alone Single Promised Seed. & this being the Case the Doctrinall Conclusion, that I take up from the Words is this, that Doctrine: Isaac is an Eminent Type of Christ." Then Taylor continues: "We heard before of Christ typified as a Mediator, & as he Stands in

Relation unto the Object of His Mediatory Office. But now in Isaac we have a Type of What is necessary in order to his accomplishing his Mediatory Office" (Nebraska manuscript Sermon 5, typescript p. 4).

But for Taylor, the intellectual schema of type and antitype is not the central issue: rather, he is concerned to show how Christ's sacrifice — a personal and vital means of salvation for mankind — is eternally represented in the continuous process by which Christ's person is imperfectly manifested in human history.

> God's wrath is So great against thy Sin, as that he must have Satisfaction either in the Way of Reconciliation, or in the way of thy Damnation. 2. That there is no Reconciliation to be had: but onely in his Son, God man answering this Type in Isaac . . . In that Isaac typified Christ, Christ must answer the type . . . that Christ should be such an Extraordinary person consisting [92] of two natures, the one to purchase & Satisfy withall by active & passive Obedience. The other by its worthiness, to render this Active and Passive Obedience, Efficacious, . . . Hence, either the End of all that Christ did both as to the Union of the Natures, & also in the Natures United, in both active, & passive obedience, & so also the End of all the types, & especially this of Isaac (Nebraska manuscript Sermon 5, typescript pp. 36-37).

It is, of course, the hypostatic union of divine and human in Christ's person that makes the sacrifice efficacious for the salvation of mankind. But to prefigure this in the Isaac-Abraham episode is more for Taylor than an intellectual exercise in prophecy and fulfillment. It is part of a continuous and eternal revelation of Christ's person that renders the antitype meaningful for other moments of human history than the incarnation. He asks in the fifth *Meditation,* "Oh costly Sin! this makes mine intraills bleed. / What fills my Shell, did make my Saviour die. / What Grace then's this of God, and Christ that stills / Out of this Offering into our tills?"

The response to this question comes in the accompanying sermon, and it extends a doctrine also developed by Taylor in the *Christographia*: the doctrine of Christ's two natures. The passage illustrating this point is long but it merits being quoted in full, since it is not generally available. At the end of the sermon, just as he "applies" the doctrine to his personal situation and to that of his congregation, Taylor parallels the lines from the *Meditation* that inquire about the nature of sin and the process of redemption by saying:

> Oh! then how glorious must Christ needs be, who is typified hereby. In that hereby we See him Consisting of two Natures perfect, & Compleat and one person. Of the Godhead & the Manhood. That the Manhood could be advanced to an hight Suitable for its union to the Godhead, must needs make it the most glorious lump of Humane Nature that Ever was. & as for the God-

head it hath all the Excellency of the Godhead in it. Now then these two united what an Excellency is here? Ah! but that these two and all their Excellency should become an offering to God for man's Sins! & the Humane to die in the Fire of Gods wrath for thy Sins! Oh what a thing is this? Oh! what a Loveliness is here then in this matter manifested in Christ Jesus? . . . For what is done by Christ, is nothing more than what is right [89] And do but se here some few things as they are typified by Isaac & you will finde it thus. You may se how Sin hath constrained the whole Creation. The whole Creation is not enough to make an offering to God for thy Sin, if thou had'st it to lay down. Consider here there must be Sacrifice, & this Sacrifice must Consist of a Nature Mortall, and Immortall. Mortall, or else cannot dy Immortall or else it cannot but die, & ever get out of the Clutch of Death: Humane, or else it is not the Same that Sinned. Divine or else it cannot Satisfy for Sin. This matter is so greate that it exceeds all Created Wisdom to have imagined . . . [90] This truth is a Demonstration of God's Grace abundantly overflowing to poore Souls. Seing Such is the State of man by Sin, that he that shall Secure man from Sin, must consist of two Natures one Mortall one Immortall: one Humane, & one Divine, the one to tender the price, the other to render the Price sufficiently pretious to Satisfy, & purchase the one to Die, the other to render the Death Efficatious. Both must bee laid upon the Altar, the one burnt in the Fire of Gods justice for a burnt offering: None could be found to do this, but the Son of God & that the Son of God Should undertake, & therefore be made of Son of God &, and so do it, is the Piece of the most unmatchable Grace that ever was heard of and that God the Father should not onely permit him: but should send him forth to do it is another demonstration of the Like matchless Grace. Now then that both these two should thus joyntly put forth this Grace Oh! what Grace is here? & yet in that Isaac, & the ram should in their Sacrifice thus typify the Lord Christ; we have this grace typified to be in Christ (Nebraska manuscript Sermon 5, typescript pp. 38-40).

Thus for Taylor, the hypostatic union of divinity and humanity make possible the salvation of mankind, and this union is manifest, not represented, in various imperfect forms throughout human history, the antitype of which is Christ's eternal gracious perfection. The individual believer, understanding this process through his regenerate powers of perception, aspires to become part of this continuous process of prophecy and fulfillment, type and antitype. He seeks, in short, to recapitulate the prophetic type and to identify with the historical and eternal process of which it is a part. In a tantalizing metaphor from the Second *Meditation* of the Second Series, Taylor implores God to make him part of this figural process:

> Oh! that my Soul was all enamored
>   With this First Born enough: a Lump of Love,
> Son of Eternall Father, Chambered

> Once in a Virgins Womb, dropt from above.
> All Humane royalty hereby Divin'de.
> The First Born's Antitype: in whom they're shrin'de.
>
> Make mee thy Babe, and him my Elder Brother,
>   A Right, Lord grant me in his Birth Right high.
> His Grace, my Treasure make above all other:
>   His Life my Sampler: My Life his joy.
>   I'le hang my love then on his heart, and sing
>   New Psalms on Davids Harpe to thee and him (II.2, 30-44).[17]

Unlike the voice howling in the wilderness, Edward Taylor quietly extended the language of Canaan to have real metaphorical value for the process of his own salvation at a time when the efficacy of the prophecy had been all but lost for New England's errand into the wilderness. His vision of the first-born as a type of Christ is firmly anchored in conservative exegesis, as the sermon accompanying this meditation makes clear. The meditation and sermon maintain Taylor's consistently personal and Christological focus, indicating that the person, Christ, is indeed the antitype of types instituted before his coming: "That he [Christ] was indeed the Antitype of, & typified by the First Born both before the Law, & Under the Law." He then uses the *analogy* of first-born children to *illustrate* aspects of Christ's office as redeemer begotten of God, but he is extremely careful to distinguish metaphorical uses from instituted typological correspondences.

The First Born are Types of Christ as they stand in Relation unto the other Children. & so Christ is Gods first Born onely Metaphorically, Because he is properly Gods onely begotten Son: & all other Children of God are onely Adopted Children, & not naturall. Rom 8. 15. 16. 17 John 1. 12. & hence Christ is the First onely metaphoricall. Yet thus the First Born typify him in Severall Respects (Nebraska manuscript Sermon 2, typescript p. 12).

Figural writing and typology were for Taylor a means of expressing the immediate personal power of grace the poet felt so keenly. As prophetic synecdoches of the realization of the kingdom — not only on earth but in individual lives — the biblical figures provided Taylor a series of instituted images to anchor his doctrine of prophecy and fulfillment, so that his poetry resonates not only with traditional and conventional exegetical habits of mind, but also expresses his deepest conviction that Christ's saving power would soon effect his personal salvation.

III
Recapitulative Typology and Eschatology

6

THE SHAPING OF THE FUTURE: ESCHATOLOGICAL SYMBOLISM IN OLD AND NEW ENGLAND DURING THE SEVENTEENTH CENTURY

Now, the *Twentieth Chapter of the Revelation,* is, of all, doubtless, the most free from *Allegory,* and from the Involution of prophetical Figures, as describing indeed that Age and State, wherein all things relating to the *Kingdome of God,* will be most *clearly understood,* Particularly, that the First Resurrection, *which Begins the Happy State, Of the Church Upon the Earth,* is no Allegory.

> —Cotton Mather, "Problema Theologicum," in ms. letter to Nicholas Noyes of Salem, 1703 American Antiquarian Society Collection

They will so *Putt on Christ,* that there will be *Neither Male nor Female,* nor any difference between them ... there will be no more Difference of Sexes, but both sexes will be again united in *One Body* as they were before this *Deep Sleep.*

> —Cotton Mather, "Triparadisus" ms. in American Antiquarian Society Collection, ca. 1725

THE DISSOLUTION of the distinctions between "correlative" typology and "developmental" typology in the broadened exegesis of Edward Taylor suggests a conflation of allegory and figural writing that Taylor's conservative doctrine does not exhibit. The eschatological and prophetic emphasis of his imagery is firmly anchored in biblical figuralism although his ingenious conceits and convoluted metaphors have obscured this continuity from the view of modern critics. The language of Canaan as a prophetic force was indeed muted in the late seventeenth century, but its importance among a specific group of writers held firm throughout post-Reformation history and was especially crucial for historians and theologians in New England.

It was only natural that the New England Puritans would find the doctrines of millennialism compatible with their strong emphasis on the

115

cycles of prophecy and fulfillment. Eschatology and a belief in future fulfillment shone from every page of the seventeenth-century sermon, and
for the Puritan, an understanding of the future depended wholly on a
comprehension of revelation both in Scripture and in nature. The past,
always instructive for the historian, became for the Puritan historian
more than a series of moral lessons; the discernible patterns of
history—as revealed to God's instituted and appointed interpreters—were figures and types that shadowed forth the events of the
future, just as biblical type and antitype were instituted to demonstrate
providential guidance and divine continuity in human time. Moreover,
eschatological writing was organized around certain specific biblical images, like the millennium of Christ's reign over His kingdom on earth at
the conclusion of the human experience. Prophecy of the millennium
was certainly not original to New England Puritanism, but in millennial
eschatology, the Puritans found a belief about the future that cor-
responded ideally with their interpretation of past and contemporary
episodes in the history of God's chosen people. The language of Canaan
and its prophetic power were beautifully preached in sermons and
treatises concerning the millennium, so that the New England Puritans
of the first generation felt assured that God's kingdom was about to be
realized in their own time. This chiliasm continued throughout the
dominant phases of Puritanism in New England, although there were
periods of declension that led ministers to stress the judgment rather
than the more positive aspects of millennial fulfillment. The following
chapters treat specific problems in the tradition of millennial and
eschatological thought in early New England, showing how the language
of Canaan reached its most significant and sophisticated forms of expression in the chiliastic writings of these early Puritans. In millennial
writing, the figures and types follow a pattern of developmental
typology, recapitulating the experience of past historical episodes as prophetic synecdoches of future fulfillment. Recapitulative typology is thus
not a new departure in exegetical reasoning; rather, it is an extension of
the principles of developmental typology so that human history from the
incarnation to the judgment looks forward—through revealed and instituted figures—to the second coming of the eternal antitype. Millennial eschatology provides the frame of reference in which the language of
Canaan was most fully realized in colonial America. In documents as
wide-ranging as Jonathan Edwards' *History of the Work of Redemption* and
Timothy Dwight's *Greenfield Hill,* early American writers expressed
millennial hope through pastoral metaphors of peace and plenty that
were firmly anchored in biblical eschatology, thus extending the
language of Canaan beyond Puritan New England into the Federal
rhetoric of the new republic. It is the purpose of this section to trace this

important and fascinating evolution in the history of American thought.

THE MEANING OF MILLENNIAL PROMISE

Millennialism has fascinated theologians and philosophical writers since the term was first employed in the ancient Epistle of Barnabus. In seventeenth-century England, controversy over the anticipated millennium had significant political overtones, as the Puritan insurgents looked forward to the coming of Christ's kingdom. In New England, emigrant Puritans viewed their crossing of the Atlantic as a preparatory stage in the drama of world redemption through their errand into the wilderness, whose mission would be realized in the future glory of an American millennium. "The presence of *Christ* in this Kingdome shall no doubt be glorious and evident," wrote Joseph Mede in *Remaines on Some Passages in the Revelation* (1650), but he hastily qualified his enthusiasm with the caveat, "Yet I dare not so much as imagine — which some Antients seem to have thought — that it should be a visible converse upon earth. For the Kingdome of Christ ever hath been ... a Kingdome whose Throne and Kingly Residence is in Heaven." Interpretation of the few Scripture allusions to the millennium became the central question for seventeenth-century exegetical commentators, and the political application of millennial doctrine in England and America gave a new dimension to post-Reformation belief about the coming of the "new heavens and new earth" described in Isaiah and expanded in Revelation.

The symbolic language through which the Scripture reveals God's future plans was "opened and explained" to corroborate opposing views of the chiliad, and eschatological symbology therefore provides a unique perspective from which to view the changing conceptions not only of millennial hopes but also of the language used to express these beliefs. The purpose of this chapter is to trace the development of the language of Canaan in seventeenth-century millennial thought in England and in America, as it moved from *sabbatism* — a doctrine that placed the millennium of peace promised in Scripture in the seventh, one-thousand-year period after the creation of the world — through the formation of a pastoral and Edenic chiliasm that would later influence nineteenth-century American writing, to Cotton Mather's shift toward a metaphorical interpretation of the end of the world, showing how the language of Canaan remained a constant rhetorical vehicle throughout.

Doctrinally, the interpretations move away from Joseph Mede's conviction that the millennium could only occur in heaven, toward an earth-centered chiliasm, less an abrogation of earthly reality by an avenging judge and more a fulfillment of human perceptual and social potential. Thomas Shepard, Increase Mather, and Samuel Sewall all argued that the kingdom must descend from heaven to restore a corrupted earth, but they exhibit awareness of the laws of nature and demonstrate contemporary scientific interpretations of the universe, as when Sewall uses Newtonian physics for proofs in his *Phaenomena quaedam Apocalyptica*. (Given the universally accepted law of gravitation, it was reasonable to state the relationship between the "new heaven and new earth" in the language of scientific argument even though the spiritual and typological modes were also carried in Sewall's prophetic description.) Finally, the chapter builds upon Shepard's sabbatical argument in the *Theses Sabbaticae* (1649) and analyzes the important contributions of Increase and Cotton Mather to the development of millennial symbology. The "New Jerusalem," a significant manuscript written by Increase Mather in 1687 and unknown until its discovery in 1976, is analyzed in relation to his other chiliastic writings, and the concluding sections belong to Cotton Mather, who has incorrectly been linked with his father's chiliasm in a joint prediction that the judgment and millennium would commence in 1716. But the central questions treated here relate to the transformation of doctrinal changes into rhetorical strategies and the associated changes in the employment of figurative language, especially the prophetic language of Canaan. Social, political, even historical pressures are always exerted on a language, which must respond lest human expression stagnate, and the evolution of millennial symbology in seventeenth-century New England writing is a fascinating barometer of transformations in the use of biblical figures to explore patterns in American history.

Like the symbolic language used to explain millennial expectations, the eschatology of New England Puritanism in the seventeenth century had evolved from Reformation Puritan doctrine. Millennial symbolism developed out of traditional Renaissance uses of metaphor, emblem books, figures, and types. But a concern with progressive eschatology, and particularly a focus upon the second coming and judgment, followed by a millennium of harmony and peace, dominated religious writing among Puritans in England and in America. The hermeneutic tradition, with its prophetic types and allegorical parallels, provided a rich figurative mode for the American symbolic imagination. The association of Old Israel and New England (through recapitulative typology) sanctioned with divine authority the historical experience of New England emigrants, and new world Puritans used their Bibles to examine those patterns they found re-emerging in contemporary history, so that the future blessedness of New England might be predicted with the certainty of divine revelation.

From the early voyage literature, the new world was conceived to be a prelapsarian Eden, complete with "all kinds of odoriferous flowers," as described by Captain Barlow in Richard Hakluyt's *Voyages*. Most geographical metaphors were derived from scriptural foundations, and the biblical land "flowing with milk and honey" suggested the new-world promised land that Puritans sought to transform into the kingdom of Christ. The primary symbolic and scriptural figure around which these prophetic visions were developed was that of a millennium, Christ's thousand-year reign of peace and prosperity that would occur at the end of human time, following the downfall of Antichrist. Moreover, from John Foxe's *Book of Martyrs,* Thomas Brightman's *Apocalypsis Apocalypseos,* and Joseph Mede's *The Key of the Revelation* to Samuel Sewall's *Phaenomena quaedam Apocalyptica* and Cotton Mather's *Magnalia Christi Americana* and *Theopolis Americana,* the theme of a messianic national destiny is prominent. New England eschatology reflects the conventional Puritan conviction of national election, God's predestining of the community for the providential purpose of waging war against Satan and subsequently sharing the benefits of Christ's kingdom. Indeed, during the eighteenth century, the Great Awakening extended this paradigm to the time of the American Revolution and enlarged what had been a parochial New England idea into a national conception of America as the location of Christ's millennial fulfillment.

Millennialism is a tremendously complex subject, and it would hardly be appropriate to my purposes here to survey the history of doctrine relating to the end of the world and Christ's kingdom of a thousand years. However, some prominent characteristics of millennial thought are important to an understanding of metaphorical expressions used by writers to describe the millennium, and the prophetic force of the language of Canaan is most beautifully realized in those eschatological passages where writers employ biblical rhetorical devices to express the future promise of America.

Strictly speaking, the term "millennium" denotes in theology the thousand years of the kingdom of Christ on earth referred to in Revelation 20:16. "Millenarianism" (or the corresponding word of Greek derivation, "chiliasm") is the belief in the millennium; more specifically, the belief that Christ will reign personally on the earth with his saints for one thousand years or an indefinitely long period before the end of the world. As writers explored the metaphorical possibilities of this eschatological figure, the emphasis would shift from one biblical prophecy to another, but the rich figural language used to express future hope remained constant. The biblical prophecies of the millennium are varied, but a few central passages are repeated without end by early American writers. They are: Isaiah 65:17-25; Daniel 12:12-13; Revelation 20:1-3,7; and Psalm 90:4, which reads, "For a thousand years in thy sight, are but as yesterday when it is past, and as a watch in the night." The passage from Psalms is particularly important for early American chiliasm, since the writers were able to argue a historical scheme commencing over four thousand years before Christ and culminating in the early years of the eighteenth century, according to the numerological schemes evolved from Scripture.[1]

The earliest example of a Judeo-Christian doctrine of a millennial kingdom is found in the prophetic books of the Old Testament, though the idea of an eschatological millennium is pre-biblical and exists in nearly every primitive religion examined by the authors of *Hastings Encyclopedia of Religion and Ethics.*[2] A literal and historical expectation of the overthrow of Antichrist and the establishment of an earthly kingdom modeled on the kingdom of David in biblical Jerusalem was first advanced by the early Church Fathers, but St. Augustine undermined this teaching by imposing a metaphorical or figural interpretation on Daniel and Revelation, which lasted until the time of the Reformation of the sixteenth century. Under the Augustinian scheme, the millennium was simply the work of the Christian church on earth, and the "first resurrection of the dead" (Revelation 20:6) metaphorically denoted the change in the individual soul from sin to purity.

Thus, from the time of the early church, there has been controversy over whether the thousand years would be a literal and verifiable historical experience, or a spiritual one signifying the end of the world. Generally, the literalists held that Christ would come personally to earth to reign during the millennium and that the saints could look forward to a rebuilding of the temple and city of Jerusalem, the reinhabitation of the land of Israel by the Jews, following their conversion, and to the investiture of all the risen elect with a kingly pre-eminence over the remnant nations of the world. This chiliasm was shared by Joseph Mede and Increase Mather, both of whom looked forward to a judgment that was to precede the millennium of Christ's personal glory. This tradition persisted throughout the eighteenth century and reappears in the adventist prophecies of the Millerites in the 1840s.

Opposed to this position is the spiritual or allegorical view, which held that the millennium would consist of a spiritual transformation of the world, during which Christ was to reign in spirit but not in person. Like the literalists, the spiritualists viewed the happy paradise as being a future state, but they argued that man's estate would become so blessed that a perfect society of gathered saints could consistute the visible church of Christ on earth even before the second coming and judgment.

It is also important to clarify the two schools of thought denominated "premillennialism" and "postmillennialism." Put simply, the premillennial interpretation held that Christ's second coming would occur before the millennium could begin, whereas the postmillennial view held that Christ would come at the end of the thousand years of peace and prosperity.[3] Obviously, there is a close relationship between the literal and premillennial, the spiritual and postmillennial, but the association is not as clear as it might seem. The tensions between attempts to maintain a literal veracity in prophetic interpretation and the tendency to endow biblical figures with allegorical and metaphorical value were present in both pre- and postmillennialism throughout the seventeenth and eighteenth centuries. A conservative tradition shared by John Cotton, Thomas Shepard, Increase, Samuel, and Cotton Mather, Thomas Bray, Samuel Langdon, Abraham Cummings, and even William Miller, attempted to hold together a view of Scripture and history that leaned heavily on biblical typology for "proof," and resulted in a premillennial eschatology articulated in the rich, biblical symbolism of the prophetic types and figures. Meanwhile, Jonathan Edwards and his postmillennial followers were also Calvinists who argued from a strong scriptural foundation, but they succeeded in transforming typology by renewing the prophetic authority lost in the static imagery of the jeremiad. The postmillennial New Lights argued that through Christian agencies the Gospel would gradually permeate the entire world and become immeasurably more effective than at present, without the personal arrival of Christ, and that eventually, after a thousand year period of peace and prosperity, there would simultaneously occur the advent of Christ, the general resurrection, the judgment, the destruction of the old world by fire, and the revelation of the new heavens and the new earth foretold by Isaiah. Obviously, this view was influential in the thinking of progressive idealists of the eighteenth century in New England.[4] A consequence of their success was the resurrection of typology as prophetic language, one that could describe their vision of a glorious society soon to be built on earth.

Both groups embraced advocates of the utopian view of America as a future paradise, a theological idea that bore secular fruit in the edenic, pastoral visions of the United States so popular in the early nineteenth century. They also supplied a host of metaphors that reappear in the mythology of America's wilderness from the time of the earliest settlements to the Civil War,[5] when all such utopian dreams were dashed on the battlefields of Gettysburg and Atlanta. For example, the metaphorical interpretation was adopted by Samuel Sherwood, who observed in his own time the fulfillment of Scripture promises by citing current events and the growth of the church in the American wilderness:

When that God, to whom the earth belongs, and the fulness therof, brought his church into this wilderness, as on eagle's wings, by his king, protecting providence, he gave this good land to her, to be her own lot and inheritance forever ... God has, in this American quarter of the globe, provided for the woman and her seed, a fixed and lasting settlement and habitation, and bestowed it upon her, to be her own property forever . . . He was not conducting them from a land of liberty, peace, and tranquility, into a state of bondage, persecution, and distress; but on the contrary, he wrought out a very glorious deliverance for them, and set them free from the cruel hand of tyranny and oppression, by executing his judgments in a most terrible and awful manner, on the Egyptians, their enemies, and was, by his kind Providence, leading them to the good land of Canaan, which he gave them for the everlasting inheritance.[6]

The thousand-year period during which the forces of evil will be bound and the righteous saints will enjoy abundance and plenty, peace and tranquility became so dominant an image in sermons and literature of the seventeenth and eighteenth centures that commmentators saw in contemporary events "signs of the times" which indicated the beginning of the grand and prosperous period.[7]

It is the language of the scriptural allusions to the millennium that allowed commentators the paradoxical freedom to recreate the vision of the thousand years provided by Daniel and St. John, while restricting the boundaries of the vision to those scanty references contained in the Bible. If the millennium was revealed in only a handful of prophetic Scripture verses, it has been one of the most broadly interpreted visions in the Judaeo-Christian tradition. Thus when the Puritans of the first two centuries in New England turned to their Bibles for assurance of the future fulfillment of those promises, they drew heavily upon typology to give their arguments the kind of literal authenticity that a typological adumbration would supply. And they brought to New England the conventions of Continental and English figural exegesis of those Scripture passages that adumbrate the world's transformation into a peaceable kingdom governed by Christ. As heirs to the rhetorical traditions of the Renaissance, their sermons and histories echoed not only the Bible but also the language of reformed exegesis of Revelation.

The Reformation produced important changes in the metaphorical approach to millennial prophecy. The vision of Daniel consisted of Four Beasts, representing the world empires (Babylon, the Medes and Persians, Greece, and Rome). The last beast had ten horns, or kings, and a little horn that destroyed the ten. After the destruction of the last beast, the kingdom was to be given to the saints forever, for example, the "Fifth Monarchy." But because the establishment of this penultimate kingdom was to usher in the end of human time, the saints advancing such interpretations were in the paradoxical position of joyously realizing their own participation in divine history and interpreting the prophetic figures of Daniel and Revelation as signs of their own imminent destruction. Particularly in the new world, "they [millennialists] saw themselves at once in a New Jerusalem, at the ends of the earth, and momentarily in limbo—in fact, in a sort of triple jeopardy, where affliction was proof of being in the right place."[8] In Cromwell's interregnum, millennialism and chiliasm were popular prophetic modes, and Cromwell himself was deeply influenced by chiliastic thought, including the writings of Joseph Mede, Thomas Brightman, Stephen Marshall, and Thomas Parker.

ENGLISH MILLENNIAL FIGURALISM

The prominence of millennial figuralism in post-Reformation England has been established by recent scholarship.[9] Both Mede and Brightman wrote of the figural significance of Daniel's prophetic vision, and for the purposes of this study, the importance of these lengthy commentaries is not the doctrinal positions they advance concerning the coming of Christ's kingdom but the uses they make of typological and figural language found in the Old Testament passages examined by the writers. For example, Thomas Brightman presented a metaphorical reading of Daniel's vision, as one would expect any Christian commentator to do, in his *A Most Comfortable Exposition of the Last and Most Difficult Part of the Prophecie of Daniel* ... (1635). But he directly associated the figures of Daniel with Christ's incarnation, thereby endowing the prophetic images with typological significance. Like William Ames, he viewed the ceremonies of the Old Testament, for example, the sacrifices, as prefigurative of Christ's ultimate sacrifice, and in a very revealing passage, he associated these elements directly.

> Christ therefore is to be understood, who by his death hath abolished the ceremoniall lawe of sacrificing; which is also made plaine by the maner of speaking . . . He by violatinge the daily sacrifice did abolish and take away the lawe, but when Christ is spoken of, it is only said absolutely, He shall make the sacrifice to cease or take it away as in this place, because he did abolish it, not by violatinge and breaking it, but by fulfilling it.[10]

And, as though to speak for all the English commentators who were trying to sort out the figural relationship of the "elect nation" to the prophetic images of the Scripture, Brightman concluded: "It is hard and hidden indeed what time these wordes doe meane: yet we must labour to fish and finde it out by comparing it with other places" (p. 94).

One of those "other places" might possibly be Brightman's own *A Revelation of the Revelation* (1615), where he argued a figural interpretation of the apocalyptic vision: "Hearken, therefore, diligently awhile and receive out of this Prophecy not some obscure signs but most evident arguments, that thy husband (Christ) is about to arise even now for the avenging of thy grief, and that he may give over this whore (Papacy) into thy hands to pour out upon her the whole rage of thy jealousy . . . And lest any thing should yet be wanting to the full heap of joy, here thou mayest know that the calling of the Jews to be a Christian nation is hereunto joined and withall a most happy tranquility from thence to the end of the world."[11]

This echo of Canticles exegesis illustrates how closely linked the Old and New Testaments were when figural interpretation is applied to both. Indeed the Song of Solomon would be a pagan love song with highly erotic imagery were it not for the typological and allegorical interpretations of the book, and the vision of Daniel would have a direct, prophetic level of meaning through an examination of the mysterious figures that appear in the vision itself; however, the typological mystery advanced by Daniel and interpreted by the commentators of post-Reformation Europe and England is well illustrated in a highly imagistic passage found in Thomas Parker's *The Visions and Prophecies of Daniel Expounded* (1646), where Parker, in attempting an exegesis of Chapter 8, verse 15, suggests that

> *Daniel,* signifying to Type the Witnesses of Truth in the last time, is first moved to seek for the meaning of the Vision; and thereupon *Gabriel* appeareth in the similitude of a man, being sent at the voice of Christ . . . which signifieth the unsealing of this and other mysteries to the Saints of the last time (for Unto *Daniel* himself they were to be unknown, and to all other before the last time, *Acts* 1.7, *Matth.* 24.36, onely to *Daniel,* as in a Type, an explication is given, to be fully perfected in the Antitype, the later Saints, who were alone to understand the same.[12]

Parker, like most of his Puritan contemporaries (Parker preached in Newbury in Berkshire, England, as well as in the church at Newbury in Massachusetts Bay Colony), saw a direct connection between the prophetic images of Daniel and the imagery of Revelation. Nothing was original or new in this correlation of the Old and New Testament prophecies. But for Parker, as for most Puritans, the figural meaning of Daniel was incomplete; it was only by reading the book typologically, in terms of a scheme of partial revelation and complete revelation mounted on the historical pattern of linear time, type to be concluded by antitype, that Daniel and Revelation both foretold the coming of Christ in the incarnation and the kingdom. "The mysteries were to be unsealed in the meaning, as here unto *Daniel* typically in the bark of words, and at the voice, that is, the command of Christ, . . . Christ also signifieth the *Revelation* by His Angel, *Revel.* 1.1; and *Michael,* the great Prophecie, by the ministery of an Angel in the similitude of a man, *Dan.* 10" (p. 46).

Similarly, Joseph Mede, author of the most influential work on the millennium to appear in the seventeenth century (*Clavis Apocalyptica,*

1627), not only read the figures of Revelation and Daniel as having a literal fulfillment in the future but also saw in them figural and typological metaphors of the spiritual eternal presence of Christ and his kingdom.

It has long been known that Joseph Mede was a premillennialist, influencing such later American writers as John Cotton and Increase Mather, both of whom shared his view that Christ would come personally and literally to judge the world and to establish his kingdom on earth. It is also a commonplace that Mede's greatest contribution to millennial eschatology was his theory of a synchronism of prophecies, by which he meant "when the things therein designed run along in the same time; as if thou shouldest call it an agreement in time or age."[13] Mede was able to show, convincingly, the three central divisions to the prophecy in the book of Revelation, and he proved through synchronism of the prophecies that those things foretold in the vision of John were applicable to other times and other ages which had corresponding events and circumstances to those described symbolically in the Apocalypse. However, Mede's breakthrough for the figural writers of the seventeenth century was that he also saw in Daniel and Revelation a "double resurrection" — not only in the bodily dead at the judgment but also of those saints remaining at the end of the thousand year kingdom, and this meant that Mede had interpreted the literal prophecy of a resurrection figuratively, that is, the prophetic image had not only a literal and historical meaning for a future time, but it also had a metaphorical and spiritual sense which radically altered his view of the last days.[14]

The significance of this challenge to accepted authority cannot be overemphasized. Not only did Mede posit conclusions that would long influence millennial thinking among the Puritans in Old and New England; he had also opened the floodgates for writers who were seeking ways to find in Scripture a literal truth and a metaphorical or spiritual meaning that would not violate the integrity of the literal interpretation. In his *Treatise on Psalm 50.14,* for example, Mede argued openly that "The Book of *Psalms* is a Book of *Prophecies; . . .* I say the *Psalms* are *Prophecies,* and that both *Concerning Christ himself,* and also the Church which should be after him."[15]

Predictably, typology provided the key to this view of Psalms as in his general interpretation of Old Testament figures.

But as in *typical speeches* it often comes to pass that the things which are spoken are true both in the *type* and *antitype,* as that in Hosea 11.1, *Out of Egypt have I called my Son,* was in some sense true both of *Christ* and *Israel,* and that in Exod. 12.46, *Thou shalt not break a bone thereof,* was true *literally,* both of *Christ,* and the Paschal Lamb; and that in Psal. 22.18, *They parted my garments among them,* was true figuratively in *David* and *literally in Christ;* Even so it comes to pass in the *prophecies,* and namely in this, that so it foretells of things to come, that it is concerned also with the time present; it foretells the estate of the Church in the Gospel, and yet meant something that concerned the present Church of the Law.[16]

Mede's figural reading was followed by English and American millennialists throughout the seventeenth century. But the *double sense of the literal* released in his exegesis was also found in the work of other dissenters who were "literalists" in their rejection of the medieval, Roman Catholic mode of spiritualizing Scripture. Stephen Marshall, for example, a radical dissenter whose writings were as politically significant as they were theologically influential, declared emphatically that

> the *building of Zion is the Lords own work;* . . . *Zion* you know is in the Scripture taken sometimes in a *literall,* but ordinarily in a *mystical* and *spiritual* sense; *Zion* in a literall sense was that strong part of the City of *Jerusalem,* which *David* did take from the *Jebusites,* . . . and called it the *City* of *David,* the most beautiful part of *Jerusalem;* this is *Zion* literall; . . . The *Zion* which my text means is *Spiritual Zion,* mystical *Zion,* the *Zion* whereof the City of *David* was a type (as *David* himself was type of Christ) and that is, the Church of God, which in a hundred places at least in the Old and New Testament is called by the name of *Zion.*[17]

Marshall read into the establishing of Zion not only the correspondences between the Old Testament figure of Jerusalem, and the New Testament kingdom promised in the Messiah's incarnation, but also the whole range of church history following Christ's founding the gathered church:

> This is the *Zion* that we are to speak of; and this *Zion,* this Church of God is then built . . . when the elect are called in, Churches gathered and established, the worship and government of Christ set up, for the perfecting of the Saints, for the work of the Ministry, for the edifying of the body of Christ, till all the Saints come in the unity of the Faith . . . then doth hee build up *Zion.*[18]

This English Puritan millennial tradition was shared by the settlers of New England, and arguments about the nature and extent of Christ's kingdom raged on both sides of the Atlantic among adherents of the millennial vision. As in other areas of doctrine and interpretation, the Puritans in Old and New England shared a common vision of the extension of reformed theology into the new world, and the language of Canaan developed so fully by Perkins and Ames, Brightman and Mede, pervades John Cotton's millennial discourses, some of which were composed before he left England, providing, with his American writings, a clear view of the correspondences between England and America on this important subject.

The changes in typological reasoning during the seventeenth century resulted in a conservative restriction of the types to scriptural
boundaries, although some literal exegetes extended the figures to
modern times through analogy and allegorical correspondence. The
decline in piety so painfully evident in the jeremiads of the end of the
century would eventually lead writers to practice caution in their
association of New England with Old Israel while looking to the future
with an apprehension of the judgment that would have to precede millennial glory; the eschatological imagery of the early settlers soon lost
much of the prophetic optimism it had once enjoyed. Early in the century, when John Cotton chose II Samuel 7:10 as the text for *God's Promise
to His Plantations,* he had been exploring the analogy between the departure of Winthrop's Puritans and the movement of Old Israel out of
Egyptian bondage into the Land of Canaan. "Moreover, I will appoint a
place for my people Israel," the Scripture reads, "and I will plant them,
that they may dwell in a place of their own, and move no more." As the
individual soul is provided the grace to escape bondage in sin, so the nation Israel was to move from Egyptian bondage to a land of milk and
honey. This type was not only a literal event; it was also a prefiguration
of that eternal moment when Christ would lead his people out of bondage into eternal freedom. In the spiraling and progressive dispensations
revealed to man about the future of God's saints, the New England
Puritans figured prominently as a recapitulation of those primitive, prophetic, typological Israelites. And as they fulfilled the promises of Scripture in Cotton's exegesis, so they were also prophetic themselves of the
dawning of a new day, one in which the saints would be gathered by
Christ in a glorious moment when all peoples would speak the language
of Canaan.

JOHN COTTON AND NEW ENGLAND'S ERRAND
INTO THE NEW HEAVENS AND NEW EARTH

In New England, Mede's most prominent early apostle was John
Cotton, minister to the Massachusetts Bay Colony and one of the most
important figures in the founding of the Puritan commonwealth. Cotton
was a critical influence not only in theology but also in affairs of state,
and his understanding of law was based largely on his figural reading of
Scripture. It was in disagreement with Roger Williams, for example,
that Cotton established principles for the foundation of a theocratic
government in New England that were argued by Williams against Cotton in an essentially typological framework.[19]

Among his numerous sermons and treatises Cotton wrote *A Treatise
Concerning the Covenant of Grace* (1645), in which he articulated a covenant
foundation for the reading of God's dispensation as continuous
throughout human history; two documents relating to the last days: *The*

Keyes of the Kingdom of Heaven (1644), in which he argued a literal interpretation of the first beast of chapter 13:1-9, as being the contemporary
"Roman Catholick Visible Church," and *The Churches Resurrection* (1642),
a significant document in which he followed Mede in declaring that
there were two (literal and figural) resurrections.

Throughout Cotton's writings on millennial typology there exists a
tension. On the one hand, Cotton seems to regard his own removal from
England, and that of his fellow emigrants, as a fulfillment of the types
and an extension of the New Testament antitypes. On the other hand,
he seeks to preserve the historical value of scriptural typology, so that the
parallels he finds between Israel and New England would have no more
value than their relation as analogues. It would be allowable, for example, to erect a Congregational Church on American soil with governing
ordinances derived from the practices instituted among the Israelites,
but it would be improper to make more of the Old Testament figures
than their moral examples would allow. Extending these parallels into
allegories is what the medieval spiritualizers had done, and the Puritan
mind rejected any notion of abstracting from Scripture any more than
the meaning God had intended. Since the "errand into the wilderness"
was divinely instituted, the relations between Israel and New England
were providentially determined. Although Cotton's early writings reflect
the Puritan habit of regarding New England as an antitypical fulfillment
of the Old Testament types, by which the "errand into the wilderness"
was a continuous extension of the Church Militant, he made it clear in
his later work that typology would not allow such a loose interpretation
of Scripture.

When Cotton began his ministry in 1612, the biblical typology was
commonly used in the understanding of Scripture's place in the history
of redemption. Therefore Cotton felt compelled to define the term, and
there are a number of early attempts by Cotton to clarify the use of Old
Testament figures. However, unlike the typology of the Puritan
theologians of the second and third generations in New England, Cotton's system is so integrated with his total theological belief that it is
almost impossible to take any one of these definitions out of context and
conclude much about Cotton's uses of the types. For example, in *Some
Treasure Fetched Out of Rubbish,* Cotton indicates that in the Old Testament Christ was revealed in the types and extraordinary signs, and in
the New Testament in baptism and the Lord's Supper, the only allowable sacraments. But all were shadows of those heavenly things to come.
This was "developmental" typology at its best. He continued by defining
a sacrament as a "sign or form of invisible Grace . . . teaching or
shadowing by representation."[20] This rhetorical fusion of the type and
sacrament allowed Cotton to justify the types by their ceremonial relation to Christ's mystical body, and he employed the types to reinforce his

view that Christ's second coming was imminent. The Old Testament types and the New Testament sacraments both contained moral value for the future kingdom of God, which they also prefigured.

Cotton's early typology was closely linked to the Puritan conception of the "errand into the wilderness," but his later controversy with Roger Williams and the Antinomians forced him to clarify his views about the polity of the New England Way. The most important statement he made during this pamphlet exchange was a declaration about the value of Old Testament types. In *The Bloudy Tenent of Persecution,* the apostate Roger Williams had argued that the abrogation of *all* types in Christ meant that no ceremony or ordinance in New England should be modeled on the Old Testament practices. In his rejoinder to Williams, *The Bloudy Tenent Washed and Made White with the Blood of the Lambe,* Cotton makes himself quite well understood on the matter of types and their relation to the theocracy of Massachusetts Bay. Like Milton, he would regard the types as moral or spiritual examples but asserts that the Old Testament types were fulfilled in Christ:

> For all Figures in the Old Testament have their accomplishment in the New. Now evident it is, *Ahab* (apostate Idolater) was no type of Christ, nor was Israel (after the apostasy) a type of the true Church of Christ. A Tabernacle it was, but not a Tabernacle of Christ. *Aholah,* but not *Aholiah.* To make this act in Israel a type of Christ's act in the Christian state, or church, is to make darkenesse a type of light. Ceremoniall Lawes were generally Typicall: not so Moses his Judicialls, especially those which had in them morall equity.[21]

If the types were in any sense abrogated or fulfilled in Christ, they possessed a measure of moral value that allowed their perpetuation in New England:

> The Magistrates to whom God hath committed the charge of bodies, and outward man of the subject, are they not also to take care to produce faithfull teachers to be sent amongst them? *Jehosaphat* tooke faithfull care for the soules of his people in this kind, 2 *Chron.* 17:7,8,9. Neither did he this as a *Type* of Christ, but as a Servant of Christ. Those things are said to be done as *types* of Christ which being ceremoniall duties, were afterwards done by Christ, in his owne person, and so were in him accomplished, and abolished: And it would be sacriledge to performe the same after him.[22]

As Perry Miller has indicated in his *Roger Williams,* the controversy between Cotton and Williams had much to do with their varying opinions of typological exegesis and its role in determining a rationale for the practices and governing of the theocracy in Massachusetts Bay. Williams held firmly that "if the Kings of Israel were types of Christ, then they were not examples of pious conduct for modern sovereigns."[23] Cotton contended that there was nothing mutually exclusive about a type being fulfilled in one sense and continuing to serve as a moral or ethical example for later generations, provided that the types were followed in imitation only, rather than as extended prophetic or typological adumbrations of Christ, in whom they had been abrogated. But more important, he saw a clear distinction between the typical ceremonies of the Old Testament, many of which were imitated slavishly in the Catholic and Anglican ceremonies, and the judicial laws of the Decalogue, which were not typical only but also provided moral equity. Thus the only proper sacraments for the worship of Congregationalists were those newly instituted by Christ: baptism and the Lord's Supper. All other sacraments and ceremonies were abrogated in Christ. However, the law was not abrogated in the Gospel, but fulfilled and extended to cover that historical period between the first coming and the millennium.

This tendency to find more in the biblical type than a simple adumbration of Christ is characteristic of the line of exegesis from Calvin and Cotton to Cotton Mather and Jonathan Edwards. Though varying emphases alter our impressions of each figure as being conservative or liberal in his approach to the exegesis of Scripture, there is no doubt that they all share the Puritan penchant for discerning the spiritual as well as the literal meaning in a text and for extending the Word to have moral and metaphorical application in New England. Until the 1640s, John Cotton had been a member of a company of ministers who regarded typology as a way of reading their own history as a prefiguration of the coming of Christ's kingdom on earth. It was not difficult for them to abandon this conception when Cotton's prophecy of the millennium failed to materialize in 1655. Cotton himself had not lived to see the failure of his prediction, and by 1655 the Congregational Way had become an imperfect model and image of Christ's kingdom, so that a reading of New England's history as the antitypical fulfillment of the Old Testament, so important to earlier Puritan exegesis, had lost its importance. While Cotton's later works were emphasizing the moral and exemplary value of types derived from the Old Testament, the "errand into the wilderness" was ceasing to dominate the rationale for the New England Way, and a new generation of theologians and writers, including Samuel Mather and John Davenport, began to explore the possibility of returning typology to its original use as a means of exegeting Scripture.

It is through Cotton's *The Churches Resurrection* and his *Keyes of the Kingdom of Heaven* that the influence of English millennial figuralism reaches into New England, just as typology also was transmitted to the "American strand" through Cotton's *Treatise on the Canticles*. By giving a literal and figurative meaning to the concept of resurrection as it is delivered in the Scripture, he provided a means and an explanation for metaphorical interpretations of New England's contemporary history, and for the association of the seventeenth century with biblical times through the analogies and figures of each.

The First Resurrection:
There is a double Resurrection; the word first implieth, that the first Resurrection is of mens soules and bodies dead in sinne . . . that's the first resurrection . . . Now of this first Resurrection, there are two parts . . . first, it is of particular persons; the houre is coming and now is when the dead shall heare the voyce of the Sonne of God, and they that heare shall live . . . Secondly, there is a first resurrection also of Churches, when as they are recovered againe from their Apostatical and dead estate in Idolatry and Superstition . . . the calling home of the Jewes it will be the Resurrection of the Churches.[24]

Cotton's examination of this idea is very long and highly imagistic. It depends on an association he makes between the metaphorical resurrection of the church and the Resurrection of Christ, after His crucifixion. "It is called the first Resurrection because of the resemblance of the Resurrection of Christ and the Faithfull in him," Cotton declares, but it is also seen as being "the House of Israel, rising out of their graves of Ignorance and Apostacie, to a Church estate: but I call this a branch of the first resurrection, because it is a Ressurection of the Soules of men, and their bodyes, not out of the Grave, properly so called, but out of the grave of Ignorance . . . it is also with particular persons, if they rise out of the grave of Ignorance and Idolatry" (*Churches Resurrection,* p. 12).

The distinctions drawn here by Cotton, following Mede, are absolutely critical to the development of figural and historical writing in the New England colonies during the seventeenth century. The essential point here is the relationship between Cotton's view of the resurrection, his millennial eschatology, and what would later appear in the writings of Increase Mather and Edward Taylor. Cotton viewed the first resurrection as a "resemblance to Christ's," which he clearly articulated in *The Churches Resurrection.* Increase Mather viewed the first resurrection as Christ's literal resurrection from the grave, that is, he adopted a literal rather than a figural view (see Mather's *The Dying Legacy of a Minister, The Mystery of Israel's Salvation,* and the *Meditations on the Glory of the Heavenly World*). Other than this crucial literal versus figural difference, their interpretations of the resurrection and its relation to the millennial scheme were doctrinally quite similar. However, this transition between Cotton and Increase Mather is important because it is the real measure of differences between the first generation of New England Puritanism and the second generation, indicating a more static pattern of interpreta-

tion in the second and a more rigid reliance on the literal veracity of
Scripture, where John Cotton's interpretation was fluid, prophetic—both in the communal and individual senses—and highly imagistic.

In *The Keyes of the Kingdom of Heaven*, John Cotton once again shows
his skill in bringing life to Scripture through a careful exegesis of the letter and the spirit of a text. The book is legalistic and highly structured; it
does not at first glance resemble a spiritual treatise nearly so much as it
gives the impression of a manual for church polity which, in fact, it was.
Larzer Ziff, who has edited several of Cotton's texts concerning church
government, remarks that

> Three hundred years after its publication, *The Keys of the Kingdom of Heaven*
> presents an outmoded facade; its pages appear at first glance to be unrelieved
> by any element of what one might consider ordinary human interest. Here
> the seventeenth-century theologian, at ease in the Zion of scriptural inter-
> pretation, seems to set forth his argument in a dead language. Recalling the
> remote days of the apostles, he seems scarcely to glance at the history of his
> own day. For the modern reader, he seems to deal in invented rather than in
> documented events.[25]

That dead language to which Ziff refers is, of course, the language of
Canaan, a seemingly archaic form of discourse for those who do not
recognize the patterns through which words are raised by God's spirit up
into life. Ziff recognizes this paradox, though he does not examine it,
when he says "but the tensions of the times are in *The Keys,* and they
drive the argument onward. Although the chief purpose of the treatise is
to demonstrate that the church founded in apostolic times was indeed a
Congregational one and although the chief arguments are scriptural, yet
The Keyes takes its strength from contemporaneity" (p. 27). That contemporaneity is Cotton's power to see the literal and the figurative at once,
the Augustinian strain of figural interpretation that pervades his
writings on eschatology and even is found throughout his arguments for
church government in New England. For example, in describing the efficacy of the keys themselves and what they represent for modern
history, he clearly associated the literal and the metaphorical meanings:

> The acts of these days, are said to be binding and loosing, which are not the
> proper acts of material keys; for their acts be opening and shutting, which
> argueth the keys here spoken of be not material keys, but metaphorical; and
> yet being keys; they have a power also of opening and shutting; for Christ
> who hath the sovereign power of these keys, He is said to have the key of
> David, to open, and no man to shut; to shut, and no man to open, Rev. iii, 7,
> which implieth, that these keys of Christ's kingdom, have such a power of
> opening and shutting, as that they do thereby, bind and loose, retain and
> remit; in opening, they loose, and remit; in shutting they bind, and retain.[26]

Of course it is the divine law that binds man in sin and grace that loosens those bonds—Cotton's way of saying that there is a process of development connecting the Old and the New dispensations. However, his metaphorical reading of the image of the keys makes this association for him and for those readers who also see in the language of Canaan the prophetic power of words transformed into metaphors for God's transforming spirit.

THOMAS SHEPARD AND THE MATHERS

Modern scholarly books and journals are filled with assessments of the role of this prophetic force in New England history. The Mathers are particularly prominent subjects in attempts to demonstrate the strong tradition of biblical metaphor that extends into the eighteenth century. Perry Miller observed that "the two Mathers were . . . possessed by the rule of the true apocalyptic spirit; they marched into the Age of Reason loudly crying that the end of the world was at hand."[27] Sacvan Bercovitch has shown how Cotton Mather fused a vision of his personal destiny with the future promise of New England, so that his desperate efforts to turn the city on a hill from Babylon to Jerusalem must be understood as part of the larger process of his personal millennial eschatology.[28] Emory Elliott argues that "Cotton Mather firmly believed that he had been sent on a special mission by God to lead his own and his father's generations out of their years of confusion and doubt and into a new time which would see the coming of Christ and the establishment of the New Jerusalem in America."[29] Moreover, many of the original documents produced by Increase and Cotton Mather reveal changes in their attitudes toward Scripture and its efficacy to support their views of the last days. Increase Mather explored the typical significance of Samson and David in *Meditations on the Glory of Our Lord Jesus Christ,* concluding that their exemplary virtues had been fulfilled and abrogated by Christ's earthly ministry, but he argued the importance of typology as a prophetic system in *The Mystery of Israel's Salvation,* which treated the future of the Jewish nation at the time of the millennium.[30] "It is evident," he wrote, "that the salvation of Israel will be wonderful, if we compare it with those former deliverances which in the days of old have been vouchsafed unto the Tribes of Israel. It is indeed true, that God hath in former times bestowed more eminent and wonderful salvations upon the Israelitish Nation than upon any Nation in the world . . . but because their deliverance was a TYPE of this, therefore this will be the more eminent and wonderful, for the TYPE must needs come short of the ANTITYPE."[31] Similarly, Cotton Mather early in his career anticipated the imminent return of Christ and a literal fulfillment of the scriptural promises, though his late position moved away from so literal an anticipation:

Good News for the *Israel* of God, and particularly for His *New English Israel.* The Devil was never more let *loose* than in our Days; and it proves the *Thousand Years* is not very *far off. Shortly,* didst thou say, Dearest Lord! O Gladsome word! I may Sigh over *this* Wilderness, as *Moses* did over *his.* We are *consumed by thine Anger,* yet if God have a Purpose to make here a *Seat for any of Those Glorious Things, which are spoken of Thee, O Thou City of God;* then even thou, *O New-England,* are within a very little while of Better Dayes than ever yet have Dawn'd upon thee. *Our Lord Jesus Christ shall have the uttermost parts* of the Earth for his Possession, the last shall be the *first,* and the Sun of Righteousness come to shine *Brightest,* in Climates which it rose *Latest* upon.[32]

The historical metaphors adopted by the Mathers were primarily scriptural, arising out of their concern to identify for New England the peculiar providential role established for the saints in the first dispensation and revealed to a regenerate understanding through a proper interpretation of the biblical types and prophetic figures. The tensions present in the typology of Cotton Mather indicate the pressures on him to accommodate his traditional reading of Scripture to the revelations of God in the natural world, and the image patterns of his writing associated with the New Jerusalem reinforce the central idea through which he explained how, in the cyclical process of history, New England might assume a role analogous to Old Israel's prophetic role. The Mathers extended the biblical type into contemporary times not only by declaring its emblematic significance but also by showing how its typological promises were still to be fulfilled. Thus the prophetic value of the Old Testament figures was sustained even while other commentators employed them as "meer metaphors and moral examples."

In the early years of the colony some ministers, like John Cotton, had expressed the hope that New England might one day become the scene of Christ's triumphant kingdom, and the process of analogy to Old Israel was clearly stated by Thomas Hooker in the *Application of Redemption* (1657), where the first generation minister justified the parallel through typological reasoning:

There must be Contrition and Humiliation before the Lord comes to take possession ... This was typified in the passage of the Children of Israel towards the promised Land. They must come into and go through a vast and roaring Wilderness, where they must be bruised with many pressures, humbled under many overbearing difficulties, before they could possess that good land which abounded with all prosperity, flowed with Milk and Honey ... The Truth of this Type, the Prophet *Hosea* explains, and expresseth at large in the Lords dealing with his People in regard of their Spiritual Condition, Hos. 2.14, 15. *I Will Lead Her into the Wilderness and break her heart.*[33]

For Hooker, the soul and Israel were analogous; the process of transformation through which Israel of old was led by God's Providence exemplified the process through which the soul must pass in undergoing regeneration. But the contemporary, seventeenth-century experience of the Christian Pilgrim moving toward millennial fulfillment through Christ is more than exemplified by Israel's pilgrimage through the wilderness to Canaan; it is typified, or foreshadowed according to the cycles of providential dispensation.

Millennial expectations flourished in this psychological context, where ministers and people together looked to the dispensations of the past to provide themselves with certain and sure projections for the future. Congregations turned to their Bibles to receive assurance that they were indeed living in the last days. They were able to identify signs of the times in contemporary events that corroborated the patterns they had perceived in scriptural revelation, thus rendering double proof of God's prophetic dispensations and giving the New England Puritans a participatory role in the evolution of God's redemptive and historical plan.

But it was the Mathers' chiliasm that "clearly and emphatically expressed the belief that the glorious day was at hand and that New England was certain to be the site of the New Jerusalem: the coming of the Lord was not a 'metaphor,' Cotton Mather declared, 'it was the next thing to be looked for.'"[34] The primary concerns of the Mathers—particularly Increase—would be to establish that the millennium had been prefigured in Scripture and to prove that it was about to take place by examining such signs of the times as the conversion of the Jews, an aspect of the millennial promise that was regarded to be a crucial prerequisite by which the advent of the last things might be identified. Their chiliasm, in turn, depended on assumptions provided earlier by Thomas Shepard and Samuel Mather. Because the sabbath was considered by some to be a type of the millennial rest, and since all commentators used the concept of a day as a thousand years freely, the typology of the sabbath figured centrally in arguments about the time of the approaching end.

Thomas Shepard carefully presented the case for the abrogation of Old Testament types of Christ's incarnation in *Theses Sabbaticae* (1649). He then proceeded to show how the types might still have efficacy in the scheme of world history, despite their abrogation by the coming of the flesh. The *Theses* provide exhaustive arguments for the conclusion of ceremonial, legal, and judicial types, but they also present a logically persuasive statement endorsing the moral authority inherent in the biblical figures, because they possess eternal and perpetual equity.

Although the distinction between moral perpetuity and exegetical typology in the figures of the Old Testament was not original to Shepard, his *Theses Sabbaticae* is the classic Puritan defense of the use of types in perpetuating the New England way. Shepard showed how the types are actually of two kinds, the "*typus fictus* . . . or *arbitrarius* (which is all one with a similitude)," and the "*typus destinatus* . . . purposely ordained to shadow out Christ." The example Shepard selected to contrast the two kinds of types shows how the true types may only be observed under the Covenant of Grace:

> The Covenant of Works, by which Adam was to live, is directly contrary to the Covenant of Grace by Faith in Christ, (Rom. xi. 6) by which we are to live. Christ is revealed only in the Covenant of Grace, and therefore could not be so revealed in the Covenant of Works directly contrary thereunto. Adam therefore was not capable of any types then to reveal Christ unto him; of whom the first Covenant cannot speak, and of whom Adam stood in no need . . . hence, it follows, that he stood in no need of Christ or any revelation of him by the types; no, not to confirm him in that covenant.[35]

The central theme of the *Theses Sabbaticae* involves Shepard's effort to establish legitimate limits for typology under the covenant of grace, and his arguments seek to restore the significance of the sabbath as it had been ordained by God in the Decalogue. Shepard does not deny that the types were originally instituted to shadow forth events and persons that were fulfilled in the earthly ministry of Christ; however, he refused to accept the view adopted by his contemporaries who argued that the abrogation of the typical sabbath in Christ was a termination of its efficacy for Christian history. He was careful to clarify the distinction between the Old and New Testament dispensations, and then distinguished equally carefully the moral value of the sabbath from its typological significance:

> If therefore the sabbath was given to Adam in innocency before all types, nay, before the least promise of Christ, whom such types must shadow forth, then it cannot be in its first and native institution typical and ceremonial, but moral; and therefore in its first and original institution of which we speak, it did not typify either our rest in Christ from sin in this life, or our rest with God in heaven in another life, or any other imagined rest which man's wit can easily invent and invest the sabbath with (2, 171).

Even if the sabbath were considered typologically, Shepard argued, so that its ceremonial nature would have been abrogated in Christ's incarnation, its moral value was derived from its eternal institution in the providential scheme:

But the question is . . . whether it be not therefore of perpetual and universal obligation, binding all Nations and persons in all ages, in their Hearts, Lives, Manners, to the observance thereof, as a part of that Holiness we owe to God, and which God required of all men according to the rules of moral equity; or, on the contrary, whether it be not rather a typicall, ceremoniall, figurative, and temporary precept, binding onely some persons, or that one nation of the Jews for some time, from obedience of which law, Christians (in respect of any law of God) are now exempted (1, 35).

Shepard's answer to this question was that the sabbath carries the whole authority of moral equity for Christians in all times, and his objective in the *Theses* was to solve once and for all the problem of justifying the institution in a society whose few ceremonies were being challenged by the Antinomians as instituted extensions of the Old Testament types. The core of his arguments for the moral equity of the sabbath consisted of his distinctions among the kinds of laws given under the old dispensation. While disclaiming a typical significance for the sabbath in modern times, he emphasized strongly the moral equity inherent in the institution:

Thesis 38: There were three sorts of laws which are commonly known, and which were most eminently appearing among the Jews: 1. Moral. 2. Ceremoniall. 3. Judiciall.
Thesis 39: The moral respected their manners as they were men, and are therefore called moral. The ceremonial respected them as a church, and as such a kind of church. The judicial as a commonwealth, and as that particular commonwealth. Moral laws were to govern them as a human society, ceremonial as a sacred society, judicial as a civil society (1, 51).

Shepard then indicated how the moral law was derived from the law of nature, and because it was divinely instituted, it has a perpetual value for Christian history and society that is eternal and continuous:

Thesis 40: The moral law, contained in the decalogue, is nothing else but the law of nature revived, or a second edition and impression of that primitive and perfect law of nature, which in the state of innocency was engraven upon man's heart, but now again written upon tables of stone, by the finger of God (1, 151).

The law of nature and the moral obligations of that law are to be obeyed because they were instituted to have eternal and perpetual value. The sabbath belongs both to the moral and the ceremonial systems and is therefore preserved under the continued efficacy of natural cycles.[36] Shepard's doctrine draws the old and new dispensations close together, minimizing their differences. He understood that the sabbath may be an "accidental" or an "affixed" type, but this designation was unimportant in comparison to its eternal, moral signification. If the sabbath held ceremonial importance for the Jews of the Old Testament and its typological value was abrogated by Christ's incarnation, it was even more richly endowed with a moral equity that is perpetual and universal, complementary to the typological scheme. Since the first sabbath was given before there was any real promise of Christ, that is, before the Fall, then "in its first and native institution, the Sabbath is not typicall and Ceremoniall but morall onely" (2, 165). Although the ceremonies were "types and shadows of things to come and therefore being to cease when the body was come," because of its natural institution, the sabbath continued to have value for the New English Israel.

Shepard's continuous efforts to distinguish between the *typus fictus* and the *typus destinatus* represented a conservative victory for exegesis, because it established clearly the boundaries of typology in the early theocracy. If the sabbath were instituted before sin and could only be typical by accidental assignment, then its efficacy for New England had to be reasoned from a scriptural premise other than the typological system. But Shepard preserved the integrity of typology and also gave the sabbath a perpetual, figurative prominence by relieving typology of the burden of providing moral and spiritual authority for sabbatical justification. The Old Testament types seemed to be securely in place, and the sabbath continued to be celebrated, sanctified by God, and prophetic of the millennial rest that is to come, not abrogated or concluded by Christ.

Shepard's resolution of the sabbatical controversy was important because it extended, morally, figuratively, and metaphorically, the value of the Old Testament into modern times. His argument was supported by others. Samuel Mather taught that the sabbath had both moral and prophetic value, and he declared it to be typical:

The general Notion of a Sabbath is a *time of Rest.* They had *three sorts of Sabbaths:* their *weekly Sabbath,* every seventh day; their *yearly Sabbath,* every seventh year; and their *great sabbatical Year,* reckoning seven times seven years, which was their *Jubilee,* every *fiftieth year.* In every one of which was something of a Shadow of things to come, the Apostle is express, *these things are a Shadow of Things to Come . . . Their weekly Sabbath on the seventh Day of the week;* this was partly *Moral* and *Perpetual,* considered as a seventh part of weekly time, sanctified and set apart by God from common use, for Man to rest from the Works of his weekly Calling, in imitation of God, and in remembrance of the great work of the Creation of the World. But tho' the Sabbath be *partly Moral,* and it must needs be so, seeing it is one of the *Ten Commandments,* . . . therefore *Adam* in his innocent and sinless Estate needed a Sabbath; and God sanctified this Day before the Fall of Man.[37]

Unlike Shepard, Samuel Mather sought to establish both the moral and the typological significance of the sabbatical scheme, and to identify its figurative significance for the millennial kingdom: "Yet the *Jewish* Sabbath was in *some respects Ceremonial* and therefore it is abrogated, and the Christian Sabbath substituted instead thereof; for it had some typical Respects and Uses, some ceremonial Rites and Observations annexed to it" (*Figures or Types*, p. 445). Among those "typical" uses Mather cites *"the Commemoration of their typical Redemption and Deliverance out of Egypt"* (p. 445). More important, he goes on to argue, as Jonathan Edwards would later do in his *History of the Work of Redemption,* that the sabbath was indeed a type of rest, prefiguring the rest of Jesus in the grave and the eternal rest designed to be the reward of the saints: "As there was in the Jewish Sabbath a Commemoration of that typical Redemption out of *Egypt,* so secondly, it was a *typical Prefiguration of the Rest of the Body of Jesus Christ in the Grave that whole Day"* (p. 446). The Christian sabbath is established in the place of the abrogated Jewish sabbath, and the cyclical pattern of prefiguration and fulfillment continues throughout history: "From all which you may see the Morality of the Sabbath considered as in general, together with the shadowy Nature of the Jewish Sabbath of the seventh Day, having these typical Respects and Relations annexed to it; and so therein you see the Grounds for the Abrogation of it, and of the Substitution of the Christian Sabbath instead thereof" (p. 446).

This was an important achievement. Millennial theology was a prominent prophetic force during the early stages of the colonial migrations and settlement, and it enjoyed importance until the middle decades of the nineteenth century. In the rivalry between conservative and liberal typological commentators late in the seventeenth century, however, the question of the sabbath as a figure of the millennial rest became a critical focus that would later supply writers with a systematic, scriptural argument for the time and nature of the millennium. Typology and prophecy were obvious keys for understanding the relevance of the past for the present, and when applied to the cycles of history they also unlocked the secret mysteries of the future. Increase Mather continued to view the Old Testament figures and types — including the sabbath — as prophetic synecdoches of the coming kingdom, and in so doing, he echoed the theology of the seventeenth-century English commentators on the millennium, such as Joseph Mede and William Whiston. Sabbatism and the theological value of God's seventh day of rest as instituted in the Genesis account of creation, continued to dominate millennial thinking throughout the seventeenth and eighteenth centuries, culminating in Jonathan Edwards' scheme outlined in the *History of the Work of Redemption.* Moreover, the symbolic value of the millennial sabbath was realized in the typological associations found throughout the writings of commentators like the Mathers and Samuel Sewall.

Increase Mather's contributions to the evolution of American symbolic writing include his assessment of the allegorical significance found in contemporary natural events, and his compilation of case histories, *An Essay for the Recording of Illustrious Providences* (1684), dramatizes the relationship of divine authority to history by showing how Providence intervenes in human affairs to provide signs and symbols of the creator's will. In the *Doctrine of Divine Providence,* also published in 1684, and in such treatises as *Angelographia* (1696) and *Kometographia* (1683), Mather showed how the world of spirit and the world of matter are closely associated in the evolution of a single grand scheme through which the creator will effect the work of redemption.

It is, however, in Mather's chiliasm, his predictions of the future millennium, that his most concrete and specific contributions to the symbolic imagination may be measured. Closely associated with the development of the jeremiad, the Mather chiliasm placed the coming of Christ before the millennium in traditional premillennial fashion and looked forward to a literal resurrection of the saints. Moreover, he persisted in a view of the flowering of the saints in millennial glory at a time when many ministers were more pessimistic in their assessments of the end of the world:

> Mather grew to adulthood in years when revolutionary millennialism in England was at its height. Brightman, Mede, and John Cotton, the father of Mather's future bride, were all his heroes and all charismatic prophets of the imminent rule of the saints on earth. Increase was himself in the British Isles at the time of the last, fanatic effort by Fifth Monarchy rebels to overthrow Cromwell and anticipate the second coming. Then came the Restoration. For the rest of his life, Mather lived in a world of discourse where the literal promise of heaven on earth was steadily blurred over and made harmless . . . The overthrow of Antichrist and the rule of the saints was no longer preached. Increase Mather, however, never gave up the vision.[38]

For Increase Mather, the literal and metaphorical meanings of Scripture were fused in the working out of God's redemptive plan for mankind. Thus when other Puritan scholars were moving toward a wholly figural and metaphorical interpretation of those prophecies in Revelation and Isaiah, Mather held even more fervently to his view that there would be a literal restoration of the world following the second coming and judgment. The conversion of the Jews, prophesied in Revelation and looked for as a sign of the imminent fulfillment of Scripture promises, became for Mather a central symbol signifying the begin-

ning of the end of the world. But if Mather viewed the millennium as imminent, he was more reluctant than some of his contemporaries to tie
this vision to a particular date. "Imminent, he explained on several occasions, meant sometime in the next few years; and one should not
presume to calculate precisely the movement of the Lord."[39]

In his early writings on the millennium, such as *The Mystery of Israel's
Salvation* (1669) and *Diatriba de Signo Filii Hominis et de Secundo Messiae
Adventu* (1682), Mather placed the coming judgment and millennium in
the future, and argued: "that there shall be a General conversion of the
Tribes of Israel, is a truth which in some good measure hath been
known, and believed in all ages of the Church of God, since the Apostles
days" (*Mystery of Israel's Salvation*, Preface, p. 1). Interpretations of Israel's
salvation varied in Mather's time; some commentators viewed the
restoration of Israel as an event in the historical past, "conceiving that
there shall be no other calling of them, than what was at their return out
of the *Babylonish Captivity*." Like many of his contemporaries, Mather
distinguished a "spiritual Israel — such as in respect of faith and religion"
from a "carnal, natural Israel, i.e., those that are by generation of the
seed of Jacob, who afterwards was called Israel" (p. 7). But if Mather
declared that "wee must know there is a double *Israel* spoken of in the
Scripture," he was emphatic in his assertion that the national conversion
of the Jews which would precede the millennium was to be a literal,
historical event. The "doctrine" of *The Mystery of Israel's Salvation* argues
"that the time will surely come, when the body of the twelve tribes of
Israel shall be brought out of their present condition of bondage and
misery, into a glorious and wonderful state of salvation, not only
spiritual but temporal" (p. 7). This central doctrine, which places the
millennium in the future and specifies that the Jewish nation will be converted prior to its arrival, is corroborated by Mather's insistence that the
events of Scripture are typological foreshadowings of contemporary
events. "That deliverance of the Jews by Cyrus out of Babylon," he says,
"was very wonderful, yet nothing so wonderful as this will be, as is evident, because that was but a *type* of this, and therefore it is, that in many
places in the Scripture, the very same expressions are used to signifie
both that deliverance out of Babylon and this which is to come" (p. 4).
And Mather's symbology is consistent with traditional views of exegetical hermeneutics; the type must remain inferior to the antitype,
which succeeds it in historical time, and will eventually fulfill the
promises implied in the typological adumbration: "Because their
deliverance was a *type* of this, therefore this will be the more eminent and
wonderful for the Type must needs come short of the Antitype" (p. 4).

This identification of New England as the antitype of Old Israel was
not original to Increase Mather's eschatology; however, the sustaining of

this myth into the later seventeenth century was a remarkable mythic, literary, and theological achievement. Since the formulation of the Half-Way Covenant in 1662, New England ministers had stressed the declension of the New English Israel from her original errand into the wilderness, and Samuel Danforth, the Boston minister who preached the election sermon of 1670, *A Briefe Recognition of New England's Errand into the Wilderness,* represents a tradition of jeremiads that culminated in Mather's own *Ichabod: or, The Glory Departing,* preached and published in 1702. Thus the public acknowledgment that New England could possibly fulfill the promises of Scripture by becoming the antitype to Old Israel's typological prefigurations was an affirmation of the vision of the first generation, conceived in traditional prophetic terms and articulated through the exegetical methods conventionally employed to assert the correspondences between New England and the cycles of ancient history. *The Mystery of Israel's Salvation* is important because it distinguished between a literal restoration of Israel and a figurative fulfillment of the Scripture promises. But Mather was insistent that the imminent events would include the real, historical, spiritual transformation of the Jewish nation:

> It is evident, that the Tribes of Israel shall partake of a spiritual salvation if we consider the visible Church estate which they shall be in after their conversion. Albeit now there is no Church amongst the Jews; but the time is at hand, when God will erect many glorious Churches amongst them, and upon every dwelling place of Sion, and upon all the glory he will be a defence. And the Church polity which Israel shall then be under, will not be a carnal one such as was from Moses to Christ, but a very spiritual polity, for they shall be no more under Josiacal paedagogy, no more under ceremonial law (*Mystery of Israel's Salvation,* p. 113).

In the 1690s while other Puritan exegetes were beginning to view the millennium and judgment as a metaphorical prophecy, suggesting that the times were too corrupt to provide an appropriate setting for the spiritual peace and harmony suggested in the eschatological passages of Scripture, Increase Mather held firmly to his belief that God would commence the last days with a restoration of Israel as a nation, both spiritually and temporally. He dismissed the declension in piety—which he acknowledged and used to theological advantage in *Ichabod: or, The Glory Departing*—by showing that "it is evident, that the salvation of Israel will be wonderful, if we compare it with those former deliverances which in the days of old have been vouchsafed unto the Tribes of Israel. It is indeed true, that God hath in former times bestowed more eminent and wonderful salvations upon the Israelitish Nation than upon any Nation in the world" (*Mystery of Israel's Salvation,* 1669, p. 77). He knew that "it will be in a time of very great trouble when Israel shall be saved" (p. 34), but he argued that

The *Wolf* and the Lamb shall feed together, and the Lion shall eat straw like the bullock, and dust shall be the serpent's meat, they shall not hurt nor destroy in all my holy mountain, saith the *Lord* (Isa. 65.25). Before the Fall, the Wolf and the Lamb, the Bullock and the Lion could live quietly by one another; man was not subject to hurt by serpents or venomous creatures, there was not that enmity in any of the creatures to seek the destruction of one another. Even thus shall it be again: as *Adam* was a *Type* of Christ, Rom. 5. 14. So was *Adams* world, a *Type* of Christ, the second *Adam* his world, when he shall come to judge the earth (*Mystery of Israel's Salvation,* p. 125).

Thus Mather's anticipation of the forthcoming millennium is argued from the Scripture types in a linear, historical movement toward the last days while his description, though brief, of the millennial period is couched in the language of Old Testament prophecy.

These positions are corroborated by his *Dissertation Concerning the Future Conversion of the Jewish Nation* (1709), until recently the clearest known statement of Mather's millennial beliefs. Written between 1692 and 1695, the *Dissertation* affirms the second coming, the resurrection of the elect in bodily form, the thousand-year reign of the saints and angels on earth, to be concluded by a general resurrection. Moreover, the *Dissertation,* like much of Mather's eschatological writing, argues against the allegorizing of Scripture as a way of predicting the future. As he wrote when speaking of Richard Baxter, "If Men allow themselves this liberty of *Allegorizing,* we may at last Allegorize Religion into nothing but Fancy, and say that the Resurrection is past already. How much safer it is to keep to the Letter of Scripture, when for us so to do is consistent with the Analogy of Faith?" (p. 27). Mather surveys the history of millennial interpretations and concludes that "*it is a known, received Maxim among Divines, that in the interpretation of Scripture we may not depart from the literal sense, if it will stand with the analogy of Faith.* For Men to make *Allegories* where there are none, is to obtrude their own Imaginations instead of Scripture . . . The 20th of *Apocalypse, of all the Narrations in that Book, seems to be the most plain and simple, most free of Allegory, and of the involution of prophetical Figures.* How can a Man then take a Passage of so plain, and ordinarily expressed Words as those about the *First Resurrection* are, in any other sense than the usual and Literal?" (*Dissertation,* p. 19). Thus he adopts the typological reading of Revelation as an extension of the literal sense, not to be confused with the allegorizing of the Apocalypse that has confused scriptural interpretation since the early days of the church fathers. The millennium, or chiliad, he cites, is literal and future, not metaphorical and past. "If the Millennial Reign began a Thousand Years ago, then Christ's Reign on Earth and Antichrist's would be at the very same time, which cannot be" (p. 25). The pastoral visions of peace prophesied in Isaiah and restated in Revelation would occur following the second coming and Judgment of the world, after which there would be a general or "second resurrection."

The doctrinal positions of the *Dissertation* are important because they indicate how strongly Increase Mather defended the literal reading of scripture promises, which he identified with the typological or figural instead of the allegorical. While the *Dissertation* treats a specific portion of the apocalyptic vision, two documents explore the whole range of millennial expectations, tracing the history of reformed interpretation and declaring authoritatively that the thousand-year reign is soon to be expected. Curiously, the first of these documents, the "New Jerusalem," is a manuscript written in 1687, now housed in the collections of the American Antiquarian Society.[40] The second is the well-known treatise, *A Discourse Concerning Faith and Fervency in Prayer and the Glorious Kingdom of the Lord Jesus Christ,* (1710), which Perry Miller has described as "the finest of his Chiliastic hymns."[41] Both these treatises affirm that Mather ancitipated an imminent millennial kingdom and that he viewed the figures of Scripture as types foreshadowing the second coming:

> When this Kingdom of Our Lord Jesus Christ shall come and prevail over the World, *There Will Be Peace and Tranquility Throughout the Earth.* Psal. 72.7 . . . Not only Peace, but *Abundance of Peace.* Such happy tranquillity was the like was never yet known in the world. One of Christ's glorious Titles is, *The Prince of Peace,* Isai. 9.6. Solomon was a *Type of Christ* in this respect: His Name has *Peace* in the signification of it; God said to his Father David, A Son Shall be *Born to Thee Who Will be a Man of Rest* . . . What happy days of Peace did the Children of Israel enjoy in his days, and under his Reign, Typifying the Peace of Christ's Kingdom (*Discourse,* p. 51).

Throughout the *Discourse,* typological and prophetic figures abound. If they conform to the traditional linear and historical patterns established for typological exegesis, they incorporate into the literal reading of Scripture a figural sense that derives from God's divine dispensation in Scripture revelation. Mather makes this point extremely clear when he discusses the City of God, for example,

> *They of the City,* viz., the Citizens of Jerusalem, who are a *synecdoche* put forth for all the Subjects of the Kingdom, *Shall Flourish Like the Grass of the Earth,* they shall increase and become very numerous and very happy. All these Expressions are used *Emblematically* to set forth the success of the Gospel, and the wonderful growth and flourishing of Christ's Kingdom (*Discourse,* p. 14).

Christ's kingdom to come is everlasting, and the Mathers declared its imminence against alternative evidence provided by contemporary ministers of the jeremiad, who saw in the future a bleak judgment with little hope for the "new heavens and new earth" prophesied by Isaiah. The chiliasm of Increase Mather, beautifully preached from his exegesis of scripture figures, made him unusual in New England at the close of the seventeenth century. Ironically, the Mather declarations were supported by some of the more scientific explanations of the coming of the end of the world, such as Thomas Burnet's *The Sacred Theory of the Earth* and William Whiston's *A New Theory of the Earth,* composed by a professor of mathematics at Cambridge, which argued that the world was about to be consumed by the advent of a comet. Thus the language of Canaan drew authority from a wide variety of theological and scientific documents.

For example, the most intriguing of Increase Mather's chiliastic writings is the "New Jerusalem" manuscript, because it treats the actual sequence of events during the millennium rather than academic arguments about the timing of the second coming or the possibility that the millennium has already commenced. For the "New Jerusalem," the future expectations of premillennialism are a *donné;* "the New Jerusalem, Mather wrote, would 'excel the literl Jerusalem' in several ways: first, its maker and builder is God; second, only God's elect, members of the 'mistical church' may inhabit Jerusalem and 'miserable degenerates' would be excluded; third, unlike the Old Jerusalem which was destroyed, the New Jerusalem, the spiritual Jerusalem, 'shall stand forever' as 'an eternall excellence.' "[42] The crucial point developed in the document is that the New Jerusalem shall be a restoration and renovation of the earth, a fulfillment of that prophecy in Isaiah that "new heavens and a new earth" shall be joined together. Nothing, Mather argues, can evolve from the contemporary scene to fulfill this prophecy. Rather, the millennial state, like salvation, must come from heaven in a divine dispensation. "When the New Jerusalem comes downe from heaven, it is saide that the heaven and the earth that now are, shall be no more, but a new heaven and earth, *Rev.* 21. 1, 2. there will then be a *New World,* another world wonderfully differing from what this is at present where wee now live. And so will the resurrection world bee, it is in the Scripture saide to be another world, It is expressly distinguished from this present world" ("New Jerusalem," p. 29).

The achievement of the "New Jerusalem" manuscript is that it establishes Mather's position on the specific conditions of the millennial paradise and shows clearly his premillennial faith in the future perfection of God's society of saints. To those postmillennial believers who thought that New England would evolve into the city of God without the assistance of grace, Mather declares, "It is in Vaine for men to *think* or dream of perfection before that day, 1 John 1:8, *If Wee Say Wee Have No Sin Wee Deceive Ourselves and the Truth Is Not In Us.* There are none that have more sin in them, than they that Say or Imagine that they have none att all" (p. 32). He is emphatic about the process of the millennial dispensation; the "new heavens and the new earth" result from the descent of the New Jerusalem from heaven to earth. On this point, Mather is insistent and repetitious: "That the New Jerusalem doth intend ye resurrection world is further evident from Severall things. First, *In That When New Jerusalem Doth Come Downe from Heaven, There Are Such Things To Be Done, As Shall Not Be Done Untill the Resurrection World Shall Begin*" (p. 28).

> *Againe,* when New Jerusalem comes down from heaven, it is saide that the heaven and the earth that now are, shall be no more, but a new heaven and earth: Rev. 21:1, 2. there will then be a *New World,* another world wonderfully differing from what this is at present where wee now live. And so will the resurrection world bee, it is in the Scripture saide to be another world, It is expressly distinguished from this present world, Luke 20:34, 35 . . . *Wee Look for a New Heaven and a New Earth* (A New World, that is) for the Hebrews were wont to express the world by those termes of heaven and *earth Wherein Righteousness Shall Dwell. Righteousness Shall be There* (p. 29).

The "New Jerusalem" is to be a perfect society, one in which "all faithfull Christians shall one day partake in the glorious privileges and happiness of the New Jerusalem which comes downe from heaven" (p. 25). In this respect, Mather takes John's vision quite literally, asserting that "in *Rev.* 21:2, 10, [John] had a vision wherein hee did behold the New Jerusalem descending from God out of Heaven, whereas if it had intended the church triumphant in heaven only, it had been seen rather ascending to God in Heaven than descending and coming downe from God out of heaven" (p. 25). It is clear that the characteristics of the "New Jerusalem" differ from those of the Church Triumphant "in heaven above"; namely, it is to be an earthly rather than heavenly church, "compassed bout [by] the nations of the world," and it is to be a national and visible church. Above all, it is to be a literal and historical expression of God's Providence, an earthly manifestation of His divine dispensation that appears in perfection at the end of human time. It is therefore eternal and immortal, a victorious figure of God's triumph over evil:

> But the day is coming when *All the World Shall Become Christ's Kingdome,* Rev. 11:15. When the Seventh Angel doth sound the trumpett, a Voice is heard from heaven saying *The Kingdomes of the World Are Become the Kingdomes of Our Lord and of His Christ.* This will be a glorious day when there shall not be a kingdome in all this world, but shall be Christs when all this world shall become Christ's Kingdome (p. 55).

Doctrinally, this view is neither original to Mather nor unorthodox. However, that so affirmative a position on the coming of Christ's kingdom should be expressed in 1687, when many of Mather's contemporaries were voicing the day of doom that would imminently arrive to destroy the corrupt world of Satan's kingdom, creates a paradox. Indeed, Mather's own jeremiads, such as *The Day of Trouble is Near* or *Ichabod,* would stress the other side of this future glory by emphasizing, in Jonathan Edwards' terms, that the future punishment of the wicked is unavoidable and intolerable. Mather titled one of his own denunciatory treatises, *The Wicked Man's Portion* (1675).

The "New Jerusalem" offers a superb view of Mather's use of the figural language of Canaan to prove his vision. We have seen that the literal interpretation of Scripture provided his narrative a descriptive authority and that, following St. John's words, Mather anticipated a literal resurrection and a descent to the earth of the heavenly city. But several features of the treatise show that he followed closely the orthodox figuralism of typological exegesis in order to give his interpretation the authority of Scripture prophecy and to ground his vision in the revelation of God's will. First, he is very specific about the origins of certain important words, as seen in his primitive etymology of the term "Jerusalem": "The notation which some give of the Name, *Jerusalem,* is, from the Hebrew word, *Jare,* which signifieth *fear.* and *Salem,* the original name of that city, as much as to say, *Fear Ye Salem.* In Salem is Gods Tabernacle, & his dwelling place in Sion. Be therefore afraid to sett yourselves against Salem, where God & his heavenly Angels are able in a moment to destroy all Salem's enemies" (p. 21). This trope, which is in the narrative, is reinforced by an amplification appended to it in a marginal note, emended and inscribed by Increase Mather's own hand, as he was rereading the copy transcribed by his son, Cotton. The emendation reads:

> That is the way to be secure and save whatever may become of the world . . . They shall repaire thither as to a place of safety and security. The church of God is the securest place to be in, that possibly can be. So on the other hand, it is a dangerous thing for men to sett themselves against Gods people. They sett themselves against Jerusalem and what became of those that did so of old whilst It was a cittie beloved of God (p. 21n).

The question of "Jerusalem of Old" is answered through typological exegesis of the text, and Mather clearly shows how the early Jerusalem was but a figure of that which is to come. *"If Jerusalem the Most Glorious Cittie in the Whole World Was a Tipe and Figure of the Church of God, How*

Then the Church Must Needs Excell in Glorie. The antitipe must needs be more glorious than the Tipe. The substance must needs outdoe that who was but a figure and shadow of it" (p. 14).

This is conventional reformed doctrine concerning typology. The verifiable historical figure must foreshadow, imperfectly, that substance of which it was but a shade. When the veil is finally lifted, and all resurrected Saints view eternal glory with what Edward Taylor called "bodilie eyes" — those soul's eyes made perfect through regeneration and grace but those resurrected in bodily form — then the magnificence of God's holy city would be manifest to those elected for salvation. Mather is quite specific about the differences between the typological figure of the Old Jerusalem and the fulfilling antitype of the New Jerusalem:

> There are three things especially in which the Church of God doth exceed and go beyond the old Jerusalem. The Spirituall excells the Literall Jerusalem. *First,* in respect of the builder and founder of it. As for the old Jerusalem that was Built by man . . . To be sure it was some man. But as for the *Spiritual Jerusalem* God hath laide the foundations thereof. *His Foundation Is the Holy Mountaines.* Psalm 87.1. As for the church of God, it is he that hath laid the foundations thereof . . . what shall one answer the messengers of the nations . . . that *God Hath Founded Sion* (p. 14).

This proof is typical of Mather's method. The Scripture text is the foundation for a prophetic assessment of contemporary times, and the Old Testament figures are methodically explored as prophetic synecdoches of the coming of the future kingdom. And Mather is very clear about the abrogation of the type that prefigured the New Jerusalem:

> *As For the Old Jerusalem: That Hath Been Destroyed Long Ago.* It was destroyed first by the Babylonians, and after it was rebuilt it was destroyed again by the Romans, and when about three hundred years after that, Julian the Apostate out of his hatred of Christ, and the Christian names did Incourage the Jewes to build Jerusalem, . . . it was destroyed by the Immediate hand of God from heaven . . . a mighty earthquake overturned all so that there was not so much as a stone left upon a stone (p. 17).

The Old Jerusalem "did miserably degenerate," so that its godly perfection was no longer possible. Thus had New England degenerated in her "errand into the wildness," so that now the saints could only hope for the coming of Christ's future kingdom, that "new heaven and new earth" that would descend at the end of human time in fulfillment of the Scripture promises. If the Puritans were to continue their imitation of Old Israel, a theocracy modeled on the revealed laws of God, then they could only, like Old Israel, look forward to the coming of the Messiah to redeem them and to establish a holy society out of the corruptions of contemporary life. Mather goes into great detail on this in both *Meditations on Death* and in *Meditations on the Glory of the Heavenly World*. He tells the saints it is obvious the millennium must come to rectify the present situation in which the church is downtrodden even in Boston.

Typology made this figural association possible; without it, the prophetic images of the Old Testament would be abrogated, condemned, pagan patterns of idolatrous degeneration. As Sacvan Bercovitch put it, "typology emphasizes the *imitatio*, it translates secular history, whether of individuals or of communities, into spiritual biography, and it recalls the tradition of the Saints' lives . . . Typology recommended itself to the Reformers as an ideal method for regulating spiritualization, since it stressed the literal-historical (as opposed to a purely allegorical) level of exegesis, and then proceeded to impose the Scriptural pattern."[43]

By extending the symbolic significance of scriptural typology to contemporary history, Increase Mather expanded the possibilities of biblical interpretation in New England. Although the typological method was used early in New England to assert the historical authority of the New English Israel, not all ministers were convinced that New England would indeed usher in the long-awaited millenium. By comparing Increase Mather's writings and Samuel Sewall's chiliasm with Cotton Mather's uses of metaphor, the typological symbology of the late seventeenth century was not fully shared even by the father and his son, though both freely applied biblical figures to contemporary history. As Robert Middlekauff suggested, "Cotton Mather never commented on this dream of his father. Typology remained for him a rhetorical device, not an instrument to be used in the analysis of history."[44] But for Increase Mather, writing of the "New Jerusalem" or *The Mystery of Israel's Salvation* only a few years earlier, "Israel's future promised to be important in the end of the world: Christ's Second Coming and the destruction of Antichrist would be signalized by the salvation of the exiled Jews who would be gathered from the four corners of the world. Obviously New England would be affected by these last climactic events, and in the meantime she could profit much by Israel's example."[45]

Mather's typological scheme was not inconsistent with the traditional premillennial reading of John's apocalyptic vision. But his insistence that a harmonious balance could be maintained between *litera* and *figura* continued the expanding possibilities of New England's sustained analogy between her experience and that of the Old Testament Israel. The typological method added prophetic dimension to the static figures of the first dispensation and gave contemporary history a vital role in the continued history of the work of redemption.[46] Thus Mather's historiography pivoted on the typological reading of the Old Testament, and his vision of the future redemption of the world was presented in the prophetic language of Israel's fulfillment. It was not, of course, the progressive historiography that later developed among postmillennial Calvinists like Jonathan Edwards, but it shared with Edwards a view of America's promise that was rooted in the figural language of the Scripture types.

As a statement of late seventeenth-century millennial figuralism Mather's ideas were fully corroborated by one of the most graphic impressions of the end of the world to be rendered during this era: Samuel Sewall's *Phaenomena quaedam Apocalyptica, Or, some few Lines towards a description of the New Heaven As It makes to those who stand upon the New Earth* (1697). Sewall's *Phaenomena*, like Mather's "New Jerusalem" manuscript, is a climactic seventeenth-century statement of typology's importance in the historical process through which mankind's redemption would be achieved. Sacvan Bercovitch calls it a document "where history is prophecy in process, where the Redeemer is the antitype of Jesus, and where the New World is an actual locale awaiting its glorification."[47] And Sewall himself intrudes the question rhetorically that had been implied in the original, first-generation "errand into the wilderness": was America intended to be the seat of the New Jerusalem prophesied in Scripture?

> New Jerusalem will not straiten, and enfeeble; but wonderfully dilate, and invigorate Christianity in the several Quarters of the World; in *Asia*, in *Africa*, in *Europe*, and in *America*. And one that has been born, or but liv'd in *America*, between thirty, and fourty years; it may be pardonable for him to ask, Why may not that be the place of New Jerusalem? . . . Why may not *New-Spain* be the place of *New Jerusalem?* Its being part of the New World, one would think, carries with it no contradiction thereunto. Places are usually called new from the newness of their situation; and not from their being built anew; as *New Spain, New England, New London* (p. 2).

Sewall follows traditional prophetic commentators like Thomas Thorowgood and John Downame in establishing the prefigurative value of Old Testament typological systems for New Testament times, in which the New English Israel was immersed: "Mr. [John] *Eliot* was wont to say The *New English* Churches are a preface to the New Heavens: and if so, I hope the preface and Book will be bound up together, and this *Mexican* Continent shall comprehend them both" (p.2).

Increase Mather had been concerned to demonstrate the imminence of the coming kingdom and to establish 1716 as the precise date for its fulfillment, but Sewall was more occupied with the geographical location and setting, which Mather had assumed to be America from the tradition of *translatio studii*, the classical theory that civilization moves in a westward course, from Greece to Rome to Western Europe and thence, according to seventeenth- and eighteenth-century European thinkers, to the New World.[48]

Sewall, too, assumed this *translatio* in the composition of his treatise about the millennium and its pastoral realization on earth. "May it not . . . be argued," Sewall declared, "*New-Jerusalem* is not the same with *Jerusalem;* but as *Jerusalem* was to the westward of *Babylon;* so *New Jerusalem* must be to the westward of *Rome;* to avoid disturbance in the Order of these Mysteries" (*Phaenomena*, p. 29). The *translatio studii* of course is manifest in the errand motif and in its later symbolization as "manifest destiny" in the westward course of empire. As Mather's typological reasoning had led to the prediction of an imminent fulfill-ment of Scripture promises of the millennium, Sewall's typology, less overt in its development of a figural relationship, articulates the cor-respondence between the Old Testament Jews and the New English Israel.

The Apocalypse is a most illustrious Epithalamium suited to the stately Magnificence of the Bridegroom, and of the Bride. Now the *Jews* upon their Return, will eminently sustain that Character. The *New Jerusalem* is that which the Old and New Testament do ring of. This City of God is especially made up of *Jews*, and from thence it hath its Name . . . Therefore, seeing the Parchments belong to those who have the Estate; this book must needs belong to the *Jews;* because the glorious Things that are spoken of therein, are eminently spoken of them (*Phaenomena*, p. 28).

But the supreme achievement of the *Phaenomena* is that through the author's concern to establish America as the seat of the New Jerusalem, a pastoral vision corroborated by Scripture prophecy develops and sug-gests a future paradise that would resemble that lost in Eden:

The Land Was as the Garden of Eden, or Paradise, Before Them; and Behind Them a Desolate Wilderness. They have fulfilled, and surpassed the Mischievousness of old Babylon, in Making the World as a Wilderness, and Destroying the Cities Thereof. Now the Good Lord by His Good Spirit Lift Up a Standard Against the Cruel Enemy of Christ and Mankind: That Such Enemies May Be Scattered. And Let the Lord Lift Up His Hand: Declare His Power To the Gentiles, that They May Be Gathered To, and By the Standard of the Gospel (Phaenomena, p. 57).

The world of gentile saints shall comprise a nation of the elect, fulfilling the prophecy of Scripture for a national conversion of the Jews before the millennium, now a figure or type of the true conversion of the world and its transformation into a spiritual kingdom. If for Increase Mather the kingdom of God would come down from heaven to the "new earth," for Sewall it would evolve from the present nations of the world as an antitypical fulfillment of those prophetic synecdoches designed to reveal its future realization to fallen mankind.

Sewall's theological reasoning was complemented by his contributions to the development of symbolic language among the Puritans. Unlike many of his contemporaries who saw in the Bible promises of doom and images of eternal destruction, Sewall imaged a future of hope and fulfillment, and he argued not only from the prophecies of Scripture but also from the facts of history and the details of contemporary exploration in the New World. His argument that America would be the seat of the New Jerusalem was proved typologically, but it was also reasoned from current events and from the history of America's discovery and exploration. This fusion or conflation of the *litera* and the *figura* was significant because it brought to contemporary affairs the flavor of Scripture history. Not only was New England a prophetic synecdoche for the coming of the kingdom of God — an abstraction that would be intelligible to Sewall's ministerial contemporaries but possibly obscure to some of his congregation — America was for Sewall a literal place of transporting beauty and edenic promise, so that the meanest of his readers might catch the sense of God's promise to his plantations, that Christ's eternal kingdom would be realized in beauty, splendor, and glory rather than in the doomsaying of the jeremiad.

Of all the parts of the world, which do from this Charter entitle themselves to the Government of Christ, *America's* Plea, in my opinion, is the strongest. For when once *Christopher Columbus* had added this *fourth* to the other *Three* parts of the foreknown World; they who sailed farther Westward, arriv'd but where they had been before. The Globe now failed of offering anything New to the adventurous Travailer; Or, however, it could not afford another new World. And probably, the consideration of *America's* being *The Beginning of the East, and the End of the West*; was that which moved *Columbus* to call some part of it by the Name of *Alpha* and *Omega*. Now if the *Last Adam* did give Order for the engraving of his own Name upon this *Last Earth*; 'twill draw with it great Consequences; even such as will, in time, bring the poor *Americans* out of their Graves, and make them live[49] (*Phaenomena*, p. 61).

The types had come full circle. Sewall's perception of the coming millennium was a fulfillment of the figures of Scripture in the literal details of current events, such as Columbus' discovery of America, and as such, all historical events became part of the process of providential dispensation, just as the types had prefigured the antitypes in the first and second dispensations. Thus the correspondence cited above, between Eden and America, continues the process of divine revelation by developing parallels between Old and New Testament times that were divinely instituted. It would be the business of Cotton Mather and Jonathan Edwards to give typology a new epistemological foundation through which the coming of the kingdom might be realized without the literal presence of Christ. As Cotton Mather was to argue in the "Biblia Americana" and to illustrate in the *Magnalia Christi Americana*, prophecies of the millennium and typological correspondences between Old Israel and New England were metaphors of God's future transformation of the corrupt world of men; no longer would men be able to say that the kingdom had come to New England. But for Edwards and the New Light Calvinists, the kingdom arrived not through a cataclysmic descent from heaven to earth, but through a process of transformation of men's hearts so that the spiritual presence of Christ pervaded "the American desart."

Millennial figuralism in Cotton Mather's writing abounds, but it must be distinguished from Increase Mather's chiliasm, and this difference is important to the development of millennial symbolism and the language of Canaan. Although the *Magnalia Christi Americana* (1702) looks to the past to find recapitulations of the Old Testament types among the settlers of early New England, the typological structure of the book develops out of a traditional, biblical historiography that Mather employed. Cotton Mather's application of Scripture to contemporary events is closely allied to the practices of his father; however, for Cotton Mather, the earthly realization of a heavenly kingdom no longer carried the full authority of prophetic fulfillment, so that his symbology of the millennium is less convincing of an imminent, earthly experience. Rather, his writing is richly endowed with metaphors drawn from Scripture figures, so that distinguishing a prophetic typology from a metaphorical allusion is more difficult than in an exegesis of his father's chiliasm. For example, in the "Harmony of the Gospels" in the "Biblia Americana," Cotton warns

To Earthly Creatures this world is their own countrey, & their Father's House. *Tho' There Are Many Places, Which They Know Little Of, Yett in General, They Know What Ye World Is, and What Its Enjoyments Are.* Here They Are at Home, *& with Their Kindred: With People Disposed Like Themselves.* Heaven *Is a Country More Unknown to Them, Than* Canaan was *To Abraham. It Is Only God That Can Discover the Countrey Unto Us, & The Way To It, as He Led Abraham into Canaan. Abraham's Action Is in the Scripture Made a Figure of a Christian's Life in This World: Who Is But* a Pilgrim and Stranger here . . . Tho' the Patriarchs did certainly believe, *That Their Posterity Should Inherit the Earthly Canaan, Yett They Understood* Better Things, *Contained in This Promise, Even an Heavenly Countrey, Which They Expected, as Their Inheritance* (n.p.).

Here Abraham is perceived in two distinct ways. First, he is an allegorical *peregrinus* making his way from the earthly city of Babylon to the heavenly city of Jerusalem, an *exemplum* — in the moral sense — to be imitated by saints in all ages. But he is also seen as a "Figure of a Christian's life in this world," which carries not only the authority of moral example but also the prefigurative value of a typological association. Mather is not clear about preferences, but he concludes his passage with the suggestion that even the Old Testament patriarchs "did certainly beleeve that their posterity should inherit the earthly *Canaan*, yett they understood *Better Things* contained in this promise, even an *Heavenly Countrey*, which they expected, as their *Inheritance*."

Thus Cotton Mather clearly anticipated, with his father, a millennial kingdom to come, but one that would be modeled on the Promised Land of old and a Canaan for which the errand into the wilderness would be a necessary prerequisite. Four relatively late documents clarify this position and should be regarded together in an assessment of Cotton Mather's millennial symbology. *Theopolis Americana: An Essay on the Golden Street of the Holy City . . . with Some Good Hopes of Better Things to be Yet Seen in the American World* was published in Boston in 1710. The following year, Mather issued a conventional jeremiad called *Perswasions from the Terror of the Lord*, but the subject, "a Sermon Concerning the Day of Judgment," provided an opportunity to develop specific eschatological images. Mather returned to the millennial theme in *The City of Refuge: The Gospel City Explained* (1716), but curiously skirts the issue of America's possible fulfillment of the millennial promises of Scripture, dwelling more particularly on the image of Jesus as a "city of refuge." Finally, in *India Christiana: a Discourse Delivered unto the Commissioners for the Propagation of the Gospel Among the American Indians . . .* (1721), Mather shows that the Scripture prophecies are metaphors in "an Entertainment which they that are *Waiting for the Kingdom of God* will receive as Good News from a Far Country." The progression of eschatological images in this group of treatises clearly shows Mather's movement away from his father's argument that the "new heavens and new earth" would be realized in the immediate future of New England. Indeed, it is surprising that he never changed the predictions of his commentary on Revelation in the "Biblia Americana," which followed William Whiston and Increase Mather in citing 1716 as the year of New England's millennial fulfillment.

Theopolis Americana does identify New England as the spiritual seat of the New Jerusalem but moves quickly to condemn contemporary apostasy which would prevent the realization of prophecy. "Glorious Things are spoken of thee, *O Thou City of God! The Street Be in Thee, O New England: The Interpretation of It, Be Unto You, American Colonies*," Mather declares emphatically, and his doctrine is simple, conventional, reformed chiliasm: "There is an Heavenly *City*, to be inhabited by an *Innumerable Company of Angels*, and by the *Spirits of Just Men Made Perfect* by a Resurrection from the Dead, with *Jesus* the *Mediator of the New Covenant Shining Upon Them; A City*, where, *God Shall Dwell with Men, God Himself Shall be with Them, and We Shall Inherit All Things*. There will be a Time, when that *Holy City* will be nearer to this *Earth* than it is at this Day" (p.2). And that America was once selected for the realization of these promises is echoed throughout the doctrine sections of the sermon-treatise in rhapsodic passages like these: "There is not a *Street* of more *Pure Gold* upon the Face of the Earth at this day, for the *Gospel* generally Preached in the true *Purity* of it, than the *Churches* of *New England*" and "*Praise the Lord, O New England, Praise Thy God*, O American *Zion*, in that He has Bestow'd so many such Gifts upon thee" or "O *America*, will no Share of the Lords *Garments* and *Glories* and the *Righteousness of the Saints*, fall to thee . . .? Yea, the Day is at hand, when that Voice will be heard concerning *Thee, Put On Thy Beautiful Garments, O America, The Holy City!*" (pp. 1-46). Geographic images are drawn from contemporary exploration and shipping to reinforce the prominence of America's fulfillment and destiny: "and as the *Ships Cover the Sea, the Earth*, and thou, *America, too Shall be Filled with the Knowledge of the Glorious Lord*" (p. 47). There is here a sense of unfulfilled promise, the falling short of a predetermined standard that characterized all the jeremiads, and Cotton Mather's eschatology carried the burden of dashed promises, but in one particularly rich passage, he images America's future fulfillment of the Jerusalem eschatology by linking the unfulfilled portions of America's destiny to specific geographical areas of the known world:

There are many Arguments to perswade us, That our Glorious *Lord,* will have an *Holy City* in *America: a City, the Street Whereof will be Pure Gold*. We cannot imagine, that the brave Countries and Gardens which fill the *American Hemisphere,* were made for nothing but a *Place for Dragons*. We may not imagine, That when the *Kingdom of God* is come, and *His Will is done on Earth as it is done in Heaven* . . . a *Balancing Half of the Globe,* shall remain in the Hands of the *Devil* . . . *America* is Legible in these Promises . . . The Kingdom of our *Saviour* becoming a *Great Mountain, that must Fill the Whole Earth,* does particularly fill, and Change, and Bless those Countries which Belong to the *Ten Kingdoms of the Roman Empire* . . . Now, the *American Countries* do belong to some of those *Ten Kingdoms* . . . There have been *Martyrs* of *Christ* in *America* . . . Tho' Austin knew nothing of *America,* yet no *American* could have made a better descant on the Mystery of Our Lords *Garments* . . . than *His* . . . The World, says he, which does *Consist of Four Parts,* will have the *Church of Our Lord Jesus in every Part* (pp. 44-45).

Mather clearly protests too much. His other writings, even the *Magnalia*

Christi Americana (which Perry Miller calls "the most imposing jeremiad of them all") conclude that New England's apostasy has led too far away from the original mission to warrant looking to the future for a fulfill-ment of Scripture promises. But Scripture will also be fulfilled in the coming of the judgment, and Mather's *Perswasions from the Terror of the Lord* warns that the "Day of Judgment [was] typified, in the Fate of the Five Wicked Cities, Gen. XVIII.15. *Will Not the Judge of All the Earth Ex-ecute Judgment?* Yes, there will be a day wherein He will be the Judge of all the Earth; wherein He will Execute Judgment!"[50]

Of course the eschatology of the jeremiad and the chiliasm of Cot-ton and Increase Mather were closely linked, but it is important to distinguish the views of the millennium from those predictions of future doom. Moreover, it is crucial to differentiate between the authoritative certainty with which Increase Mather looked forward to the descent of the new heavens to a restored earth and the insecurity with which Cotton Mather's images suggest eschatological fulfillment. For example, in the richly imagistic *The City of Refuge: The Gospel City Explained,* Mather shows that "The *Land* promised for, and bestowed on, the *Israelitish* Na-tion by the Glorious God, was a *Land Full of Mysteries* . . . And one Remarkable *Glory* of that *Land* was this, that the *Mysteries* of the *Glorious Gospel* were notably represented in the Circumstances of it" (pp. 3-4). But he returns to the typological figure of Canaan as a prefiguration of the New Jerusalem by echoing the trope originally articulated in the "Biblia Americana."

> The *Land* in General was a *Type* of a *Better Country,* that is, *an Heavenly.* The Godly Believers, who *Sojourned* in it, *so considered it!* So Accounted It . . . I am now to point you unto a Glorious *Christ,* as to a *City of Refuge.* It is not with an Arbitrary Conjecture or Opinion, that we propose our *Jesus* as the *Antitype* of such a *City.* We do it upon that sufficient Invitation, Heb. VI.18, *We Have Fled for Refuge, to Lay Hold on the Hope set before Us* (p. 5).

Here Mather invokes the typological scheme to endow the Canaan of Old with prophetic value in terms of the heavenly kingdom to come. But he anchors his association in Scripture, though he departs markedly from the conservative typological scheme by indicating that the faith of the old Israelites included a prophetic knowledge of their Canaan's "typ-ing out" the "better country" that was to come. The remainder of the ser-mon treats the parallels between the Old Testament cities of refuge, those places where accused criminals might retreat to and the antitypical role of Christ as a refuge from sin. It is straightforward exegesis and not especially imagistic if contrasted with the more deliberate metaphors of the *India Christiana.*

India Christiana is Mather's late attempt to reconcile the prophecies of Scripture with the presence of Indians on the American continent before it was settled by the New English Israel. But it also identifies, metaphorically, America as part of the scriptural scheme of chiliastic fulfillment, and it resonates the figural language of Canaan. Composed on the text of Psal. 89:15, "Blessed is the People, that Know the Joyful Sound," the sermon-treatise explores the typology of the trumpet's sound that will (or has already) usher in the millennium. "There is a *Joyful Sound,*" Mather says, "which is to be heard among the Children of Men, where the Gospel is published, and where the *Ordinances* of it are established. The *Sound* of the *Silver Trumpets* which Entertained the Ancient *Israelites* was no less *Typical* than *Musical.* In these Days of the New-Testament, we have the *Substance* of the *Instrumental Musick,* which was of old used in the Worship of God. The *Shadow* vanished away" (p. 2). If this figural assessment indicates why there was no music in the Puritan churches, it also sets the stage for Mather's commentary on the metaphorical value of the ancient sound itself. The "sounding trumpets" are not imminent harbingers of the millennium, as they had been for Increase Mather, but metaphors for grace and the power of salvation. "The *Trumpets* of the *Gospel* call us . . . the *Sound* of this *Trumpet* fetches back the Lost Souls of all the Elect, *From the Power of Satan Unto God.* They are not *Silver Trumpets* that are now *Sounding* unto us; But they are *Saving Trumpets!*" (pp. 4-5).

This conflation of the type and emblem is particularly prominent in one passage where Mather associates the sound of the trumpet with that "new sense of things," as Edwards would call it, that the elect must possess in order to respond to the overtures of grace.

> There are People who *Discern* the *Joyful Sound.* The *Silver Trumpets* of old, were *Distinct and Signal* in the *Sound* thereof . . . There are those under the *Gospel,* to whom our Lord says, . . . *Have Ye Understood All These Things?* And they can reply, *Yea, Lord!* We may say concerning the *Trumpets* of the *Gospel* as was of old said concerning the *Pauline Epistles,* there are in Them, *Some Things Hard to be Understood.* But there are people who do competently *Understand Them.* They readily perceive the *Language of the Trumpets,* about the whole *Mystery of Christ* and the Homage that we owe unto Him. 'Tis not a *Strange Language to Them* . . . Truly, in the *Trumpets* that we have *Sounding from Zion,* we have the *Lord Speaking from Heaven unto Us,* and we have *Right Judgments* in them (pp. 5-14).

This liberal association of allegorical image and type gave Mather's eschatological symbology a new direction. Unlike his father, he was unable to see in the "signs of the times" a clear indication that the kingdom of God, the "New Jerusalem," or "heavenly kingdom," was about to be realized on earth. Rather, he used the figural language of the

Old Testament and New Testament to establish metaphors of God's redemptive process, to prove, through analogy, that the elect might "hear" the sound of the trumpet and "see" the glorious kingdom, even as the world was nearing the time of judgment and destruction.[51] In this process, the epistemological powers of the regenerate perception would understand the sounds and signs of God's approaching climax of earthly history and the commencement of the last days. The imagery of the *India Christiana* agrees with the expanded use of typology found also in the "Biblia Americana," which was composed during the last two decades of Mather's life, reflecting the changing exegetical positions he affirmed from 1710 to 1728. The imagery in both seem to indicate that the heavenly kingdom is not imminent but far away and that its coming will be heralded by a trumpet that will be intelligible only to a regenerate, elect perception. As with the "images and shadows of Divine things" that Edwards would soon find in the natural world, this auditory revelation was restricted to those having the implanted power to receive, through the senses, the impulses of God's divine dispensation. It is significant that the emphasis in *India Christiana* is not on the trumpet's sound as an overt signal of the coming kingdom; rather, it is the sound of an invitation to repentance, out of which will eventually emerge the community of saints gathered into the heavenly kingdom. And the work of the reformed church was to continue the westward course of God's progressive historical pattern: "We may truly say, the *First Planters of New England,* are the *First Preachers* of the Pure Gospel to the *Americans,* that we certainly know of. This *Good Work,* O New-England, thou hast the Honour of making the *First, Right, Fair, and Genuine Beginning* upon it" (*India Christiana,* p. 27). The literal and historical colonizing of America by the Spaniards and the Puritans is subordinated to a metaphorical reading of the past experience. The abrogation of the types of the Old Testament in the destruction of Jerusalem signals for Mather the promise possible in America's future fulfillment of those prophecies, though the fulfillment is treated less literally and more metaphorically or analogically than it had been by Increase Mather:

> The *Jewish Nation* have now lost their *Silver Trumpets* for these many Ages. And in their long Dispersion, how pathetical is their Cry unto us . . . Yea, And how many Protestant Churches have in our Days, had their *Silver Trumpets* forced from them; and instead thereof heard the *Enemies Roaring in the Midst of the Congregations!* Yea, How many Nations are there that never heard the *Joyful Sound!* (pp. 18-19).

But with the coming of truth through the Reformation extended into New England, the sound of the trumpet assumes a new role in signaling the evolution of progressive dispensation:

Blessed the People, who *Know the Joyful Sound:* then we are a *Blessed People* and at the same time we are to be taught to continue so. By Brethren, we have the *Joyful Sound* at such a rate, that it may almost be said of us, as in Deut. IV. 7., *What Nation is There, Who hath God so nigh unto Them?* For the *Silver Trumpets* to be heard sounding as they are in the *American* Regions; *Verily,* 'Tis the Lords Doing, and *Marvellous in Our Eyes* (p. 22).

Thus Cotton Mather's employment of the biblical types extended their meaning, not only in terms of significance for New England history, but also in the context of figural symbolism. Though Increase Mather had held fast to the principles of conservative typological exegesis in his eschatology and his figural reading of contemporary events, Cotton Mather had begun with his father's eschatological vision and had transformed it into historical allegory, so that the events of contemporary history had not only a prefigurative value but were also "spiritualized" to suggest, allegorically, a meaning in the historical perspective if not a realization and fulfillment in the prophetic sense.[52] The apocalyptic vision shared by prophets of the imminent millennium was evolving toward a perception of the end as a spiritual phenomenon, *real* and *true* but not the *literal* coming of heaven down to earth that Increase Mather had predicted. Rather, the apocalyptic metaphors were drawn as parallels to earlier history in order to demonstrate how redemptive patterns would spiral forward toward a teleological future point. As the following chapter will show, the *Magnalia Christi Americana* corroborates this vision, even in its assessment of the events of the seventeenth century, which were past at the time of its composition. In so appearing, the *Magnalia* advanced the course of metaphorical exploration by liberating the biblical figures from the linear confines of Scripture history.[53] In the *Magnalia Christi Americana,* itself a formidable jeremiad, Cotton Mather displayed his most significant use of the biblical analogy, and revealed a penchant for metaphorical construction that would give rise to Jonathan Edwards' transformation of the biblical types into images or shadows of divine things that he found not only in the biblical but also in the scriptural universe.

7

COTTON MATHER'S
MAGNALIA CHRISTI AMERICANA,
"BIBLIA AMERICANA," AND
THE METAPHORS OF
BIBLICAL HISTORY

Modern communities, we have come to learn, have as much need for spiritual cohesion as did the communities of the past; and that need was particularly strong in the new republic: a nation without a past, a people without common customs, a territory without clear boundaries, and an economy without a stable center — variously agrarian, urban, pre-modern, and in transition toward modernization — but with extraordinary opportunities for personal aggrandizement. Surely a major reason for the triumph of the republic was that the need for a social ideal was filled by the typology of America's mission. As this was translated into the language of the times, it provided what we might call the figural correlative to the theory of democratic capitalism. It gave the nation a past and future in sacred history, rendered its political and legal outlook a fulfillment of prophecy, elevated its "true inhabitants," the enterprising European Protestants who had immigrated within the past century or so, to the status of God's chosen, and declared the vast territories around them to be their chosen country.

— Sacvan Bercovitch,
The American Jeremiad

MILLENNIALISM PROVIDES a frame of reference through which modern readers may compare the uses of figural language in the seventeenth and eighteenth centuries. But it is often tempting to conflate the early, literal vision of fulfillment with the more spiritual and metaphorical understanding advanced by transitional writers like Cotton Mather and Jonathan Edwards. The purpose of this chapter is to examine changing conceptions of the language of Canaan as they are reflected in Cotton Mather's *magnum opus,* the *Magnalia Christi Americana* and his manuscript Bible, the "Biblia Americana." Both documents gave new range and power to the eschatological authority of millennial symbols found in Scripture and in contemporary events.

If the dissenters in Europe felt the unifying force of disapprobation and persecution, the immigrants to the New World expressed their purpose in the phrase "an errand into the wilderness." But this sense of mission, the "errand" that was to be performed, provided the first generation of Puritan settlers with more than a principle of unification. This was the New Israel, fleeing the tyranny of Egypt, cast upon the wild seas of the Atlantic by Providence to carry on the work of the Reformation that was yet incomplete in Europe and England, an antitype of Old Israel's shadowy type.

The enthusiasm of the errand is clearly seen by contrasting the sense of retreat that attended William Bradford's writing *Of Plimouth Plantation* with the sense of purpose contained in *A Modell of Christian Charity,* which John Winthrop delivered aboard the *Arbella* as his company journeyed to America in 1630. The theme was a persistent one throughout the vicissitudes of apostasy and faithfulness among the Puritans during the seventeenth century. As late as the 1690s, we find Cotton Mather composing for his *Magnalia Christi Americana:*

> I write the *Wonders of the Christian Religion,* flying from the depravations of *Europe* to the *American Strand;* and, assisted by the Holy Author of that *Religion,* I do, with *Truth* itself, report the *Wonderful Displays* of His *Infinite Power,* Wisdom, Goodness, and Faithfulness, wherewith His Divine Providence hath Irradiated an Indian Wilderness.[1]

Just a few years later, in 1700, Mather delivered the election sermon in Massachusetts Bay Colony on a similar theme:

> There was a people, of whom the God of Heaven said, *This people have I formed for myself, they shall shew forth my praise.* And if there be such a people anywhere under the Cope of Heaven at this Day, 'tis the *English Nation.* But of the *English Nation,* certainly there is no Colony, or Plantation that hath more cause to *Shew Forth the praise* of the Almighty, than that which is now and here Convened.[2]

This account of the New English Israel is conventionally developed with rich metaphors comparing Massachusetts Bay to the Israel of old. Finally, Mather turned to his audience and humorously suggested that the parallels are so exact, that the two elect nations are virtually indistinguishable:

> A people there has been, of whom that Account may be given, *O Lord, Thou hast brought a Vine thou has cast out the Heathen, and planted it: Thou didst cause it to*

take deep *Root, and it filled the Land: She sent out her Boughs unto the Sea, and her Branches unto the River.* My Hearers all this while know not, whether I am giving an Account of *Old Israel,* or of *New England:* So Surprising has been the Parallel![3]

Even in this election sermon, in which Cotton Mather went on to chastize New England for having fallen away from God's commission, the frame of reference is the original "errand into the wilderness."

But if the "errand into the wilderness" had allowed the early immigrants to conceive of themselves as analogous to the Israelites in their exodus from Egypt, it also provided serious problems for the professional theologians among the Puritans, including Cotton Mather, who sought to maintain a proper relation between exegesis, prophetical fulfillment, and the New England experiment. Cotton Mather's grandfather, John Cotton, was fully aware of the numerous analogies between the Israel of the Old Testament and the contemporary Puritan Israelites, but he was continuously striving to define his own migration as a more personal response to God's providential calling. In his writings, John Cotton had stressed the importance of the analogy between Israel and New England in an attempt to predict the imminent coming of Christ and in an effort to prove that New England was the antitypical fulfillment of both Old and New Testament prophecy. Biblical types were invoked to reinforce this parallel at the beginning and at the end of the seventeenth century, but by the 1640s, the emphasis had shifted from purely typological to figural, moral, and exemplary value contained in the types. The Congregational Way became more than a fulfillment of the types; it was also a model for the kingdom of God on earth. For the grandson, the Old Testament parallels to the experience of New England rested entirely on a figural reading of Scripture, an application of the language of Canaan that represented a late effort to restore to contemporary history the authority of Scripture prophecy.

For example, in the afternoon of November 17, 1689, when Cotton Mather stood before his congregation at the North Meeting House in Boston and delivered the sermon on the Old Testament subject of Noah and the ark, his text was Genesis 6-9, but his treatment of the Scripture reflected a tension between his desire to provide a straightforward exegesis and his temptation to offer, through analogy, an application of the Old Testament lesson to the New English Israel.

After an introductory statement, Mather approached the subject of Noah with a metaphor drawn from the New Testament, consistent with the Puritan habit of mind that found resemblances and correspondences between events recorded in the Old Testament and those provided in the New. The preacher declared that "the wise men that of Old were travelling and Enquiring after the Lord Jesus Christ found Him a Babe in Swadling Cloaths and paid Respect unto Him, King of the World. As many as are, and God forbid that any should not be inquisitive after the Holy Child Jesus, may behold Him in the Swadling Cloaths, which the *types* of the Old Testament Enwrapped Him in."[4] He could hardly have done otherwise. The events or persons prefigured, the antitypes, fulfill the earlier shadows and establish a spiritual bond between the two subjects, and Mather's adaptation of the linear paradigm from biblical history resulted in a spiraling, recapitulative model for establishing connections between Old Testament and modern times. This progressive historical association was utilized by Mather to dramatize God's continuous concern for His chosen "New English Israel." Figural writing in Mather's *Magnalia Christi Americana* (1702) is a transformed typological symbolism, an important adaptation of the language of Canaan.

Conservative exegesis and liberal spiritualizing continued to influence each other throughout the latter part of the seventeenth century, so that a number of works represent a mixture of the spiritualized Old Testament and an orthodox exegesis of the types within the same narrative. Moreover, by Cotton Mather's time, the scientific approach to the natural universe not only provided a wholly new epistemology but also tempted writers to combine their perception of God's revelation in nature with more rational explanations of the natural phenomena. Thus the role of Scripture and typology as a pattern for New England's experience in the wilderness became less a vital force in the colonial culture and more an abstracted myth that was nurtured by the guardians of tradition. Although conservative lines of scriptural exegesis were maintained throughout the period by such men as Samuel and Increase Mather, John Davenport and Thomas Shepard, the barriers between spiritualizing and typology were lowered and it had become easier for exegetes to draw upon a variety of epistemological sources in determining the nature of God's revelation. Cotton Mather, whose life bridged the seventeenth and eighteenth centuries, attempted a reconciliation of the scriptural and natural, the typological and the allegorical, even while he continued to read history according to the instituted scheme of type and antitype. Cotton Mather's understanding of the doctrine of the types and the tensions resulting in his epistemology may be seen in his use of the ideas posited by his uncle Samuel in the *Figures or Types of the Old Testament* and in his employment of scriptural analogues as metaphorical symbols in the *Magnalia Christi Americana*.

The congregation before which Mather stood that day in 1689 would have been well prepared to receive a sermon on Noah in which the ark and the church were compared. Among the Puritans of New England, the ark of Noah was commonly regarded to be a type of the

Christian church, but Mather still felt compelled to clarify the typological method of exegesis with a terse explanation:

> Those Christians, that Lived before the Incarnation of Our Lord, had a *Glorious Gospel,* in *Shadows of Good Things to Come.* A *Type* is in short, an *Instituted Resemblance of Gospel Mysteries.* The things which the *Gospel* gives us a naked *Representation* of were veiled under many *Signs* and *Seals* which God made unto his Ancient People as it were Sacraments of *Good Things to Come.* And not only the *Person* of the *Messiah,* but His *Conditions, Endowments,* His *Benefits,* and His *Ordinances,* too, yea, and the *Miseries,* and the *Enemies* from which we are by Him delivered; all of these were preached in and by those *Types* of Old.[5]

Although he tended to exaggerate the particular aspects of Christ's life that were usually included in more conservative systems of typological exegesis, Mather's basic definition corresponds to that set forth earlier by Samuel Mather, whose *Figures or Types* had provided Puritanism with a systematic and conservative approach to the doctrine of typology. Cotton Mather spiritualized the biblical type, or sometimes allegorized a type outside its biblical context and applied it to an issue of life in New England, but he always possessed a sound understanding of scriptural typology and figural language as a basic system of linking the Old and New Testaments. However, his *Work Upon the Ark* explores the ark of Noah as a type of the Congregational Church in New England, which becomes, only by way of analogy to the New Testament Church, its spiritual corollary. By using the types analogically, Mather exceeded the bounds of his father's literal expectations for New England, particularly in Increase's millennial and eschatological treatises, but he balanced some of the traditional distinctions between typology and allegory in composing the *Magnalia* and in writing the "Biblia Americana."

Cotton Mather's most important works reflect this tension in exegesis. The *Magnalia Christi Americana,* first published in 1702, is an ecclesiastical history of New England, complete with individual biographies of the leading persons, cast in the framework of the providentially designed *translatio studii.* It is written with a continuous emphasis on the role of New England in history, which is no more than the earthly fulfillment of God's cosmic design. The second document, the "Biblia Americana" (1700-14?), a manuscript on deposit at the Massachusetts Historical Society, is a translation of the Bible and a ponderous biblical commentary, with numerous digressions to discuss specific matters like the figural language of the Old Testament. This work is especially important in understanding Mather's typology and in showing the significance of Scripture and nature in his reading of New England's providential history.

Mather exhibits very conservative approaches to typology in the "Biblia Americana," and the tightening of his exegetical method is perhaps understandable because he is attempting to explain specific correspondences between the Testaments as they arise in his tedious exegesis. In the "Biblia," he is not specifically concerned with the relations between Old Israel and New England, although there are frequent echoes of the parallels he had established earlier in the *Magnalia Christi Americana*. Cotton Mather was occasionally a "spiritualizer" of the biblical types, and he did indulge a penchant for allegorizing nature (*Agricola*) and he sometimes used the biblical types as simple illustrative examples so that parallels between Old Israel and the New English Israel would appear to have been providentially instituted. In the *Magnalia*, these exegetical correspondences are used as metaphorical controls, and throughout the work, the sense of providential destiny is strong.

Mather's restatement of the "errand" theme as late as the end of the seventeenth century is an important commentary on the development of attitudes among Puritans toward their original mission. Not only was the *Magnalia* designed to glorify the founders of New England; it was also conceived with an awareness that the mission of New England had been designated by Providence, and with a concern for her apostasy from that calling. Mather seems concerned to establish the analogy between New England and the Israel of old, without insisting that New England was the antitypical fulfillment of the scriptural types. While on the one hand he considered New England to be a fulfillment of the promises of Scripture, he was too conscious of the contemporary decline from the Reformation ideals to view her as wholly antitypical. Although Mather's reading of contemporary history in the light of biblical exegesis represents an extension of scriptural typology into modern times, his *use* of the types was only illustrative and spiritual. Unlike John Cotton, who had regarded New England to be the antitype of Old Israel and who expected the imminent return of Christ, Cotton Mather established the analogy between New England and Israel without insisting so strongly that Massachusetts Bay was to be transformed into the millennial kingdom. Therefore his use of the types suggests that imitation of the Israelite theocracy would have only moral or spiritual significance, so that New England could not flatter herself into believing that she had come to fulfill all the promises of Scripture. Nevertheless, Mather's belief in the divine appointment of New England and the resonances of prophetic, figural language are found throughout the *Magnalia*: "The *leader* of a *People* in a *Wilderness* had need been a *Moses*," he declares, "and if a *Moses* had not led the people of *Plymouth Colony*, when this worthy person was their governour, the people had never with so much unanimity and importunity still called *him* to lead them."[6] William Bradford is only one of the many Puritan leaders for whom such biblical analogues have been established. Throughout the *Magnalia*, Mather associates Israel with New England and indicates the correspondences between their leaders. Of John Winthrop, he writes:

> Accordingly when the *noble design* of carrying a colony of *Chosen People* to an *American* Wilderness, was by *Some* Eminent Persons undertaken, *this eminent person* was, by the consent of all, *chosen* for the *Moses,* who must be the leader of so great an undertaking; and, indeed, nothing but a *Mosaic spirit* could have carried him through the *temptations,* to which either his *farewel* to his *own land,* or his *travel* in a *strange land,* must needs expose a gentleman of his *education.* [7]

In a history that so naturally emerges from the lives of eminent persons, the leaders of Israel were natural scripture-analogues for Mather to employ. But with such divergent contemporary figures as Bradford and Winthrop being compared to the same biblical type, the value of the comparison would have to be moral and spiritual rather than typologically precise. In the life of John Cotton, another Moses analogue is presented, and Mather even included Woodbridge's poetical description of John Norton, Cotton's successor, who is compared to Joshua, Moses' successor:

> Though *Moses* be, yet *Joshua* is not dead:
> I mean renowned *Norton;* worthy he,
> Successor to our *Moses,* is to be.
> O happy *Israel* in *America,*
> In such a Moses, such a Joshua. [8]

Rather than establish New England as a typological reincarnation of ancient Israel, Mather uses the biblical figures metaphorically and morally, to organize the *Magnalia* around certain prominent themes that were common to the scriptural and the contemporary situations. For example, he declares that "the most *crooked way* that ever was gone, even that of *Israel's* peregrination *through* the *wilderness,* may be called a *Right Way,* such was the *way* of this *little Israel,* now going into a wilderness," and he uses the parallel between Israel and New England to accommodate and illustrate God's providential concern through the history of redemption. [9]

The lives of eminent men become Mather's most prominent means of securing New England's place in providential history. "Mather dissolves history into biography," concluded Peter Gay in *A Loss of Mastery,* but the objective remained constant: to prove that New England and her people stood in a particular relation to God. In the introduction to the biography of his father, Increase, Mather posits a methodology for historical writing that he had earlier followed in composing the *Magnalia:*

I know not how the *Pen* of an *Historian* can be better Employ'd, than in Repor-
ting the *Vertuous* Tempers and Actions of the Men that have therein *shown forth
the Vertues of* our Blessed *Redeemer,* and been the *Epistles of Christ* unto the rest of
Mankind. Nor indeed has Mankind generally found any sort of *History* more
Useful and more *Grateful,* than what has been given in the *Lives* of Men that
have been distinguished by an *Excellent Spirit.* The *Best of Books* does very
much Consist of such an *History!*[10]

Mather is here answering John Oldmixon's attack on the *Magnalia,* but
his conviction that history should be the biography of saints derives from
a belief that scripture history worked in this manner. While establishing
the analogues for the life of William Phips, he was even more explicit in
revealing his method. "So *obscure* was the *original* of that memorable person, whose *actions* I am going to relate," he says, "that I must, in a way of
writing, like that of *Plutarch,* prepare my reader for the intended relation,
by first searching the *archives* of antiquity for a *parallel.*"[11] These archives
included the Old Testament, Greek and Roman mythology, and a
number of figures from ancient history. The sense that history has
become for Mather a spiraling process of progressive regeneration in no
way violates his view that the types of Scripture were fulfilled and
abrogated by Christ; rather, it complements his traditional and conservative interpretation of the biblical figures. Not only did Mather regard
the history of New England to be evidence of God's continuing Providence as a leader for his New Chosen; he attempted to use the Scripture
parallels metaphorically and spiritually to establish specific parallels between New England and Israel. This represented a desperate cry for a
return to the original mission in an age when natural science and other
modes of historical epistemology were coming into prominence, and the
metaphorical control of an "errand into the wilderness" provided the
ideal setting for the writing of history by way of biography. Not only are
personal analogies developed with biblical types; the wilderness itself is
employed as a metaphor for the natural environment of New England
throughout the work. Puritans considered the forests to be the dwelling
place of Satan and frequently justified their expeditions against the Indians by ascribing to them satanic influences. In the *Magnalia,* one learns
that the wilderness is an aspect of the eternal war between good and evil;
it provides a setting in which the Christian *peregrinus* may find his way
back home to God. If the *Magnalia* is read closely, one can discover the
systematic linking of the wasteland and its natural elements to spiritual
(and sometimes scriptural) analogues. For example, the "*wilderness* having always had *serpents* in it" is compared to the forces of evil and to the
devil.[12]

   Cotton Mather used his Old Testament in two distinct senses in the
Magnalia. First, he was thoroughly aware of the abrogation of the types

in Christ, and he recognized the totally distinct mission of New England in her errand into the wilderness. But his sense of history and his conception of the progressive nature of God's revelation led him to make continuous associations between the Old Testament, the ancients, and contemporary events. Since he did not affirm that New England was antitypical or a fulfillment of the scripture types and since he avoided suggesting that New England was a *fulfillment* of the future kingdom, his use of typology was designed to establish a system of analogues between historical periods, the one illuminating the other. Moreover, if contemporary events could be identified by reading ancient and biblical history to discover parallels, it could also be asserted that New England was moving forward toward a preordained end, known only to God. In this context, the new world, New England, and the "errand into the wilderness" were repeated historical episodes in the larger framework of the history of redemption. His foremost objective was to show that New England was under continuous providential guidance, and the purpose of the parallels with pagan history was primarily illustrative; Mather did not consider Greek or Roman history to be guided by Providence, from which both Israel and New England received direction. Mather's adaptation of Plutarch's reading of history by way of the lives of prominent individuals and special events was not unique; however, his sense of history as a process of repetition within a teleological destination must be understood in the unique context of Puritan eschatology. The warning implicit in this magnificent jeremiad is that only by a return to the original calling would New England enjoy release from current disaster, which was surely the reproof of a displeased Lord. Reorientation, however, would insure the role of New England in the grander history of the work of redemption.

Typology, then, becomes the key by which moral examples from the Old Testament are accommodated to the New English Israel and to posterity. Cotton Mather's way of reading history may have utilized the types to elucidate contemporary events, but it did not destroy his scholarly sense of biblical and exegetical typology. In the *Magnalia*, we find a few allusions to typological exegesis as a system for interpreting Scripture, and sometimes the allusions help clarify the reader's understanding of the doctrine as Mather conceived it: "In our asserting, a matter of the *Old Testament*, to have been *typical*, 'tis not needful, that we be always able to particularize any *future mysteries* of the *New Testament* therein referred unto; *truths* which were then of a *present* consideration, were sometimes represented in the *types* then used among the people of God, which helps to understand the case."[13] In the tradition of exegesis established by the early Church Fathers, Mather attempts to show how the types of the Old Testament were a means of God's revelation to those people living before the incarnation:

Although the *Work* of *Redemption* was not actually wrought by Christ, till after his incarnation, yet the virtue, efficacy, and benefits thereof, were communicated unto the elect in all ages successively from the beginning of the world, in and by those promises, types and sacrifices wherein he was revealed and signified to be the seed of the Woman, which should bruise the Serpent's head, and the Lamb slain from the beginning of the world, being yesterday and to day the same, and for ever.[14]

More often, however, Mather is concerned to employ typology for moral and illustrative purposes. In the general introduction to the *Magnalia,* he posits a methodology for utilizing the types in the *Magnalia* and asserts the way that he intends to relate the history of Israel to that of other ancient peoples in establishing analogues for New England:

Assisted by the Holy Author of that *Religion,* I do, with all conscience of *Truth,* itself, report the *wonderful displays* of His Infinite Power, Wisdom, Goodness, and Faithfulness, wherewith His Divine Providence hath irradiated an *Indian Wilderness* . . . Certainly, it will not be ungrateful unto good men, to have innumerable *Antiquities, Jewish, Chaldee, Arabian, Grecian* and *Roman,* brought home to us, with a *sweet light* reflected from them on the *word,* which is our *light;* or, to have all the *typical* men and things in our *Book of Mysteries,* accommodated with their *Antitypes:* or, to have many hundreds of references to our dearest *Lord Messiah,* discovered in the writings which *testifie of Him,* oftner than the most of mankind have hitherto imagined: or, to have the *histories* of *all ages* hitherto, of the divine *Prophecies,* as far as they have been fulfilled; and not meer *conjectures,* but even mathematical and incontestible *demonstrations,* given of *expositions* offered upon the *Prophecies,* that yet remain to be accomplished.[15]

Although Cotton Mather published no document similar to Samuel Mather's *Figures or Types of the Old Testament,* so that we cannot examine his typology by comparing a single work with his uncle's treatise, it is possible to discern in the *Magnalia* the influence of the *Figures or Types* and to explore further the continuity of conservative exegesis in the "Biblia Americana."

On February 10, 1714, Mather wrote in his *Diary,* "It seems now high time for me, to come into Action, and to do what my Hand finds to do, that the *Biblia Americana,* may be brought forth into the World. Lett me therefore publish a Sheet, entitled, *A New Offer, to the Lovers of Religion and Learning* [published in 1714], therein giving an Account of the work, and so an Opportunity for Subscriptions towards the Encouragement of it; and not only spread Copies of that *offer,* thro' this Countrey, but also send them to *Europe*" (ii, 283). A less specific proposal for the "Biblia Americana" had appeared in *Bonifacius* in 1710, and as early as 1706, Mather had written in his *Diary* (i, 570), "I compose (and by the Fleet now going for *England*, I send over to be published,) an Account of my *Biblia Americana*" (i, 570).[16]

The projected American Bible never materialized. The manuscript occupies six ponderous volumes and has never been organized or catalogued and indexed. But in the *New Offer to the Lovers of Religion and Learning*, Mather had predicted twelve divisions for the "Biblia Americana," including "IV. The TYPES of the Bible, accommodated with their *Antitypes*: And this Glorious Book of God, now appearing a Field, that yields a marvellous Mixture of Holy *Profit* and *Pleasure*, in those Paragraphs of it, which have sometimes appeared the least Fruitful with Instruction."[17] Not only was the "Biblia Americana" never published, it hardly achieved the impressive format outlined in the *New Offer*, even in manuscript.

Despite Cotton Mather's immense energies, the projected plan in the *New Offer* when compared to the six-volume manuscript of the "Biblia Americana" would indicate that the project was too formidable for a single man to complete. Although materials are included in the "Biblia Americana" that are foreshadowed under the titles designated by the *New Offer*, most appear to be digressions from the main business of exegeting the Scriptures in a most ordinary manner. Here and there Cotton Mather's genius for synthesizing wide-ranging ideas is evident; for example, in handling the many problems of the Exodus, he presents a clear summary of the ceremonies and persons to be given typological recognition in his exegesis. His position throughout the "Biblia Americana" is extremely conservative, and his reliance on the typology of Samuel Mather is everywhere present. Moreover, he sometimes directly refers to his uncle's work by suggesting that the reader turn to the *Figures or Types* for further illumination. In his conclusion of a lengthy discussion of the typology of feasts and ceremonies, for example, he remarks: "It is now time for mee to acknowledge, that in those *Illustrations*, the discourse of my uncle, *Samuel Mather*, on *ye Types of Ye Old Testament*, have not a little assisted mee."[18]

Typology as a separate subject was only a facet of the overall design of the "Biblia Americana." Originally planned to be a translation of the Bible and an exhaustive commentary on the whole body of Scripture, the six folio volumes are subdivided into many seemingly diverse parts. They contain no table of contents or index to specify the classification of information. However, Mather's literal-minded approach to the historical episodes of the Bible is reflected in his inclusion of a variety of tables and graphs. This kind of fidelity to historical truth is central to a conservative doctrine of typology, and Mather's opinions concerning the types appear frequently enough in the "Biblia Americana" to show his latent conservatism as a biblical exegete; even while his eschatological writings were less literal in their anticipation of a spiritual millennium:

Book VII. This *First Promise* was afterwards expanded in very many prophecies of the *Messiah*. The *Prophecies* are with an amazing artifice interwoven
with other matter. God instructing . . . [of the] Glorious one. The Bible is
filled with the *Prophecies* and the most particular circumstances of the *Glorious* . . . Coming anew with the *New Testament* we find them all most punc-
tually accomplished.[19]

But Cotton Mather was the product of a generation that had been ex-
posed to the rationalist philosophy of John Locke, so that he could
hardly have read either Scripture or nature in precisely the same manner
as his uncle Samuel. For example, in a digression entitled "The Harmony of the Gospels," Mather provides a somewhat scientific appraisal
of the creation and its perception by man:

There is in the creation, abundance of *Invisible* matter and motion. The Great
God could have made ye matter which is most *Invisible* by man, to have been
seen, in all the minute and curious terms, of it. He who found the *Light*, and
the *Soul*, could have made ye fibre of ye *nerves*, in such a delicate manner, even
in this life (which probably may be done, for ye Celestial Body) as to give man
a kind of *Natural Microscope*. But for His own *Divine Substance*, we cannot see it.
We cannot hope for the sight.[20]

Moreover, there are occasional places where the typology of Samuel
Mather appears to have been allegorized, abstracted from the Old
Testament context for the purpose of illustrating a point of argument. In
some instances, Cotton Mather has subverted the biblical types as exegetical instruments and has used them as moral or representative examples, even as Samuel Mather had allowed when a type was initially
endowed with moral equity. For example, there is the discussion of
Abraham, where the patriarch serves not only as a type of Christ to
come but also as a Christian *peregrinus* making his way from the earthly
city of Babylon to the heavenly city of Jerusalem.[21]

This extension of the typological symbol beyond the limits of the
biblical context to represent a Christian pilgrimage was not unknown to
either Samuel or Cotton Mather; John Bunyan's *Pilgrim's Progress* was
popular literature throughout the late seventeenth century. Although in
the preface Bunyan declares that he "speaks by types," his work is clearly
a sustained allegory, and his narrative a fiction representing the progress
of the Christian soul toward salvation. It is interesting to find this kind of
extended typology in Mather's "Biblia Americana," where aspects of the
literal and historical situation are endowed with allegorical significance,
suggested in Mather's final remarks on Abraham. In all other respects,
the treatment of Abraham is thoroughly historical in its presentation of
the typological correspondences.

Occasionally, we find Mather's deliberate attempts to reconcile
typology and the allegorizing of the Old Testament. His mystical inter-

pretation of the creation story approaches spiritualizing in certain parts. He declares, for example, that

> The marriage between *Adam* and *Eve* was a Sacrament. (Eph. 5:32) of the Intercourse between the Lord Jesus Christ, and his church. There is a *Mystical Marriage* between the Lord and His people; the Song of Solomon, the Forty-Fifth Psalm (with 2 Cor. ii:2) are lively descriptions of it. *Eve* was taken out of Adam, and the Lord with His Church, makes but *one* (Eph. 5:30). *Adam* was *Asleep* when *Eve* was formed out of him; and yee Lord was cast into a deep, dead *Sleep*, for three days, by which means *Hee* procured a Church unto himself (Tit. 2:14). The side of *Adam* was opened, that Eve might be fetched out, and the Blood of Our Lord, which purchased His Church for Him, came out of *His Opened Side* (Joh. 19:34).[22]

In the same allegorical vein, there is a particularly illuminating allusion to the Garden of Eden in which Mather abandons typological correspondences altogether and finds only metaphorical value in the Garden, which he endows with specific allegorical significance: "And ye Church is the *Tillage* of Our Lord Before Christ, as the *Garden* was of *Adam*. (Compare Gen. 2:15 with Cant. 4:16)" (I, n.p.).

Generally, however, Mather's whole aim in the "Biblia Americana" was to develop a conservative doctrine of scriptural exegesis through allusion to pagan mythology, typology, and commentaries by other hands. Therefore his digressions into allegorizing, while significantly different from his exegesis of Scripture typologically, must be viewed as being representative of his concern to utilize every available epistemological means for the accommodation of spiritual truth. For example, without discarding the typological significance of the sabbath, Mather insists on the moral equity of the instituted day of rest and shows how it has meaning for the Massachusetts theocracy. In commenting on Paul's Epistle to the Hebrews, he says:

> There is a state of Glorious and Wonderful Rest. Which our Blessed Jesus, which will give unto His Church in that *Great Millennial Sabbath* . . . every Rest mentioned in the Scripture as already obtained by the People of God, was but a *Type* of the *Rest* which *Yett Remains* to *bee*, expected and obtained . . . It followes, then, that there must *Remain a Rest*, beyond all this, which Our Lord Jesus Christ, will bring his people unto, even that *Rest* all this was a *Figure* of (IV, n.p.).

The problem that Thomas Shepard had devoted several hundred pages to solving was no stranger to Cotton Mather. After Christ's coming, should the sabbath be observed despite the abrogation of all types and ceremonial institutions by the coming of the flesh? Both Cotton and Samuel Mather show how the sabbath as an instituted day of rest was not wholly abrogated by Christ, because it is a perpetual symbol shadowing forth the rest that is to be given the true believer at the conclusion of all history.

Mather's reading of the types does not render isolated images of Christ. The preacher makes clear that the Old Testament has a teleological role in the redemption of the world and that it is incorporated into a broader scheme of creation and restoration than the literal narrative would indicate. He insists that the law and the Gospel are dispensations by the same author, just as Samuel Mather had regarded the Old and the New Testaments to be products of a single spirit. He says that

> The *Law of Moses* was established on many rites, to be observed nowhere but in the *Land of Canaan* . . . But yett we must consider these things, as a method of providence, working toward the *great end always in view*, even the *Generall Restoration of Mankind from the Curse of the Fall*, and the opening of that *Scheme* of the *Divine Proceedings*, which was to bring a blessing upon all the *Nations of the Earth*. Accordingly, when *Abraham* received the promises, he had assurance given him, not only of *Peculiar Blessings to Himself* and his *Offspring* but also of a *General Blessing* to be convey'd thro' him to all Mankind (IV, n.p.).

Both the law and the Gospel, their covenants and the typological correspondences through which they are manifested to mankind, are part of a divine plan for the reorientation of mankind in the post-lapsarian condition. In a concluding paragraph treating the typological significance of the creation, Mather asserts that *"Adam in Losing, Adam in Hurting,* is a figuration of *our Lord Jesus Christ in Gaining, Helping, Saving.* From *Adam wee derive sin* (Gen. 5:3) but *Grace* (Joh. 3:16) from *Our Lord Jesus Christ*, From *Adam*, wee derive *Death;* (Rom. 5:18), but *Life* (Joh. 3:36) from Our Lord Jesus Christ. Yea, the Confusion which is brought upon the World by *Adam*, shall bee one day, by our Lord Jesus Christ, repaired" (I, n.p.).

Once this basic pattern of exegetical correspondences has been established, it is easier for the reader to see how the "Biblia Americana" reflects a systematic typology in other specific instances of exegetical commentary. Mather's doctrine of the types appears prominently in his exegesis of the Old Testament, and in his treatment of the book of Hebrews in the New. Moreover, his commentary on certain passages from Galatians, provided in connection with his exegesis of Genesis, gives an impression of the kinds of correspondences he sought to establish between the Testaments. In the exegesis of Galatians 4:24, he writes:

> The differences and the properties of the *Two Covenants* are from *Abraham*

exhibited unto us. (Gal. 4:24) In *Hagar*, wee see the *Covenant of Works. Hagar was a Bondwoman;* Thus, wee are entangled in *Bondage* if wee are united unto the *First Covenant. Hagar* had a child, by the *Strength of Nature.* Thus, wee are under the *Old Covenant* . . . [which] must be *Cast off* . . . *And Abraham* indeed may turn aside unto *Hagar,* thus a beleever may have some Acting, as under the *Covenant of Works.* But, hee was with *Sarah.* The *Covenant of Grace,* wee see, in her. This *Covenant* has the *Freedom of Sarah in it,* the *Divine Assurance & Influence* that *Sarah* had (I, n.p.).

This interpretation of the relationship between the covenants is the traditional one, first established by St. Paul in Galatians and preserved in the exegesis of more orthodox commentators. But the framework within which Cotton Mather developed his own conception of the typological correspondences was extended to incorporate some rather fanciful analogies. Like Samuel Mather, Cotton was concerned to accommodate not only the literal and figurative meaning of Scripture to his readers but also to open to them the doctrine of the types. Samuel Mather had explained Samson as a type of Christ, for example, by comparing him to the mythical Hercules; Cotton Mather provides a similar kind of exegesis when he interprets Abraham's sacrifice of Isaac. Although he would have the sacrifice typify God's willing sacrifice of His own son, Mather allows his penchant for explaining the spiritual meaning of a literal text to carry him away from the straightforward correspondences recorded in the two Testaments. Characteristically, he begins with a thorough and detailed analysis of the biblical text itself, so that we have no doubt of the historical veracity of the story about Isaac and Abraham given in Genesis 22, nor should we misunderstand the typological correspondences between Isaac and Jesus:

Amazing the History, which we have, of Isaac's obedience *His Father* said, *My Son You Must Bee A Burnt Offering Unto the Lord.* Behold, without any Replying without any repining, hee submitts unto that strange demand. This hee did, tho' hee were twenty-five years old at least. And yett, this was but a little shadow of what Our Lord Jesus did. His *Father* said, *My Son, Become Thou a Burnt Offering that My Justice May be Satisfied, & Glorified Forever.* Well, Hee complies, without any resistance, without any reluctance. His answer was, *Lord, I come* (Isa. 53:7 and Joh. 10:18).[23]

Once the general correspondences have been established, however, Mather proceeds to examine the text in such detail that he digresses into a discussion of some fanciful analogies between the Old and New Testament episodes that borders, at times, on allegory. For example, when he explains the origin and purposes of the ram in the sacrifice, he not only indicates a mysterious prefiguration of the atonement, but specifically asserts that the ram and Isaac together represent the dual nature of Christ, the Divine and the Human Jesus:

> Q. What singular Mystery was there in ye *Ram,* caught & kill'd by *Abraham,* for a *Sacrifice?*
> A. In the sacrifice offered by *Abraham,* wee must consider it was the *Ram* that felt the *Knife.* This admirably answers to the two natures of Our Lord Jesus Christ; both of which together contribute unto the Sacrifice of the New Covenant. The *Divine Nature* of Our Lord, suspending the Expressions of His Power & His Glory, was the Mystery of Isaac ty'd. The *Humane Nature* of Our Lord, crucify'd, was the mystery of the Ram slain, So Remarkable a concurrence of things, that it is ascribed entirely unto the contrivance of Almighty God, *The Lord Will Provide.*[24]

This interpretation of the role of the sacrificial ram in the Genesis account of Isaac's sacrifice represents a departure from the typological correspondences established by Samuel Mather in the *Figures or Types.* Although the type has not itself been "spiritualized" to represent an abstraction in the Platonic manner, an aspect of the type has been endowed with allegorical significance extraneous to the usual typological adumbration. In Samuel Mather's account, there are no references to the special powers of the ram in the sacrifice of Isaac, and there is no attempt to indicate that the ram and Isaac adumbrate the dual nature of Christ.

In the 1689 sermon, *Work Upon the Ark,* Cotton Mather had stated that "Noah's Ark was a Type of the Church." His interest in the typology of Noah and the ark had not diminished over the years between 1689 and the completion of the "Biblia Americana." One of the most extensive examples of his typology is given in the exegesis of Genesis 7, 8, and 9 and it is interesting to compare his views of the types provided in the earlier sermon with his judgments about typology abstracted from this portion of the commentary in the "Biblia Americana."

In the *Work Upon the Ark,* Mather had indulged his penchant for allegorizing details, although he had ostensibly set out to define typology and to provide his congregation with some examples of orthodox typological correspondences taken from the Genesis account of the ark. One example will suffice here; while explaining how the ark became a type of the Christian church, Mather begins to record the significance of each part of the ark and to allegorize all the physical dimensions of the construction. He says:

> As a ship is by *Humane* ingenuity, often made a Resemblance of the *Church,* so the *Ark,* which was a *Sort of Ship,* is by *Divine Authority,* exhibited as a Figure or Shadow of it. They compare the *Pump* in a *Ship* to *Repentance,* which fetches

out the *Corruption* that endangers our souls. They compare the *Sails*, to our *Affections*, in which when the *Wind* of the Holy Spirit Blows, we are carried swiftly on to the *Harbour of Eternal Blessedness*. The *Rudder,* that *May* be *Compared* unto the *Tongue of Man;* the *Compass,* that *May* be *Compared* unto the *Word* of *God*. But These *Comparisons* are innumerable, as they that have read *Navigation Spiritualized* by some worth[y] English Writer must needs be sensible; and I hope ever[y] Gracious Mariner does accustome himself to such reflections.[25]

Mather has provided his congregation with excerpts from John Flavel's *Navigation Spiritualized* as a gloss for his presentation of the typological significance of Noah's ark. Although he would not have us abandon the historically oriented pattern of prefiguration and fulfillment, he does concede the value of allegorizing in the accommodation of spiritual truth. This was, of course, an important achievement. The direct mention of Flavel's companion piece for *Husbandry Spiritualized*—the model for his own *Agricola, or the Religious Husbandman*—indicates how Mather had drawn some of his own metaphors from Flavel's practice of allegorizing nature, and that he would attempt a synthesis of the kind of metaphorical analogies drawn by Flavel and the spiritualizers with the more conservative emphasis on biblical typology.

In the "Biblia Americana," Mather also used allegorical and metaphorical comparisons to reinforce his exegesis of the typological correspondences, despite the generally conservative plan of the work. However, the thrust of this massive commentary was to establish figural language within the framework of an orthodox and traditional exegesis, so that the examination of Noah and the ark is more straightforward than the earlier mixture of typology and spiritualizing had been. There is a tightening of his typology into a quasi-systematic form in the "Biblia Americana," which can partially be explained as a late effort by Mather to hold together a way of reading history and a method of exegeting Scripture that had already been weakened when he first came to know it. "The *Ark* will prove a *Type* of Our *Saviour* out of whom there is no *Salvation*," he declares, and his way of accommodating this doctrine is to link the flood to Christian baptism in a manner that utilizes ingenious allegorical correspondences.[26] As the water buoys up the ark, so the soul of the regenerate is buoyed up by the water of baptism. However, the correspondences established for the flood and baptism within this framework are always set in a linear, historical relation to each other, and they are metaphorically associated in such a way that the antitypical significance of the latter concludes the former.

This systematizing of the typological correspondences in the "Biblia Americana" should not be construed as a change in Mather's exegetical method late in his career. Cotton Mather was significantly influenced by his father's more conservative doctrinal positions, and it must be remembered that the earlier *Work Upon the Ark* was written in the same period when he composed the diatribe against witchcraft, *Providences Related to Witchcraft and Possessions.* Throughout his writing, there is a sense that underneath the natural universe there lies a spiritual significance that wants explanation. However, Mather's interest in the allegorical meaning of natural events was characteristically Puritan; it does not conflict with a reading of Scripture that rejects the allegorical mode for a system of correspondences that are related through historical time. On the contrary, Mather combined the allegorical sense with the typological reading of the two Testaments to render an exegesis that was clearly traditional if occasionally accommodated by the establishing of an allegorical analogy. In the earlier sermon, for example, the features of the ark were allegorized to reinforce the typological correspondence between the ark and the church; in the "Biblia Americana" the important correspondences are maintained throughout the exegesis, while spiritualized aspects of the Genesis account receive only limited attention. The range of Mather's theological concerns was bound to lead to an exploration of alternative modes of epistemological fulfillment; however, the mainstream of his exegesis from the *Work Upon the Ark* to the *Magnalia Christi Americana* to the "Biblia Americana" reflects a respect for the traditional correspondences of orthodox typology, with only an occasional interest in the spiritualized symbols used by writers like John Flavel. He never abandoned his strong faith in a prophetic and eschatological view of history, in which his doctrine of the types was firmly rooted. All human history was to be assessed in the light of its relation to God's divine plan. Cotton Mather himself said, "The *Covenant* of God lives at ye *Bottom* of *All.*"[27] Figural writing—typological and allegorical— was designed by God as a vehicle for revealing the divine plan to a regenerate perception, as Jonathan Edwards was to articulate in his *Treatise Concerning Religious Affections* and dramatize in the sermon-series that formed the *History of the Work of Redemption.* Cotton Mather's *Magnalia* and "Biblia" were clear examples of the tensions present in millennial thinking and figural expression at the end of the seventeenth century. The jeremiad dominated sermon literature and influenced the writing of history as theologians looked less forward to the optimistic fulfillment of scriptural promises and found increasing evidence of impending doom in signs of the times. Cotton Mather's employment of scriptural language in a new metaphorical context provided the possibility of a spiritual millennium and gave rise to interpretations of history that would restore to the language of prophecy the authority of Scripture. It would remain for Edwards and the New Light Calvinists to make full use of the synthesis between natural and scriptural revelation begun in Cotton Mather's writings.

8

JONATHAN EDWARDS
AND THE GREAT AWAKENING

Mors stupebit et natura
Cum resurget creatura
Judicanti responsura

— Hector Berlioz, *Grande Messe des Morts*

Biblical history is completely internalized and the entire text becomes
no more than a sustained metaphoric vehicle for the powers, states,
conflicts, and processes of individual minds in the course of their experience on earth . . . No less than its beginning and middle, the
apocalyptic end of the Biblical text signifies a personal and inner experience, not a generic and outer event. "Now the second *Adam* Christ,
hath taken the Kingdom my body, and rules in it; *He makes a new heaven,
and a new earth, wherein dwells Righteousnesse*, . . . And this is to be made a
new creature, in whom old corrupt lusts are passed away, and every
power in him is a new power." When in the fulness of time this power
shall triumph in the spirit of all individuals, then shall the prophecies
of Revelation be fulfilled: "And when this universall power of
Righteousnesse is spread in the earth," the world shall be *"a Land
flowing with milke and honey,* plenty of all things, every one walking
righteously in the Creation to another . . . as it was in the beginning."
. . . Consonantly, the restored paradise of the Apocalypse will not be a
location outside this world to which we will be transferred after death;
it will be this world itself, as experienced by our redeemed and glorified
senses in our earthly existence. "And now in this new heaven and new
earth, he himself who is the King of Righteousnesse doth dwel and rule
. . . O ye hear-say Preachers, deceive not the people any longer, by
telling them that this glory shal not be known and seen, til the body is
lain in the dust. I tel you, this great mystery is begun to appear, and it
must be seen by the material eyes of the flesh: And those five senses
that is in man, shall partake of this glory."

— M. H. Abrams, *Natural Supernaturalism*

THE TYPOLOGICAL systems developed by New England
writers from 1630 to 1650 were necessary precedents for their
understanding of America's historic role in establishing the
kingdom and planting the seeds of the New Jerusalem. But the typology
of the millennium and the rich imagery associated with it in early

American writing have often been overlooked because millennialism, like typology, is an inexact prophetic system that needs constant clarification. Millennial symbols provided a host of interpretations for current events from the early New England Puritans to the Civil War, affirming that the pressure on language to explain historical movements arose not only out of the changes brought by the events, but also out of the necessity for each generation to reconcile traditional scriptural mythology with contemporary developments in the interpretation of God's revealed will. For example, premillennial writing, with its emphasis on the judgment, developed visions of the future with proofs derived from selected scriptural prophecy, with imagery drawn primarily from Daniel and Revelation. But Jonathan Edwards and his postmillennial disciples argued a historical sequence from the scriptural types that placed the millennium before the judgment and put the Calvinists in the position of providing American theology with a radical justification for early nationalism.[1] Though the premillennialism of the Mathers stressed the decline of contemporary piety and the imminence of the judgment, Edwards argued that the beauty and perfection revealed through nature *and* Scripture to a regenerated perception was a prophetic synecdoche of the future redemption of the world. Like modern charismatic and "born again" Christian groups, Edwards and the New Lights regarded man's life after rebirth to be an instrument of the Spirit. The conviction that their present lives prophesied future fulfillments was the deepest impulse of the New Light movement. New Lights read their Bibles to understand what future blessings God had revealed in the words and lives of His chosen peoples. Unlike the premillennialists, they used sermons, histories, poetry, autobiography, and biography not to lament the present order so much as to propel their audiences toward the realization of the New Jerusalem. The Great Awakening aroused millennial spiritualism, and Edwards' party showed that paradise could be realized in America by a transformation of society and a restoration of the human soul. Moreover, they justified their conclusions with scriptural arguments that extended the historical boundaries of the typological system into the modern world even while they explored the contemporary scene for signs that the cycles of millennial revolution were about to commence.

The two American dreams—those of the spiritual "errand into the wilderness" so commonly associated with the Puritan impulse to establish a "city upon a hill," and the more contemporary economic democracy that has attracted waves of immigrants to American shores since the first writing of the *Constitution*—have more to do with each other than one might think. The rationalist eighteenth century witnessed a secularizing of the original errand impulse, a transformation reflected in the contrast between Joel Barlow's own *Prospect of Peace* (1778) and *The Columbiad* (1806), but the language of America's mission remained spiritual and biblical, pastoral and edenic, even following the loss of pietistic force that accompanied the rise of technological progress and promised a new form of millennial order and harmony at the close of the eighteenth century.

The seventeenth-century writers had not employed the Bible as a contrivance by which they would give their "errand into the wilderness" prestige or divine sanction; rather, they believed that history worked in cycles and that their own historical period could foreshadow the second coming of Christ just as ancient Israel had prefigured his first coming. In the first-century histories, culminating in Mather's *Magnalia Christi Americana* (1702), New England leaders are not only made analogous to Old Testament patriarchs; they are also drawn as exemplary saints who possess an instituted continuity with their earlier prefigurations in Old Testament history. Thus, as Sacvan Bercovitch has shown, John Winthrop was transformed by the rhetoric of Cotton Mather's *Magnalia* into *Nehemias Americanus,* not merely likened unto Nehemiah; rather, Nehemiah becomes a prototype of the American self.[2] The comparison of Old Israel to New England did not end with a few obvious parallels like the metaphorical associations found in the histories. Once accepted and understood to be the foundation of early New England's self-conception, the typological system allowed the settlers to predict future events based on a reading of the Bible and an evaluation of "signs of the times" prophesied in the two testaments. If the Old Testament is filled with prophecy about the coming of the Messiah, then the Puritan migration, so clearly a recapitulation of the first dispensation, must foreshadow the second coming and the millennium.

The biblical frame of reference out of which New England had been developed stated clearly that all human history was a divine drama, and that life was simply a pilgrimage from Babylon to the holy city of Jerusalem. Thus the expectations were always futuristic, and the Great Awakening provided another opportunity for renewal that projected for Americans a millennial eschatology as powerful as that generated by the first generation one hundred years earlier. The preachers of the last half of the seventeenth century regarded their primary task to be a defense of what the first generation had created. They used biblical metaphors and the language of Canaan to preserve the old order, to lament the state of the present, and to look for a renewal of God's holy purpose in the coming judgment and millennium. Thus the progressive millennial impulse is less pronounced in the literature of New England between 1660 and 1730, and the jeremiads, like Increase Mather's *Ichabod* (1702), and the histories, like Cotton Mather's *Magnalia* (1702), are heavily retrospective. They anticipate a universal transformation, as we have seen in Samuel Sewall's *Phaenomena quaedam Apocalyptica*; however, the change is to come as a result of worldwide destruction. Still, one of the late seventeenth-century assumptions, often spoken but more often unspoken, was that the errand mission begun by the first planters would yet be fulfilled; a corollary of the declension theme was that renewal could only come through a wholesale societal regeneration.[3] The issue was less whether such a transformation was possible than how it could be accomplished. If premillenialists like Increase Mather argued that Christ's judgment would rectify the evils of the present world, making possible millennial harmony and peace, the New Lights, with Jonathan Edwards at their helm, argued a postmillennial eschatology that was rooted in the possibility of social perfection on earth. The expectations that the history of redemption had yet to reach a climax and that New England had an important role to play within it never wholly disappeared, and, contrary to received opinion, the jeremiad acted to intensify enthusiasm for millennial order and peace. "The divine wrath, in short, which lighted up the saints' way of trial, and so called attention to the disastrous pitfalls along the journey, also revealed the New Jerusalem at the end of the road."[4]

Referring to this important transition from declension to awakening, Sydney Ahlstrom has stated "Although Jonathan Edwards was surprised in 1734 when a revival of religion became manifest in Northampton, that event was neither accidental nor strange; the soil had in many ways been prepared. In the first place, Puritanism was itself, by expressed intention, a vast and extended revival movement. Few of its central spirits had wandered far from a primary concern for the heart's inward response, and its laity inwardly knew that true religion could never be equated with dutiful observance. Even in years of most lamented declension the churches were informed by a carefully reasoned theology and warmed by a deeper faith than the jeremiads acknowledge."[5] The sources ran deep, but to tap them, the New Lights had to live through self-surrender without absolute knowledge of what was ahead. "The New Lights, with Edwards' quiet leadership, made a fearful leap into the unknown to gain assurance that the future would receive them lovingly, and those that found they had been reborn, became convinced that whole societies might do the same. Just as they had been severed from their individual pasts, so, they believed, an entire nation might shed its former self and surrender to the future, trusting it would find joy."[6] Thus the New Lights read their Bibles prophetically and metaphorically to understand what future realities God had revealed in the words of his chosen people, and the conviction that their own lives prophesied a future fulfillment of God's will in America became the deepest impulse of the New Light movement.

It is therefore no coincidence that Joseph Bellamy could develop a progressive teleology in his sermon-treatise on *The Millennium* (1758) or that Samuel Hopkins, in *A Treatise on the Millennium* (1793), would adopt the same spiraling paradigm to describe the *revolutions* so necessary to the evolution of world history. Revolution and change have long been regarded to be vehicles of Providence, and no American historian was more aware of that principle than Jonathan Edwards, whose *History of the Work of Redemption* employs biblical typology and the standard divisions of patristic theology for the history of the universe to provide an interpretation of the past and a vision of the future consistent with the myth created in the seventeenth century of America's teleological destiny. It is important to explore this traditional eschatology in the millennial writings of Jonathan Edwards, contrasting the Christian myth with secular adaptations written by Joel Barlow and Philip Freneau. It is the same myth that governs Barlow's early *Prospect of Peace* (1778) and the *Vision of Columbus* (1787). This essential American millennial vision and its conventional biblical symbolism, the paradigm for which was established in the early New England Puritan interpretation of the Bible, operates throughout American historical writing until the Civil War, when the unity and order so important to the millennial visions of Edwards, Bellamy, David Austin, and the Whig historian George Bancroft was shattered on the battlefields of Gettysburg and Atlanta. It was a unifying vision, spoken in the figures of the Old and New Testaments, shared with the mythographers of the seventeenth century, William Bradford, John Winthrop, William Hubbard, Edward Johnson, Thomas Shepard, Samuel Sewall, and Increase Mather—best represented in the prophetic jeremiad by Cotton Mather, the *Magnalia Christi Americana,* fittingly published and written near the close of the century, as though it were a "century sermon" preached by Mather for posterity as well as his contemporaries.

The language of Canaan through which these millennial historians expressed their views forms an epistemological and symbolic continuity that also runs throughout American writing, and Perry Miller has demonstrated how Walden Pond is an extension in the teleology of the errand into the wilderness.[7] The examples of this biblical symbology in the poetry of Freneau, Barlow, and Dwight—to mention only the most prominent late eighteenth-century poets—are endless, and an examination of these eschatological patterns in the images of these three writers will follow. But the imagistic value of the Bible was not confined to religious writings and their secular counterparts. In a few specific instances, the language of Canaan actually entered the political arena—as distinguished from performing a rhetorical service—to influence America's self-conception at the earliest stages of Federal and Republican debate. One example will suffice here, one for which I am indebted to my colleague John Seelye of the University of North Carolina at Chapel Hill. It has to do with the selection of the seal that would best represent the newly formed nation.

Despite strong neo-classical influences during the early years of the nation, the biblical influences of New England extended to an important symbolic action in the summer of 1776:

> The common evangelical errand that became a national mission is no better illustrated than by the record of a meeting between Thomas Jefferson, Ben Franklin, and John Adams, on July 4, 1776, a date usually associated with another, though related, event. Having declared the sovereignty of the Thirteen States, the three representatives of the southern, middle, and eastern sections met for the purpose of designing a Great Seal which would symbolize the purpose and legitimize the presence of the new nation. What they each proposed was far different from the imperial eagle and Roman motto that eventually graced a manifestly neoclassical icon. Only John Adams chose a classical motif, an allegorical emblem borrowed from an illustration in Shaftesbury's *Characteristics*—Hercules resting from his labors. As an Enlightenment symbol, it was well suited to what Adams regarded as America's ordering purpose, and as a personal choice it testifies to his perpetual minority view. It is significant that both Jefferson and Franklin, independent of each other, suggested images taken from the Mosaic Exodus: Franklin the Red-Sea whelming of Pharoah's army, Jefferson the Providential pillar of smoke leading the Jews toward their Promised land. Though these prophetic symbols eventually were transformed, these Exodus scenes graphically prefigure both the Republic's sense of grand isolation and the westward movement that became codified, and later explained, by Manifest Destiny.[8]

It was, of course, the American Revolution that focused all historical and biblical precedents and gave the earlier writings on millennial themes a prophetic sense, and both the New Lights and the secular poets were aware of correspondences between biblical symbols, prophecy, and the "signs of the times."

The symbolic and metaphorical value of the American Revolution was not lost on those advocates of the millennium who saw in America an opportunity to promote the new nation as a divinely sanctioned society.[9] In 1794, for example, David Austin brought together under one cover several millennial documents that argue the perfection of society as a sign of the coming millennium. Included were Jonathan Edwards' *The Millennium, or, The Thousand Years of Prosperity Promised to the Church of God in the Old Testament and in the New, shortly to Commence and to be Carried to Perfection under the Auspices of Him, who, in the Vision, was Presented to St.*

John and Joseph Bellamy's *Prophecy of the Millennium,* which had originally been published in Boston in 1758.[10]

Nor were Edwards and his followers the only ones to establish an association between the millennium and the Revolution. Isaac Backus, writing in 1786, argued that biblical prophecy was currently being fulfilled, and that "some have attempted to prove that a *Nation Was Born at Once,* according to prophecy, when the *Independence of America* was declared; but that glorious event is yet before us. Necessity brought Pharoah to send Israel away with rich treasures, on the very night which God had told Abraham of four-hundred and thirty years before, and necessity will bring the world to relinquish their tyranny over the church, when that prophecy is fulfilled."[11] Samuel Hopkins' beatific vision of the millennium differed from the Calvinist position on the timing of these eschatological events, and yet his treatise was detailed and comprehensive, less typological than allegorical and derived from straightforward biblical prophecies.

Figural and typological associations abound in Samuel Sherwood's *The Church's Flight into the Wilderness,* preached in January of 1776, the same month that Thomas Paine issued *Common Sense.* Sherwood, like many of his contemporaries, made the conventional association between New England and Old Israel, but his special interest became the figure of the woman found in the book of Revelation, who, according to the text (Revelation 12:14-17), was "given two wings of a great eagle, that she might fly into the wilderness, into her place." Sherwood's exegesis is straightforward: "The woman in this passage, is represented as a pregnant state, travailing in birth, and in violent pangs to be deliver'd, which is doubtless designed as an emblem of the true Church of Christ."[12] And the passage of Christianity from east to west in the tradition of *translatio studii* is clear: for Sherwood, the woman moving into "her place" in the wilderness is America's fulfillment of the prophetic destiny:

> This passage, in its most natural, genuine construction, contains, as full and absolute a promise of this land, to the Christian church, as ever was made to the Jewish, of the land of Canaan. It is, in an appropriated sense, "her place"; where she is nourished, from the face of the serpent. And the dealings of God in his providence, in bringing his church from a state of oppression and persecution, into this good land, are very parallel and similar to his dealings with the Israelites, in delivering them from the tyrannical power of the haughty, cruel, monarch of Egypt, and conducting them to the good land so promised in Canaan (Sherwood, *Church's Flight into the Wilderness,* p. 23).

It is clear that for Sherwood, as for many of the ministers of the American Revolution, the *translatio studii* convention was more than a "meer metaphor," it provided, indeed, the biblical connection for associating the events of the Revolution with the prophecies of Scripture.

America was not only to be the seat of the New Jerusalem; it was also to be a millennial fulfillment through the predestination of Providence for a geographical shift of the center of Christianity from Europe to the American strand. "This American quarter of the globe," Sherwood concludes, "seemed to be reserved in Providence, as a fixed and settled habitation for God's church, where she might have property of her own, and the right and rule and government, so as not to be controul'd and oppress'd in her civil and religious liberties, by the tyrannical and persecuting powers of the earth, represented by the great red dragon" (p. 24). The dragon is monarchy and tyranny, not the papacy as Congregationalists and Puritans had long argued, so that for Sherwood and his contemporaries, the American Revolution provided that very sign that the concluding phase of God's historical drama was about to commence, and their roles in the perpetuating of revolution were thus sanctioned by the dictates of Scripture and the extension of biblical prophecy into modern times. Until the period of the Civil War, millennialism continued to enjoy some authority and the Revolution was viewed as a past historical event.

Though the millennial idea had passed into the hands of minor sects like the Millerites, some traditional arguments for its imminent arrival were advanced in such documents as William Miller's *Evidence from Scripture History of the Second Coming of Christ about the Year 1843* (Troy, N.Y.; Kemble and Hooper, 1836) and *A Lecture on the Typical Sabbaths and Great Jubilee* (Boston: Joshua Himes, 1842).[13]

The Great Awakening and American Revolution gave new life to millennial eschatology in eighteenth-century American thought, and the most prominent spokesman of Calvinist millennialism in eighteenth-century America was Jonathan Edwards. Much of what Edwards said concerning the millennium lies buried in the language of biblical typology, through which he interpreted Scripture and by which he understood God's revealed will in the Book of Nature and in the Old and New Testaments. The New Light millennial writers of the eighteenth century reflect the tensions present in the transformation of typology from a literal and historical exegesis of Scripture to an allegorical symbolism, but they restore to typology the authority of prophecy by extending prophetic power to natural symbols.

Although primary loyalties were to colony and empire in 1750, the images of emerging nationalism that are prominent in the literature indicate how strongly a governing conception of civil union was challenging earlier Puritan visions of theocracy and religious uniformity. The ministers reflect the insecurity of this transformation by recalling the glories of the past while they deplore the degeneracy of the present. The millennial writers, however — especially the New Light Calvinists of the

Great Awakening—were able to insure continuity in their visions of history by establishing their future expectations in the language of the biblical past. On the one hand, they gave precision and specificity to arguments concerning the millennium by anchoring their visionary constructions in scriptural typology and the language of biblical prophecy. On the other, some ministers were able to develop new ways of understanding the future by restoring prophetic value to typological figures that they found not only in Scripture but also in nature. Moreover, the prophetic correspondences were developed by a wide variety of writers and thinkers.

For example, the librarian and jurist, James Winthrop, developed a series of exegetical treatises each of which attempted to bring contemporary history into focus with ancient revelation. In the spring of 1794, he wrote *An Attempt to Translate the Prophetic Part of the Apocalypse of St. John,* which established a traditional exegetical foundation for his later writings on the millennium. In 1795, Winthrop penned *A Systematic Arrangement of Several Scripture Prophecies Relating to Antichrist, with their Application to the Course of History,* in which he showed clearly a direct association between the ancient nations specifically mentioned in biblical prophecy and the new nations more recently created in the American and French Revolutions. Finally, in 1803, he published *An Attempt to Arrange, in the Order of Time, Those Scripture Prophecies yet Remaining to be Fulfilled,* in which Scripture prophecies are applied to contemporary history from 1792 to the end of human time.

Similarly, Thomas Bray developed a biblical argument justifying the American experience in *A Dissertation on the Sixth Vial* (1780), where, in the brief introduction, he says, "The Grand Scene is chiefly the vast Roman Empire; within the limits of which, and its appendages, the principal great and interesting scenes and changes of the church of Christ would be exhibited down to the time of the Millennium." The Roman Empire, in turn, is more specifically defined to include America: "By the appendages of the Roman Empire, I intend those acquisitions in any part of the world, to all, or either of those kingdoms, of which the empire was made up at the time of the vision. This takes in America, which is undoubtedly comprehended in these prophecies. This is one of the grand divisions of the earth, where great and interesting scenes, respecting the church of God, have already opened, and no doubt, still greater ones yet to follow . . . America is plainly comprehended, and has a grand part, in some of the greatest and most interesting scenes" (vii, n). Though there were contemporary movements in Europe and in England that attempted to prove a connection between ancient prophecy and modern historical developments, American millennialism enjoyed a unique opportunity to associate "signs of the times" with the revelations of Scripture.

Even as New England society was being transformed from a Puritan theocracy to a political republic, the ministers' writings and ser- mons—all widely distributed from pulpit and press—developed a millennial utopianism that is rooted in traditional scriptural promises. By employing typology and the traditional language of figuralism, they restored to exegesis the authority of prophecy at a time when many theologians were busy looking for allegorical symbols throughout the Bi- ble. In so doing, the millennial thinkers stressed the historical and literal veracity of Scripture, extending the tradition begun by the Puritans in England and reinforced by John Cotton, Thomas Shepard, and the Mathers in New England. Moreover, they provided the early American imagination with a symbolic mythology and a prophetic force that allow- ed writers to predict future events through a process of historical analogies.[14]

The tradition of typological and prophetic language extending from scriptural figures to more recent images like Freneau's graphic descrip- tion of the millennium in *The Rising Glory of America* (and other poems of the "rising glory" tradition) was critically important to early America, since it provided a foundation for arguments about the nature of America's destiny. For seventeenth- and eighteenth-century American Puritans, who placed faith in the truth of Scripture and whose beliefs about the future depended on their understanding of God's dispensa- tions in the past, the revelations of the Bible were interpreted both figuratively and literally, with early emphasis on the restricted boun- daries of biblical dispensation and the rules governing typological ex- egesis. They saw in the Bible a *linear* teleology, with God leading his chosen people from Babylon to Jerusalem through the perils of earthly existence. However, through an evolving awareness of the cyclical pat- terns in human history and through a perception of themselves as the New English Israel, instituted to continue God's providential design, the later Calvinists like Joseph Bellamy and Jonathan Edwards developed a *spiraling* vision of the future and of post-Reformation history. More im- portant, they saw in America not only the progressive fulfillment of scriptural promises, but a conclusion to God's plan and a locus for the building of the earthly Jerusalem, that "New heavens and new earth" prophesied by Isaiah. For these "New Lights" history would culminate in the establishment of the millennial kingdom of God so that the distinc- tions between heaven and earth would ultimately disappear.

The prophetic writers of old had been able to develop a beatific vi- sion of the millennium by transmitting the contents of revelatory visions, and the commentators of the early church reinforced this eschatology by viewing the Scriptures as a progressive series of inspired dispensations, all which would culminate in fulfillment at the end of human time. Recent studies provide the grounds for linking this tradition of interpretation to exegetical customs prominent in England during the late Middle Ages and early Renaissance.[15] By extending the Puritan emphasis on a typological exegesis of Scripture and history, one by which the authority of the past could be employed to understand the process of the future, American millennial writers posited convincing conclusions about the nature of America's destiny, and there is statistical evidence to support at least the dissemination of these ideas from the pulpits of New England in 1750. Even while the eschatological forces of typology and prophecy were gradually transformed from the conservative, historical, and linear teleology prominent in the early seventeenth-century commentaries to the more allegorical and Platonic imagery found in the eighteenth century, most advocates of the American millenium rooted their conclusions firmly in Scripture-oriented exegesis that allowed little variation from a designated Scripture pattern. Even so secular a writer as Philip Freneau employed biblical eschatology to describe the coming fulfillment of America's promise:

> And when a train of rolling years are past,
> (So sung the exiled seer in Patmos isle)
> A new Jerusalem, sent down from heaven,
> Shall grace our happy earth, — perhaps this land,
> Whose ample bosom shall receive, though late,
> Myriads of saints, with their immortal king,
> To live and reign on earth a thousand years,
> Thence called *Millennium.* Paradise anew
> Shall flourish, by no second Adam lost,
> No dangerous tree with deadly fruit shall grow,
> No tempting serpent to allure the soul
> From native innocence. — A *Canaan* here,
> Another *Canaan* shall excel the old,
> And from a fairer Pisgah's top be seen.
> No thistle here, nor thorn, nor briar shall spring,
> Earth's curse before: the lion and the lamb
> In mutual friendship linked, shall browse the shrub
> And timorous deer with softened tygers stray
> O'er mead, or lofty hill, or grassy plain;
> Another Jordan's stream shall glide along,
> And Siloah's brook in circling eddies flow:
> Groves shall adorn their verdant banks, on which

The happy people, free from toils and death,
Shall find secure repose. No fierce disease,
No fevers, slow consumption, ghastly plague,
(Fate's ancient ministers) [shall] again proclaim
Perpetual war with man: fair fruits shall bloom,
Fair to the eye, and sweeter to the taste;
Nature's loud storms be hushed, and seas no more
Rage hostile to mankind — and, worse than all,
The fiercer passions of the human breast
Shall kindle up to deeds of death no more,
But all subside in universal peace . . .
And such AMERICA at last shall have
When ages, yet to come, have run their round,
And future years of bliss alone remain.[16]

The images of the last days drafted by these harbingers of the millennium were generally conservative in the development of scriptural patterns, and they employed some traditional methods of typological exegesis by which a type or figure would anticipate a future event in a linear and historical continuum. Although contemporary pressures on the language to abandon a literal reading of Scripture for a figurative and allegorical interpretation were increasingly strong, the millennial visions developed out of very narrow scriptural contexts and some echoed earlier assessments of the end of the world. If the piety of New England was truly declining as ministerial hermeneutics turned toward the jeremiad, then the imagery of eschatology held even more firmly to those traditional patterns of exegesis by which commentators had understood the last days from the time of the primitive church. Put another way, "If the figure most often repeated in the sermons of the late seventeenth-century was the departing of the father, usually symbolized by the abandonment of New England by God the Father, the most prominent figure during the eighteenth century was the eschatological symbol of the millennium, usually figured by anticipation of the return of the son."[17] These mythopoeic and archetypal symbols were employed successively by the early writers to produce a systematic vision of the future of New England based on the patterns discernible in her biblical and historical past.

At the same time, the Great Awakening and Jonathan Edwards produced a revitalized typology optimistically transformed to explore the prophetic figures of the natural world. While rooting their conclusions in Scripture parallels, the Calvinists argued an eschatology that was derived from prophetic images found in nature and current events, so that the millennial expectation became less a fear of the judgment than an awareness of God's transforming power over men's hearts. During the mid-eighteenth century, and just prior to the American Revolution, the force of the prophetic arguments was intense and animated reassertions of America's future in the writings of Edwards and his disciples, Joseph Bellamy, Timothy Dwight, and David Austin. The thousand-year period during which the forces of evil would be bound and the righteous saints were to enjoy abundance and plenty, peace and tranquility became so dominant an image in sermons and literature of the eighteenth century that commentators throughout the Western world saw in contemporary events "signs of the times" which indicated the beginning of the grand and prosperous millennial period. John Williston, a Scottish divine whose *Balm of Gilead for a Diseased Land* (1742) shows what power—internationally—such a constellation could have:

> We have very late and well attested accounts of glorious effusions of the Spirit in several parts of America, and particularly New England, and some of them I have dated within the last few months . . . These showers of the spirit, which are falling just now on several places, do encourage many to hope that they are forerunners of God's giving a general revival to his work, and of his bringing about the glory of the latter days, which he had promised to his church when he will make his Gospel everywhere a glorious manifestation of the Spirit (*Balm*, p. 97, 1804 edition).

And Edwards himself, like Cotton Mather before him, used "extraordinary prayer" as a millennial sign, linking the millennial hope with the rising tide of enthusiasm so prominent in the west.

> I have often said, as I say now, that I looked upon the late wonderful revivals of religion as forerunners of those glorious times, so often prophesied in Scripture, and that it was the first dawning of that light which, in the progress and issue of it, would at last bring on the church's latterday glory; but there are many that know I have from time to time added, that there would be many changes, revivings and intermissions, and returns of dark clouds and threatening circumstances, before the work shall have subdued the world and Christ's kingdom shall be everywhere established and settled in peace.[18]

One of the New Lights who assumed the typological justification for the sabbatical millennium was Joseph Bellamy, a follower of Jonathan Edwards in Bethlehem, Connecticut, who published some *Sermons on the Millennium* in 1758. Bellamy begins cautiously by explaining the precise role of the types in prefiguring the events of the New Testament:

> Hitherto God had supported his People's Hopes chiefly with Promises, with verbal predictions; but from the Days of Moses to the Days of Solomon King of Israel, to assist his People's Faith, God did, besides repeated promises of

the same Thing, by a great Variety of wonderful works shadow forth the glorious day; and at the same time shew, that he had sufficient Wisdom to accomplish the greatest designs.[19]

Almost immediately, however, Bellamy extends the typological system to provide an argument for the time of the coming millennium:

> But when shall the Son of David reign? and the Church have Rest? When shall the cause of Truth and Righteousness thus prevail? Perhaps the very Time was designed to be shadowed forth in the Law of Moses, in the Institution of their holy days. The *Seventh Day*, said God, "The Seventh Day shall be a Sabbath of Rest, the Seventh Month shall be full of Holy Days, and the seventh Year shall be a Year of Rest"; So, perhaps, after *Six Thousand* years are spent in Labour and Sorrow by the Church of God, the Seventh-Thousandth shall be a Season of spiritual Rest and Joy, an Holy Sabbath to the Lord. And as God the Creator was *Six Days* in forming a confused Chaos into a beautiful world, and rested the *Seventh*; so God the Redeemer, after *Six Thousand* Years Labour in the Work of a New Creation, may rest on the Seventh, and then Proclaim a General Liberty to an Enslaved World . . . And as surely as the Jews were delivered out of the babylonish Captivity, and Babylon itself destroyed; even so surely shall all these Things be accomplished in their Time. And mystical Babylon shall "sink as a Mill-stone into the sea" (pp. 50-52).

In the lengthy discussion that follows, David becomes a figure of Christ's kingship in the millennial vision, and his kingdom in Jerusalem prefigures the New Jerusalem. Biblical figures were extended into modern times prophetically and typologically, and the sabbatical pattern liberated by Thomas Shepard and Christianized by Samuel Mather provided Bellamy and Edwards a foundation for numerological predictions about the time of the fulfillment of millennial promises.[20]

    For the Calvinists, the millennium seemed imminent, and most broke with Samuel Hopkins over what they considered to be his Federalist-inspired postponement of the millennium to the end of the nineteenth century.[21] But for Abraham Cummings, a post-Revolutionary premillennialist, the millennium was very near, and the prophetic image of the sabbatical rest offered typological proof:

> Under the old dispensation, the Jews had a Millennium in prospect as well as we. They were in constant expectation of a glorious time, in which holiness and happiness should be general, if not universal; but they considered that glorious time only as the continuation of their own dispensation, and expected that the nations would embrace their religion and their kind of government, that all flesh would worship at their temple, from one *New Moon* to another, and from one *Seventh Day Sabbath* to Another. They expected as a

nation to have a portion of this promised glory with the rest of mankind. And in general it appears, that both the righteous and the wicked among them had the same leading sentiments on this subject. The nature of our dispensation was doubtless as well known to the Apostles when Christ arose as to any of the pious Jews; and yet they ask, Lord, wilt thou at this time restore again the kingdom of Israel? Of the like nature are the views and expectations of Christians in general at this day. THE MILLENNIUM IS AT HAND, SAY WE, TO MAKE OUR POSTERITY HAPPY, AND ALL NATIONS HAPPY, UNDER THE IMPERFECT GOVERN-MENT OF MERE MEN, BY THEIR EMBRACING THE EXTERNALS AS WELL AS THE IN-TERNALS OF OUR RELIGION: THE MILLENNIUM WILL BE A GLORIOUS CONTINUANCE OF OUR OWN DISPENSATION.[22]

Though Cummings disagreed with Edwards by specifying the personal appearance of Christ in a premillennial dispensation, he argued the cyclical institution of types and figures in the progressive revelations of history:

Now, since it is allowed that our gospel glory typifies the Millennium and that the destruction of the Jewish world typifies the destruction of the Christian world; with equal propriety we may consider the first coming of Christ as a type or representation of his second coming; . . . the first coming of Christ to destroy the Jewish world and introduce our dispensation; and the second coming of Christ to destroy the Christian world and introduce the millennium, the former being a type of the latter. We have seen in what order the type has been fulfilled; what doubt then can remain of the completion of the antitype in the same order (p. 33).

What doubt, indeed. Typology was providing the millennial advocates scriptural foundations for their numerological predications, and the cyclical patterns of history advanced by Cotton Mather were no longer metaphorical representations of an earlier dispensation proved by analogy. Rather, the prophetic emphases of typical adumbration and antitypical fulfillment were restored to show how America would be the setting for a grand millennial conclusion. Nor was the typology of the sabbath unique in its restored efficacy. If the jeremiads had employed biblical figures to indicate how the magistrates and leaders of New England should return to the moral examples they exhibited, mid-eighteenth-century preachers were convinced that the leaders of Massachusetts Bay could prefigure Christ's leadership of his elect, as Joseph Bellamy used David to adumbrate Christ's millennial kingship. In 1758, the Loyalist minister, Thomas Frink, preached the election sermon in Massachusetts and set out a doctrine in the language of Canaan to argue his own interpretation of the role of modern magistrates.

Frink's employment of biblical figures to eulogize contemporary magistrates has a long history in western culture. However, the Puritans were especially fond of typological analogies to the leadership of ancient Israel, whether or not the biblical figures were viewed as types of the fulfilling New England antitypes. It seems natural that in an effort to give vitality and meaning to the treacherous journey across the Atlantic Ocean and into the "howling wilderness," the settlers would derive trust and confidence from a perception of their own leaders that gave their mission not only providential sanction but also a mythic dimension. The early ministers and historians realized that the leaders were not strict parallels to the biblical leaders, nor were they instituted antitypes for the Old Testament typological correspondences. Even in extreme cases, the authors realized that Christ alone was the fulfillment of the images or shadows and that His antitype — whether eternal or temporal — would be necessary to the completion of the divine drama. Nevertheless, a systematic borrowing of these analogies persisted in the sermons and histories of the first and second generations, so that the later writers, like Frink, would have inherited a long tradition of analogy similar to that of the New English Israel and the ancient Israelite parallel. In these later years, indeed, the types invoked are less often Moses and Joshua of the wilderness journey to Canaan and more often are David, Hezekiah, Solomon, and Nehemiah, who ruled over the established, but embattled, kingdom and would deliver Israel from Babylon to a New Jerusalem. In some cases, even the millennial emphasis was implied in the typological parallel to the Old Testament figure, and the use of biblical leaders as examples for the New English Israel provided fertile soil for controversy, recalling the dispute between John Cotton and Roger Williams concerning typological significance and instituted leadership in the first generation of New England Puritanism. Thomas Frink's sermon is not important in historical or social terms, but it does provide an argument wholly from typology and figural exegesis for a prophetic determination of the millennium, and it provides a brief parallel to the writings of Edwards and the Calvinists of the Great Awakening who used typology — particularly the typology of kingship — to predict the coming millennium and heavenly kingdom.

Prophetic typology was Frink's system for proving the future realization of scriptural promises of the millennium, and he restated the progressive, cyclical historiography so prominent in the writings of Jonathan Edwards when he asserted, "It is very evident, and I suppose universally agreed, that Jerusalem the Metropolis of Judea, was a Type of the Christian visible Church (as the Temple and Sacrifices of other Ceremonial Services thereof, were a Type of the Pure Gospel service and Worship) and *David* under this Figure, celebrates the beauty and glory of the Gospel-church in the latter days."[23] The temple worship of the Old Testament becomes typical of the whole Christian church in the kingdom of God, of which the history of New England is a part. The "Millennial State of the Gospel Church, represented under the figure of the City of Jerusalem and the Temple," is attended by a total reformation of the society of Christian believers, and Hezekiah is "a most lively emblem of what shall be done in the latter times, when the Christian Church shall be restored to its State & Worship, according to the Gospel" (pp. 38-39).

Hezekiah is, therefore, both a prefigurative type and a moral example. Frink's subtle exegesis established the ancient figure as an emblematic example for all rulers who would regard their tenure as part of the progressive prefigurations of the second coming. In a section generally overlooked by modern students of the election sermon, Frink justified the use of biblical typology in the interpretation of contemporary historical events, showing how historical cycles of adumbration and fulfillment are repeated:

> All types or figures being to have a respect to the things figured; if we consider them as figures, we speak at the same time of that which they represent; so that which is said, has necessarily two proper and natural senses; one that agrees to the figure, and another to the thing figured: . . . The Old Testament is a Figure of the New, and all those things which befell the Jews, were figures of whatever should happen to Jesus Christ, and his Disciples. (pp. 6-7).

Frink has distinguished the two senses of Scripture and has assigned the label "mystical" to typology. "They are capable of two senses, that of the Figure and that of the thing Figured," he reasons, and he concluded with the distinction that "the words themselves shew that the Design of the writer was to represent by a Figure something more sublime" (p. 21). That "something more sublime" is the kingdom of Christ, both earthly and heavenly. "And therefore I consider this Prophecy as typical of that happy state of the Church and the world in the latter days," he continued, and his sense of the broadened typological correspondences outside the boundaries of Scripture led immediately to an argument for the coming of the kingdom. The church of the visible kingdom of Christ is therefore prefigured in the Old and New Testaments and will be fulfilled in the course of human events by divine intervention:

> If we look into the *Prophecies* of the Old Testament, we shall find they speak of the vast extent of Christ's visible Kingdom on Earth, and seeing those Prophecies have never yet been accomplished, we must conclude that there is a Time yet to come, before the Consummation of all Things, wherein our Saviour will once more display the glorious Banner of his *Cross*, and like a mighty man of war, march on conquering and to conquer, 'till he has

compleated his Victory over the Powers of the Earth, and brought all the world into a State of Subjection and Obedience to him and His Gospel; when the Kingdoms of the World shall become the Kingdoms of the Lord and of his Christ (pp. 29-30).

Prophetic typology became Frink's system for proving the future realization of scriptural promises of the millennium, and he restated the progressive, cyclical historiography so prominent in the writings of Jonathan Edwards:

It is very evident, and I suppose universally agreed, that Jerusalem the Metropolis of Judea, was a Type of the Christian visible Church (as the Temple and Sacrifices of other Ceremonial Services thereof, were a Type of the Pure Gospel service and Worship) and *David* under this Figure, celebrates the beauty and glory of the Gospel-church in the latter days (p. 31).

The temple worship of the Old Testament becomes typical of the whole Christian church in the kingdom of God, of which the history of New England is a part. The "Millennial State of the Gospel Church, represented under the figure of the City of Jerusalem and the Temple" is attended by a total reformation of the society of Christian believers, and Hezekiah is a "most lively emblem of what shall be done in the latter times, when the Christian Church shall be restored to its pure State & Worship, according to the Gospel" (pp. 38-39).

Hezekiah is, therefore, as Frink's exegesis established, an emblematic example of the progressive reformation of society leading to the final emergence of Christ's kingdom. "The Reformation begun and brought to Perfection by *Hezekiah,* an eminent Type of Christ, in this glorious display of his regal power does most graphically set forth in Figure this wonderful Reformation of the Church and of the World in the latter days" (p. 38). All secular history, particularly that of the Roman Empire before Constantine, is denoted "anti-Christian," and the purification of the church that was begun with Luther and Calvin is thought to have been carried to New England under the continued history of the work of redemption.

The significance of Frink's use of typology to interpret the events of world history lies in his working out a scheme of revelation based on the eschatological value of the Old Testament dispensation. His eschatology is based entirely on scriptural revelation and the fulfillment of scriptural promises in world history after Christ's incarnation, but he has rejected the conception of a type as a figure of specific events or persons having its conclusion in the coming of the flesh. Frink used Hezekiah not only as a moral example that all magistrates should endeavor to follow but as a typical prefiguration of Christ's millennial purification of the world. He saw the role of the New England magistrates as obedience to the example of Hezekiah, an original type in the tradition of Reformation rulers through which Christ would eventually usher in His kingdom. Frink's emphases on the prefigurative value of Hezekiah's figure indicate how strong the tradition of typological exegesis had remained in the conservative setting of Massachusetts Bay.

The millennial harbingers continued to explore the prophetic types for evidence of God's imminent return, and in the 1840s when Emerson had virtually concluded the association of typology with historical prefiguration by declaring a type and a symbol to be synonymous, William Miller grounded his whole adventist prophecy in a typological scheme exhaustively argued from Scripture. Millennial schemes were common to periods of revival enthusiasm. There were Adventists during the 1830s and 1840s who prophesied the imminent return of Christ and the commencement of the earthly kingdom. The Millerites predicted the commencement of the millennium in 1843 and would argue from Old Testament prophecy and the book of Revelation, also incorporating the typical figures commonly used by Shepard, Mather, and the early Puritans.[24]

The typical efficacy of the sabbath as a figure of the millennium was extended into modern times, and the moral authority of the Old Testament types was employed as an example for the magistrates of New England, but the renewed prophetic power endowed typology by Jonathan Edwards gave it an even greater scope. Moreover, Edwards' declaration that the millennium would occur on earth prior to the second coming and judgment nurtured utopian enthusiasm during the Great Awakening and foreshadowed a society of God's saints out of which the millennium would emerge. This progressive and evolutionary view of prophetic fulfillment was most fully developed in Edwards theology, making him the most prominent exponent of millennial utopianism in America before the Revolution. His writings on the millennium and his numerous attempts to construct a synthetic typological doctrine were centered on a transformation of the typological figures themselves to give meaning to the events of contemporary history. For Edwards the types were instituted to be organic and vital; they became richer images than the static metaphors of the jeremiad tradition, exceeding the extension of typical efficacy into modern cycles of history because they were not just reflections of God's grand design but harmonious prophecies of the world's redemption.

Edwards extended typology beyond the boundaries of the two Testaments by minimizing the distinction between the figure and the thing figured.[25] However, he always retained an eschatological sense of a future fulfillment of the promises made through natural and scriptural revelation. While orthodox typology applied to this historical scheme established between the Old and New Testament dispensations, for Edwards it also embraced correspondences between external representations and the spiritual ideas they shadow forth. Typology was for Edwards "a denial of the possibility that the universe is devoid of meaning . . . it served the classic purpose of giving coherence and unity to history. Just as the events and personages of the Old Testament foreshadowed the Redeemer, so too did all that transpired in Edwards' own day strike him as being prophetic of the coming Kingdom."[26] Edwards perceived a progressive "harmony between the methods of God's Providences in the natural and religious worlds, in that as when day succeeds the night, and the one comes on, and the other gradually ceases, those lesser lights that served to give light in the absence of the sun gradually vanish as the sun approaches."[27] Edwards was not allegorizing the types into static metaphors or emblems; rather, he was revitalizing them by using typology as a renewed prophetic language for God's promises revealed in nature.

Unfortunately, some of Edwards' most illuminating passages on the subject of typology remain in manuscript. In Miscellany 119, for example, he observed that:

> The things of the ceremonial law are not only things whereby God designedly shadowed forth spiritual things; but with an eye to such a representation were all the transactions of the life of Christ ordered. And very much of the wisdom of God in the creation appears, in his so ordering things natural, that they livelily represent things divine and spiritual, . . . as also, much of the wisdom of God is in his Providence, in that the state of mankind is so ordered, that there are innumerable things in human affairs that are lively pictures of the things of the gospel . . .[28]

Edwards' ultimate aim throughout his unpublished writing on typology was "to show how there is a medium between those that cry down all types, and those that are for turning all into nothing but allegory and not having it to be true to history."[29] His reasoning about the distinctions between typology and allegory was always clear, and he restored to typology its original historical and prophetic meaning while applying earlier dispensations to contemporary and future ones. He gave a cautious warning in his "Notebook on the Types" that "persons ought to be exceeding careful in interpreting of types, that they don't give way to a wild fancy; not to fix an interpretation unless warranted by some hint in the New Testament of its being the true interpretation, or a lively figure and representation contained or warranted by an analogy to other types that we interpret on sure ground."[30] However, he regarded typology to be a "certain sort of language, as it were, in which God is wont to speak to us."[31]

Consistent with his published declarations about the natural universe being typical and prophetic of God's future redemption of the world, he concluded the "Types" notebook by observing:

> To say that we must not say that such things are types of those and these things unless the Scripture has expressly taught us that they are so, is as unreasonable as to say that we are not to interpret any prophecies of Scripture or apply them to those and these events, except we find them interpreted to our hand, and must interpret no more of the prophecies of David, etc. For by the Scripture it is plain that innumerable other things are types that are not interpreted in Scripture (all the ordinances of the law are all shadows of good things to come), in like manner as it is plain by Scripture that those and these passages that are not actually interpreted are yet predictions of future events.[32]

Several clear declarations of typological doctrine illuminate Edwards' theory of God's revelation in cycles of historical dispensation. Edwards' writings are richly endowed with conclusions about the coming millennium, and they also abound in typological proofs of its imminent fulfillment that show how the biblical figures were revitalized to strengthen the case for the coming kingdom.

Two published documents are central in Edwards' millennial prophecies: the *History of the Work of Redemption,* a series of sermons first preached in 1739 but not published until after his death, and *An Humble Attempt to Promote Explicit Agreement and Visible Union Among God's People* (1747), which gave the Great Awakening a prophetic role in calling for civil as well as religious union. Edwards declared: "*Union* is one of the most *amiable* things that pertains to human society; yea, it is one of the most beautiful and happy things on earth, which indeed makes earth most like heaven," and thus he suggests the image of God's perfection that would be reflected in a perfect civil union and prophesies the harmonious earthly kingdom that is to be an image of heavenly beauty.

This kind of millennial emphasis is exceedingly strong throughout Edwards' writing. For example, in *Some Thoughts Concerning the Present Revival of Religion in New England* (1742), we find:

> It is not unlikely that this work of God's spirit . . . is the dawning or at least a prelude of that glorious work of God, so often foretold in Scripture . . . and there are many things which make it probable that this work will begin in America . . . And if we may suppose that this glorious work of God shall

begin in any part of America, I think if we consider the circumstances of the settlement of New England, it must needs appear the most likely of all the American colonies.[33]

And in the same year that he had preached the *History of Redemption* sermons, 1739, he stated in his *Personal Narrative* that the relation he perceived between the present and the future could be determined by analyzing prophetic images in Scripture:

> My heart has been much on the advancement of Christ's kingdom in the world. The histories of the past advancement of Christ's Kingdom have been sweet to me. When I have read the histories of past ages, the pleasantest thing in all my reading has been, to read of the kingdom of Christ being promoted. And when I have expected, in my reading, to come to any such thing, I have rejoiced in the prospect, all the way as I read. And my mind has been much entertained and delighted with the scripture promises and prophecies, which related to the future glorious advancement of Christ's Kingdom upon earth.[34]

It should not be surprising, then, that Jonathan Edwards' central spiritual and intellectual endeavor became the unearthing of those harmonious correspondences prophesied in Scripture and, in his resurrection of typological patterns, that he should apply the types and antitypes to the natural world. The close relationship he understood to exist between Scripture, history, and nature is clearly seen in the letter he wrote to the Trustees of the College of New Jersey (later Princeton University) when they offered him the presidency:

> I have had it on my mind and heart (which a long ago began, not with any view to publication), a great work, which I call a *History of the Work of Redemption* — a body of divinity in an entire new method, being thrown into the form of a history . . . wherein every divine doctrine will appear to the greatest advantage, in the brightest light, in the most striking manner, shewing the admirable contextual harmony of the whole . . . I have also for my profit and entertainment, done much towards another great work, which I call the *Harmony of the Old and New Testaments,* in three parts. The first, considering the Prophecies of the Messiah, his redemption and kingdom . . . showing the universal, precise, and admirable correspondence between predictions and events. The second part, considering the Types of the Old Testament shewing the evidence of their being intended as representations of the great things of the gospel of Christ; and the agreement of type and antitype. The third and great part, considering the Harmony of the Old and New Testament, as to Doctrine and precept.[35]

Edwards' assumption of the Princeton presidency and his subsequent death prevented his completing this ambitious work.[36] But he did leave us the redemption sermons and some manuscript fragments of the "Harmonies" in addition to the manuscripts called "Prophecies of the Messiah" and "Fulfillment of the Prophecies of the Messiah," all of which corroborate with detail those exegetical principles advanced in the *Types of the Messiah* and the posthumous *History of the Work of Redemption.* The vision of the last days provided by the *History* is yet more important, since this may be explicated by those assertions in the typology and prophecy manuscripts. Although his son, Jonathan Edwards, Jr., and his friend John Erskine had a substantial hand in reshaping some of the sermons to complete the book, which was finally published in 1774, the views are those of Edwards, since they may be checked by opinions he offered elsewhere on the same subject.

Following the example of the "late expositor" Moses Lowman, whose *Paraphrase and Notes on the Revelation of St. John* had been to Edwards' eschatology what John Locke's *Essay Concerning Human Understanding* had been to his epistemology, Edwards asserted that the fifth vial (of the seven prophesied in Revelation which would destroy Satan's kingdom), had already been unleashed.[37] This interpretation, incorporated into the redemption sermons, placed the work of redemption very far along in its progressive course. The prophecy is proved by a scheme of typological adumbration and antitypical fulfillment. In the events of the last days, Edwards saw an extension of the prophetic fulfillment that has been progressive and continuous from the creation. In the figure of David, for example, he perceived a foreshadowing of Christ and His kingdom:

> David, as he was the ancestor of Christ, so he was the greatest personal type of Christ of all under the Old Testament. The types of Christ were of three sorts: instituted, providential, and personal. The ordinance of sacrificing was the greatest of the *instituted* types; the redemption out of Egypt was the greatest of the *providential;* and David the greatest of the *personal* ones. Hence Christ is often called David in the prophecies of Scripture.[38]

Another typological correspondence Edwards develops fully is that of the holy city. The traditional conception of Jerusalem as a prefiguration of the heavenly city is repeated in the *History,* but it is not merely a literal reincarnation as some earlier millennial typologists had suggested. Rather, it is both a literal and a spiritual city, a type of God's spiritual kingdom, which was to be established after the defeat of Satan at the end of human time. That the Jerusalem of the Old Testament was prophetic of this spiritual state in Edwards' vision is made quite clear:

> This city of Jerusalem is therefore called the *holy city;* and it was the greatest type of the Church of Christ in all the Old Testament. It was redeemed by

David, the Captain of the Hosts of Israel, out of the hands of the Jebusites, to be God's city, the holy place of his rest forever, where he would dwell. So Christ, the Captain of his people's salvation, redeems his church out of the hand of devils, to be his holy and beloved city. And therefore how often does the scripture, when speaking of Christ's redemption of his church, call it by the names of Zion and Jerusalem? This was the city that God had appointed to be the place of the first gathering and erection of the Christian church after Christ's resurrection, of that remarkable effusion of the spirit of God on the apostles and primitive Christians, and the place whence the gospel was to sound forth into all the world; the place of the first Christian church, that was to be, as it were, the mother of all churches through the world.[39]

Edwards' perception of the church as a progressive historical movement leading to the gathering of the saints in Christ was supported by his reading of the biblical types. Just as Jerusalem signified typologically the holy city and the center of Christ's spiritual kingdom on earth in the continuum of human time, so it would also signify the coming of the church-kingdom that will be established for eternity at the end of human time.

Throughout the *History of the Work of Redemption,* these typological associations abound. Edwards envisions the setting up of Christ's kingdom as a succession of great events, each revealed in the prophecies of Scripture and each having a spiritual significance for his own time. The *History,* moreover, contains a vivid description of the arrival of millennial peace and the coming of the kingdom. This conclusive interpretation of the prophecies and the types is dramatically conceived and beautifully preached; the conviction with which Edwards approached his own last days is resonant throughout the climactic scenes depicting the arrival of God's glory. The gathered church of God's elect saints is brought forward to enjoy forever the beauty of redeemed creation in a period of perfect peace. "Then shall the whole church be perfectly and forever delivered from this present evil world," Edwards says, and the sense of religious community that has characterized the Puritan vision of God's holy city from primitive times to the present echoes throughout his vision of the end: "Now they shall all be gathered together, never to be separated any more. And not only shall all the members of the church now be gathered together, but all shall be gathered unto their Head, into his immediate glorious presence, never to be separated from him any more."[40]

Similarly, in Miscellany 262, Edwards develops a millennialism that clearly suggests the fusion of civil and religious forces in the fulfillment of God's glory:

Millennium: 'Tis probable that the world shall be more like Heaven in the millennium in this respect: that contemplation and spiritual enjoyments, and those things that more directly concern the mind and religion, will be more the saint's ordinary business than now. There will be so many contrivances and inventions to facilitate and expedite their necessary secular business that they shall have more time for more noble exercise, and that they will have better contrivances for assisting one another through the whole earth by more expedite, easy, and safe communication between distant regions than now. The invention of the mariner's compass is a thing discovered by God to the world to that end. And how exceedingly has that one thing enlarged and facilitated communication. And who can doubt that yet God will make it more perfect, so that there need not be such a tedious voyage in order to hear from the other hemisphere? And so the country about the poles need no longer be hid to us, but the whole earth may be as one community, one body in Christ.[41]

Thus the millennial vision and progressive eschatology were joined in a comprehensive image of a future paradise in which human relations, scientific invention, and earthly achievement would be developed under the guidance of divine Providence. The vision was progressive and utopian. The proof of its revealed promise was governed, however, by the truths Edwards received from Scripture and nature, and from the typological associations he perceived between the two.

The prophetic language of the Bible, this language of Canaan, which John Cotton knew the saints would all speak at the final resurrection, was for Edwards instituted at the beginning of time in the building of the natural world in God's image, so that all creation resonates with prophetic images of God's ultimate glory and his redemption of the saints. Similarly, the incarnation was for Edwards more than the arrival of the Word as flesh; the antitype is eternal, not temporal, so that Christ's fulfillment of the prophetic figures, like the figures themselves, operates throughout human time, from alpha to omega. In a little-known passage from the *Miscellanies* that confirms this view, Edwards says:

479. WORK OF REDEMPTION: TYPES. Things even before the fall were types of things pertaining to the gospel redemption. The old creation, I believe, was a type of the new. God's causing light to shine out of darkness, is a type of his causing such spiritual light and glory by Jesus Christ to succeed, and to arise out of, the dreadful darkness of sin and misery. His bringing the world into such beautiful form from out of a chaos without form and void, typifies his bringing the spiritual world to such divine excellency and beauty after the confusion, deformity, and ruin of sin.[42]

If the millennial writers of the first and second generations had restricted their arguments to specific scriptural promises or to the allegorical metaphors derived from them, and if those millennial seers during the eighteenth century had also viewed the historical process as a fulfillment of specific passages in the Bible, seeking signs of the times that would corroborate their predictions, Edwards also found scriptural authority for his vision of the millennium, but he transformed the typological system by extending it to embrace the natural and historical universe. And the typology of nature set forth in Edwards' numerous writings on the subject becomes more than an academic extension of the biblical figures into modern time. It is an original epistemology by which Edwards and his successors learned to read the vast and complex Book of Nature, in which they found prophetic figures of the imminent millennium and kingdom of Christ. Like John Cotton, they envisioned a time when all the saints would understand and speak this prophetic language of Canaan, by which God's revealed will had been dispensed to regenerate perceivers through a glass, darkly. And they looked forward with joy to that time when the veil would be lifted, and all the prophecies and types would be fulfilled in a time of peace and harmony. But the significance of Edwards' vision was that it brought together the new science with earlier, traditional models for the coming of the New Jerusalem. Through Edwards' unique insight, writers like Dwight and Barlow were able to utilize the scriptural figures of traditional exegesis to describe the coming commercial and technological revolution. Although enthusiasm for a commercial millennium was muted in Dwight's writing, it reached full flower in the epics of Joel Barlow. And Edwards' little-known *Miscellanies* contain numerous examples of the fusion of technology and religion that would provide a transition from a spiritual to a natural millennial fulfillment. Two brief examples will suffice, numbers 146 and 147, where Edwards is discussing the quality of life in the era to come; reinforcing his spiraling paradigm for the world's historical cycles:

> The late inventions of telescopes, whereby heavenly objects are brought so much nearer and made so much plainer to sight and such wonderfull discoveries have been made in the heavens, is a type and forerunner of the great increase in the knowledge of heavenly things that shall be in the approaching glorious time of the Christian Church (146).
>
> The changing of the course of trade and the supplying of the world with its treasures from America is a type and forerunner of what is approaching in spiritual things, when the world shall be supplied with spiritual treasures from America (147).[43]

It is the vitality and adaptability of this symbolic millennial vision, recalling the typological systems and spiritual conviction with which the first New England Puritans had interpreted their Bibles, that gives Edwards' typological argument an organic life that would later inspire

Timothy Dwight's conception of America and his figural reading of contemporary history, Barlow's commercial vision of America's future promise, Emerson's reading of the Book of Nature, and Whitman's celebration of the fulfillment prophesied in earlier cycles of the dramatic plan.

> The Genius of the Eastern nations, and particularly of the *Jews,* was in many respects, different from that of the *Greeks* and *Romans.* Situated in a climate nearer to the vivifying rays of the Sun, his beams acted with a more enlivening influence on the intellectual, as well as vegetable world, and lit up a more bright, glowing Genius in the human breast. Born in a region which enjoyed this advantage in the happiest degree, and fired with the glorious thoughts and images of Inspiration, can we wonder that the divine writers, though many of them illiterate, should so far transcend all others, as well in style, as in sentiment? Can we wonder that these superior advantages should be displayed on every page, in the boldest metaphors, the most complete images, and the most lively descriptions? No writers abound so much in passionate Exclamation, in that striking way of communicating sentiments, Interrogation, or in metaphors taken from sublime objects, and from action, of all others the most animated. Unencumbered by Critical manacles, they gave their imaginations an unlimited range, called absent objects before the sight, gave life to the whole inanimate creation, and in every period, snatched the grace which is beyond the reach of art, and which, being the genuine offspring of elevated Genius, finds the shortest passage to the human soul.[44]

This passage, which appears in Dwight's commencement address to Yale College in 1772, effectively summarizes the author's view that biblical surpasses classical writing. The treatise goes on to distinguish the genres of Scripture narrative while comparing selected texts to classical counterparts. Dwight compares the imaginative qualities of the ancients to those of the "divine authors" and he finds the classics wanting. "In every page," he declares, "we are astonished by glorious and supernatural displays of divine power—in every page, we are charmed by fanciful, yet just, poetical descriptions of a great variety of scenes. By these methods their History has every advantage of Poetry for affecting the Imagination, with this happy circumstance, that it is all reality" (p. 6).

But Timothy Dwight, like most of his contemporaries, attempted a synthesis of classical and biblical systems of style, with the result that many passages in the *Dissertation* sound remarkably like conventional neo-classical dicta: "The great end of History is instruction" (p. 5). The achievement of Dwight's *Dissertation* is that it provides a critical and theoretical perspective for his own epic poem, *The Conquest of Canaan,* while also developing a viable context for a discussion of Joel Barlow's secularizing of the biblical metaphors in *The Vision of Columbus* and *The*

Columbiad. Dwight, one of Yale's greatest presidents and a leading theologian of the eighteenth century, represents one literary vector in the evolution of American writing following the Great Awakening, while Barlow and Philip Freneau, "that rascal" of a poet who, with his classmate Hugh Henry Brackenridge aroused the Princeton commencement of 1771 with a poem that announced "The Rising Glory of America," represent the secularizing of biblical conventions and a transformation of the scriptural patterns to speak and sing the Federal, progressive theme. In Barlow and Freneau, the "rising glory" theme utilized biblical conventions to explore new dimensions in America's historical scheme of progressive fulfillment; in Dwight, the Bible continued to serve, as it had for Edwards and the Puritan commentators before him, as the most formidable dispensation available to man of God's divinely instituted scheme for the redemption of mankind.[45] If the language of Canaan were the key to understanding scriptural writing, the epic form of the Bible and poetry gave Scripture literary depth and prophetic power missing in the dry pages of prose historical narratives, thereby justifying the exegetical endeavors of Dwight and his colleagues who sang the fulfillment of America's promised prophetic destiny.

> The prophecies are always certain, the events referred to future; their Hero is the *Messiah,* the wonderful Counsellor, the mighty God, the everlasting Father, the Prince of Peace. The Empire, that of the Universe, its extension immensity, its duration eternity. The City, the new *Jerusalem,* the Heaven of Heavens, the seat of light and blessedness; its walls of gold and precious stones, its splendor that of Almighty God. And this advantage attends all their writings, that every possible Reader, every one of us is infinitely more interested in the subject, than the *Romans* were in that of *Virgil;* as we are candidates for an immortal existence in that region of felicity, where the Sun doth not give light by day, nor the Moon by night, but the Lord himself is an everlasting Light, and the God of *Zion* her Glory (p. 16).

The millennial theme is pervasive in Dwight's writing, and his *Conquest of Canaan* views the biblical experience of Israel as an analogue for the continuous historical fulfillment of America's destiny. However, it is in some of the lesser known prose writings and sermons that Dwight affirms the millennial-progressive idea, always linking his prophetic announcement to Scripture precedent without departing from the progressive teleology also renewed in Edwards' *History of the Work of Redemption.* In his "century sermon"—a conventional and popular form through which ministers frequently reviewed the past century to assess its place in the larger frame of historical development—Dwight, like Edwards and the New Light millennialists, looked forward to a period of peace, harmony, and natural virtue:

But while we look forward with faith, consolation, and transport, to rising periods of order, peace, and safety; in which truth shall triumph, justice preside over the concerns of men, and mercy pity and assuage the sufferings of this agonizing world; while we forsee seasons of general happiness and universal virtue, a vernal growth of moral beauty, and an autumnal harvest of converts to holiness; while the eye travels through a new era in the universe of man, and beholds a rebellious world voluntarily resuming its allegiance to the Creator, the great family of Adam acknowledged as the children, God declaring himself the common Father, and the earth confessedly the temple, in which he is loved, obeyed, and worshipped, we cannot fail to revert to the "troublesome times" which now are revolving.[46]

The critical word here is "revolving," as Dwight perceived the teleology of the world and the progressive destiny of America to be at one with each other. Like Edwards' *History,* Dwight's *Discourse* and the *Conquest of Canaan* affirm a progressive, cyclical paradigm for the course of American events, and the revolutionary model sanctions disruptive change and the troublesome signs of the times as signals that the end — though now a transformation to be looked forward to — will soon come. It is an echo of an old theme, one that Dwight sang with all his rhetorical power and believed with all his heart, having earlier, like many other ministers during the American Revolution, declared the war with England to be a stage in the progressive fulfillment of millennial expectations. "May we not then, with singular propriety," he argues in 1777, "address AMERICA in the words . . . of our text, *Fear not, O land! be glad and rejoice, for the Lord will do great things.* Have we not the best reason to hope, that God will not leave such mighty beginnings unaccomplished, but will hasten them to a glorious and happy completion."[47]

It is not, indeed, in the *Conquest of Canaan* that Dwight's most successful conflation of poetic form, biblical vision, and millennial theme occurs. In *Greenfield Hill,* ostensibly a neo-classical pastoral poem celebrating the virtues of life in New England, Dwight affirms the vision that he has anchored in biblical rhetoric through his sermons by recasting paradise in the future tense:

> See the wide realm in equal shares possess'd!
> How few the rich, or poor! how many bless'd!
> O happy state! the state, by *Heaven* design'd
> To rein, protect, employ, and bless mankind . . .[48]

The millennial state is an earthly paradise, not a heavenly fulfillment in eternity but a renewed, restored state in human time informed by the design of heaven; however, the architect is clearly the Creator, whose plan for restoration as revealed in Scripture becomes the paradigm for historical fulfillment:

Yet there, even there, Columbia's bliss shall spring
Rous'd from dull sleep, astonish'd Europe sing,
O'er Asia burst the renovating morn,
And startled Afric in a day be born;
As, from the tomb, when great *Messiah* rose,
Heaven bloom'd with joy, and Earth forgot her woes,
His saints, thro's nature, truth and virtue spread,
And light, and life, the *Sacred Spirit* shed;
Thus, thro' all climes, shall Freedom's bliss extend,
The world renew, and death, and bondage, end;
All nations quicken with th'ecstatic power,
And one redemption reach to every shore (p. 158, ll. 303-315).

The neo-classical motif etched in the pastoral paradise of an edenic garden is informed throughout by the vision of Isaiah, and the "sacred spirit" pervades the order and bliss of *Greenfield Hill* just as the Holy Spirit appears in the metaphors and similes of the Old Testament prophetic account.

As in Edwards' writing, the biblical visions of paradise are conceived in earthly terms, conflating the classical and Christian motifs that would appeal to audiences steeped in Homer, Virgil, the Bible, and Puritan sermons. *Greenfield Hill* becomes a realization of Scripture promises, "no meer metaphor, but the next thing to be looked for." The cycles of history that bring the restoration of paradise are anchored in God's millennial dispensation, and the progress of human time evolves toward a teleological state of fulfillment that is dramatically conceived and poetically realized in the richest images of the language of Canaan. It remained for Joel Barlow to spend his career developing an appropriate vehicle for the transformation of scriptural millennial figures to the new, secular teleology. For with the coming of the American Revolution, millennial eschatology — and those biblical symbols so prominent in the language of Canaan — were under pressure to reflect the enlightenment version of a postmillennial paradise, a society perfected by progress without the assistance of divine grace.

9

JOEL BARLOW AND THE
RISING GLORY OF AMERICA

I hope to see our young America in possession of an Heroick Poem,
equal to those most esteemed in any Country.

— John Adams

Why sleep'st thou, Barlow, child of genius, why?
See'st thou, blest Dwight, our land in sadness lye?
And where is Trumbull, earliest boast of fame?
'Tis yours, ye bards, to wake the smother'd flame—
To you, my dearest friends! the task belongs,
To rouse your country with heroic songs.

— David Humphreys,
*A Poem on the Happiness
of America,* 1786

On wings of faith to elevate the soul
Beyond the bourn of earth's benighted pole,
For Dwight's high harp the epic Muse sublime
Hails her new empire in the western clime.
Tuned from the tones by seers seraphic sung,
Heaven in his eye and rapture on his tongue,
His voice revives old Canaan's promised land,
The long-fought fields of Jacob's chosen band.
In Hanniel's fate, proud faction finds its doom,
Ai's midnight flames light nations to their tomb,
In visions bright supernal joys are given,
And all the dark futurities of heaven.

— Joel Barlow,
The Columbiad, Book IX, 1807

THE PROBLEM of language and its relation to genre or form
was resolved in Puritan New England by writers and preachers
whose rhetorical responses to political, social, and spiritual conditions were governed by biblical precedent. For example, just as the
theocracy of early Massachusetts Bay Colony had been established
following the model of the Old Testament theocracy and was originally
sanctioned by God's law, the historians and ministers of early New
England attempted to model their rhetorical styles according to the
language of Canaan by which the writer, with God's grace, might raise

208

words up into life, giving the colonies a specific, ordered relationship to the prophetic writings of Scripture. As a part of the process of fulfillment in divine history, the Puritans were certain that the biblical models would give their literature the didactic purpose that guided the originals. Thus William Bradford's *Of Plimouth Plantation* is an attempt to write providential history from the perspective of a leading participant, and Edward Johnson's *The Wonder Working Providence of Sion's Saviour in New England* is a metaphorical accounting of the New England experience that has the structure and form of myth. Cotton Mather's *Magnalia Christi Americana* "dissolves history into biography," as Peter Gay reminds us, and brings together the classical and Judeo-Christian historical method in an attempt to create an authentic epic of New England.

For the writers of the late eighteenth century, particularly those considered here, the poets of the American Revolution, the task of finding the appropriate form to express a conflation of biblical and classical theme was much more complex. The dominant genres were neoclassical, and the influence of English writers like Alexander Pope and the Christian humanist John Milton was strong. If Milton had found a satisfactory form in the epic-dramatic structure of *Paradise Lost* to "justify the ways of God to men," the poets of the revolutionary era were faced with the problem of reconciling a secular, enlightened, and progressive view of America's future with more traditional and theological positions, expressed in the figures, symbols, and forms of biblical language, that prophetic language of Canaan which had given America's writers spiritual conviction from John Winthrop to Timothy Dwight. The transition to a secular version of this richly metaphorical, highly figural biblical language was not achieved at once, nor were writers consciously scheming to utilize the rhetorical framework of the past in order to generate enthusiasm among their contemporary readers. Rather, the expectations of America's national future seemed to respond well to the rhetorical strategies of earlier models, and it was natural that the millennial enthusiasm so prominent in the writings of Jonathan Edwards and the New Light movement should reappear in the progressive, optimistic neoclassical epics of Joel Barlow and the early federalist and republican poets. Millennialism, indeed, may be found in the expansionist poetry of Walt Whitman, who could hardly be linked to William Bradford or Cotton Mather in any way other than that they all shared a common expectation of America's fulfillment of the idealistic prophecies of Isaiah and Revelation.

Thus the problem became one of emphasis and imagery. For Bradford, Mather, and Edwards, the real possibility that a religious millennium might be realized in North America energized fantastic visions of the future glory of New England. But Dwight, Barlow, and Freneau anchored their beliefs in the progressive optimism of federalist or republican expectations, while utilizing the Scripture rhetoric they had inherited from the early settlers through Jonathan Edwards and the New Lights.

The crux of the problem became the composition of an epic poem to celebrate the rising glory of America, and a full-fledged genre of epic writing resulted from the numerous attempts made between 1760 and 1807, when Joel Barlow's *Columbiad* consummated all previous efforts. It was not simply a matter of establishing a form, which, after all, was provided by the ancient writers—both biblical and classical—who had already developed literary structures that would bring together. the elements of psychology, history, religion, and human drama to represent the values and attitudes of a culture. The Puritans were certainly aware of these precedents, and Cotton Mather argued, as we have seen, the necessity of utilizing biblical biographical models in writing the history of New England. Epic and history were inseparable, but the rhetorical patterns of epic writing had to be adapted from scriptural and figural usage to herald the evolving emphasis on America's secular glory.

It is therefore no creative or artistic flaw that caused Joel Barlow to experiment with a proper epic language and an appropriate form. Like his predecessors among the Puritans, and like Walt Whitman whose epic grandeur is resonant in every line of his newly liberated "free verse" form, Joel Barlow was accommodating the language of Canaan to its new theme—the glory of America's technological and political future. To distinguish this from the earlier prospects for America's spiritual fulfillment of Scripture prophecy, and to express the result in language consonant with America's epic greatness, became the focus of Barlow's career. It is the purpose of this chapter to trace the development of that transformation, and to specify the changes in the language of Canaan from a spiritual to a secular context.

Millennial symbolism continued to appear in the composition of narrative poems throughout the period of the American Revolution. Though such divergent patterns of interpretation would emerge as Timothy Dwight's premillennial convictions in *The Conquest of Canaan* and Philip Freneau's postmillennial optimism in *The Rising Glory of America*, the constant use of biblical images to explore the future promise of the new nation developing its new land appears pervasive. As William Andrews has shown, such diverse figures as John Trumbull and the poet-philosopher William Smith all employed the neoclassical *translatio-studii* theme, which had been Christianized by the Puritans and then was being secularized again by the writers of late eighteenth-century America, even as they retained the biblical images that were not fused with classical and neoclassical iconography. Smith's *A General Idea of the*

College of Mirania, a polemic on the subject of public support for general education, and his *Poem on Visiting the Academy of Philadelphia* (1753) both anticipate Joel Barlow's conviction that in education lies the key to true participatory democracy. The anonymous pamphlet, *Some Thoughts on Education*, published in 1752 and attributed to Smith, conflates prophecy of America's rising glory and the advancement of learning, a convention of the *translatio* motif that by Barlow's time was an accepted view of the relations between the old and new worlds.[1]

The American Revolution of course, gave rise to predictions of continental unity that extended the *translatio* idea into political arguments for separation from Britain, just as the New Light sermons had cited the "paradise in America" theme as an extension of the earlier "errand into the wilderness" idea, whereby the European Reformation would be continued on the American continent as a beacon and example to the earlier segments of the western world, which were now to lose the central position they had occupied as sites for the New Jerusalem. These themes are prominent in the poetry of Freneau, Dwight, and Barlow, but they are also pervasive in the sermon literature of the time, especially in Congregationalist writing of the revolutionary era, though other colonial ministers and some loyalists saw in America both a literal and spiritual fulfillment of Scripture prophecy. For example, Theodore Frelinghuysen, a theologian who saw in the defeat of the French at the time of the French and Indian War a prospect for American national development, argued that

As thou Sun givest Light from East to West, so shall Man, whom I have created in the East, people the Earth still Westward on; and with him shall go polish'd Life, Arts, and Science, and real Religion, by which Glory redounds to my Name, Salvation to my Creatures. — Two Thousand Years may expire before I give my Law in Form; Two Thousand before *Messiah* come unto whom is to be the Gathering of the Nations: when through manifold and divers Vicissitudes, my Gospel reach remote America; all the While as the Light advances to the West, leaving the more Eastern Parts of the Earth darker and darker, until a Time of Apostacy, together with its deserved Punishment from Heaven, close the Eve of Two Thousand Years more.[2]

Frelinghuysen represents an extension of the *translatio studii* theme into prerevolutionary times, and the background for his assertions lay in the sabbatism of Thomas Shepard and the chiliasm of Increase Mather. Theologians continued to make specific predictions about the timing of the millennium, and some explored the rich symbolism of those prophetic books in the Bible which contain numerological schemes for determining the exact date of the end of the world. For example, in 1724 William Burnet of New York analyzed the twelfth chapter of Daniel in great detail in *An Essay on Scripture Prophecy* and divided the great history of the work of world redemption into predictable stages, the first of which he assumed to have passed in the year 1715, one year earlier than the Mathers had predicted the commencement of the millennium. Like his predecessors, Burnet was concerned with figural writing, but only in so far as it revealed to him the mechanisms for dating the last days. The Great Awakening emphasis on fulfillment of Scripture types and prophecies stressed the spiritual significance of America's rising glory, and well into the 1750s, writers and jeremiad preachers continued to urge Americans to return to the original mission of the first and second generations. Through the mid-century and continuing well into the post-meridian decades of the American Revolution, the jeremiad emphasis on regeneration and restoration continued to haunt writers who saw in America's transformation a possibility of fulfillment and progressive spiritual, social, and political improvement. But these writers and ministers were not able to assert America's millennial promise in the same terms that had been employed by John Cotton, Thomas Shepard, the Mathers, and Jonathan Edwards. America was now a secular and enlightened land, as well as a locus for the fulfillment of Scripture promises. And yet, these seemingly irreconcilable interpretations of her destiny were to be brought together in the nationalistic verse of the revolutionary era, 1765-1789.[3]

Reconciliation — or transformation — occurred in the composition of an epic poem celebrating America's current greatness and her future potential. Poets like John Trumbull and David Humphreys celebrate America's promise in nationalistic verse composed largely out of undergraduate enthusiasm, but before the epic poem could be realized in Barlow's *Columbiad*, a synthesis and transformation had to occur — a synthesis of the spiritual and secular versions of the early American dream and a transformation of biblical types and figures endowed with wholly spiritual significance into the rhetorical symbols appropriate to secular prophetic verse. The language of Canaan, in a word, would become for a time the language of a secular American destiny.

The 1760s and 1770s provided new directions for writers of all types, from secular millennialists like Philip Freneau, who saw in the possibility of revolution a fulfillment of Scripture promises, to ministers like Samuel Sherwood and Abraham Cummings, who argued that America was to become a spiritual paradise following the biblical model. "The important role which the clergy played in furthering the cause of the Revolution by their writings and sermons tended to reinforce the conception of the author as minister," suggests Emory Elliott, noting that

When the political and economic situations worsened in the 1760's and early 1770's, the leaders of colonial interests called upon the preachers to use their rhetorical skills to voice the discontent of the people and to arouse the apathetic to action. The influence of ministers like Jonathan Mayhew, Samuel Langdon, and John Witherspoon was not lost upon the young men in the colleges, nor did they fail to recognize the effect upon the people of the old Puritan idiom which the preachers revived. The young men trained in the classics and cognizant of the new critical theories were impressed that traditional verbal patterns of the Puritan sermon — the imagery, religious metaphors, and biblical types — continued to hold vital meaning for the great mass of Americans.[4]

Thus the rhetoric of the revolutionary era conflated progressive secular historiography and a revitalized sense of America's spiritual destiny, so that the imagery of Puritan theology — especially the biblical types and figures — these important symbolic forms, became the rhetorical vehicles through which ministers, poets, pamphleteers, and patriotic writers fused the Puritan past with progressive destiny to mold a new national American mythology: "The Revolutionary historians . . . used Puritan imagery as a metaphoric device to justify the War of Independence; it was part of their moral and legal self-vindication. They show us how ideology arises out of social conflict."[5]

The emergence of a concept of revolution as an inevitable historical process had begun in the Reformation, where theologians and historians treated the concept of national election as an extension of individual salvation, and the American dream of independence for continued progress nurtured this historical and traditional model. But the crucial translation of the "errand into the wilderness" into a national myth embracing armed revolt and separation from Great Britain is found in the late eighteenth-century distinction between the religious and the secular view of revolution, prominent from Aristotle through Karl Marx, which sees a societal upheaval and violent overthrow of existing government as a means to a political end. Alternatively, "the religious meaning of revolution stems from the tradition of ecclesiastical or sacred history," according to Bercovitch.

It pertains both to the individual believer and to mankind in general, and on both levels it is emphatically and unequivocally progressive. Despite the vanity of man's earthly efforts, he has a great *spiritual* destiny. Individually, each believer has the promise of heaven, through what Augustine termed the *revolutio* of the soul toward God. Collectively, mankind is advancing toward New Jerusalem in accordance with God's redemptive plan, through a series of revolutionary upheavals . . . The New England Puritans, who inherited this

millennial-revolutionary outlook, applied it directly to their own errand into
the wilderness. In effect, they fused secular and sacred history in the context
of American Progress.[6]

This conflation of sacred and secular constituted an important
achievement for the Puritans and their eighteenth-century followers,
whether secular or spiritual. By providing the adherents of the revolutionary ideology with a traditional authority and a rational, enlightened
view of their own progressive times, the fusion of sacred and secular
history appeared in such divergent documents as Samuel Sherwood's
The Church's Flight into the Wilderness and Philip Freneau's *Rising Glory of
America*. Some of these works heralded a restoration of the grand design
for America that the original settlers had deduced from their reading of
Scripture and had consummated in their "errand into the wilderness",
and the arguments in both the secular and the sacred literature followed
a biblical pattern, through which the American Revolution was viewed
as "Armageddon," that final confrontation between the forces of good
and the Antichrist foretold in Revelation. Armageddon was a necessary
precedent for the arrival of millennial peace and the transformation of
society into the kingdom of God on earth, and the proponents of a postrevolutionary millennial society anchored their predictions in the relevant passages from Isaiah 53 and Revelation 21. Thus the American
Revolution became an integral part of the eternal historical process, the
critical key to the establishment of a pastoral kingdom on earth where
God's saints would "beat their swords into ploughshares" and enjoy eternal peace. It was the historical pattern that Timothy Dwight had
perceived and articulated in his composition of the biblical *Conquest of
Canaan*, which was followed by *Greenfield Hill*, the pastoral elegy of
millennial peace, set in America. Americans were able to view their
history and the events of their times in the traditional and orderly context of Jonathan Edwards' 1739 sermons on the *History of the Work of
Redemption* (edited and published by his son, Jonathan Edwards, Jr., in
1774), which espouses the concept of revolution as an inevitable part of
the cycles of the historical process. Utopian views of America's historical
destiny were centered in the prophecies of Scripture, and the ministers,
who argued for separation from England as an extension of God's divine
plan for the advancement of the Reformation, as well as pamphleteers
like Thomas Paine invoked biblical rhetoric in defending the revolutionary cause. For the ministers, this adaptation of biblical patterns of
history to modern times was conventional, from Cotton Mather's use of
typological figuralism in the *Magnalia Christi Americana* in 1702 to Samuel
Sherwood's exegesis of Revelation and assertion of its application to contemporary America in *The Church's Flight into the Wilderness* (1776). Less

obvious, perhaps, is Thomas Paine's employment of the bondage trope, which the Puritans had used in 1630 to show how England was analogous to Egypt of old, to show how England, in her role as tyrannical despot, was the Antichrist incarnate, which must be overthrown before the millennium could begin. The millennial theme is not overwhelming in Paine's writing, but he uses it enough to indicate a familiarity with its rhetorical importance for the audience he was attempting to reach. Moreover, the Puritan emphasis had demonstrated a condemnation of Rome as Antichrist during the seventeenth century, with English writers like Joseph Mede and Thomas Brightman arguing the necessity of overthrowing that power as a precedent to millennial tranquility, while American Puritan writers in the eighteenth century — Jonathan Edwards and the New Lights particularly — seemed equally concerned with the despotism of England as a threat to the fulfillment of millennial prophecies. Indeed, Thomas Paine's *The American Crisis* essays are filled with the rhetorical strategies of the jeremiad and are richly endowed with images of Britain that are rhetorically associated with the forces of evil in Scripture, which must be overthrown by the forces of good in God's divine plan for world history. This is particularly evident in *The American Crisis,* Number II, where Paine argues the logic of the jeremiad in relation to national election and national punishment in a passage that is particularly reminiscent of Puritan writing:

If ever a nation was mad and foolish, blind to its own interest and bent on its own destruction, it is Britain. There are such things as national sins, and though the punishment of individuals may be reserved to *another* world, national punishment can only be inflicted in *this* world. Britain, as a nation, is in my inmost belief the greatest and most ungrateful offender against GOD on the face of the whole earth . . . All countries have sooner or later been called to their reckoning; the proudest empires have sunk when the balance was struck; and Britain, like an individual penitent, must undergo her day of sorrow, and the sooner it happens to her the better. As I wish it over, I wish it to come.[7]

And again, in *The American Crisis,* Number V (1778), Paine reaches a rhetorical flourish that is characteristically biblical and Puritan rather than neoclassical or enlightened: "From such men and masters may the gracious hand of Heaven preserve America! And though the sufferings she now endures are heavy and severe, they are like straws in the wind compared to the weight of evils she would feel under the government of your king, and his pensioned parliament . . . The will of God hath parted us, and the deed is registered for eternity. When she shall be a spot scarcely visible among the nations, America shall flourish the favorite of Heaven and the friend of mankind."[8] Obviously, Paine could hardly be grouped with the ministers and poets of the American Revolution whose primary purpose was the establishing of signs of the times that would corroborate Scripture prophecy of a forthcoming and imminent millennium. However, the influence of these rhetorical patterns was strong, and in Paine's political writing occasional flourishes of biblical and Puritan rhetoric are clear. In *Common Sense*, for example, Paine employs rhetorical strategies commonly used by scriptural exegetes despite the overwhelming political and social sentiment of the piece. Even the anti-Christian *Age of Reason* suggests parallels between sacred and profane history that can be employed to argue the reverse of Paine's position, namely, that the "Christian mythographers," as he derisively denotes the writers of Scripture, are following a pattern already established in the mythology of the ancient Greeks, so that their claim to an original and "revealed" historiography is false. On the contrary, the synthetic writers of the revolutionary era—those poets like Freneau and Dwight and the ministers like Sherwood—would see in the historical process a fusion of sacred and secular that was being brought to a dramatic climax in the parallels between the scriptural prophecy of Armageddon and the overthrowing of Antichrist in the American Revolution. William Hedges wrote, "A closer look . . . suggests that the motives behind the more purely political and the more purely literary endeavors were much the same . . . A widespread utopianism in politics parallels millennialism in *belles lettres* and religion. Indeed, both before and after 1776 political theorizing in America often seems a kind of pastoralism, . . . An idealized rural environment and the sense of an ideal political order are of course brought together in Jefferson's *Notes on Virginia* and Crevecoeur's *Letters from an American Farmer*."[9]

Thus all kinds of literary expression during the era of the American Revolution conspire to develop a vision of the elect nation's future promise that is rooted in Scripture prophecy, typology, and figuralism modified by the enlightenment belief in order, harmony, and a pastoral simplicity that is classical in origin despite its association with the pastoral harmony of Isaiah. Even poetry designed to anticipate reconciliation rather than revolution adapted the pastoral mode and biblical figuralism of nationalistic verse. For example, Nathaniel Evans conceived the future in a vision of pastoral, millennial harmony, structured according to biblical prophecy, but energized by science and commerce rather than faith:

> HASTE then, O haste, thy soft'ning Pow'r renew,
> Bless ev'ry Clime, the *Old-World* and the *New!*
> In friendly League unite each distant Shore,
> And bid Mankind with Anger burn no more:

> COMMERCE shall then expand without control,
> Where coasts extend, or farthest Oceans roll;
> These spacious Realms their Treasures shall unfold,
> And *Albion's* Shore shall blaze with *Indian* Gold.
> HAIL! happy *Britain*, in a Sovereign blest
> Who deems in Kings a virtuous Name the best;
> Guardian of Right and sacred Liberty,
> *Rome's* glorious NUMA shall be seen in Thee,
> Beneath thy smile fair SCIENCE shall increase,
> And from one Reign of LEARNING and of PEACE.
> E'en we who now attempt the Muse's Shell
> Great GEORGE's sweet Munificence can tell,
> Tho' far, far distant from his glorious Throne,
> Yet has our Seat his regal Bounty known,
> So universal shines the God of Day,
> Each Land enlight'ning with his genial Ray.[10]

And the writers who "see bolder genius quit the narrow shore," look to America and to science, as did John Trumbull in "The Prospect of the Future Glory of America" (1770), to uncover "hiding in brightness of superior day,/ The fainting gleam of Europe's setting ray." An inverse proportion between Europe's decline and America's rising glory was established in these nationalistic verses, and for David Humphreys, a Revolutionary poet and contemporary of Joel Barlow, "Columbia! daughter of the skies" needed only to "Awake to Glory, and to greatness rise!"[11]

Humphreys' three "rising glory" poems— *The Glory of America* (1773), *A Poem Addressed to the Armies of the United States of America* (1780), and *A Poem on the Happiness of America* (1786)— are characteristic of the genre and representative of the transformation from millennial symbolism that prophesied a spiritual progression to the use of the traditional language of Canaan in a secular context. In *The Glory of America,* the poet sees a pastoral scene of millennial tranquility, "A lovely scene—Ye who in waters lie/ And bask and gambol in noon's flaming ray/ In silent joy to Peace your homage pay." But the diatribe against "Deluded Britain" shows the political cast of the poem, and the concluding verses display a secular vision in which science and learning are the instruments of evolving social and political perfection:

> Another theme I now attempt to sing,
> Of rising genius, and the source whence spring
> Delicious fruits, a mental feast of joy,
> Fair Science and her train, which never cloy . . .
>
> All human greatness shall in us be found,

> For grandeur, wealth, and honor far renown'd;
> While thus the nation boasts its powerful state
> Endow'd with all which constitutes it great
> In calm security, the land shall rest,
> He people blessing, by her people blest.

This theme of human evolution through learning and science is repeated in *A Poem Addressed to the Armies of the United States*, which was, by Humphreys' own prefatory declaration, designed "To inspire our Countrymen now in arms, or who may hereafter be called into the field, with perseverance and fortitude, thro' every species of difficulty and danger, to continue their exertions for the defence of their country, and the preservation of its Liberties."[12] It is clear, however, that "liberty and independence" are to be preserved not only by force of arms in the revolution against British tyranny, but also in the commercial expansion of North America, and in the advancement of learning so prominent in a secular and enlightened society:

> Then shall rich commerce, court the fav'ring gales,
> And wond'ring wilds admire the passing sails,
> Where the bold ships, the stormy Huron brave,
> Where wild Ontario rolls the whitening wave,
> Where fair Ohio, his pure current pours,
> And Mississippi laves the extended shores.
>
> The oh, blest land! with genius unconfin'd,
> With polish'd manners, and the illumin'd mind,
> Thy future race, on daring wing shall soar,
> Each science trace, and all the arts explore;
> 'Till bright religion, beck'ning from the skies,
> Shall bid thy sons to endless glories rise (p. 15).

The invocation of "bright religion" at the close of the poem restores to the poem's argument the original sense of a spiritual fulfillment, but by now, the true hero is clear: science and learning will bring about the anticipated era even though God's assistance is asked in the concluding stanza:

> And thou Supreme! whose hand sustains the ball,
> Before whose nods, the nations rise and fall,
> Propitious smile, and shed diviner charms,
> On this blest land, the queen of arts and arms;
> Make the great Empire rise on wisdom's pean,
> The seat of bliss, and last retreat of Man (p. 15).

The neoclassical, pastoral society and Judeo-Christian millennial symbolism are again fused in Humphreys' *Poem on the Happiness of*

America, which celebrates George Washington as a classical and biblical hero. It is the genius of the western world — suggesting the *translatio studii* motif that has animated many of these nationalistic poems — that will accelerate social and scientific improvement in America, but the result is celebrated in a vision of perfection that is cast in biblical language:

> Oh happy people, ye to whom is given
> A land enrich'd with sweetest dews of Heaven!
> Ye who possess Columbia's virgin prime,
> In harvests blest of ev'ry soil and clime!
> Ye happy mortals, whom propitious fate
> Reserved for actors on a stage so great . . .
>
> Thrice happy race! how blest were freedom's heirs,
> Blest if they knew what happiness is theirs,
> Blest if they knew, to them alone 'tis given
> To know no sov'reign but the LAW AND HEAVEN! (p. 29).

Humphreys again employs the life-as-drama metaphor at the poem's conclusion, where the millennial paradise is brought to fulfillment in the fusion of heaven and earth, echoing Increase Mather's conviction that the New Jerusalem would result from the "new heaven" coming down to earth. The meaning here, however, is very different; unlike Mather, Humphreys is using the language of Canaan to explore the possibility of America's destiny in secular terms, utilizing the transformed biblical symbols to reinforce his conviction of America's future promise:

> Why turns the horizon red? the dawn is near —
> Infants of light, ye harbingers appear!
> With tenfold brightness gild the happier age
> And light the actors o'er a broader stage!
> See Heav'ns perennial year to earth descend!
> Then wake, Columbians! fav'rites of the skies,
> Awake to glory and to rapture rise! (p. 44).

Here, Humphreys develops the synthesis of science and revelation that would inform Barlow's *Columbiad* and bring together the spiritual and secular millennial expectations. As James Davidson put it,

The history of redemption, which served as a vehicle of optimism in times like the peak of the Great Awakening, also became the framework which men used to answer the question of how it was possible to reconcile injuries done to the innocent and righteous with God's omnipotent and benevolent character . . . God was completely just, as well as aesthetically perfect in showing the glory of the Millennium by setting it in contrast with the evil times which would precede and follow it.[13]

Joel Barlow was to echo the moral emphasis of millennial expectations by fusing, in a symbolic vision that drew heavily from biblical figures of the last days, the political and religious future of America. This vision is neoclassical in design, a pastoral paradise of harmony and proportion; biblical in theme, issuing from the eschatology of Isaiah and the Book of Revelation; and a product of the eighteenth-century enlightenment in its secular, progressive view of history.

> But chief their moral soul he learns to trace,
> That stronger chain which links and leads the race;
> Which forms and sanctions every social tie,
> And blinds or clears their intellectual eye.
> He strips that soul from every filmy shade
> That schools had caught, that oracles had made,
> Relumes her visual nerve, develops strong
> The rules of right, the subtle shifts of wrong;
> Of civil power draws clear the sacred line,
> Gives to just government its right divine,
> Forms, varies, fashions, all his lights increase,
> Till earth is fill'd with happiness and peace.[14]

Of the writers considered in this chapter, Joel Barlow is the most representative of the transformations that occurred, following the Revolution, from a religious and typological scheme of historical revolutions to a secular, progressive historiography. Like Edwards and Dwight, Barlow prophesied the millennium or universal order and peaceful harmony, and he saw in America's future the secular fulfillment of prophetic promise in commercial and technological terms. But Barlow's vision did not rest on the power of grace or the strategies of divine wisdom to effect this fulfillment; rather, he developed, through successive revisions from the writing of *The Prospect of Peace* (1778) to *The Columbiad* (1807), a supreme expression of the Jeffersonian vision of America as a pastoral and commercial utopia. It is significant that all three of the poems in the Barlow vision of an evolving millennial paradise—the *Prospect, The Vision of Columbus* (1787), and *The Columbiad*—are essentially neoclassical in form, composed in rhyming, heroic couplets that affirm the order and harmony prophesied in the verses themselves. Barlow was crucially transitional; he provides that essential link between the pastoral visions of a millennial paradise that precede him in the eschatology of Jonathan Edwards and the New Light movement, and the mystical and regenerative figuralism of Henry David Thoreau and the Transcendentalists. Barlow's vision derives much from the Puritan millennialism that informed American symbolic writing before the American Revolution; however, he was certainly no Puritan and substitutes commercial progress for grace in his history of the work of free enterprise. On the one hand, he looks forward to Thoreau and Emerson without fully sharing their mystical insight into the cycles of nature and the typological configurations of historical time; on the other, he accepted a linear teleology based on the progressive evolution of commerce, industry, and technology, which would culminate in the early nineteenth-century visions of a pastoral America transformed by the machine in the garden. His angle of vision resulted in a secular and progressive prophecy for America's future, but he adopted the earlier Christian model for its prophetic and poetic language, and even, on occasion, anchored his vision in specific, typological parallels.

It is important to treat the three poems chronologically, using his prose writings to corroborate the visions developed in the epic verses, because Barlow reused much of the material from the *Vision* in *The Columbiad*. By comparing selected passages, we can form not only a sense of Barlow's method of composition—important for aesthetic and literary history—but we can also see just how the prophetic symbol was transformed from an earlier use that relied heavily on biblical precedent to a later, more secular use in which the theological value has yielded to images of commercial, scientific, and technological improvement. For Barlow, the millennium is still an important psychological force; however, the realization of millennial promises will take place in secular, rather than spiritual terms.

The Prospect of Peace begins with characteristic neoclassical themes, anticipating the restful phase of history when the world will be transformed into a bower of bliss; but even here, industry plays a significant role in holding together the order that is to come:

> Along these shores, amid these flowery vales,
> The woodland shout the joyous ear assails;
> Industrious crouds in different labors toil,
> Those ply the arts, and these improve the soil.
> Here the fond merchant counts his rising gain,
> There strides the rustic o'er the furrow'd plain,
> Here walks the statesman, pensive and serene,
> And there the school boys gambol round the green.[15]

The vision fuses pastoral images of classical harmony and abundance with the work-ethic of America's rising commercial glory:

> See ripening harvests gild the smiling plains,
> Kind Nature's bounty and the pride of swains;
> Luxuriant vines their curling tendrils shoot,
> And bow their heads to drop the clustering fruit;

> In the gay fields, with rich profusion strow'd,
> The orchard bends beneath its yellow load,
> The lofty boughs their annual burden pour,
> And juicy harvests swell th' autumnal store (p. 5).

The dominant image-patterns of the first stanzas of *The Prospect of Peace* are agricultural metaphors, designed to affirm a new American landscape that will follow "The closing scenes of Tyrants fruitless rage, / The opening prospects of a golden age." But the poem moves forward to an anticipation of the peace expected at the conclusion of the revolutionary hostilities, which are viewed as an inevitable movement in the historical process:

> Historic truth, our guardian chiefs proclaim,
> Their worth, their actions, and their deathless fame . . .
> And soon, emerging from the orient skies,
> The blisful morn in glorious pomp shall rise,
> Wafting fair Peace from Europe's fated coast;
> Where wand'ring long, in mazy factions lost,
> From realm to realm, by rage and discord driven,
> She seem'd resolv'd to reascend her heaven (p. 4).

Similarly, the concluding lines of the poem affirm the Christian myth of a transforming, regenerative millennial process, one in which the conventional symbology is derived from John's vision in Revelation, and reinforced by Milton and other Christian poets and theologians through the centuries. Barlow concludes:

> Thro' the broad East, the brightening splendor
> Reverses Nature and illumines heaven;
> Astonish'd regions bless the gladdening sight,
> And Suns and Systems own superior light (p. 12).

The light imagery here is thoroughly conventional Renaissance doctrine that appears in Milton's *Ode on the Morning of Christ's Nativity* and Jonathan Edwards' sermon, *A Divine and Supernatural Light*. And here, in the final stanza, Barlow overlays the classical motif and the natural formula with the symbology of Christian doctrine:

> As when th' asterial blaze o'r Bethl'em stood,
> Which mark'd the birth-place of th' incarnate God;
> When stern priests the heavenly splendor view'd,
> And numerous crouds the wonderous sign pursu'd;
> So eastern kings shall view th' unclouded day
> Rise in the West, and streak its golden way (p. 11).

The birth of Christ, traditionally viewed as a rising eastern morning star, is here established as the type prefiguring the antitype of His second coming: "THAT signal spoke a Saviour's humble birth, / THIS speaks his long and glorious reign on earth!" (p. 11).[16] In this blessed time of spiritual fulfillment, the elect shall rise to enjoy those promised pleasures they have long awaited:

> THEN Love shall rule, and Innocence adore,
> Discord shall cease, the Tyrants be no more;
> 'Till yon bright orb, and those celestial spheres,
> In Radiant circles, mark a thousand years;
> 'Till the giant FIAT that burst th'etherial frames,
> Worlds crush on worlds, and Nature sink in flames!
> The Church elect, from smouldering ruins, rise,
> And sail triumphant thro' the yielding skies,
> Hail'd by the Bridegroom! to the Father given,
> The Joy of Angels, and the Queen of Heaven! (p. 12).

These concluding lines and the imagery of Christian millennialism are misleading, although they certainly indicate how strong the influence of Puritan rhetoric was in the early poetry of Barlow's evolving vision. The true center of *The Prospect of Peace* appears in the middle panel of this tryptich: the "new Messiah" is science, through which the new millennial glory will soon be realized. It is science, not religion, that will bring fulfillment to America, and it is "Fair Science," not religion, that moves forward into *The Vision of Columbus* and *The Columbiad* to provide imagery of prophetic consummation.

> Fair Science then her laurel'd beauty rears,
> And soars with Genius to the radiant stars.
> Her glimmering dawn from Gothic darkness rose,
> And nations saw her shadowy veil disclose;
> She cheer'd fair Europe with her rising smiles,
> Beam'd a bright morning o'er the British Isles,
> Now soaring reaches her meridian height,
> And blest Columbia hails the dazzling light! (p. 7).

The new American genius is realized in Benjamin Franklin, while *"Rittenhouse* appears/ To grace the museum with the rolling spheres" (p. 8). And another realization of "that young Genius, that inventive soul," is Jonathan Edwards, whose own millennial vision corroborates Barlow's description of his role in realizing America's destiny:

> These last Displays the curious mind engage,
> And fire the genius of the rising age;

> While moral tho'ts the plas'd attention claim,
> Swell the warm soul, and wake the virtuous flame;
> While Metaphysics soar a boundless height,
> And launch with *Edwards* to the realms of light (p. 8).

Although the "Virgin's Offspring and the *Filial God*" are celebrated as instruments in the progress of divine history, the force of Barlow's argument is that science and her representative genius figures will usher in the millennium. Edwards is depicted as a rationalist, a metaphysician, rather than a Puritan theologian, and he will not even appear in *The Vision of Columbus* or *The Columbiad*.

Rationalism and Christianity have been freely mixed in this neoclassical poem, and Barlow was not atypical in fusing these elements into an epical, artistic design. Milton, after all, had drawn heavily on classical allusions that were conflated with Christian figures in *Paradise Lost*, but for Barlow, the traditional Christian millennium is only possible after the achievements of science have been realized:

> With Science crown'd, shall Peace and Virtue shine,
> And blest Religion beam a light divine.
> Here the pure Church, descending from her God,
> Shall fix on earth her long and last abode;
> Zion arise, in radiant splendors dress'd,
> By Saints admir'd, by Infidels confess'd;
> Her opening courts, in dazzling glory, blaze,
> Her walls salvation, and her portals praise (p. 10).

Obviously, Barlow shared imagistic habits of mind with the New Light ministers though his conclusions and beliefs were radically different from theirs. His imagery and millennial overlay are distinctly Christian although his vision moves toward a secular fulfillment of Scripture promise. Barlow delivered *The Prospect of Peace*, we must remember, as a commencement address at Yale College in 1788 at his senior exercise. It was typical of a genre of "rising glory" poetry composed by college students of the revolutionary era, and it is affirmative in its view that a peaceful conclusion to hostilities will soon arrive, bringing the millennium of order and harmony also awaited by the New Light Congregationalists. That America is to be the seat of this millennial fulfillment is characteristic of the New Light emphasis, as we have seen, following the *translatio studii* motif adapted so clearly from earlier models like Samuel Sewall's *Phaenomena quaedam Apocalyptica*. It was a breakthrough for Barlow, and for the secular millennialists who would follow him in the nineteenth century, such as Daniel Webster and Edward Everett. Here the imagery of Christian mythology—especially that of the millennial fulfillment long employed to offer a vision of future glory for the American enterprise — is itself adapted to a new purpose, the celebration of an American technological glory that was not to appear until the following century. In his later poems, or, rather, the next two versions of this lifetime effort to resolve the millennial theme in epic form, Barlow would eventually abandon any pretenses to a Christian eschatology and adapt the historical process of biblical dispensations to a purely secular goal. This transformation — or adaptation — is the critical link between the "errand into the wilderness" and "manifest destiny," and it remained for Barlow to prove the connection in the shaping of America's epic poem. A brief glance at some selections from Barlow's prose, contemporary with his composition of *The Columbiad*, which should be used as a gloss on the poetry, will clarify his intent. His was a profoundly nationalistic theme with all the high seriousness of epic grandeur.

That Barlow took this personal mission seriously cannot be disputed, regardless of the critical reading one may wish to give his epic productions. In *An Oration Delivered at Washington, July 4th, 1809*, he recapitulated the motive forces that have driven him through the years to define the American national destiny and to articulate this purpose in verse and prose. "To prepare the United States to act the distinguished part that Providence has assigned them," he argued, "it is necessary to convince them that the means are within their power. A familiar knowledge of the means will teach us how to employ them in the attainment of the end. Knowledge will lead to wisdom; and wisdom in no small degree is requisite in the conduct of affairs so momentous and so new. For our situation is in many respects not only new to us, but new also to the world." This conviction is pervasive throughout the millennial poetry, and the symbolic constructions utilized by Barlow to show America that Providence had prepared them for great things are conventional images that emerge from Puritan New England through the New Light movement. The end of a perfect society provided a viable goal for the revolution that could indeed draw upon the eschatological emphasis of Puritan millennialism, and Barlow seized the opportunity to join this millennialism to republican optimism in a way that stressed continuity rather than disjunction. The perfectibility of human society was, to Barlow, a primary one. It "is not a subject of idle speculation, fit only to adorn the pages of a book; it is a truth of the utmost importance in its practical tendency. No maxim is more essential to the legislator of a nation or to the negotiator of treaties; and it ought especially to be present in the minds of all men who are called to administer a representative government."[17]

For Barlow, social perfectibility could only be accomplished in the context of republican principles, and throughout a literary career that provided the *Vision* and *The Columbiad,* he organized his views toward a republican order that should replace universal monarchy. In his appeal to Europe's enlightened and educated elite, the *Advice to the Privileged Orders* (1792), Barlow traced the history of feudal monarchy and deplored the principle of birthright, the attendant moral corruption, and the military system that monarchy established to support its unwarranted power. The *Advice* appeared only a few days before the second part of Thomas Paine's *Rights of Man,* and contained many of the same sentiments. Ironically, though the *Advice* was not circulated as widely as Paine's inflammatory writings, at the time it was considered even more seditious by the British government and was ranked with Paine's writing for condemnation and attack. In the same year, in a brief poem entitled "The Conspiracy of Kings: a Poem, Addressed to the Inhabitants of Europe, from Another Quarter of the World," Barlow satirized monarchy, and announced that "From western heav'ns th' inverted orient springs, / The morn of man, the dreadful night of kings." Indeed, Barlow's democratic energies condemned Federalism as subversive of true republican order, but his *Advice* was never banned nor was his printer indicted for printing it, as had Paine's publisher been for printing the *Rights of Man.*[18]

Barlow's system, moreover, was rational and enlightened. If Paine occasionally blurs his purpose with extraordinarily articulate, inflammatory diatribe, Barlow sets his goals clearly and intelligently so that readers are persuaded by the sense of his argument rather than the justice of his cause. He is persuaded, for example, that "there is no absolute independence of nations, any more than of individuals. Men are everywhere surrounded with wants, and everywhere incumbered with superfluities; the necessity of asking aid and the ability of granting it are mutual, perpetual, and universal; they keep-up a constant exchange of commodities, a circulation of the vital fluid of society."[19] And though he claimed that "with respect to men, I am of no party," he was in fact "a Republican in theory and practice, notwithstanding the disgrace into which that principle seems to be falling in America. I consider it as my unalienable right, as well as my indispensible duty, to render a service to you whenever I find occasion . . . And I shall not relinquish this right, nor neglect this duty, whoever may be the men, and whatever the party, to whom you may choose to delegate your powers."[20] Despite such political outbursts — or perhaps because of them — Barlow remained a theoretician and visionary, so that his proposals for the perfect society had less the practical planning found in Paine's *Common Sense* and *Rights of Man* and more of a visionary quality projecting the poet's ideal future society. On one specific feature of this society, however, Barlow was quite clearly a pragmatist: the necessity for universal public education.

In the Fourth of July Oration in 1809, he looked forward to a time when America would have two hundred million inhabitants, and he eulogized her potential greatness, commercially and socially. He talked of "improvements," by which he meant physical improvements like roads and canals, but he also emphasized public education: "A universal system of education . . . is incontestably one of the first duties of government, one of the highest interests of the nation, one of the most sacred rights of the individual . . . without which your republic cannot be supported."[21] The obligation of government to provide education stems from Barlow's belief that only an informed voter could make a right decision, so that universal public education was a practical consideration as well as a fundamental human right. Moreover, education would increase the ability of citizens to have intercourse with other nations with whom Americans were interdependent, thereby affirming the principle of mutual agreement and organic, harmonious relationships among the nations of the world. In his *Two Letters to the Citizens of the United States,* this principle is articulated as an organic process of nature:

> Prosperity creates certain relative superfluities, which being exchanged between the parties, supply their relative wants. This interchange of commodities creates an interchange of affections; it begins among individuals, and extends, in regular progression with their knowledge, to every country and every portion of mankind.
>
> Nature has certainly placed no barrier in this long course of improvement. Whatever barriers are perceived in it are unnatural and accidental; they will therefore be removed by the development of the human faculties, though by slow degrees. There is no reason why civilization, after having softened the temper of individuals, and harmonized the component parts of a state, as acting among themselves, should forever stop short at that point, and leave the state a savage without, while it is social and peaceful within (p. 50).

Barlow's vision of progress and prosperity was amplified by his plan for creating a national system of education, and he would have been delighted with the Morrill Land-Grant Act of 1862 that did establish a form of federal assistance toward a public system of education. In the *Prospectus of a National Institution* (1806), he saw in an established, central, educational system a potential for harmony, balance, proportion, and happiness in the perfect society. Just as his verses were balanced by neoclassical rhyming couplets, the society they heralded would be balanced by a sensible management of human faculties, and each citizen would be trained for rational living as well as for sound judgment at the ballot box.

> It is most essential to the happiness of the people and to the preservation of their republican principles, that this tendency to a separation should be over-balanced by superior motives to a harmony of sentiment; that they may habitually feel that community of interest on which their federal system is founded. This desirable object is to be attained, not only by the operations of the government in its several departments, but by those of literature, sciences, and arts. The liberal sciences are in their nature republican; they delight in reciprocal communication; they cherish fraternal feelings, and lead to a freedom of intercourse, combined with the restraints of society, which contribute together to our improvement.[22]

For Barlow, education was both a practical means to provide each citizen with that "first right he possesses, after that of breathing the vital air, . . . the right of being taught the management of the power to which he is born"[23] and a way of bringing about universal harmony, order, and peace — a social millennium.

Although Barlow's public addresses were conceived as visionary projections of a social program delivered to enlightened audiences who were implored to act on his proposals, they may be used as a gloss on the visionary poetry, for throughout his life Barlow attempted to shadow forth the dawning of a new day in America, a period when the pastoral scenes of neoclassical poetry would be realized and the prophecy of biblical millennialism would be fulfilled in the commercial progress of America's social and political growth. Leon Howard argues that "Barlow never saw the international commerce as bitter competition but only as the peaceful means of satisfying mutual wants, and as such he glorified the American ideal of commercial expansion and incorporated it into his new vision. Barlow viewed the prospect of a new world, established on the principles of freedom and equality already achieved in America, developed through the growth of reason, and spread by an increasing commercial intercourse."[24] It is no surprise, therefore, that the images of the millennial poetry are both classical and Christian, and that the ultimate objective of the poet is the prophesying of America's new destiny, as he viewed his nation's commercial potential, political and social perfectibility, and articulated the vision in a series of related epic poems. The goal of all was a realization of the spiritual and earthly paradise eloquently preached in Barlow's 1787 Fourth of July Oration, which he delivered at the North Church of Hartford:

> Under the idea of a permanent and *happy* government, every point of view, in which the future situation of America can be placed, fills the mind with a

peculiar dignity, and opens an unbounded field of thought. The natural resources of the country are inconceivably various and great; the enterprising genius of the people promises a most rapid improvement in all the arts that embellish human nature; the blessings of a rational government will invite emigrations from the rest of the world, and fill the empire with the worthiest and happiest of mankind; while the example of political wisdom and felicity here to be displayed will excite emulation through the kingdoms of the earth, and meliorate the condition of the human race.[25]

Indeed, Barlow even invokes the language of Canaan as that medium through which we may come to understand America's prophetic destiny, a vehicle through which he would articulate the grand design as revealed to him through his vision. "In the pleasing contemplation of such glorious events, and comparing the scenes of action that adorn the western hemisphere, with what has taken place in the east," he asserts, "may we not apply to our country the *Language of the Prophet of Israel*, . . . 'The glory of this latter house shall be greater than of the former, saith the Lord of Hosts,' peace to any disorders that may at present subsist among us, peace to the contending passions of nations, peace to this empire, to future ages, and through the extended world."[26] Although Barlow's two great poems differed in form—one a narrative vision and the other an epic—they are essentially similar in predicting for America a glorious future, brilliantly depicted and graphically articulated in a secular modification of the language of Canaan.

THE VISION OF COLUMBUS

The Vision of Columbus is introduced by a statement of purpose in which Barlow argues that he "formed an idea of attempting a regular Epic Poem, on the Discovery of America."[27] But he soon "rejected the idea of a regular epic form, and has confined his plan to the train of events which might be represented to the hero in vision." In this way, he continued, he would avoid the pitfalls of conformity to the epic scheme while keeping a single poetic design constantly in view, "which is to gratify and soothe the desponding mind of the hero," Christopher Columbus. The early sections of the poem are a conflation of primitive, neoclassical, and Christian imagery, and Barlow depicted Columbus despondent over the evolution of America since its discovery. But the early books of the *Vision* are also richly endowed with images taken from the Bible and from Judeo-Christian commentators, so that America is cast as the New English Israel of Puritan exegesis:

> As that great Seer, whose animating rod
> Taught Israel's sons the wonder-working God,
> Who led, thro' dreary wastes, the murmuring band

> To the fair confines of the promised land,
> Oppress'd with years, from Pisgah's beauteous height,
> O'er boundless regions cast the raptured sight;
> The joys of unborn nations warm'd his breast,
> Repaid his toils and sooth'd his soul to rest;
> Thus, o'er thy subject wave, shalt thou behold
> Far happier realms their future charms unfold,
> In nobler pomp another Pisgah rise,
> Beneath whose foot thine own Canaan lies;
> There, rapt in vision, hail the distant clime,
> And taste the blessings of remotest time.[28]

However, the poem does not move toward a millennial fulfillment in scriptural terms. Instead, the first two books provide a tedious geographical description of North and South America which is used to introduce the central narrative myth of the poetic vision, the story of Manco Capac and his wife Mama Oella and their founding of the Incan dynasty and civilization in Peru. Capac becomes Barlow's central symbol of a messiah for his primitive paradise, a pastoral, primitive paradise that will come to fulfill the potential of the earth for enlightenment. Barlow's discarding of the epic form—an established genre with the sophisticated restrictions of his own civilized order—suggests a new beginning, and the visionary process would also introduce a new perspective gained by examining an older, more traditional model. Indeed, sandwiched between Books II and III, a prose *Dissertation on the Genius and Institutions of Manco Capac* brings together Christian and pagan, ancient and modern traditions in a representative formula for universal enlightenment and progress. Paramount in this historical process are the leaders whom Barlow associates freely: "The most distinguished characters in history, who have been considered as legislators among barbarous nations, are Moses, Lycurgus, Solon, Numa, Mahomet and Peter of Russia. Of these, only the two former and the two latter appear really to deserve that character."[29] Barlow argued that "the establishments of Manco Capac carry the marks of a most benevolent and pacific system; they tend[ed] to humanize the world, and render[ed] his people happy; while his ideas of the Deity were so perfect, as to bear a comparison with the enlightenment doctrines of Socrates or Plato" (82).

This conflation of figures is crucial to Barlow's method, and it has a precedent in Cotton Mather's association of ancient and biblical figures in his writing the history of New England as the *Magnalia Christi Americana,* where contemporary persons such as William Bradford and John Winthrop are made analogous not only to Moses the biblical lawgiver, but also to Lycurgus, the Greek. Scriptural parallels and classical myths are drawn close together by both writers, though their resulting objectives were opposed. Robert Richardson said, "Typology helped create a climate of acceptance for mythic thought, encouraged a historical view of myth, and provided a technique for interpreting and integrating various bodies of myth. Joel Barlow's comparison of the Peruvian Manco Capac to both Moses and Lycurgus is certainly made easier by the American tradition of typological interpretation."[30] The relationship between typology and early New England mythology has been explored at length by Sacvan Bercovitch in his recent book, *The Puritan Origins of the American Self* and in chapter 7 of this study, where the realization of John Winthrop as "Nehemias Americanus" by Cotton Mather is shown to be characteristic of a method of writing history as myth among New England Puritans. What is fascinating in the Barlow *Vision*—especially in the "Dissertation"—is that the same process of association that Mather employed is being used to celebrate Capac's virtues as representative of enlightened leadership and progress. Capac is a recapitulation of primitive virtue just as John Winthrop is a typological recapitulation of Moses and Lycurgus. Capac is a republican lawgiver, as was George Washington, therefore the American Republic is shown to be an ideal society after the manner of primitive models in which Judeo-Christian, classical, and pagan images are conflated.

> Until the institution of representative republics, which are of recent date, it was always a fact confirmed by experience, that those constitutions of government were best calculated for immediate energy and duration, which were interwoven with some religious system. The legislator, who appears in the character of an inspired person, renders his political institutions sacred, and interests the conscience, as well as the judgment, in their support (pp. 84-85).

Although Barlow cynically suggests an intentional strategy by which the ancient lawgivers were able to canonize their schemes without having the sanction of authentic, divine authority, he quickly points out that "the Jewish lawgiver had this advantage over the Spartan: he appeared not in the character of a mere earthly governor, but as an interpreter of the divine will . . . by forbidding usury, and directing that real property should return to the original families in the year of Jubilee, he prevented too great an inequality of property, and by selecting a particular tribe, to be the guardians and interpreters of religion, he prevented its mysteries from being the subject of profane and vulgar investigation" (p. 85).

The ancient patterns—especially those classical myths that parallel the Judeo-Christian scheme—are made analogous to the drama of God's revealed will, and in the process, just as Cotton Mather had utilized the ancients metaphorically to corroborate the historiography of his

Magnalia Christi Americana, Barlow's *Vision* transforms the religious epic figures into metaphorical representations. The cycle of prophetic symbolism adapted from the typological tradition is retained, but its purpose is now to anticipate that revolution which will provide an American commercial ascendancy. If for Thomas Paine, mythology — pagan or Judeo-Christian — was suspect, artificial, and devious, for Barlow myth was a way of perceiving reality, and he used both ancient systems to prophesy America's commercial destiny. Paine argued that "the Christian mythologists, calling themselves the Christian church, have erected their fable, which for absurdity and extravagance is not exceeded by anything that is to be found in the mythology of the ancients."[31]

The Vision of Columbus, like the *Magnalia Christi Americana*, affirms the reality and importance of symbol and myth in the expression of religious belief, although Barlow would abandon this perspective in his writing of *The Columbiad*. The imagery of the vision is traditional and conventional; the primitive sun worship of Manco Capac's people is to be associated with the light imagery of Milton's "Ode on the Morning of Christ's Nativity," not because it represents grace and regenerative power, as it so clearly does for Milton, but because the process of rational association allows the reader to perceive in the Capac mythology an analogy for Christianity's progressive hold on the American imagination. "This rationally recommended and enthusiastically endorsed sun-worship pervades *The Vision of Columbus*, and is carried through in literary ways. The image of the sun of enlightenment (a commonplace of the period to be sure) rising to dispel the dark night of error occurs at least fifteen times in Book One alone. Book Three is chiefly taken up with a battle between the forces of light and the forces of darkness, the battle pivoting around an eclipse and subsequent reemergence of the sun. The sun is the crucial link between Capac's Peruvian civilization and the eighteenth-century enlightenment. Capac himself becomes the New World's mythical founder of the earliest form of the enlightenment."[32] This process is nowhere more evident than in the text of *The Vision of Columbus*, and an examination of a few, selected passages will clarify the pattern that pervades the whole poem.

Like Dante, Barlow's Columbus is provided with a "blest Immortal" guide, who points to "lands yet unknown, and streams without a name," which "Rise into vision and demand their fame."[33] But the association Barlow intends for the secularized myth is clear. His next line develops the metaphorical analogy to the Judeo-Christian tradition and *compares* the experience of Columbus with conventional, religious versions:

> As when some saint, in heav'n's sublime abode,
> Extends his views o'er all the works of God;
> While earth's fair circuit, in his presence rolls,

> Here glows the centre, and there point the poles; . . .
> With equal glance, the great observer's sight
> Rang'd the low vale, or climb'd the cloudy height,
> As, led by heaven's own light, his raptured mind,
> Explor'd the realms that here await mankind.[34]

It is important to note that *The Vision of Columbus* was itself altered significantly by Barlow between the publication in 1787 of the Hartford edition and the publication in 1793 of the Paris edition. The intervening years had witnessed the French Revolution and the distinct ascendancy of Enlightenment rationalism, which appears to have influenced some of the changes Barlow made during those five intense years. For example, a significant passage appears in the ninth book in both versions, one which describes fully the anticipated period of millennial prosperity, and in the 1787 Hartford edition, the metaphorical analogies are developed through a vision that reads like an eighteenth-century paraphrase of the sixty-fifth chapter of Isaiah:

> At this blest period, when thy peaceful race
> Shall speak one language and one cause embrace,
> Science and arts a speedier course shall find,
> And open earlier on the infant mind.
> No foreign terms shall croud with barbarous rules,
> The dull, unmeaning pageantry of schools;
> Nor dark authorities, nor names unknown
> Fill the learn'd head with ign'rance not its own;
> But truth's fair eye, with beams unclouded, shine,
> And simplest rules her moral lights confine;
> One living language, one unborrow'd dress
> Her boldest flights with happiest force express;
> Triumphant virtue, in the garb of truth,
> Win a pure passage to the heart of youth,
> Pervade all climes, where suns or oceans roll,
> And bid the gospel cheer the illumined whole.
> As the glad day-star, on his golden throne,
> Fair type of truth and promise of the sun,
> Smiles up the orient, in his rosy ray,
> Illumes the front of heaven, and leads the day;
> Thus soaring Science daughter of the skies,
> First o'er the nations bids her beauties rise,
> Prepares the glorious way, to pour abroad
> The beams of Heaven's own morn, the splendors of a God.[35]

In the 1793 version, the "glad day-star," so prominent an image in Increase Mather's traditional premillennial interpretation of the "Book of Revelation," is dropped altogether, and a classical allusion is substituted for the biblical figure of the morning star; the line thus reads: "As early Phosphor on his golden throne, / Fair type of truth and promise of the Sun." Phosphor on his throne is here depicted as a "fair type of truth," associating the classical figure metaphorically and historically with the prophetic system of typology by which the figures of biblical exegesis were endowed with value for contemporary Puritan America. The image is conventional and echoes the Miltonic trope once again; yet in this second version of the *Vision*, the classical type foreshadows the emergence of science-as-hero, which, when leagued with religion, can bring the world out of darkness just as for Edwards, light imagery was used to depict Christ's leading the world from darkness to eternal light. In both the 1787 and 1793 editions, this millennial moment is followed by a passage that shows Barlow's tension between a purely enlightened resolution and those assurances provided by Scripture prophecy:

> Then blest Religion leads the raptured mind,
> Thro' brighter fields and pleasures more refined;
> Teaches the roving eye, at one broad view,
> To glance o'er time and look Existence thro',
> See worlds, and worlds, to Being's formless end,
> With all their hosts, on one dread Power depend . . .
> His boundless love, his all-pervading soul
> Illume, sublime and harmonize the whole; . . .
> Instructs the heart a nobler joy to taste,
> And share its feelings with another's breast,
> Extend its warmest wish for all mankind,
> And catch the image of the Maker's mind;
> While mutual love commands all strife to cease,
> And earth join joyous in the songs of peace.[36]

This adaptation of the millennial vision of Isaiah, with its harmony, balance, and decorously harmonized proportion, holds science and religion in juxtaposition as unequal powers in the advancement of mankind's progress. It is clear that Barlow has attempted to reconcile the rival forces of faith and reason, but his result is a conflation of the two rather than a synthetic resolution. Epistemology is the key; Barlow wishes to show how illumination and knowledge will result from scientific achievement which will be delivered in the millennial context. In the 1787 version the "day-star" and in the 1793 version "Phosphor" are "fair type(s) of truth," preparing for the advent of Science, which, with the aid of religion, will illumine the darkness of unenlightened mankind, long held in the prison of this "darksome house of mortal clay," as Milton wrote in the "Nativity Ode." The "light" for Barlow is provided not through grace or the restoration of man's fallen vision but through the progressive evolution of the scientific method of investigation and its conclusive pursuit of truth, as it lies hidden in the unexamined world of nature.

The millennial psychology and the anticipation of a new dawn for mankind are resonant throughout the ninth book of *The Vision of Columbus*. However, though religion and science are seemingly paired in an effort to understand hidden truth, Barlow's own vision is clear: the ignorance of mankind can be dispelled not through the tyranny of religious dogmas, found throughout the pagan (classical) and the Judeo-Christian worlds, but only through the enlightenment of science, the true messiah-figure capable of penetrating the darkness of human ignorance. Thus Barlow's continuous emphasis on the importance of universal education is echoed indirectly through the assertion that enlightenment will eventually triumph over ignorance in the millennial state. These images are traditional, scriptural, and conventional, but their recasting to provide a new meaning is clearly intended in *The Vision of Columbus*, particularly if the two versions are collated to determine those substantive changes the poet made between 1787 and 1793. However, the adaptation has been completed and is fully realized in Barlow's supreme poetic effort, the epic *The Columbiad*, through which he finally brought together a form, a consistent pattern of modified images, and his pervasive millennial theme to celebrate America's fulfillment of prophetic promises in commercial and technological splendor. These transformations would not be more than the literary history of one writer's growth and development if Barlow were not so very representative of his time; his poetic metamorphosis and his obvious alterations in the growth of the text show clearly how America was changing during the federal and early republican phases of her national development.

THE COLUMBIAD

The writing of *The Columbiad* and its publication on Christmas Eve, 1807, may have been the grandest extravagance in American literary history. It is well known that Barlow revised the early drafts numerous times, incorporating whole sections of *The Vision of Columbus* and reworking his theme to fit the new epic format. But the book's production and design also consumed the poet. He personally selected the fine paper on which it was printed, contributed one thousand dollars (and solicited another five thousand from the inventor Robert Fulton) to commission paintings by Robert Smirke which would decorate the book as engravings. As though its form celebrated the content in the way that the content celebrated America, the book was a magnificent product in every way. "Even the caustic Francis Jeffrey in the *Edinburgh Review* said he

never had seen a more attractive book published in England. He conced-
ed: 'The infant republic has already attained to the very summit of
perfection in the mechanical art of bookmaking.' "[37] But in order to complete the epic poem—an achievement which had eluded Barlow as he
struggled with other forms to celebrate America's promise—he was
forced to refuse other commissions that would have probably given him
a more exalted place in the evolution of national literature in the United
States.

> Barlow squandered his months in fanning the thin, feeble coals of poetic fire
> when he might have been writing the history of the United States. In so do-
> ing, he missed a chance that comes to very few men. Jefferson and Madison
> were urging him to write the history and were offering the resources of the
> government archives and their own files. They were also ready with their
> memories and interpretations of men and events. In July, 1806, the President
> sent Barlow four boxes of papers and pamphlets for use in the history, but
> always there was another more pressing project, and at this moment it was
> *The Columbiad.*[38]

Moreover, the poem was not received as an outstanding achievement,
although the author had made unusual sacrifices to complete his life's
ambition of establishing the epic grandeur of the new nation. In the
Edinburgh Review, Francis Jeffrey, who had praised the technical aspects
of the book's production, had this to say:

> As a great national poem, it has enormous—inexpiable—and, in some
> respects, intolerable faults. But the author's talents are evidently respectable:
> and severely as we have been obliged to speak of his taste and his diction in a
> great part of the volume, we have no hesitation in saying that we consider him
> a giant, in comparison with many of the puling and paltry rhymsters, who
> disgrace our English literature by their occasional success. As an Epic poet,
> we do think his case is desperate; but as a philosophical and moral poet, we
> think he has talents of no ordinary value; and, if he would pay some attention
> to purity of style, and simplicity of composition, and cherish in himself a cer-
> tain fastidiousness of taste, —which is not yet to be found, we are afraid, even
> among the better educated Americans, — we have no doubt that he might pro-
> duce something which English poets would envy, and English crtitics ap-
> plaud.[39]

Barlow's critics—contemporary and modern—are all aware that
The Columbiad was no mere rewriting of the narrative vision composed in
1787. "*The Columbiad* [is] more than a revision of *The Vision of Columbus*,"
writes William Andrews. "Underlying the second poem is an increased
optimism about the capacity of society to improve itself and move of its
own accord toward perfection . . . *The Columbiad* articulates a vision of

universal peace and happiness which replaced the strictly nationalistic one founded on the application of the *translatio* exclusively to America."[40] And Leon Howard, who has given Joel Barlow special tribute for his contributions to the development of an American national literature, sees in *The Columbiad* an expression of Barlow's sense of national optimism at the turn of the century: "The system of philosophy Barlow adopted for *The Columbiad* was that used in his more speculative, less practical political writings. It was, of course, optimistically progressive; and, as in *The Vison of Columbus*, the progress was in accord with a predetermined plan. In the latter poem, however, the plan was Nature's rather than God's."[41] This alteration was significant; by moving away from the divine drama that had provided a structure for the millennial and figural writings of prerevolutionary America, Barlow was obligated to find new ways to use the language of Canaan, which he had employed in the earlier poem, to celebrate the progressive, secular evolution of America's national destiny.

The external differences between the two poems are simple: the historical introduction was retained, but Barlow added a lengthy philosophical preface in which he explained that "*The Columbiad* is a patriotic poem; the subject is national and historical" but that his "object is altogether of a moral and political nature. I wish to encourage, and strengthen, in the rising generation, a sense of the importance of republican institutions; as being the great foundation of public and private happiness, the necessary aliment of future and permanent meliorations in the condition of human nature."[42] This grand design was accomplished by expanding the original eight books to nine, even though Barlow did not alter much of the original plan in the first five books, where both poems describe parts of America and trace the development of western civilization from its beginnings in the Inca empire. But Books VI, VII, and VIII are changed significantly; the treatment of the American Revolution, confined to Books VI and VII in the *Vision*, fills all three in *The Columbiad*, thus necessitating the addition of a final, or ninth and concluding book.[43]

In assessing the changes Barlow made in the text of the *Vision* when he began to compose *The Columbiad*, it is useful to compare selected passages from the two prominent editions of the *Vision*, the 1787 Hartford and the 1793 Paris, with the 1807 Philadelphia printing of *The Columbiad*. Some of the shifts are subtle, others blatant and obvious; nearly all are substantive. Clearly, an extensive textual analysis is beyond the scope of this study; however, a few relevant passages reveal clearly Barlow's later emphasis on a more rational development than *The Prospect of Peace* and the *Vision* had displayed, and the later stanzas show a renewed emphasis on learning as a resolution of those human problems

that millennial paradise was originally designed to redress. Barlow's progressive vision is clearly postmillennial in that he asserts the perfectibility of society through projects of self-improvement such as universal
education. In the final book of the 1787 *Vision*, for example, Columbus
sees a perspective of the apocalypse and commencement of the millennial period:

> Now, fair beneath his view, the important age
> Leads the bold actors on a broader stage;
> When, clothed majestic in the robes of state,
> Moved by one voice, in general council meet
> The father of all empires: 'twas the place,
> Near the first footsteps of the human race;
> Where wretched men, first wandering from their God,
> Began their feuds and led their tribes abroad.[44]

The language of Canaan so prominent here, invoking the original sin
through which mankind has historically departed from God's predetermined plan, is dropped completely in the final book of *The Columbiad*,
where the passage reappears in modified form to reflect a more rational
explanation for social problems based on an understanding of primitive
social organization:

> Fill'd with unfolding fate, the vision'd age
> Now leads its actors on a broader stage;
> When clothed majestic in the robes of state,
> Moved by one voice, in general congress meet,
> The legates of all empires. 'Twas the place
> Where man first sought to socialize his race;
> Ere yet beguiled, the dark delirious hordes
> Began to fight for altars and for lords;
> Nile washes still the soil and feels once more
> The works of wisdom press his peopled shore.[45]

Similarly, Barlow shifts the imagery and meaning of comparable
passages by altering several important words from 1787 to 1793 to 1807.
In Book VIII of the *Vision* (which becomes Book IX in the expanded version of *The Columbiad*) we find:

> To whom the Angelic Power; to thee 'tis given,
> To hold high converse, and enquire of heaven,
> To mark uncircled ages and to trace
> The unfolding truths that wait thy kindred race.
> Know then, the counsels of th' unchanging Mind,
> Thro' nature's range, progressive paths design'd,

> Unfinish'd works th' harmonious system grace,
> Thro' all duration and around all space;
> Thus beauty, wisdom, power, their prats unroll,
> Till full perfection joins the accordant whole.[46]

The fusion of progressive improvement and revealed religion is even more explicit in the 1793 version, but both retain the "Angelic power" through whom the vision is accomplished, and the harmonious perfection achieved remains the product of a divine power, either "th' unchanging Mind" (1787) or "the Maker's mind" (1793). The concluding line of the stanza in the 1793 version, cited below, makes clear Barlow's continued emphasis on a reconciliation between faith and progress:

> To whom th' Angelic Power: — To thee 'tis given
> To hold high converse and enquire of Heaven,
> To make untravers'd ages, and to trace
> The promis'd truths that wait thy kindred race.
> Know then, the counsels of the Maker's mind,
> Thro' nature's range, progressive paths design'd.
> Progressive works at every step we trace,
> Thro' all duration and around all space;
> Till power and wisdom all their parts combine,
> And full perfection speak the work divine.[47]

The Columbiad, however, represents a shift away from this attempted reconciliation toward an Enlightenment interpretation of nature's progressive course that is clearly guided more by truth and wisdom than by God's grace:

> To whom the guardian Power: To thee is given
> To hold high converse and enquire of heaven,
> To mark untraversed ages, and to trace
> What'er improves and what impedes thy race.
> Know then, progressive are the paths we go
> In worlds above thee, as in thine below.
> Nature herself (whose grasp of time and place
> Deals out duration and impalms all space)
> Moves in progressive march; but where to tend,
> What course to compass, how the march must end,
> Her sons decide not; yet her works we greet
> Imperfect in their parts, but in their whole complete.[48]

The slight changes in syntax and the substantive alterations in nominative form are significant. "Angelic" becomes "guardian," "(a)wait" becomes "improves" and the "progressive march" becomes a

secular, natural phenomenon that is independent of divinity and does
not rely on the "Maker's mind" to provide harmonious design or completion. It is the piecing together of the puzzle that renders the whole, and it
is man's reason that enables individuals and civilizations to develop
toward this goal of harmonious perfection. Indeed, in his notes for *The
Columbiad*, Barlow cites the advancement of learning and the progressive
evolution of technology as hallmarks of societal improvement:

> I conceive it no objection to this theory that the progress has hitherto been
> slow; when we consider the magnitude of the object, the obstructions that
> were to be removed, and the length of time taken to accomplish it. The future
> progress will probably be more rapid than the past. Since the invention of
> printing, the application of the properties of the magnet, and the knowledge
> of the structure of the solar system, it is difficult to conceive of a cause that can
> produce a new state of barbarism; unless it be some great convulsion in the
> physical world, so extensive as to change the face of the earth or a con-
> siderable part of it.[49]

Ultimately, it is the spirit of commerce that complements science as
the generator of millennial prosperity and progress; the cycles of
spiritual regeneration and progress that were so apparent in the
historical patterns of biblical dispensation have been replaced by a new
force — the advancement of society through education and politics and
the progressive improvement of the world through commercial intercourse. If for Edwards, the mariner's compass had been invented to
facilitate the spreading of the Gospel, for Barlow the mariner's compass
enabled nations to conduct commercial affairs more expeditiously and
efficiently.

> The spirit of commerce is happily calculated to open an amicable intercourse
> between all countries, to soften the horrors of war, to enlarge the field of
> science, and to assimilate the manners, feelings, and languages of all nations.
> This leading principle, in its remoter consequences, will produce advantages
> in favor of free government, give patriotism the character of philanthropy, in-
> duce all men to regard each other as brethren and friends, and teach them the
> benefits of peace and harmony among nations.[50]

In spite of these pressures on the language to accommodate a new
system of belief and new forms of expression, the language of Canaan
continued to be a vehicle for carrying the progressive, millennial vision
of future times. If it was now endowed with new value and meaning, and
if the old figures were now used to render new meanings, the forms
themselves were firmly held as metaphorical structures through which
the new values were expressed. Barlow continued to utilize biblical

figures in his *Vision of Columbus* but he was clearly moving away from the typological value these figures had carried in the contemporary writing of the New Light movement. A brief examination of Barlow's specific program for societal improvement will make this clear.

Like Jonathan Edwards, Barlow envisioned a perfect society wrought from history in cycles of dispensation; however, this postmillennial, progressive vision was expressed in the language of scriptural prophecy but realized through the agency of scientific improvement and commercial expansion. It is an indication of the power of the biblical language to hold on during a time of transformation that in the notes to *The Vision of Columbus*, Barlow provides a prose gloss for his view that progress would come through scientific advancement rather than through spiritual regeneration, though the language of the poem clearly exemplifies biblical analogies and is resonant with figures drawn from the types and figures:

> It has long been the opinion of the Author, that such a state of peace and happiness as is foretold in scripture and commonly called the millennial period, may be rationally expected to be introduced without a miracle. *Nec deus intersit nisi dignus vindice modus*, is a maxim, as useful to a Christian Philosopher as to a Heathen Poet. Although, from the history of mankind, it appears, that the progressive improvement has been slow and often interrupted, yet it gives pleasure to observe the causes of these interruptions, and to discern the end they were designed in the course of Providence to answer, in accelerating the same events, which they seemed for awhile to retard.[51]

Barlow excised this passage from his notes to *The Columbiad*, further indicating his focus on a technological scheme of progress that had no corollary in Scripture prophecy. And he attributes, in the notes to Book IX of *The Columbiad* (1807; p. 438), the happiness of society to the expansion and growth of commerce and to the progress of science rather than any further stage of divine dispensation. "The spirit of commerce is happily calculated by the Author of Wisdom to open an amicable intercourse between all countries," Barlow argued, echoing some of the sentiments Jonathan Edwards had announced in the *Miscellanies* as he attempted a reconciliation between the dispensations of the "Divine Author" and the inevitable cycles of historical progress. But Barlow's emphasis is clearly secular; he argues that commerce will "soften the horrors of war, enlarge the field of science and speculation, and assimilate the manners, feelings, and languages of all nations." And the secular emphasis is transformed immediately into political and social patriotism, exhibited throughout in Barlow's republican enthusiasm through which both commerce and agriculture became allies in the progressive realization of a perfect society.

This leading principle, and its remoter consequences, will produce a thousand advantages in favor of government and legislation, give Patriotism the air of Philanthropy, induce all men to regard each other as brethren and friends, eradicate all kinds of literary, religious, and political superstition, prepare the minds of all mankind for the *rational reception of moral and religious truth* [italics mine] and finally evince that such a system of Providence, as appears in the unfolding of these events, is the best possible system to produce the happiness of men.[52]

The progressive cycles of history are clearly designed to culminate in a perfect ordering of society which is enlightened, harmonious, and future. But the language of Barlow's earlier poem reflects the strong influence of biblical imagery in the realization of this vision, so that we may also contrast passages that have no specific parallels in the companion poem but which reflect, nevertheless, dramatic changes of emphasis. For example, in the *Vision*, Barlow discusses the source of the system in the full flower of Canaan's metaphors, a section which he dropped altogether from *The Columbiad:*

> Progressive thus, from that great source above,
> Flows the fair fountain of redeeming love.
> Dark harbingers of hope, at first bestow'd,
> Taught early faith to feel her path to God;
> Down the prophetic, brightening train of years,
> Consenting voices rose of different seers,
> In *shadowy types* display'd the accomplish'd plan,
> When filial Godhead should assume the man,
> When the pure Church should stretch her arms abroad,
> Fair as a bride and liberal as her God;
> Till warm benevolence and truth refined,
> Pervade the world and harmonize mankind.[53]

The scriptural language and patterns of typological prophecy and fulfillment are clear; Barlow intends not only a vision of progress but one that is at least partially derived from the historical authority of divine dispensation. But it is equally clear that he anticipates the wholly secular version of progress offered by *The Columbiad*, because the lines above are followed by these:

> And thus fair Science, of celestial birth,
> With times long circuit, treads the gladsome earth;
> By gradual steps to mark the extended road,
> That leads mankind to reason and to God.[54]

It is important that the passage had been deleted entirely from the 1793 edition, and it is omitted in *The Columbiad*. The strong biblical references and the prophetic force of the language were not appropriate to Barlow's more enlightened and rational purpose. Instead, the imperial course is guided by science and reason, so that in the Paris edition of the *Vision* we find the following stanza in place of the "shadowy types" cited above:

> 'Tis thus meek Science, from creation's birth,
> With time's long circuit treads the darksome earth,
> Leads in progressive march th' enquiring mind,
> To curb its passions and its bliss to find,
> To guide the reas'ning power, and smoothe the road,
> That leads mankind to nature and to God.[55]

Thus religion — in this case specifically the spiritual dispensations understood by the Judeo-Christian work of redemptive history — is subordinated to "rational reception of moral and religious truth"; piety is supplanted by moralism, "that only criterion of truth that we are able to obtain."[56] Barlow laments the slow progress of the past unfolding of God's plan and seems to explain it by showing how rational science was not until recently available to assist the divine author: "It is possible that some considerable revolutions are yet to happen, before the progress will be entirely free from embarassments. But the general system appears so *rational and complete*, that it furnishes a new source of satisfaction, in contemplating the apparent dispensations of Heaven."[57] But Barlow adheres to the historical scheme of cyclical dispensation when he prophesies that progress will be attained through a movement toward universal harmony and perfection:

> It seems necessary that the arrangement of events in civilizing the world should be in the following order: *first*, all parts of it must be considerably peopled; *second*, the different nations must be known to each other; *third*, their wants must be increased, in order to inspire a want for commerce. The first of these objects was not probably accomplished till a late period. The second for three centuries past has been greatly accelerated. The third is a necessary consequence of the two former.[58]

It is significant that rational perception, as contrasted with spiritual revelation, has become the vehicle of epistemology, the means through which individuals are to know and to understand truth. Of course, Jonathan Edwards had already done much to reconcile Lockean epistemology with divine revelation, as the following chapter explains in detail, but Barlow is here shifting the emphasis away from Scripture altogether, citing the physical world and its condition as the standard for measuring stability and change in the cycles of revolution. It is equally significant that Barlow retained much material from these notes in the ninth book of *The Vision of Columbus* in his revision of the notes to *The Columbiad*, Book X. In short, the prophetic books of both the *Vision* and *The Columbiad* are reflections of the changes in language that had taken place even as Barlow composed the earlier poem. Although biblical images are used in the *Vision* to suggest progressive evolution and development, by 1806 much of this had been stripped away. Leon Howard said, "Barlow no longer felt that man's hope depended upon some internal sense: it depended, instead, upon the overthrow of error by scientific investigation and the formation of new, more trustworthy habits of thinking."[59] The poet himself had warned in the Preface, "There are two distinct objects to be kept in view in the conduct of a narrative poem: the *poetical* object and the *moral* object. The poetical is the fictitious design of the action; the moral is the real design of the poem."[60] The traditional imagery of *The Vision of Columbus*, the "poetical" design or "fictitious" design of the earlier poem, has been supplanted by a more wholly neoclassical design, an epic structure rather than a narrative vision, and the poem's content—what he chooses to call the "moral design"—is clearly more philosophical and political than it had been in the earlier prototype.

> This brave new world which Columbus was allowed to see was, physically, very much like the one he had seen in the earlier poem. Intellectually, however, it was different. Barlow had become more clearly utilitarian in his social philosophy and more completely a rationalist in morals. He placed more emphasis upon "interest" as a force for uniting the world and less upon "sympathy" and "friendship." And he expressed greater confidence in the ability of men's minds to expand beyond "local" limits and consider the "strength and happiness of all humankind." Instead of "blest Religion" leading the "raptured mind," he saw a rational "Moral Science" conducting the inquisitive, "lively" mind toward its proper goals.[61]

Similarly, Barlow's image patterns shifted away from a spiritual use of the language of Canaan toward a secular meaning and a secular employment of those types and figures which had earlier, in other contexts, exhibited altogether different interpretations and meanings. The transformation was complete; America's future promise was often sung in the prophetic images of biblical verse; but no longer did the metaphors carry the freight of biblical meaning or scriptural typology and prophecy. If the parliament of man in Book X of *The Columbiad* resembles the commencement of millennial harmony and peace, it no longer signifies a spiritual millennium which must be wrought by the author of history. Rather, the figures provide Barlow's readers with a comforting, traditional system for understanding the greatness of

America and the brightness of her future, without the added expectation
that God's millennial paradise will be realized, either spiritually or
literally, in this "American quarter of the globe."

The continuity of Puritan imagery was not lost, however, in the
transformation of the early American dream into federalist and
republican visions of American glory. Concurrent with the development
of the rising glory genre of poetry and the political transitions that
marked the era of the American Revolution was the gradual influence of
Jonathan Edwards and the New Light epistemology on late eighteenth-
century American thinking. Edwards successfully wrought a new
epistemology out of a new understanding of nature provided by scientific advances without violating the integrity of Scripture or his belief in
a millennial future. It was Edwards, rather than Barlow, who survived
the industrial revolution in America, though Barlow's epic verses are
echoed in Whitman's epic *Song of Myself*. The secular promise of America
was indeed derived from the spiritual and eschatological visions of the
Puritans, and Edwards' "new sense of things" would provide the
transcendental thinkers with a prophetic vision of the future that was
rooted in the epistemology of New England's Puritan past. The secular
and spiritual progressivists thus continued to parallel each other, and the
heralds of America's scientific and technological progress — men like
Jedediah Morse, Noah Webster, and Edward Everett, had antiphonal
voices to those of Emerson, Thoreau, and Whitman, who, following Edwards' earlier example, developed a language grounded in the language
of Canaan so prominent in America's first two centuries. Meanwhile,
the prophets of technological progress explored America's future
promise with a new vocabulary, too — one evolved from neoclassical and
enlightenment rhetoric of the eighteenth century, which either
transformed the images and figures of biblical rhetoric into a secular and
progressive myth, or abandoned the Scripture figures altogether. Barlow
himself wrote,

Our language is constantly and rapidly improving. The unexampled progress
of the sciences and arts for the last thirty years has enriched it with a great
number of new words, which are now become as necessary to the writer as the
ancient mother tongue. The same progress which leads to further extensions
of ideas will still extend the vocabulary; and our neology must and will keep
pace with the advancement of our knowledge.[62]

For Barlow and the technological progressivists, the language of Canaan
was now a system of metaphors for analogical use only, lacking the deep
conviction and prophetic meaning that governed its use during the
seventeenth and eighteenth centuries in New England. The alternative

and parallel strain, from the early Puritan settlers through Jonathan Edwards to Ralph Waldo Emerson and the transcendentalists, extended this rich language into the nineteenth century and provided Walt Whitman with a prophetic vocabulary that would soon sing America's continental expansion and imperial design.

IV
*Epistemology and the Biblical Symbol
from the Great Awakening to the
American Renaissance*

10

JONATHAN EDWARDS
AND THE
KNOWLEDGE OF GOD

The book of Scripture is the interpreter of the book of nature two ways,
viz., by declaring to us those spiritual mysteries that are indeed
signified and typified in the constitution of the natural world; and
secondly, in actually making application of the signs and types in the
book of nature as representations of those spiritual mysteries in many
instances.

> —Jonathan Edwards,
> Image 156

If future years shall raise the roving mind;
Progressive arts exalt the soul on high,
Peace rules the earth, and faith unfold the sky;
Say, how shall truths like these to man be given,
Or Science find the limits mark'd by Heaven?

> —Joel Barlow,
> *The Vision of Columbus*
> 1793

JOEL BARLOW defined a new, secular vision of America's future
promise, contrasting the image of confusion provided by the
biblical tower of Babel with the harmony and order of that universal language to be spoken by all peoples during the millennial
peace. But his epic vision was wrought from an evolving usage of the Bible that gradually abandoned biblical meaning while retaining scriptural
images and figures. For Jonathan Edwards, Barlow's predecessor in
eighteenth-century American thought, the language of Canaan retained
its original meaning and Edwards' interpretations of historical events
were anchored in the promises of Scripture revelation. However, Edwards' contributions to the development of American symbology were
not confined to millennial and eschatological writings or to the highly
metaphorical *History of the Work of Redemption*, though one could argue
that everything Edwards wrote had some relation to principles of
eschatology and images of future fulfillment. One continuity between
the eighteenth and nineteenth centuries may be drawn in the transformation we have traced between Edwards' eschatological vision and

Barlow's epic sense of America's pastoral and technological or commercial fulfillment. Another equally important development took place in the search for an understanding of the principles of revelation.

For seventeenth-century Puritans, God's teleological purposes were revealed in Scripture, which, in turn, might be corroborated by His wisdom in the created universe or in the "remarkable providences" which signaled God's direct involvement in the affairs of the natural world. But for Jonathan Edwards, the influence of an early reading of John Locke's *Second Essay Concerning Human Understanding* was exceedingly strong, so that Edwards devoted much of his energy to the development of a language that would reconcile those truths received through God's holy writ and those impressions made on man's rational and empirical senses through natural revelation. The result of this reconciliation was crucial for the symbolic tradition in American writing, particularly for the symbology later developed by the transcendental writers Ralph Waldo Emerson and Henry David Thoreau. Thoreau and Emerson clearly represent one significant pattern in the movement from rationalism to transcendentalism, and the symbolic language defined by Emerson and employed by Thoreau may be traced to those questions articulated by Jonathan Edwards in his epistemological arguments for a synthetic reading of Scripture and the Book of Nature.

The following two chapters analyze the connections between New Light Calvinism and nineteenth-century New England transcendentalism by examining the central question concerning man's power to know the divine: through what specific vehicles or means is the world of spirit revealed to man? What are the exact correspondences between the world of spirit and the world of nature? Although these questions might ultimately be subsumed under a vision of millennial perfection, the symbolic language through which such a vision could be expressed depended primarily upon the "new sense of things" through which Edwards liberated biblical figuralism and fused natural with scriptural revelation. If millennial eschatology provided one critical focal point through which transitions from spiritual to secular thinking might be measured, transformations in epistemology from Edwards to Thoreau are equally important indices of change in the evolving history of the language of Canaan. Even Barlow, whose obsession had been the creation of an appropriate American epic form, offered a critical comment on this central epistemological question and objected to the veiled writing that had characterized spiritual and iconographic symbolism in religious history. In his notes to the ninth book of *The Columbiad*, we find:

The art of painting ideas, being arrested in the state in which the use of the alphabet found it, went into general disuse for common purposes; and the works then extant, as well as the knowledge of writing in that mode, being no longer intelligible to the people, became objects of deep and laborious study, and known only to the learned; that is, to the men of leisure and contemplation. These men consequently ran it into mystery; making it a holy object, above the reach of vulgar inquiry. On this ground they established, in the course of ages, a profitable function or profession, in the practice of which a certain portion of men of the brightest talents could make a reputable living; taking care not to initiate more than a limited number of professors; no more than the people could maintain as priests. This mode of writing then assumed the name of *hieroglyphic*, or *sacred painting*, to distinguish it from that which had now become the vulgar mode of writing, by the use of the alphabet. This is the source of that ancient, vast, and variegated system of false religion, with all its host of errors and miseries, which has so long and so grievously weighed upon the character of human nature (*The Columbiad*, 1807, p. 392n).

Jesus himself spoke in parables in order to prevent those for whom God's revealed word was not intended from hearing and understanding, and commentators from the time of the early church have been concerned to retain the exclusive qualities of Judeo-Christian revelation. To this abuse of the symbolic mode Barlow and Paine might have justifiably objected; however, the rich traditions of symbolic writing that they inherited through New England Puritanism provided an epistemological foundation for postrevolutionary symbolism which was impressively reasserted in the American transcendental movement. Once again, typology as a system for comprehending God's symbolic mode in Scripture was utilized, and Edwards' fusion of scriptural and natural revelation necessitated his adaptation of this traditional typological system to the Book of Nature.

From the beginning, there have been schools among the typologists that reflect conservative, or traditional and orthodox exegesis, and these place great emphasis on the historical veracity of the type and the specific correspondence between type and antitype within the bounds of Scripture. More liberal typologists sometimes employ Platonic, ahistorical symbols, thus bordering on spiritualizing or allegorizing. It was Edwards' task to reconcile the two extremes.

For the literal-minded Puritan, the conservative exegesis had a particular appeal. For Jonathan Edwards, however, a Calvinist and a mystic, typology as a key to the mysteries of the universe was not so simple a matter. Conservative and liberal modes of exegesis were continuously at war during the late seventeenth and early eighteenth centuries, so that a number of Edwards' contemporaries were inclined toward a mixture of the spiritualized Old Testament narrative and an orthodox exegesis of the types. Moreover, scientific interest in the natural universe provided a radically new approach to epistemological problems and tempted theologians to combine their perceptions of nature with their reading of Scripture. Some conservative theologians, like Cotton Mather, while thoroughly grounded in the conservative orthodoxy, experimented with new forms of perception and accepted some new methods of understanding even while they continued to read Scripture according to the instituted scheme of type and antitype.[1]

Jonathan Edwards is a particularly interesting figure to consider in the context of this epistemological change because he sought to know God through a wide variety of sources during his lifetime. In comprehending and exegeting Scripture, Edwards was essentially a conservative; his display of scholarly, textual, critical methods in *A History of the Work of Redemption* combines with his intense Calvinism to render a document of orthodox and traditional conviction. The *History* was written in the 1730s and first appeared as a series of sermons preached in 1739. It was left in manuscript by Edwards at the time of his death and was not published until 1774 when his son edited the manuscript. It provides the most complete summary of Edwards' orthodox and conservative approach to the eternal work of the Holy Spirit and contains a particularly illuminating section on the typology of Scripture, by which the author understood the work of the spirit to be the same in both Testaments. But Edwards' interest in human psychology and his continuous probing of philosophical theories of knowledge resulted in a varied use of the biblical types. If he endorsed and explained the conservative doctrine of typology in *A History of the Work of Redemption*, he transformed the types in his *Images or Shadows of Divine Things* so that nature became an alternative source of revelation. In the *Miscellanies,* Edwards presented the types in the two distinct senses he employed elsewhere: he asserted their value as historical figures within the instituted scheme of type and antitype, and he suggested their significance as allegorical symbols. Despite this apparent loosening of the doctrinal position, Edwards' writing always carried a prophetic and eschatological emphasis.

It is toward an understanding of these three documents that the present chapter is addressed. However, it should be stated that one's views of Edwards' typology should not determine the theologian's position in the spectrum of exegesis and doctrine generally. In the essential matters of Puritan theology and Calvinist doctrine, Edwards moved from the liberalism of Stoddardeanism toward the conservatism of his own final position. When it came to man's sinfulness and God's restorative grace, Edwards endorsed the extremely traditional positions of Reformation Calvinism. But in his epistemological documents, the concern with God's accommodation of the divine idea through a natural revelation is strong, so that a number of documents may be viewed as supportive of his liberal typology even though they are not directly involved with the positing of a doctrine. *A Faithful Narrative of the Surprising Work of God* (1737), *The Distinguishing Marks of a Work of the Spirit of God* (1741), and *Some Thoughts Concerning the Present Revival of Religion in New England* (1742) treat separate aspects of revivalism during the Great Awakening, and each provides a defense of the work of the Holy Spirit in contemporary New England. And the epistemology of the Great Awakening, as Edwards understood it, is best summarized in his *A Treatise Concerning Religious Affections*, (1746) in which the "new sense of things" — by which the transformed member of the elect could comprehend God's revelation through nature as well as Scripture — is fully explained and exhaustively argued. These documents, and the numerous allusions throughout Edwards' writing that also reflect the influence of John Locke, are of vital interest in assessing Edwards' position in the development of American thought; and they provide some assistance in establishing Edwards' place in the debate between liberal and conservative typologists.

Edwards' conservatism is everywhere present in the *History*. The "doctrine" of the first sermon states clearly what he means by redemption:

I would show how I would be understood when I use the word *redemption*. And here it may be observed, that the work of redemption is sometimes understood in a more limited sense, for the purchase of salvation; for so the word strictly signifies, a purchase of deliverance; . . . It was begun with Christ's incarnation, and carried on through Christ's life, and finished with his death, or the time of his remaining under the power of death, which ended in his resurrection . . . But then sometimes the word of redemption is taken more largely, including all that God works or accomplishes tending to this end; not only the purchasing of redemption, but also all God's works that were properly preparatory to the purchase, or as applying the purchase and accomplishing the success of it; so that the whole dispensation, as it includes the preparation and the purchase, and the application and success of Christ's redemption, is here called the work of *redemption* . . . in one word, all that is wrought in execution of the eternal covenant of redemption; that is what I call the work of redemption in the doctrine; for it is all but one work, one design. The various dispensations or works that belong to it, are but the several parts of one scheme.[2]

The continuous scheme of redemption that Edwards observed in human history is nevertheless centered specifically in Christ's eternal power. The unique design may have a variety of aspects or manifestations, both before and after Christ's historical presence on earth; however, the continuity of history provides a linear setting within which the great work is developed. "It is but one design that is formed, to which all the offices of

Christ do directly tend, and in which all the persons of the Trinity do conspire, and all the various dispensations that belong to it are united; and the several wheels are one machine, to answer one end, and produce one effect."[3]

Edwards developed a tightly wrought, well reasoned argument for commencing the history of the work of redemption with the fall of man. The historical period from the time of the fall to the incarnation constitutes "Period I" of the *History*, and the justification for its inclusion in the scheme is presented in terms of its typological significance. "The church was under various dispensations of Providence, and in very various circumstances, before Christ came," Edwards declared, "but all these dispensations were to prepare the way for his coming."[4] By adopting a traditional division of the period into six units, Edwards isolated the major providential dispensations before the incarnation, then delivered judgment on the relative significance of each. The examples of typological adumbration and fulfillment are legion, and the governing force throughout the document is God's intentional preparation of the world for the coming of the antitype. Ultimately the dispensations are all one.

Thus we see how the light of the gospel, which began to dawn immediately after the fall, and gradually grew and increased through all the ages of the Old Testament, as we observed as we went along, is now come to the light of perfect day, and the brightness of the sun shining forth in his unveiled glory.

And Christ and his redemption are also the great subject of the history of the Old Testament from the beginning all along; and even the history of the creation is brought in as an introduction to the history of redemption that immediately follows it. The whole book, both Old Testament and New, is filled up with the gospel; only with this difference, that the Old Testament contains the gospel under a vail, but the New contains it unvailed, so that we may see the glory of the Lord with open face.[5]

In clarifying the relations of the two dispensations under the law, Edwards followed earlier models and distinguished "moral" from "typical":

The next thing observable in this period was God's giving the *typical* law, those precepts that did not properly belong to the *moral* law. Not only those laws which are commonly called *ceremonial*, which prescribe the ceremonies and circumstances of the Jewish worship, and their ecclesiastical state; but also those that were political, for regulating the Jewish commonwealth, commonly called *judicial* laws, were many of them *typical*. The giving of this typical law was another great thing that God did in this period, tending to build up the glorious structure of redemption . . . Thus the gospel was abundantly held forth to that nation; so that there is scarcely any doctrine of it but is particularly taught and exhibited by some observance of this law; though it was in shadows, and under a vail, as Moses put a vail on his face when it shone.[6]

Like Thomas Shepard and Samuel Mather before him, Edwards has here distinguished the "ceremonial and typical" law of Israel, which was abrogated and fulfilled in the incarnation, from the "moral" law dispensed eternally, having a perpetual historical value. By making this distinction, he succeeded in establishing a typology of adumbration and fulfillment without violating the significance of Scripture for generations succeeding the Old Testament period but preceding the millennium. It is this kind of conservative and traditional approach to exegesis and typology that characterizes *A History of the Work of Redemption*, and the linear, historical setting accorded the types in this document is rarely manipulated toward an allegorical interpretation. The eschatological presence of Christ is everywhere apparent, and while Edwards never lost sight of eschatology in his other writings, he did sometimes move in the direction of allegorizing or spiritualizing the manifold works of creation. The historiography implied here — that since the fall mankind has been involved in the revelation of one immutable and completed act — is another subject closely related to the typological interpretation of those events; however, it sheds light on Edwards' doctrine of the types only in a peripheral way.

Standing between *A History of the Work of Redemption* and *Images or Shadows of Divine Things* in a spectrum of conservative-to-liberal typological exegesis are Edwards' "Miscellaneous Notebooks" particularly the entries numbered 119, 479, and 1069.[7] Number 1069, otherwise known as "Types of the Messiah," suggests a number of variations on the more conservative doctrine posited in the *History*. The first two entries in the *Miscellanies* entitled "Types," and the only two of this kind before number 1069, use the term loosely for images or representations of spiritual things, not unlike the use of the term in *Images or Shadows*. Like medieval allegorizing of the biblical types, the definitions delivered in these two miscellanies hint at the prospect of spiritual revelation represented in the types of the natural universe. Both entries are brief, and may be presented in full:

119: TYPES. The things of the ceremonial law are not the only things, whereby God designedly shadowed forth spiritual things; but with an eye to such a representation were all the transactions of the life of Christ ordered. *And very much of the wisdom of God in the creation appears, in his so ordering things natural, that they livelily represent things divine and spiritual,* [such as] sun, fountain, vine; as also, much of the wisdom of God in his Providence, in that the state of mankind is so ordered, that there are innumerable things in human affairs that are lively pictures of the things of the gospel, such as shield, tower, and marriage, family [italics mine].

479: WORK OF REDEMPTION. TYPES. Things even before the fall were types of things pertaining to the gospel redemption. The old creation, I believe, was a type of the new. God's causing light to shine out of darkness, is a type of his causing such spiritual light and glory by Jesus Christ to succeed, and to arise out of, the dreadful darkness of sin and misery. His bringing the world into such beautiful form out of a chaos without form and void, typifies his bringing the spiritual world to such divine excellency and beauty after the confusion, deformity, and ruin of sin.[8]

Now the habit of mind by which men could discern the activity of God in the natural universe was neither unique nor new; the Puritan penchant for discovering remarkable providences in natural events and their belief that behind everything physical lay some spiritual truth is present in the tradition of Puritan symbolism from the beginning. However, this tradition is clearly a different avenue from the attitude toward typological exegesis as a means of reading history providentially. Edwards has thus brought together these two distinct provinces in his above definitions; for all Puritans the wisdom of God appeared in the lively representation of the ordered natural universe. However, more conservative exegetes were careful to indicate how the biblical types had been abrogated and fulfilled in the incarnation. Like the medieval allegorizers before him, Edwards here seems to be moving toward an interpretation of the spiritualized natural universe, which contains analogues of the scriptural types. Moreover, he suggests that the types of the Old Testament operate analogously to Platonic symbols in their revelation of Christ.

"Miscellany 1069" opens with a statement that is misleading. One assumes that Edwards would proceed to an exegesis of the types according to the historical scheme of adumbration and fulfillment:

We find by the Old Testament, that is has ever been God's manner, from the beginning of the world, to exhibit and reveal future things by symbolical representations, which were no other than types of the future things revealed. Thus, when future things were made known in visions, the things that were seen were not the future things themselves, but some other things that were made use of as shadows, symbols, or types of the things.[9]

So far, so good; Edwards has simply introduced the idea that types are indeed symbols or shadows of "good things to come." But he moved away from this initial position rather quickly, offering as examples of the types a number of allegorical figures in the Old Testament that could only relate to New Testament matters in a Platonic fashion. "We find that God was often pleased to bring to pass extraordinary and miraculous appearances and events, to typify future things," Edwards said, in a passage that corroborates the conservative notion that history is an instituted process of continuous relevation. But he immediately followed with an example which violates the historical principle: "Thus God's making Eve of Adam's rib, was to typify the near relation and strict union of husband and wife, from one to the other."[10] Yet throughout the "Types of the Messiah," Edwards asserted the prefigurative role of the Old Testament in its typological adumbration of Christ, the antitype:

> Now since it was, as has been observed, God's manner of old, in the times of the Old Testament, from generation to generation, and even from the begin- ning of the world to the end of the Old Testament history, to represent divine things by outward signs, types, and symbolical representations, and espe- cially thus to typify and prefigure future events, that he revealed by his Spirit, and foretold by the prophets, it is very unlikely, that the Messiah, and things appertaining to his kingdom and salvation, should not be thus abundantly prefigured and typified under the Old Testament.[11]

Throughout "Miscellany 1069," Edwards seems inclined to rely on the linear and historical analogy between the testaments, and his ex- amples are largely drawn from historical events and a few outstanding "personal types," like David. However, as the narrative progresses, it becomes evident that Edwards is also concerned to indicate the close prox- ximity between the typological revelation and allegorical representation.

> It is an argument that many of the historical events of the Old Testament are types of the great events appertaining to the Messiah's coming and kingdom, that the Spirit of God took occasion from the former to speak of the latter. He either takes occasion to speak and foretel the Messiah, and the great events appertaining to his salvation, upon occasion of the coming to pass of these an- cient events, or on his speaking of these events, celebrating or promising them, he takes occasion to speak of these latter and greater events, joining what is declared of the one with what he reveals of the other in the same discourse; which is an argument that one has relation to the other, and is the image of the other.[12]

Finally, in the summarizing argument of this highly organized and logical piece, Edwards stated clearly that he intends to regard the types in an allegorical as well as historical sense:

> The principles of human nature render TYPES a fit method of instruction. It tends to enlighten and illustrate, and to convey instruction with impression,

conviction, and pleasure, and to help the memory. These things are confirmed by man's natural delight in the imaginative arts, in painting, poetry, fables, metaphorical language, and dramatic performances. This disposition appears early in children.

This may be observed concerning types in general that not only the things of the Old Testament are typical; for this is but one part of the typical world; the system of created beings may be divided into two parts, the typical world, and the antitypical world. The inferior and carnal, i.e., the more eternal and transitory part of the universe, that part of it which is inchoative, imperfect, and subservient, is typical of the superior, more spiritual, perfect, and durable part of it, which is the end, and, as it were, the substance and consummation, of the other. Thus the material and natural world is typical of the moral, spiritual, and intelligent world, or the city of God . . . And those things belonging to the city of God, which belong to its more imperfect, carnal, inchoative, transient, and preparatory state, are typical of those things which belong to its more spiritual, perfect, and durable state; as things belonging to the state of the church under the Old Testament were typical of things belonging to the church and kingdom of God under the New Testament.[13]

The importance of this passage cannot be overemphasized. In a single statement, Edwards here indicated that while typology applies to the historical scheme established between the two testaments, it also embraces the correspondences between external representations and the spiritual ideas they shadow forth. By indicating how Christ's life radiates a typological significance, or how the Christian ordinances are symbolic of deeper spiritual principles, he consciously applied the nomenclature of orthodox typology to the allegorical correspondence, however proximal, and thus opened the floodgates for the interpretation of the universe in terms of types (the symbol) and antitypes (the idea behind the symbol). The methodology becomes clear in reading the miscellaneous notebook that Perry Miller edited in 1948 and titled *Images or Shadows of Divine things*. The work is a revealing account of impressions Edwards received from the natural universe and a record of his attempt to utilize the framework of typological exegesis as a means of interpreting these impressions. The nomenclature of orthodox typology is employed throughout, but the intention of the "exegete" is clearly to expand the boundaries of scriptural typology.

Miller's edition includes a lengthy introduction, which has become almost as famous during the last twenty years as Edwards' own work. This close association has been advantageous in that it has directed many students of Puritanism to Edwards' important work through their discipleship to Miller. It has been unfortunate because the introduction itself attempts to set the record straight about Edwards' use of the types by positing a number of definitions of typology that cannot account for *all* typological usages. Thus the reader of the introduction is provided a view of typology that is not altogether adequate for assessing the transitions in Edwards' exegesis that occur in the accompanying *Images or Shadows*.

Miller shows that Edwards wanted to employ biblical typology to counteract the contemporary tendency for reading nature "tropologically," as many medieval exegetes had done. He blames the Puritan rhetoricians for a confusion between the trope and the type, noting that "it did not occur to them that the line between the trope and the type needed any further demarcation, or that as long as the rules of the plain style held sway there was any possibility of simple metaphors being so abused that to the greatest intellect among their descendants, the pious tropes would appear as much a nuisance to true piety as the scholastic types had seemed to the former."[14] The distinction here is between the tropological or allegorical reading of the natural universe, which the Puritans certainly did make under the rubric for comprehending "remarkable Providences" (the special dispensations of God through occurrences that violated the usual laws of nature), and the "typological" exegesis of Scripture and history according to the instituted scheme of prefigurative type and fulfilling antitype. However, Miller's central assertion is that Edwards employed the typological system *to reverse* regrettable tendencies toward the tropological among contemporary writers, including Cotton Mather, whose *Agricola* was seen to reflect the consummate influences of that well-known spiritualizer, John Flavel.[15] This is an inaccurate representation of both Edwards and Cotton Mather. In the first place, while the ministers who signed the Preface to Mather's *Agricola* do indicate that he had been experimenting with the process of accommodation through the "language of Husbandry," the treatise itself leaves no doubt that Mather was unable to depart from his orthodox patterns of exegesis for the "heavenly use of earthly things." The emphasis of the sermons suggests that Mather was more concerned with restating the traditional Puritan doctrine of salvation than with the Flavel process of spiritualizing the natural universe. But the most serious problem arises out of Miller's assessment of Edwards' response to this spiritualizing, which he sees as an attempt to employ typology as a correctional vehicle.

Miller sees Edwards as the leader of a "Puritan revolt against Puritanism."[16] While Edwards' modifications of Covenant theology are well known, his reassertion of Calvinism is hardly present in the very liberal document *Images or Shadows*; yet Miller goes on to argue that Edwards resurrected the *Puritan* types to turn rhetoricians away from the excesses of tropology that had infected contemporary theology. "If Edwards was to purify the art of speech in New England," Miller says, "he had not only to chastise the tropes but to clarify the types" (p. 24). Edwards thus becomes the restorer of epistemology to the straight and narrow pathway of man's response to God's direct revelation, and in the sense that Edwards indicated how God is revealed in the natural as well as the scriptural universes, Miller is certainly right. Edwards had indeed attempted to secure his new Lockean epistemology, his "new sense of things," by according it the status already established for typological exegesis by the theologians who preceded him. Miller says that "the beauty of a type was exactly that, if it existed at all, it needed only to be seen, not argued. His psychological thesis led him to typology, just as it gave him a program for the correction of New England rhetoric" (p. 26). And this is just where the Edwardsean epistemology ceased to corroborate the older, orthodox typology.

Miller indicates these distinctions. But the value he assigns Edwards' typology in the introduction to *Images or Shadows* would credit Edwards with a more conservative typology than he presents.

> In nature, said Edwards, the agreement between the animal and the divine idea would be exactly the same kind of agreement as between the types of the Old Testament and their antitype. "There is an harmony between the methods of God's Providence in the natural and religious world." Here was the central perception about which Edwards strove to organize God's creation: the Bible is only one among several manifestations of the typical system; the pattern of the cosmos is infinite representation, and thereby intelligible (p. 27).

This transformation of the typological system is a more serious matter than Miller would make it. Edwards establishes a system of analogy in *Images or Shadows*, through which natural objects have spiritual counterparts in the allegorical fashion. But Miller seems to regard this to be no more than an "extension of typology," which has its foundation and basis in the continuity of the Old and New Testaments.

Edwards' typology here is in all respects a very different order of perception from the epistemology that is based on biblical exegesis and scriptural typology. In the "naturalistic" scheme of *Images or Shadows*, there is little room for the linear and historical relation between the type and its antitype, so that what Edwards succeeds in achieving is a method of reading nature that should supplement the revelation of God's will in Scripture. The language employed to convey this idea is misleading, since he has used type and antitype elsewhere to mean the historical and prefigurative pattern by which God's progressive revelation is established in human time. Throughout his introduction, Miller has declared that in order "to attack the evils of the local scholasticism," Edwards deliberately "invoked the types to rebuke the tropes" (p. 24). He makes extremely clear distinctions between types and tropes, but everywhere he allows the word "type" to mean the symbolic representation of a spiritual idea. Miller is perfectly aware that Edwards has used the exegetical types in this sense, and he even alludes to the transformation in *Images or Shadows* from an orthodox to a spiritualized typology: "Had Edwards, even with Locke to assist him, done no more than create a new typology, he might deserve mention" (pp. 26-27). Yet he nowhere draws the distinction between Edwards' employment of the allegorical images that he labels "types" and the orthodox historical typology of *A History of the Work of Redemption*. Rather than a resurrection of biblical typology as a means of chastising the tropology of late seventeenth-century theologians, Edwards' new epistemology in *Images or Shadows* is analogous to the medieval habit of mind by which the physical universe was believed to represent the spiritual in a Platonic or allegorical fashion. More closely related to the Puritan habit of discovering "remarkable Providences" in the natural universe than to the Puritan doctrines of typological exegesis, Edwards' typology here is more like the epistemology of his empiricist contemporaries than that of his Puritan predecessors. As in Image 142, "The silk-worm is a remarkable type of Christ," the analogy between the natural image and the spiritual attributes of Christ dominates the conception. And the patterns of thought developed in the collection of images clearly argue for a new kind of typology based on the empirical psychology of John Locke.

Although there are two hundred and twelve seemingly unrelated entries comprising *Images or Shadows*, it is in fact possible to discern several underlying motifs throughout the work. Only occasionally did Edwards use an earthly image to prefigure an event of the future, although there is a controlling sense of eschatology even in the most extreme cases of his allegorizing of nature. But even where a linear and historical perspective is suggested or implied, Edwards was still not using scriptural typology as the more conservative exegetes had understood it, although his eschatological sense does represent a more conservative position than the altogether Platonic scheme through which natural objects became symbols for spiritual truths. For Edwards, there was an indissoluble continuity between revelation in Scripture and revelation through nature:

Image 156. The Book of Scripture is the interpreter of the Book of Nature in two ways, viz., by declaring to us those spiritual mysteries that are indeed signified and typified in the constitution of the natural world; and secondly, in actually making application of the signs and types in the Book of Nature as representations of those spiritual mysteries in many instances . . .

Image 169: IMAGES of Divine Things: There are some types of divine things, both in Scripture and also in the works of nature and constitution of the world, that are much more lively than others . . . God has ordered things in this respect much as He has in the natural world . . . There is a like difference and variety in the light held forth by types as there is in the light of the stars of the night. Some are very bright, some you can scarcely determine whether there be a star there or no, and the like different degrees, as there is the light of twilight, signifying the approaching sun (pp. 109-110).

In Image 168, Edwards came very close to revealing a possible source for his "new sense of things," when he asserts that natural activity, "viz., husbandry," can instruct man by representing to him spiritual truth:

Image 168: There are most representations of divine things that are most in view or that we are chiefly concerned in: as in the sun, his light and other influences and benefits; in the other heavenly bodies; in our own bodies; in our state, our families and commonwealths, and in this business that mankind do principally follow, viz., husbandry (p. 119).

This clear echo of John Flavel's process of analogy is reinforced by Edwards' many statements affirming the value of Platonic correspondences in the typological scheme. In Image 45, he says

That natural things were ordered for types of spiritual things seems evident by these texts: John 1.9, This was the true light, which lighteth every man, that cometh into the world; and John 15.1, I am the true vine. Things are thus said to be true in Scripture in contradistinction to what is typical: The type is only the representation or shadow of the thing, but the antitype is the very substance and is the true thing. Thus, heaven is said to be the true holy of holies, in opposition to the holy of holies in the tabernacle and temple, Heb. 9:24 . . . So the spiritual Gospel tabernacle is said to be the true tabernacle, in opposition to the legal, typical tabernacle, which was literally a tabernacle (p. 56).

The problem here is not that linear and historical typological correspondences have been abandoned, but that the interpretation given the type-antitype relationship is Platonic and allegorical when the orthodox pattern was apparent. Edwards' understanding of typology as an exegetical science cannot be questioned, since he elsewhere demonstrates his comprehension of the traditional scheme. But his transformation of these conservative patterns into a looser, more flexible system of analogies is clearly the design of *Images or Shadows*.

The medieval understanding of the Book of Nature is never far away; Edwards' typology of nature is significantly medieval rather than

Puritan. Although he nowhere attempted an elaborate reading of nature according to multiple levels of meaning, as the medieval exegetes had done, Edwards adopted an approach to nature whereby the natural universe came to have an allegorical significance within a typological or figural and eschatological frame of reference.

The justification for such a reconciliation between nature and scriptural typology is not found in *Images or Shadows* because this document is more a series of meditations or reflections than a philosophical treatise. In the "Miscellanies," however, there is a passage that seems to corroborate the method that emerges in *Images or Shadows*, showing exactly how the typology of Scripture operates according to the principle of analogy which Edwards finds prominent in nature. It merits being quoted in full:

> Indeed, the whole outward creation, which is but shadows of His being, is so made as to represent spiritual things. It might be demonstrated by the wonderful agreement in thousands of things, much of the same kind as between the types of the Old Testament and their antitypes; and by their being spiritual things so often and continually compared with them in the world of God. And it is agreeable to God's wisdom that it should be so, that the inferiour and shadowy parts of his works should be made to represent those things that immediately concern himself, and the highest parts of His work. Spiritual things are the crown and glory, the head and soul, the very end, the alpha and omega of all other works. So what therefore can be more agreeable than that they should be made as to shadow them forth. And we know that this is according to God's method, which His wisdom has chosen in other matters. Thus the inferiour dispensations of the Gospel was all to shadow forth the highest and most excellent which was its end; thus almost everything that was said or done, that we have recorded in Scripture from Adam to Christ, was typical of Gospel things. Persons were typical persons; their actions were typical actions; the cities were typical cities; the nations of the Jews and other nations were typical nations; their land was typical land; God's Providences towards them were typical Providences; their worship was typical worship . . . and indeed the world was a typical world. And this is God's manner to make inferiour things shadows of the superior and most excellent; outward things shadows of the spiritual; and all other things shadows of those things that are the end of all things, and the crown of all things. Thus God glorifies Himself and instructs the minds that He has made.[17]

Here the didactic function of the natural world is clear; the analogies which the medieval exegetes had perceived under the tropology of the fourfold method have been transformed into an epistemology of correspondences called "type" and "antitype." Of course, there are enormous differences in the method and intent; however, even Edwards' sense that the spiritual seals the corporeal in an immutable and timeless act cannot restore the sense that his types here are symbolic representations of spritual ideas. By examining several of the images that relate to a single topic, this methodology becomes apparent.

A characteristic motif is that series of typological correspondences given in Edwards' treatment of marriage as a sacrament symbolizing a higher type of union than that of two persons. Image 5 commences this sequence, where Edwards recorded that "marriage signifies the spiritual union and communion of Christ and the Church, and especially the glorification of the church in the perfection of this union and communion forever."[18] Image 9, the second part of the "marriage group," is more specific: "Again, as to marriage, we are expressly taught that there is a designed type of the union between Christ and the Church." (p. 45.) In Image 12, however, Edwards enlarged on the scripturally instituted typology of marriage to assert that the system of typological representation, as he conceived it, should be extended to many other things, including the natural system of the universe:

> We are told that marriage is a great mystery, as representing the relation between Christ and the Church. (Eph. 5. 32.) By mystery can be meant nothing but a type of what is spiritual. And if God designed this for a type of what is spiritual, why not many other things in the constitution and ordinary state of human society and the world of mankind? (p. 45).

One response to this inquiry might be that typology as a science of exegesis applies to divinely instituted relationships between persons or things or events, one of which adumbrates and prefigures the other, by which the former is abrogated. To extend typology beyond these limits is to accord any outward and external representation of an inward idea the value of type and antitype. Edwards clearly understood these limits, not only from what he has posited elsewhere about typology, but also from occasional references in *Images or Shadows*:

> Image 56: There is a great mystery, i.e., a mysterious typical representation which refers ultimately to the union between Christ and the Church. God had respect to Adam and Eve as a type of Christ and the church when He took Eve out of Adam and gave that institution mentioned in Genesis (pp. 60-61).

This awareness of the instituted nature of typology combined with Edwards' application of the orthodox scheme in *A History of the Work of Redemption* balances the impressions we are provided by the epistemology that underlies most of the examples in *Images or Shadows*. For example, in Image 13, Edwards was once again attempting a reconciliation between the nomenclature of typology and the psychology of Locke:

Thus I believe the grass and other vegetables growing and flourishing, looking green and pleasant as it were, ripening, blossoming, and bearing fruit
from the influences of the heavens, the rain and wind and light and heat of the
sun, to be on purpose to represent the dependence of our spiritual welfare
upon God's gracious influence and the effusions of His Holy Spirit. I am sure
there are none of the types of the Old Testament that are more lively images
of spiritual things. We find spiritual things very often compared to them in
Scripture (p. 45).

Again, in Image 8, the bare outline of a system of analogies is presented
as a methodology for reading the Book of Nature:

Again it is apparent and allowed that there is a great and remarkeable
analogy in God's works. There is a wonderfull resemblance in the effects
which God produces, and consentaneity in His manner of working in one
thing and another throughout all nature. It is very observable in the visible
world; therefore it is allowed that God does purposely make and order one
thing to be in agreeableness and harmony with another. And if so, why
should not we suppose that He makes the inferiour in imitation of the
superior, the material of the spiritual, on purpose to have a resemblance and
shadow of them? We see that even in the material world, God makes one part
of it strangely to agree with another, and why is it not reasonable to suppose
He makes the whole as a shadow of the spiritual world (p. 44).

The problem is not that Edwards has adopted a Platonic or allegorical
view of the universe, but that he has established his cosmology in
Platonism and then has adopted the nomenclature of scriptural typology
in expounding the doctrine. For example, in Image 59, where the idea of
analogy is repeated, Edwards employed the terminology he has used in
describing typology elsewhere to describe the process of analogy:

If there be such an admirable analogy observed by the creatour in His works
through the whole system of the natural world, so that one thing seems to be
made in imitation of another, and especially the less perfect to be made in imitation of the more perfect, so that the less perfect is as it were a figure or image of the more perfect, so beasts are made in imitation of men, plants are a
kind of types of animals, minerals are in many things in imitation of plants.
Why is it not rational to suppose that the corporeal and visible world should
be designedly made and constituted in analogy to the more spiritual, noble,
and real world? (p. 65).

Moreover, the transformation of nomenclature is but a small part
of Edwards' new epistemology; he clearly perceived the natural universe
to be a "mappe and shaddow" of God's eternal kingdom. In Image 64, he
declared that "hills and mountains are types of heaven, and often made

use of as such in Scripture." But immediately, he transforms the type so that it has no more than allegorical significance in a scheme of interpretation which derives from his reading of nature through ingenious comparisons. There is an echo of Bunyan in lines like these, which refer to the typology of the mountains and hills:

> These are difficultly ascended. To ascend them, one must go against the natural tendency of the flesh; this must be contradicted in all the ascent, in every step of it, and the ascent is attended with labour, sweat, and hardship. There are commonly many hideous rocks in the way. It is a great deal easier descending into valleys. This is a representation of the difficulty, labour, and self-denial of the way to heaven, and how agreeable it is, to the inclination of the flesh, to descend the hill (p. 67).

Thus the purely representational value of the natural universe is prominently stressed. "Hills and mountains," Edwards said, "as they represent Heaven, so they represent eminence in general, or any excellence and high attainment." (p. 68.) And the phraseology of *Pilgrim's Progress* is echoed in a line found in Image 67: "This may encourage Christians constantly and steadfastly to climb the Christian Hill." (p. 68.)

This kind of allegorizing is incorporated into a more specific transformation of the biblical scheme. We are prepared for Edwards' comparisons and parallels between the history of Rome and Greece and the history of Christianity by Cotton Mather's similar citations in the *Magnalia Christi Americana*. But Edwards has taken the analogy one step further than Mather; he has made the Roman Empire a type of Christ's kingdom on earth. This extension of exegetical typology appears in several of the images, but it is strongly voiced in Image 81:

> The Roman triumph was a remarkable type of Christ's ascension. The general of the Roman armies was sent forth from Rome, that glorious city and metropolis of the world, by the supream Roman authority into remote parts of the enemies' country, to fight with the enemies of the Roman state. As Christ, the captain of the Lord's hosts, was sent forth from heaven, the head city of the universe, by the supream authority of heaven, the country of heaven's enemies, to conflict with those enemies. And on obtaining some very signal and great victory he returned in triumph to the city whence he came out, entered the city in a very glorious manner. So Christ, having gone through the terrible conflict and obtained a compleat and glorious victory, returned again to heaven, the city whence he came, in a glorious triumphant manner (pp. 79-80).

Edwards' transformed typology is again illustrated in his images that treat the sacrament. Essentially, Edwards perceived the institution of the sacrament symbolizing Christ's sacrifice repeated through the natural world, as he recorded in Image 68:

> As wheat is prepared to be our food, to refresh and nourish and strengthen us, by being threshed and then ground to powder and then baked in the oven, whereby it becomes a type of our spiritual food, even Christ the bread which comes down from heaven, which becomes our food by his sufferings, so the juice of the grape is a type of the blood of Christ as it is prepared to be our refreshing drink, to exhilarate our spiritus and make us glad, by being pressed out in a winepress (pp. 68-69).

Although Edwards clearly understood the value of the sacrament as a divinely instituted rehearsal of Christ's sacrifice, he was inclined to read into the institution allegorical significance so that other activities of nature reflect Christ's body and blood.

The most ingenious series of images is that in which Christ is compared to the sun. This renaissance commonplace was used extensively by Milton in *Paradise Lost* and *Paradise Regained*, and Edwards' treatment of Christ reflected in the glory of the sun may be found throughout the seventeenth century. However, from the early images in which he asserts only the basic tenets of the analogy between Christ and the sun to his lengthy diatribes on this familiar correspondence in his "notes on the Scriptures," Edwards provided a consistent attempt to reconcile the linear and historical dimensions of exegetical typology to the unhistorical correspondences of allegorizing. In Image 40, for example, he asserted: "The gradual vanishing of shades when the sun approaches is a type of the gradual vanishing of Jewish ordinance as the Gospel dispensation was introduced." (p. 52.) This familiar analogy is reinforced by his comparison of the law and the gospel to darkness and light in the *Miscellanies*, Number 638. The clarity with which Edwards perceives the relationship between the biblical type and the antitype and the manner in which he has drawn this comparison through a sustained analogy taken from nature indicate once again that Edwards allegorized the natural universe even while retaining a sense of the differences between typology and allegory.

> There is an harmony between the methods of God's Providences in the natural and religious world, in this as well as many other things: that, as when day succeeds the night, and the one comes on, and the other gradually ceases, those lesser lights that served to give light in the absence of the sun gradually vanish as the sun approaches; one star vanishes after another as daylight increases, the lesser stars first and the greater ones afterwards, and the same star gradually vanishes till at length it wholly disappears, and all these lesser lights are extinguished and the sun appears in his full glory above

the horizon. So when the day of the Gospel dawned, the ceremonies of the Old Testament and ordinances of the Law of Moses, that were appointed only to give light in the absence of the sun of righteousness, or until Christ should appear, and shone only with a borrowed and reflected light, like the planets, were gradually abolished one after another, and the same ordinance gradually ceased, and those ordinances that were principall (one of which was the Jewish Sabbath) continued longest. There were a multitude of those ceremonies, which was a sign of their imperfection; but all together did but imperfectly supply the place of the sun of righteousness. But when the sun of righteousness is come, there is no need of any of them.[19]

As Milton had observed in his "On the Morning of Christ's Nativity,"

> The Sun himself withheld his wonted speed,
> And hid his head for shame,
> As his inferiour flame
> The new-enlightened world no more should need:
> He saw a greater Sun appear
> Than his bright throne or burning axletree could
>   bear ("The Hymn," VII).

If Edwards had left his reconciliation of nature and scriptural typology at this level he would have done little more than draw a splendid comparison between typological adumbration and abrogation and the natural phenomenon of light and darkness. But he went much further. In Image 50, Edwards declared that "The rising and setting of the sun is a type of the death and resurrection of Christ." Although his ensuing argument attempts to prove that there is more than a simple analogy between the sun rising and the coming of Christ (for example, an instituted resemblance), Edwards here has clearly abandoned the historical scheme of adumbration and fulfillment. As the medieval exegete had done before him, Edwards turned to the vast Book of Nature for a faithful image of the spiritual realm. There is not merely a historical record of providential guidance of the chosen of God; rather the minutest details of the natural creation are provided for the edification of the regenerate individual.

If we look on these shadows of divine things as the voice of God purposely by them teaching us these and those spiritual and divine things, to show of what excellent advantage it will be, how agreeably and clearly it will tend to convey instruction to our minds, and to impress things on the mind and to affect the mind, by that we may, as it were, have God speaking to us. Wherever we are, and whatever we are about, we may see divine things excellently represented and held forth. And it will abundantly tend to confirm the Scriptures, for there is an excellent agreement between these things and the holy Scripture.[20]

This manifesto provides a summarizing doctrine to which all of Edwards' images may be related. The seeming inconsistency in his attempt to retain the orthodox typological correspondences ("Miscellany 638") and his obvious departures into Platonic allegorizing beg the question of his place in the epistemological spectrum.

One of the most interesting examples of Edwards' transformation of scriptural typology into a "natural typology" appears in his "Notes on the Scriptures, Number 271," where he writes: "The Gospel light granted to the Old Testament Church in its different successive ages was very much like the light of the moon in the several parts of the revolution it performs, which ends in its conjunction with the sun."[21] Although Edwards seems to draw only an analogy between the natural object and the scriptural pattern of revelation, he has used the moon image elsewhere, that is, in "Notes on the Scriptures, No. 315," to present a purely sensory and naturalistic interpretation. In this context, the above passage is endowed with the significance of Edwards' continuous efforts to reconcile Scripture types with the typology of nature as he personally conceived it. Although in many cases the orthodox Scripture type would be a natural object, this was not a necessary prerequisite for the instituting of the biblical types, and it is in this particular aspect that Edwards' typology departs markedly from the more conservative exegesis. He was more willing than either Cotton or Samuel Mather to extend to nature the characteristics of revelation that he found in the scriptural pattern of type and antitype. Cotton Mather had half-heartedly spiritualized the natural activity of the husbandman in the manner of John Flavel, but he did not employ the nomenclature of scriptural typology in his "exegesis" of the natural text. Rather, he allowed the analogy between the activity of the husbandman and the spiritual pursuits of the converted Christian to explain each other by developing a series of ingenious parallels between the natural world and the scriptural example. Never did he violate the integrity of the continuity of scriptural types and antitypes, although he did endow with typical value some rather fanciful analogies in the "Biblia Americana." His distinctions between typological and allegorical usage remained clear.

Edwards' typology of nature represented a new departure in the epistemology of divine revelation. That he provided a conservative force against liberalism in Covenant theology, and particularly against the excesses of Stoddardeanism, does not alter his influence in typology toward a broadening of the avenues by which man might perceive the will of God. The extremes to which he was willing to carry this "new sense of things" is given in detail in *A Treatise Concerning Religious Affections*, which grew out of Edwards' experience during the Great Awakening of the early 1740s, indicating not only how God's will may be revealed through the natural universe to the mind of the alert regenerate, but also how a personal and saving knowledge of Christ might be obtained through an experience of the physical senses, out of which the Grace of God might be dispensed to the members of his elect. Although the *Religious Affections* was only one of several documents Edwards published during the period of revival interest in New England, it is the most important statement of his emerging faith in the experimental piety of sensationalism. Moreover, it is a thorough and detailed argument contained in itself, so that it needs little reference to the context out of which it was developed. Through the *Religious Affections*, we are able to understand how Edwards came to regard signs and symbols of the natural universe to be "typical" of the supernatural, and how this modified Lockean epistemology—by which man perceived God through the external senses and through his revelation in nature—prepared the way for the romantic psychology of Emerson and the transcendentalists.

The epistemology of the *Religious Affections* was no accident; the "new sense of things" had been emerging throughout Edwards' career, and isolated fragments from his other writings reveal his penchant for an epistemology based on natural revelation. He had made it clear from the beginning that revelation of the will of God in the natural universe and the corresponding dispensation of grace was to be perceived only by the regenerate man. "My affections seemed to be lively and easily moved," he records in his "Personal Narrative," "and I am ready to think, many are deceived with such affections, and such a kind of delight as I then had in religion, and mistake it for grace."[22] The receiving of grace through natural sources was for Edwards a privilege allowed only to God's chosen and elect; and it was even then only an inspiration to the natural affections out of which an experience of grace ensued. The "new sense of things" that awaited the regenerate understanding is curiously illustrated by contrasting the reaction to a thunderstorm found in Edwards' "Personal Narrative" with a characteristic response to thunder provided by Cotton Mather in the *Magnalia Christi Americana*. Mather's approach to the natural phenomenon must be understood in the context of Puritan "providences," by which God intervened in the activity of the universe he governs to speak to His creatures on special occasions. Mather begins by assessing the thunder from a quasi-empirical point of view:

First, it is to be premised, as herein implied and confessed that the thunder is the work of the Glorious God. It is true, that the thunder is a natural production, and by the common laws of matter and motion it is produced; there is in it a concourse of divers weighty clouds, clashing and breaking one against another, from whence arises a mighty sound, which grows yet more mighty by its resonances. The subtle and sulphurous vapors among these clouds take fire in this combustion, and lightnings are thence darted forth; which, when they are somewhat grosser, are fulminated with an irresistible violence upon our territories.[23]

This, he explained, is the "Cartesian account," which is comparable to the literal understanding of a Scripture narrative. It is not long before Mather turned to God as the author of all being by whom the natural universe is ultimately controlled:

But still, who is the author of those laws, according whereunto things are thus moved into thunder? yes, who is the first mover of them? Christians, 'tis our glorious God. . . . Well, and whose workmanship is it all? "Ah! Lord, thou hast created all these things; and for thy pleasure they are and were created" . . . Hence, the thunder is ascribed unto our God all the Bible over; in the Scripture of truth, 'tis called the "thunder of God," oftener than I can presently quote unto you. And hence, we find the thunder even now and then, executing the purpose of God.[24]

Once Mather had established this doctrine from his reading of the "thunder text" in the Book of Nature, he proceeded to develop seven applications of the doctrine, showing how the voice of God is present in each thunderstorm in seven different ways. One example will illustrate his methodology:

One voice of the Glorious God in the thunder is, "that he is a Glorious God, who makes the thunder." There is the marvellous glory of God seen in it, when he "thunders marvellously." Thus do these inferior and meteorous "heavens declare the glory of God" . . . If nothing be too hard for the thunder, we may think surely nothing is too hard for the Lord! The arm that can wield thunderbolts is a very mighty arm.[25]

Mather's uses of the thunderstorm are clearly more important than the natural phenomenon itself, which is only an example of God's majesty. He has begun with nature only to make nature the servant of truth that he has already found revealed in Scripture. Thus natural phenomena act as corroborative evidence for scriptural revelation; the objective investigation of nature from an exclusively empirical approach was never quite accomplished as long as theological scientists like Cotton Mather were striving to force nature to conform to the truths they had already received from their reading of the Bible.

For Jonathan Edwards, however, the revealed truth of nature might sometimes have equal value to scriptural revelation, and his own assessment of a thunderstorm indicates the prominence of nature in disclosing the "sweetness" of God's majesty to the regenerate mind. The "new sense of things" made available new worlds of understanding for the elect:

> Not long after I first began to experience these things, I gave an account to my father of some things that had passed in my mind. I was pretty much affected by the discourse we had together; and when the discourse was ended, I walked abroad alone, in a solitary place in my father's pasture, for contemplation. And as I was walking there, and looking up on the sky and clouds, there came into my mind so sweet a sense of the glorious *majesty* and *grace* of God, that I know not how to express. I seemed to see them both in a sweet conjunction; majesty and meekness joined together; it was a sweet, and gentle, and holy majesty; and also a majestic meekness; an awful sweetness; a high, and great, and holy gentleness.[26]

This sweetness culminates in Edwards' experience of God's glory as derived from his initial perception of that glory in the phenomena of nature. Even the thunderstorm provides an avenue for communion with the divine mind:

> After this my sense of divine things gradually increased, and became more and more lively, and had more of that inward sweetness. The appearance of every thing was altered; there seemed to be, as it were, a clam, sweet cast, or appearance of divine glory, in almost every thing . . . And scarce any thing, among all the works of Nature, was so sweet to me as thunder and lightning; formerly, nothing had been so terrible to me. Before, I used to be uncommonly terrified with thunder, and to be struck with terror when I saw a thunder storm rising; but now, on the contrary, it rejoiced me. I felt God, so to speak, at the first appearance of a thunder storm; and used to take the opportunity, at such times, to fix myself in order to view the clouds, and see the lightnings play, and hear the majestic and awful voice of God's thunder, which oftentimes was exceedingly entertaining, leading me to sweet contemplations of my great and glorious God.[27]

The transformation of the natural phenomenon into an object for mystical contemplation and meditation characterizes Edwards' method in *Images or Shadows*, where natural objects are endowed with allegorical significance leading to spiritual truth. Where Cotton Mather had turned to nature and the thunderstorm to find evidence for his belief in the power and majesty of the governor of the universe, Edwards has turned to nature for a direct apprehension of God's glory and majesty, through which he arrives at a sense of tranquility and an experience of the restorative power of grace. The sweetness and peace he feels is much more than simply the aesthetic satisfaction one derives from a momentary appreciation of nature's charm. Rather, Edwards' sweetness is based on his apprehension of God's restorative power, made available to his regenerate perception through the "new sense of things."

The distinction between the regenerate and the natural understanding is crucial. If for Emerson the symbolism of nature was available for anyone who had been transcendentally redeemed, for Edwards nature's revelation was possible only for an elect and regenerate sensibility. In *Religious Affections*, Edwards has made the importance of this distinction quite clear; the regenerate and the natural man are two wholly different creatures.

> There is such a thing, if the Scriptures are of any use to teach us anything, as a spiritual, supernatural understanding of divine things, that is peculiar to the saints, and which those who are not saints have nothing of. 'Tis certainly a kind of understanding, apprehending or discerning of divine things, that natural men have nothing of, which the Apostle speaks of, "But the natural man receiveth not the things of the Spirit of God; for they are foolishness unto him; neither can he know them, because they are spiritually discerned." (I Cor. 2:14) . . . And that there is such a thing as an understanding of divine things, which in its nature and kind is wholly different from all knowledge that natural men have, is evident from this, that there is an understanding of divine things, which the Scripture calls spiritual understanding; "We do not cease to pray for you, and to desire that you may be filled with the knowledge of His will, in all wisdom, and spiritual understanding"; (Col. 1:9). It has already been shown, that that which is spiritual, in the ordinary use of the word in the New Testament, is entirely different in nature and kind, from all which natural men are, or can be the subjects of.[28]

For Edwards, the natural man corresponds to the postlapsarian Old Testament man who has not received the grace of Christ. Just as the types were revealed to the chosen of God as a partial dispensation of "good things to come," the grace of God is revealed in nature only to those whom God has similarly chosen:

> From hence it may be surely inferred, wherein spiritual understanding consists. For if there be in the saints a kind of apprehension of perception, which is in its nature, perfectly diverse from all that natural nature; it must consist in their having a certain kind of ideas or sensations of mind, which are simply diverse from all that is or can be in the minds of natural men. And that is the same thing as to say, that it consists in the sensations of the new spiritual sense, which the souls of men have not.[29]

That the natural things could provide a direct sense of the beauty of the divine excellency and the "nature of divine things" is central to Edwards' epistemology. For John Flavel and Cotton Mather, the knowledge of God had ranged from an interpretation of scriptural types and their analogues in the contemporary world to an apprehension of the moral or spiritual truth represented to natural activity. That these moral truths were simply a way of corroborating scriptural revelation for Cotton Mather is proved by his frequent allusions to the Bible throughout *Agricola*. But for Edwards, nature had become an organic vehicle for the transmission of God's restorative power. The typology of Scripture was still true for those who learned of God through a reading of the Old and New Testaments; Christ was very much alive for Edwards in the figures of Moses and Aaron, Samson and David. However, an essential aspect of the total Christian experience was the personal awareness of God's overwhelming majesty and man's awful depravity in sin, both of which were apparent to the regenerate sensibility. Not only could conversion be induced by natural circumstances; the regenerate being was provided a "new sense of things" by which he continued to enjoy a special revelation of God's majesty in the natural universe. "By this is seen the excellency of the word of God," Edwards declares; "Take away all the moral beauty and sweetness in the Word, and the Bible is left wholly a dead letter, a dry, lifeless, tasteless thing."[30] If the Scripture types were to persevere, they must be accommodated in the light of natural revelation — not the nonmoral light of rationalist empiricism, or the equally barren scholasticism of exegetical orthodoxy, but through the enlightened right reason of the regenerate man, chosen by God to enjoy the sweetness of the universe through his new sense of its true meaning.

> From what has been said, therefore, we come necessarily to this conclusion, concerning that wherein spiritual understanding consists; viz., that there consists in a sense of the heart, of the supreme beauty and sweetness of the holiness or moral perfection of divine things, together with all that discerning and knowledge of things of religion that depends upon, and flows from such a sense . . . Spiritual understanding consists in this sense, or taste, of the moral beauty of divine things; so that no knowledge can be called spiritual, any further than it arises from this, and has this in it.[31]

Ultimately, the purposes behind the new epistemology were the same as they had been for the Puritan who understood nothing more than a few providences and the revealed truth of Scripture; Christ was the ultimate antitype for the Old Testament figures, and similarly, Christ stood at the center of the doctrine of moral perfection. Understanding of the natural world depended crucially on one's regeneration in Christ and on the gaining of a new spiritual sense, which, in turn, would lead to a renewed strength of perception out of which would arise increased spiritual knowledge.

Edwards avoided a seeming tautology by firmly rooting his typology of the senses in nature. The "new sense of things" emphasized the natural things just as strongly as it espoused the new power of vision. The changing processes of the natural universe became a source of revelation for those who possessed this vision, and through a knowledge of Christ obtained by natural revelation, one's ability to interpret the mysteries of the universe improved. This graduated movement, from natural type to spiritual truth, is Platonic in design, but it is also parallel to the process of revelation followed in mysticism and it shows why Edwards has been variously labeled a Christian mystic and a religious pantheist.

The typology Edwards provided in *The History of the Work of Redemption* is conservative indeed when compared to the possibilities he outlines in *Images or Shadows* and examines in *Religious Affections*. He has taken great care to caution his readers against the dangers of Antinomianism and a spiritual personalism that would nullify the concept of God's transcendent majesty and power. But his new approach to the historic problem of man's knowledge of God had led him away from traditional methods of reading Christ in all the Scriptures and further from the Puritan habit of extending the biblical types to contemporary history. Regardless of his efforts to turn New England and his Northampton congregation to a more fundamental and orthodox Calvinism, Edwards had argued a typology based on figures instituted in nature as well as types instituted in Scripture. Because of this strong penchant in Edwards' epistemology, he may be regarded as a precursor of certain attitudes among the nineteenth-century transcendentalists, notably Emerson. The trace of mysticism in Edwards' epistemology constitutes the primary parallel between his writing and the American Renaissance.

The early efforts to reconcile scriptural truth to natural revelation were later modified by Edwards' repeated insistence that the natural universe was not only a type of Christ and the kingdom of God but might also actually be a direct reflection of Christ. It is in this final step that Edwards' sense of Christian mysticism develops, and it is through his transformed typology that he most nearly approximates the total immersion in "Nature [as] a symbol of spirit" so prominent in the writings of Emerson. For Edwards, there was still the necessity of viewing nature in the context of God's merciful revelation to fallen and sinful man, whose regenerate faculties were provided with new and supernatural powers through which he might apprehend the eternal being. Edwards' scheme of using the natural types as a means of discovering spiritual antitypes provided the allegorical foundation in the nomenclature of typological exegesis, so that Emerson and the transcendentalists were not the first to distort the traditional conceptions by endowing the terms with new meaning.

The type had come full circle. In reaction against the Platonic typology of the medieval exegetes, the Reformation typologists had reasserted the linear and historical conceptions of the early church, and these, in turn, had been espoused by the Puritans who read their own history as the antitypical fulfillment of the scriptural types. But their double vision, their assumption that in nature and in the providences they would find evidence to corroborate the truths revealed in Scripture, led them to a reliance on nature as a source of revelation that would supersede Scripture in the nineteenth-century epistemology of Emerson and the transcendentalists. The biblical types, which for the Puritans had been endowed with special meaning by God alone, gradually came to be the province of a few isolated conservative exegetes, while Edwards' followers employed the Lockean epistemology to endow nature with allegorical significance outside the biblical context. If Edwards had attempted to hold in balance a reading of Scripture through type and antitype, he had also released a psychological force in New England that would soon destroy altogether the reading of Scripture as a primary source of spiritual revelation. God was not dead; but for the transcendentalists the Word was lifeless until it could be demonstrated that some correspondence existed between the truths of Scripture and the spiritual ideas revealed in the natural universe.

Thus Edwards' transformation of the Puritan types was a significant attempt to reconcile natural epistemology and scriptural exegesis. He wound up borrowing the nomenclature of typology while endowing the natural world with spiritual significance. But the habit of mind by which Emerson saw in nature a symbol of spirit is clearly present in the epistemology of Edwards, and this epistemology must be kept distinct from the Puritan reading of history and Scripture in terms of type and antitype. Edwards, after all, had rejected Puritanism's federal theology by which the New England colonies bound themselves spiritually and historically to the Israel of old. And his primary aim in *Images or Shadows of Divine Things* was to provide a record of his own awareness of God's revealed truth in the natural universe, and the typology of nature set forth in this collection becomes far more than an extension or rehabilitation of the biblical types; it is an original epistemology by which Edwards and his successors learned to read the vast and complex Book of Nature.

11

FROM EDWARDS TO
EMERSON AND THOREAU:
A REVALUATION

I can remember that I was all alive, and inhabited my body with inexpressible satisfaction; both its weariness and its refreshment were sweet to me. This earth was the most glorious musical instrument, and I was audience to its strains.

—Henry David Thoreau,
Journal

EDWARDS' EPISTEMOLOGY in the *Images or Shadows of Divine Things* allowed the reconciliation of nature and Scripture in ways that were commonplace among German pietists and continental philosophers of the Enlightenment. However, the uniquely separatist American tradition had developed two concurrent modes: the scriptural and historical-typological on the one hand, and the allegorical-providential on the other. The figural language of Canaan had been transformed by Edwards, who always retained an element of eschatology in his natural world by showing that Christ's antitype was eternal and not temporal. This distinguished Edwards from the Romantic writers, but not from Emerson, Thoreau, and the American transcendentalists. It is the purpose of this concluding chapter to demonstrate the continuity between the language of Canaan (as we have seen it develop from the early seventeenth-century historical and figural mode to the more Platonic but mystically eschatological use in the writings of Edwards) and the regenerative vocabulary of the nineteenth-century transcendentalists, especially Henry David Thoreau. The use of metaphor among the transcendentalists is a well-known and overused approach to their writing; it is not the purpose of this brief chapter to argue once again this analysis of the symbolic mode in American Romanticism. However, it is my purpose to demonstrate how those symbols relate directly to the inherited Puritan modes of the previous two centuries, to show how the language of Canaan and its figural, prophetic power, lived on in the phrases of *Walden* and *A Week on the Concord and Merrimack Rivers*, primarily through the spiraling paradigm of regeneration which Thoreau employed to communicate his mystical sense of union between literal and figurative expression.

Perry Miller has given us ample warning about the risks involved in tracing the history of an idea. In his introduction to "From Edwards to Emerson," which appeared in *Errand into the Wilderness* in 1956, he tried to set right the confusion generated by the original appearance of that essay in the *New England Quarterly* for December 1940. "There can be no doubt that Jonathan Edwards would have abhorred from the bottom of his soul every proposition Ralph Waldo Emerson blandly put forth in the manifesto of 1836, *Nature*," he says. "We may be certain that he would have regarded it, as did the stalwart Calvinists at Princeton, as an inevitable outcome of that degenerate 'Arminianism,' the initial stirrings of which he had been the first to detect and to the destruction of which he devoted his life."[1] He continued to say that "in that strictly historical regard, then, there is no organic evolution of ideas from Edwards to Emerson" and concluded that some outstanding differences between the two thinkers must be considered along with the similarities:

> The real difference between Edwards and Emerson, if they can thus be viewed as variants within their culture, lies not in the fact that Edwards was a Calvinist while Emerson rejected all systematic theologies, but in the quite other fact that Edwards went to nature, in all passionate love, convinced that man could receive from it impressions which he must then try to interpret, whereas Emerson went to Nature, no less in love with it, convinced that in man there is a spontaneous correlation with the received impressions. Edwards sought the "images or shadows of divine things" in nature, but could not trust his discoveries because he knew man to be cut off from full communion with the created order because of his inherent depravity. But Emerson, having decided that man is unfallen (except as his sensibilities have been blunted by civilization) announced that there is no inherent separation between the mind and the thing, that in reality they leap to embrace each other.[2]

This does something to set at rest the dispute over sources and analogues, but the reprinting of the essay once again asserts Miller's conviction that "certain basic continuities persist in a culture." Without arguing that Edwards was indeed a source for the thinkers of the American Renaissance, it is one purpose of this chapter to explore a single line of continuity from Edwards to Emerson and Thoreau: the epistemological science of perceiving nature and the symbolic expression of that perception. In all three of these writers there is a consistent and harmonious pattern of perception and expression, and in Thoreau's writing, there are echoes of the prophetic figuralism found in the teleological spiral of Edwards' eschatology. As we have seen, Edwards' epistemology foreshadows the modes of expression found in Emerson and the transcendentalists. Edwards' reconciliation of those symbolic habits of mind he found in Scripture exegesis with the impressions of

God's revelation he apprehended in nature established a foundation on which the later writers could build. Edwards accepted and employed the figural language of Canaan and scriptural typology, but he also explored correspondences and analogies between this historical, typological scheme and the revealed world of the natural universe.

The two vectors of historical influence between Puritanism and the American Renaissance may be seen in the connections between Edwards and Emerson in the area of epistemology, and between Edwards and Thoreau in the transformation of the prophetic language of Canaan into a viable imagery for expressing the hope of regeneration—an eschatological impulse—in natural metaphors. Emerson's Platonism is well known; Edwards' employment of scriptural terminology to express a similar Doctrine of Correspondences between nature and spirit varies primarily in its restriction to a regenerate perception in an elect saint and in the subtle impulse in all Edwards' writing toward eschatology and fulfillment. Emerson moves toward fulfillment; but his symbolism often fuses object and referent in one timeless expression. Thoreau's re-generative metaphor, however, carries the eschatological and prophetic impulse. The language of Canaan lived on primarily in the metaphor-creating process we can discern in Thoreau's highly symbolic writing, and in the spiraling paradigm that emerges as the dominant, prophetic symbol throughout his work. It is important to examine, briefly, both of these vectors in assessing the vitality of the language of Canaan in the American Renaissance.

A central feature of Edwards' "transcendental" epistemology is the way he understood the individual's sensory perceptions to be transform-ed by grace. Not only did he allow that revelation may occur through a natural object which corroborates Scripture truth; he also stated that the individual who enjoys this transformation will experience a "new sense of things" by which his appreciation of the natural self is affirmed in the process of glorifying God's majesty. Edwards was very careful to distinguish the impressions received by this transformed perception from those available to the natural man. In explaining the characteristics of *A Divine and Supernatural Light*, he asserted that "there is such a thing as a Spiritual and Divine Light, immediately imparted to the soul by God, of a different nature from any that is obtained by natural means."[3] And having warned his readers about the powerful influences of imagination on the impressions given any natural being, he reiterated the principle of uniqueness by which the saint is transformed into a creature of special prophetic and perceptive power:

> The Spirit of God acts in a very different manner in the one case, from what he doth in the other. He may indeed act upon the mind of a natural man, but

he acts in the mind of a saint as an indwelling vital principle. He acts upon the mind of an unregenerate person as an extrinsic, occasional agent; for in acting upon them, he does not unite himself to them; for, notwithstanding all his influences that they may be the subjects of, they are still sensual, having not the Spirit. But he unites himself with the mind of a saint, takes him for his temple, actuates and influences him as a new supernatural principle of life and action. There is this difference, that the Spirit of God, in acting in the soul of a godly man, exerts and communicates himself there in his own proper nature.[4]

Recent scholarship has already demonstrated the value of this kind of declaration for determining Edwards' doctrine of beauty.[5] But scholars have been too cautious about suggesting comparisons between Edwards' Romantic epistemology, a power available only to the saints, and those abilities Emerson finds latent in every man. For Edwards, early efforts to reconcile scriptural truth to natural revelation were later modified by his repeated insistence that the natural universe was not only a type of Christ and the kingdom of God, but might also actually be a direct reflection of Christ's mysteries. In this final step, Edwards' sense of Christian mysticism developed, and through his transformed typology he most nearly approximated the total immersion in "nature as a symbol of spirit" so prominent in the writing of Emerson and Thoreau. For Edwards, there was still the necessity of viewing nature in the context of God's merciful revelation to fallen and sinful man, whose regenerate faculties were provided with new and supernatural powers through which he might apprehend the eternal being. In Emerson's typology, however, nature became more than the announced "symbol of spirit"; nature herself becomes spirit, and this understanding was available to *anyone* of uncorrupted, sensitive perception, because all men, while not equally endowed with mystical insight, were emancipated from the Puritan distinction between the regenerate and unregenerate in Emerson's universe.

In Part III, "Beauty," of the 1836 essay, *Nature*, Emerson seems to echo Edwards' doctrine of divine excellence and the Calvinist's view that natural beauty was a direct reflection of God's spiritual perfection, when he writes:

This beauty of Nature which is seen and felt as beauty, is the least part. The shows of day, the dewy morning, the rainbow, mountains, orchards in blossom, stars, moonlight, shadows in still water, become shows merely, and mock us with their unreality . . . The presence of a higher, namely, of the spiritual element is essential to its perfection.[6]

It is no surprise, therefore, when later in the same essay we find Emerson adopting the nomenclature of Edwards' transformed typology and theory of analogy when he describes a natural phenomenon:

> It is easily seen that there is nothing lucky or capricious in these analogies, but that they are constant, and pervade nature. These are not the dreams of a few poets, here and there, but man is an analogist, and studies relations in all objects. He is placed in the center of beings, and a ray of relation passes from every other being to him. And neither can man be understood without these objects, nor these objects without man. All the facts in natural history taken by themselves, have no value, but are barren, like a single sex. But marry it to human history, and it is full of life . . . Throw a stone into the stream, and the circles that propogate themselves are the beautiful type of all influence.[7]

This famous passage, and the correlative scheme by which Emerson demonstrates that nature and spirit are organically united into a system of mutual revelation, show clearly how he regarded the natural world to hold the key to universal spiritual mystery. "Every natural fact is a symbol of some spiritual fact," he also declares, and goes on to show how "every appearance in nature corresponds to some state of the mind, and that state of the mind can only be described by presenting that natural appearance as its picture." In a movement from the early Puritans through Edwards to the Romantic epistemology of American transcendentalism, the scriptural foundations of revelation were wholly abandoned for a new epistemology based on a Platonic or allegorical conception of reality. Types were no longer needed as prefigurations of antitypes. Rather, the type and antitype were present together in the eternal mystical moment that transcended all time in a "sweet" and beautiful experience of union. The historical continuity so necessary to the biblical scheme of typical adumbration and antitypical abrogation was replaced by a Platonic symbolism that rejected all sense of past or future.

Like Edwards in the "Personal Narrative," Thoreau was able to recall the exact moment through which his perception was opened and his senses charged. In his *Journal* we find the following passage:

> I can remember that I was alive, and inhabited my body with inexpressible satisfaction; both its weariness and its refreshment were sweet to me. This earth was the most glorious musical instrument, and I was audience to its strains. To have such sweet impressions made on us, such ecstasies begotten of the breezes! I can remember how I was astonished. I said to myself—I said to others,—"There comes into my mind such an indescribable, infinite, all-absorbing, divine, heavenly pleasure, a sense of elevation and expansion, and [I] have had nought to do with it. I perceive that I am dealt with by superior powers. This is a pleasure, a joy, an existence which I have not procured myself. I speak as a witness on the stand, and tell what I have perceived." The

morning and the evening were sweet to me, and I led a life aloof from society of men. I wondered if a mortal had ever known what I knew, I looked in books for some recognition of a kindred experience, but, strange to say, I found none. Indeed, I was slow to discover that other men had had this experience, for it had been possible to read books and to associate with men on other grounds. The maker of me was improving me. When I detected this interference I was profoundly moved. For years I marched as to a music in comparison with which the military music of the streets is noise and discord . . . I was daily intoxicated, and yet no man could call me intemperate. With all your science can you tell me how it is, and whence it is, that light comes into the soul?[8]

The liberating conversion and transforming of the senses does more than merely unite the individual with universal consciousness; it enables him to experience life on two levels simultaneously, the literal and the figural. The regenerative process is directly associated with prophetic language in numerous documents, for example, "Autumnal Tints" and "Walking." Like all natural men, Thoreau lived out a "literal" existence; however, he also received through his experience communications of the spirit world, so that certain kinds of experience may in fact bring both the literal and metaphysical together. In this transforming process and the power that it releases, human time and spiritual or eternal time become absorbed into each other, so that a writer's expression may have metaphorical dimensions which recreate the experience at the level of spirit.

Thoreau's writing is a good example of this metaphor-creating process. A conscious and deliberate craftsman, Thoreau shaped his recollected episodes to represent the two levels of the experience he has perceived: the literal and the spiritual. Sacvan Bercovitch writes "His 'walking' in this regard divides into two literal levels, which open in turn into two modes of spiritual ascent: the private act flowers into the atemporal garden of the soul; the national action consummates the course of time. So considered, the two levels of meaning diverge as sharply from one another as do two romantic eschatologies. Thoreau's strategy of reconciliation is predictable enough in retrospect. It consists in making the subject an *American* walker."[9] According to this view, the literal and symbolic features of Thoreau's writing become fused in the consciousness of America's historical destiny; "Microcosm became macrocosm; the country was not *like* its exemplary consciousness; it *was* that consciousness, each of them recapitulating the exodus to America, each of them representing the country's 'prevailing tendency,' each of them foreshadowing the millennium at the end of the road—each of them, in Thoreau's words, refuting the literalist's here and now by embodying the symbolic 'meeting of two eternities, past and future,' that vindicated the national calling."[10]

Now this reconciliation of symbol with event, spirit with flesh, tenor with vehicle, *litera* with *figura* was practiced by Thoreau far more than it was preached. He exhibited an almost mystical faith in the power of the organic process and the poetic intuition available to him as writer, and like Emerson, he saw the moral value of his calling as writer. If the poet and his muse were allied in an organic and natural process of discovery, they were obeying a moral principle that lies at the very center of the created universe. Emerson had asserted that "every natural process is a version of moral sentence. The moral law lies at the center of nature and radiates to the circumference. It is the pith and marrow of every substance, every relation, every process . . . The moral influence of nature upon every individual is that amount of truth which it illustrates to him."[11] For Thoreau, this truth was the result of self-discovery, and the product of self-discovery was knowing one's relation to historical time and to the natural world.

This was not simply a matter of retreating from civilization in order to enjoy the blessings of a pastoral peace. Man's duty was to discover and to exploit his organic and natural powers through a probing of his own being that would result in a transformation of his consciousness. This, Thoreau believed, could only be accomplished through man's willingness to cast off the extraneous influences of civilized living and make an excursion into nature, out of which the regenerate sensibility can fashion metaphors that will express timeless and immutable truth.

For the central image that was to express this process in his writing, Thoreau turned to Emerson. In the section of the *Nature* essay entitled "Discipline," Emerson tied his conceptions together in the following way:

A rule of one art, or law of one organization, holds true throughout nature. So intimate is this Unity, that, it is easily seen, it lies the undermost garment of Nature, and betrays its source in Universal Spirit . . . It is like a great circle or sphere, comprising all possible circles; which, however may be drawn and comprise it in like manner.[12]

Later, in "Circles," Emerson established the centrality of this image to his view of art and nature: "The eye is the first circle; the horizon which it forms is the second; and throughout nature this primary figure is repeated without end."[13] This principle figure is indeed "repeated without end" throughout Thoreau's prose writing. Not only are *A Week*, *Walden*, and the *Excursions* organized around an out-and-back movement into thought, some of the passages from the *Journal* also reflect Thoreau's circular journey into his own mind.

In *Walden*, we find: "Our voyaging is only great-circle sailing." This correlates nicely with a description that is given in the essay, "Walking": "Our expeditions are but tours, and come round again at evening to the old hearth-side from which we set out. Half the walk is but retracing our steps."[14] Obviously, Thoreau's concern is with vertically moving circles, or spiral paradigms, whether he discovers his figures in nebulae, finger-prints, ferns, leaves, or in the "figures" of frost in the thawing bank. Although the brief essay does not itself reflect the metaphorical journey "out-and-back" that is the central organizing principle of *Walden* and *A Week*, it contains a number of statements that confirm Thoreau's life-long emphasis on this organic process of creative response. Consequent-ly, it provides an excellent transition from Emerson's conception of natural cycles to Thoreau's own beliefs about the relations between thought and art, nature and spirit.

> I believe that there is a subtle magnetism in Nature, which, if we un-consciously yield to it, will direct us aright. It is not indifferent to us which way we walk. There is a right way; but we are very liable from heedlessness and stupidity to take the wrong one. We would fain take that walk, never yet taken by us through this actual world, which is perfectly symbolical of the path which we love to travel in the interior and ideal world; and sometimes, no doubt, we find it difficult to choose our direction, because it does not yet exist distinctly in our idea.[15]

Thoreau here expressed the importance of the inner voyage in the pro-cess of self-discovery, and the necessity of conducting the journey with proper attention to its moral direction. The excursion into nature, the metaphorical voyage into the inner consciousness, is a temporary func-tion of the individual performed in the fulfillment of his potential as spiritual being. Later, in the same essay, Thoreau delivered a judgment that indicates more clearly the actual relationship of man and nature, symbol and event. "For my part, I feel that with regard to Nature I live a sort of border life, on the confines of a world into which I make occa-sional and transitional and transient forays only."[16] This idea is similar to the voyage metaphor found in *Walden*:

> When I wrote the following pages, or rather the bulk of them, I lived alone, in the woods, a mile from any neighbor, in a house which I had built myself, on the shore of Walden Pond, in Concord, Massachusetts, and earned my living by the labor of my hands only. I lived there two years and two months. At present, I am a sojourner in civilized life again.[17]

The passages from "Walking" indicates how the poet lived in a neutral territory on the border of nature, from which he made a periodic journey into the soul, to return once again to the neutral position. This foray resembles a circle in geometrical terms and the circle image recapitulates the traditional metaphors of regeneration. Not only does

Walden open with an indication that an identical procedure has been followed in the experience at the pond, but the structure of the paragraph reflects the out-and-back movement of the spiritual journey. Commencing abruptly, Thoreau plunges us into the immediate situation by introducing the "following pages," which will take us on a journey to the "house which I had built myself," and where "I earned my living by the labor of my hands only." The concluding sentence returns us to the immediate situation, as Thoreau asserts that again he is a part of the civilized world. As a microcosm of the whole book, the passage illustrates one of Thoreau's favorite rhetorical devices, synecdoche. As always, the passage is tightly bound to the structure and theme of the work through its organization as an out-and-back movement and by the way the metaphorical and literal experience are organically fused.

The formula for Thoreau's method in *A Week* and *Walden* is found in a brief essay that he published in *The Dial* in 1843. "A Winter Walk" was also published posthumously in the collection of *Excursions* (1863), and it reflects the out-and-back movement that characterized Thoreau's relationship to the natural world. Its essential action is the mid-winter walk of a village dweller to a hut that lies deep in the woods. It begins at daybreak and is concluded in the evening of the same day. The material that lies in between clearly indicates the writer's development of a literal experience that organically becomes a spiritual expression.

"Silently we unlatch the door, letting the drift fall in, and step abroad into the cutting air."[18] With this statement commences a succession of impressions derived from Thoreau's own observations of physical nature. The setting is a New England landscape, punctuated by the author's philosophical interpretation of his natural environment. As we "step hastily through the powdery snow, warmed by an inward heat," we enjoy an "increased glow of feeling."

Circle images are prominent in this piece, but the central episode is the retreat of Thoreau to a "woodman's hut," located deep in the woods. The source of all life seems to radiate in concentric circles, as Thoreau associates the "inward warmth" with the "slumbering subterranean fire" of nature, which emanates from the central source of power, the sun. (There are some passages of social criticism, which correspond to "Brute Neighbors" and "The Village" in *Walden*.) As the cottage is approached, Thoreau asserts: "At length, having reached the edge of the woods, and shut out the gadding town, we enter within the covert as we go under the roof of a cottage, and cross its threshold, all ceiled and banked up with snow" (p. 116). Later, in the same section of the piece, he observes: "How much more living is the life that is in nature, the furred life which still survives the shining nights, and from amidst fields and woods covered with frost and snow, sees the sun rise" (p. 118). The climax of these observations is a statement which contrasts the life-in-nature with civilized living:

> Standing quite alone, far in the forest, while the wind is shaking down snow from the trees, and leaving the only human tracks behind us, we find our reflections of a richer variety than the life of cities. The chicadee and nuthatch are more inspiring society than statesmen and philosophers, and we shall return to these last, as to more vulgar companions. In this lonely glen . . . our lives are more serene and worthy to contemplate (p. 119).

Thoreau and the reader move now into the woodman's hut, "to see how he has passed the long winter nights and the short stormy days." The hut itself is described as being "two seasons" old, and wholly harmonious with its natural surroundings. In the distance, "some invisible farmhouse" gives forth a column of smoke, which Thoreau uses as a metaphor for his organic idea: "It is a hieroglyphic of man's life, and suggests more intimate things than the boiling of a pot. Where its fine column rises above the forest, like an ensign, some human life has planted itself" (p. 123).

The most important feature of this landscape, however, is a "wooded lake," which establishes the pattern of Thoreau's conception of Walden Pond. "In summer it is the earth's liquid eye; a mirror for the breast of nature." Once again images of circularity become central, and Thoreau asserts that "the woods form an amphitheatre about it, and it is an arena for all the genialness of nature. All trees direct the traveller to its brink, all paths seek it out, birds fly to it, quadrupeds flee to it, and the very ground inches toward it." Evidently, even the conceptual metaphor of Walden Pond preceded the experience of dwelling on its shore.

Wandering further into the woods, Thoreau hears the "distant booming of ice from yonder bay of the river." This natural interruption provides an opportunity for him to develop the image of the river as an excursion into nature, and, metaphorically, an excursion into the self. He had already made this association in the *Journal* entries that recalled the voyage on the Concord and Merrimack. Here, however, the moral, aesthetic, and metaphorical dimensions of the river are given in full.

> The river flows in the rear of the towns, and we see all things from a new and wilder side. The fields and gardens come down to it with a frankness, and freedom from pretension, which they do not wear on the highway. It is the outside and edge of the earth . . . It is a beautiful illustration of the law of obedience, the flow of a river; the path for a sick man, a highway down which an acorn cup may float secure with its freight. Its slight occasional falls, whose precipices would not diversify the landscape, are celebrated by mist and

spray, and attract the traveller from far and near. From the remote interior, the current conducts him by broad and easy steps (p. 127).

Even the digression on fishes, later found in *A Week*, is present:"No domain of nature is quite closed to man at all times, and now we draw near to the empire of the fishes. Our feet glide swiftly over unfathomed depths, where in summer our line tempted the trout and perch, and where the stately pickerel lurked in the long corridors formed by the bulrushes" (p. 128). A metaphorical value for the season of winter is also established: "In winter, we lead a more inward life. Our hearts are warm and cheery, like cottages under drifts, whose windows and doors are half concealed, but from whose chimneys the smoke cheerfully ascends" (p. 133). Although the correlation between metaphors in "A Winter Walk" and *Walden* is not always exact, it would seem that the piece was some kind of experimental prototype for both *A Week* and *Walden*. Moreover, the piece itself is unified, reflecting the out-and-back movement that characterizes the later works. "A Winter Walk" is in these respects the earliest example of Thoreau's use of the "organic principle" next to his tireless work on *Walden*.

Thoreau uses the circle as a paradigm of renewal in the process of regeneration; however, the recollection of experience for the transformed sensibility becomes a recreation of the actual process communicated by words that are themselves given a "new life." Just as Edwards found in nature a new language of revelation available to the saints, so Thoreau has discovered an organic union of symbol and idea made possible because he is "transcendentally redeemed." If Edwards shared his vision through doctrinal declarations, Thoreau shapes his writing to reflect the organic process by which the *litera* and *figura* are united by his "new sense of things."

Thoreau's use of the circle image and the principle of synecdoche was more developed in *Walden* than anywhere else in his writing, and the organic relations of symbol to idea in that work have been recently demonstrated.[19] However, *A Week* also reflects the author's metaphorical journey into thought. Each piece is designed around a recapitulation of actual experience in the life of the author, and each represents a transformation through the metaphor of self-discovery. Moreover, each experience takes place at a particular period in Thoreau's life when he was unusually concerned with self-examination, so that the voyage and the visit to the pond are endowed with spiritual value at the times they were actually experienced, not simply as emotions "recollected in tranquillity."

A Week on the Concord and Merrimack Rivers began to appear in rough form in the *Journal* as early as nine months after the actual voyage of

1839. Although not published until 1849, Thoreau worked on *A Week* while he was in residence at Walden Pond, and an example from the *Journal* will indicate how early observations were later incorporated into *A Week*. "So with a vigorous shove we launch our boat from the bank, while the flags and bulrushes curtsy God-speed, and drop silently down the stream. As if we had launched our bark in the sluggish current of our thoughts and were bound nowhither" (*Journal*, I, 136). This passage clearly indicates Thoreau's method of employing a natural experience for metaphorical purposes. The "sluggish current of our thoughts" was perhaps too obvious an analogy for the opening paragraph of the final version, and we find that this phrase has been deleted. "So with a vigorous shove we launched our boat from the bank, while the flags and bulrushes curtsied a God-speed, and dropped silently down the stream."[20] As the strategic metaphor in all Thoreau's prose writing, this journey assumes a variety of forms. The circle is the dominant image of *A Week*, although it is more difficult to discern. The out-and-back motion of both *Walden* and "A Winter Walk" is present, but the river image is more readily visualized as a journey that has begun in one place and ended in another. Nevertheless, this "river of our thoughts" is cyclical in form, and Thoreau is careful to show that the little boat has returned to its "native port," where its keel "recognized the Concord mud, where some semblance of its outline was still preserved in the flattened flags which had scarce yet erected themselves since our departure" (p. 518). However, the most convincing evidence for the structural pattern of Thoreau's metaphorical journey is the simple format of the piece. The time cycle is a single week, in which there are seven complete daily cycles.

It could be maintained that to rest one's structural analysis on the similarity between days and weeks as cycles of nature is to state the obvious. It would indeed be irrelevant merely to observe that the week-long experience is divided into seven days, each of which is a microcosm reflecting the unity of the whole. In this sense, all smaller units of time are microcosms of larger ones. However, the image of the circle is fundamental to Thoreau's structural principle in *A Week*, and there is an attempt at organizing his materials around these natural cycles; just as in *Walden*, the seasons are units within the larger framework of the annual cycle, the central symbol of spiritual regeneration. For example, the sections describing Friday evening serve not only as concluding metaphors for the explorations of that particular day, but also contain an appropriate closing for the entire journey:

The sun-setting presumed all men at leisure, and in a contemplative mood; but the farmer's boy only whistled the more thoughtfully as he drove his cows home from pasture, and the teamster refrained from cracking his whip, and guided his team with a subdued voice. The last vestiges of daylight at length disappeared, and as we rowed silently along with our backs toward home through the darkness, only a few stars being visible, we had little to say, but sat absorbed in thought, or in silence listened to the monotonous sound of our oars (p. 515).

In this culminating passage, we are once again reminded that the journey is to end where it has begun, as the two oarsmen "rowed along silently" with their "backs toward home." Even here, Thoreau digresses to reflect on the meaning of silence, in the manner that he has previously used the narrative framework as a basis for speculation and dreaming. However, in one brief observation, he seems to summarize the process of his inward exploration, as he looks upward at the stars: "Let the immortal depth of your soul lead you, but earnestly extend your eyes upward" (p. 515). This might be regarded as a paradigm of the inward journey of self-discovery. Although the experience takes one deep into the human consciousness, it is never meant to be an irreversible voyage into the darkness of introspection. This feature of the relation to nature is made quite clear in *Walden*, where the arrival of spring heralds a state of spiritual regeneration. Quite possibly, Thoreau's failure to establish the purpose and limits of his metaphorical journey contributed to his failure to integrate the form and content of *A Week* any better than he did. One perceives that the episodes and digressions contained in *A Week* somehow derive from observable experience, but there are few instances where the transitions are completely natural. The frequent poetical interruptions also contribute to an appearance of disorder. If we are impressed with Thoreau's wide range of literary allusions in *A Week*, we are puzzled by his seeming lack of ability to integrate his own piece in a concise manner. Many of his poems reflect a stylistic penchant for archaism, and his random selection from earlier poets reveals a similar inclination. Moreover, several of the essays are not integrated either actually or metaphorically. This gives the work an overall shape of disjunction, despite its orderly narrative framework.

In defense of Thoreau's method in *A Week*, one should look quite closely at two of the days which reflect some structural and stylistic principles the author was later to employ in the composition of *Walden*. Once launched onto the Concord River, in "Saturday," Thoreau and his brother pass under the "North Bridge," which occasions the first poetical digression of the narrative. The experiences of the bridge are wholly reflective; however, Thoreau describes the movement by the field of battle in terms of "din of war" from the past, which is contrasted with the "noiseless stream." This passage alerts us to a very common principle in

Thoreau's prose, the principle of contrast. In this case, alternatives of time — past and present — are presented as opposite experiences of the same "sense." The past, or the Revolutionary conflict, is remembered amid the "sounds" of war; the present, on the other hand, is represented by the pastoral setting which has "long since" settled over the battlefield. Thoreau makes an unusually smooth transition in this manner: "Gradually, the village murmur subsided, and we seemed to be embarked on the placid current of our dreams, floating from past to future as silently as one awakes to fresh morning or evening thoughts. We glided noiselessly down the stream" (p. 22). Here, the actual noise of the village of Concord is metaphorically linked to the "din of war" from the past, as the voyagers move from past, through present, to future.

Within a few sentences, however, Thoreau has returned to a familiar style: the objective, empirical description of his immediate surroundings. Reminiscent of William Bartram's tediously detailed account of his journey through Florida, Thoreau tells how the "narrow-leaved willow (*Salix Purshiana*) lay along the surface of the water in masses of light green foliage, interspersed with the large balls of the button-bush" (p. 22). Shortly, we learn that "The snake-head (*Chelone glabra*) grew close to the shore, while a kind of coreopsis, turning its brazen face to the sun, full and rank, and a tall, dull red flower (*Eupatorium purpureum, or trumpet-weed*) formed the rear rank of the fluvial array" (p. 22). These descriptive passages are followed by a virtual catalog of the species of fishes that inhabit the river, but not before Thoreau has digressed in an essay on human nature, which was occasioned by passing a fisherman on the shore. "Thus, by one bait or another, Nature allures inhabitants into all her recesses. This man was the last of our townsmen whom we saw, and we silently through him bade adieu to our friends" (p. 25). The paragraphs that follow this brief encounter are reflective and speculative; Thoreau reveals his interest in human beings as character types as he remarks, "The characteristics and pursuits of various ages and races of men are always existing in epitome in every neighborhood" (p. 26). The metaphorical value of human experience pervades Thoreau's writing, and the analogical habit of mind is fully realized in a statement like "This fishing was not a sport, nor solely a means of subsistence, but a sort of solemn sacrament and withdrawal from the world, just as the aged read their Bibles" (p. 28). The rapid juxtaposition of abstraction with concrete phenomena has always been recognized in Thoreau's style; however, it is now clear that the metaphor-making process depends on the use of figures that are eternal, not temporal, and that, like Edwards, Thoreau perceives in the world of nature a prophetic synecdoche of the world that has been and the world that will be: "Whether we live by the seaside, or by the lakes and rivers, or on the prairie, it concerns us to attend to the nature of fishes, since they are not phenomena confined to certain localities only, but forms and phases of the life in nature universally dispersed" (p. 23). The cycle image that has been identified throughout his work is the central metaphor not only of renewal, but also of the eternal, natural process by which human time is defined. Like Taylor and Edwards, Thoreau has employed the imagery of nature to explore abstract principles which he believes to be eternally verifiable. Unlike his Puritan predecessors, Thoreau perceived in nature the full expression of spirit rather than a "symbol of spirit," and in this way, the transcendental mode closely approximates the epistemological discourses of Edwards, whose elect perception received impressions of divine grace through natural sources of revelation as well as from Scripture.

The fusion of literal and metaphorical experience is everywhere present in *A Week*; both the days and the circumstances provide an ideal opportunity for Thoreau to digress into philosophy, religion, mythology, and literature. His extended essay, which comprises most of the material in the philosophical section, is barely framed by the experiences of the day. The most revealing portion of the essay, and perhaps of the entire work, is the author's assertion of his beliefs about poetry:

> There is no doubt that the loftiest written wisdom is either rhymed, or in some way musically measured, — is, in form as well as substance, poetry; and a volume which should contain the condensed wisdom of mankind need not have one rhythmless line. Yet poetry, though the last the finest result, is a natural fruit. As naturally as the oak bears an acorn, and the vine a gourd, man bears a poem, either spoken or done. It is the chief and most memorable success, for history is but a prose narrative of poetic deeds (pp. 116-117).

The balance between actuality and metaphor in the prose reinforces the poetic principle, and if early manifestations of it are seen at random in *A Week*, they are harmonized and brought to fruition in the composition of *Walden*.

There is no doubt that *Walden* is the most exactingly composed of Thoreau's prose writings. The failure of *A Week* discouraged the publishers from accepting another Thoreau manuscript, and because the materials were similar to the first work, it was necessary for Thoreau to wait for over five years before his final version was accepted for publication. Fortunately, this frustrating delay afforded time and incentive for numerous revisions of the manuscript. Lyndon Shanley has demonstrated how Thoreau revised *Walden* with meticulous care, and that his habit of building on experiences recorded in the *Journal*, to which he added and from which he later subtracted, has provided a number of problems in reconstructing the precise method of composition.[21] For example, we know that in the composition of *A Week* and *Walden*, Thoreau relied heavily on his *Journal*. An extensive account of the experience as it had happened and as it had been "recollected in tranquillity," the *Journal* is the major document for a comparison of the writer's original pattern of thought with what is presented in the final account in either derivative composition. As Sherman Paul has noted, "The value of the Walden *Journal* is not in its entries, most of which were later used in *Walden*, but in the sudden perspectives it opens on the original experience there."[22]

Shanley's excellent study of the various stages in the composition of *Walden* is reinforced with evidence from the factual account of Thoreau's life and from an extremely thorough examination of the extant materials that were used in the creation of the first published version of 1854. Most important of all, in the context of this essay, is Shanley's conviction that Thoreau created *Walden* as a metaphor of his own growth and experience, and that clearly defined "stages" of composition are difficult to delineate. "The growth of *Walden* might be compared to that of a living organism that grows continuously and imperceptibly by absorbing new material into its tissue and structure."[23] Although we are not able to determine just how much advanced planning Thoreau may have done, the method of composition reveals that there was an organic relationship between the writer's process of composition and his evolving patterns of thought. If we are unable to distinguish among "successive stages of growth" in a clear fashion, we are quite able to perceive the structural principles around which the author was organizing his recollected experience. "The greatest growth in Thoreau's conception of *Walden* resulted, however, from his seeing how he might fill out his account of the progress of the seasons and describe the changes they had brought in his daily affairs and his thoughts; by doing so, he would express more adequately the richness and the completeness of his experience."[24] The dominant image in *Walden* is the circle, and it reflects a cycle of spiritual investigation that is followed by spiritual regeneration. Moreover, the circle image is carried within a linear paradigm, the spiral, so that the synecdochic figures in nature reinforce the circle image that forms the structural framework for the entire essay; they also point forward, eschatologically, to that timeless moment when the veils will be lifted and nature and spirit will be united.

This union of symbol and idea has served two useful purposes. First, it has provided Thoreau's most meaningful statement of the organic relation between man and nature. As William Drake remarks:

> The strategic metaphor of *Walden* becomes the exploration of one's own life
> surroundings, because only here has one the centrality of focus from which to
> lay out measurements in all directions. One finds himself wherever he is by

finding where he is. Walden Pond is only as deep as one's self, depending on the extent of its service to the imagination; for nature provides the only trustworthy measurement of man. The mind of man thrives and develops by meeting and coming to terms with the world he lives in. The metaphor in Thoreau's hands is shaped to express that relationship. Self-discovery is thus linked with discovery of fact outside oneself.[25]

Second, the process has prepared the reader, as observer of the experience, for the arrival of spring. Throughout the "poem," Thoreau has been building toward the climactic arrival of spring, which represents the awakening out of introspection that has been symbolized by the darkness and stillness of the winter months. Like the Puritan three-stage process of humiliation, justification, and sanctification, Thoreau's structuring of self-discovery thus becomes a multi-phase process. The darkness must be entered before awakening is possible, but darkness is not to be lingered in eternally.

Moreover, the resulting awareness of a "new sense of things" is cumulative, like Edwards' awareness that his senses had been transformed forever by an act of grace. Thoreau's growth enables him to begin again, renewed by nature's cycle of development and as a spirit reborn. The expression of this transformation has been accomplished by his organic symbolic mode, through which the "word is made flesh," and the image has the power to transform the reader by recreating the actual spiritual growth of the writer's experience, in addition to its primary function of communicating a particular meaning. In Thoreau's metaphorical writing, as in Edwards' "Personal Narrative" and *Images or Shadows of Divine Things*, the image fuses *litera* and *figura* into a single, timeless moment, out of which the spiritual power of the words emerges. The brilliant organizing capacity of his intellect had developed an "organic principle" which, in a finished product, resembled the conventional pilgrimage of Christian seekers from Dante to Bunyan. What distinguishes Thoreau's method, however, is the way in which he integrated the details of his experience in the process of extending the metaphor. After Locke and Edwards, Thoreau firmly believed that facts and words were more than representatives of ideas, and it was to the perception of these ideas that he directed his energy and attention. Consequently, the course of his writing reveals a search for meaning in the slightest details of his natural environment. The cyclical excursion into nature was more than a means to self-discovery; it represented the deepest possible perception of man's spirituality. Through the "organic principle," the axis on which Thoreau's world turned, one is able to understand something of the man and the ideas that lie beneath the surface of his writing. In doctrinal terms, Thoreau and the Puritans were far apart; however, in the employment of images to reflect the eternal process of historical revelation and fulfillment, the hermit of Concord and the reclusive minister of Westfield are exploring similar territory, the one using the Bible to discover new meaning in contemporary history and the other finding prophecy and fulfillment in the cycles of natural dispensation.

Nineteenth- and twentieth-century extensions of the prophetic mode lie beyond the scope of this study. It is clear, however, that the personalized sense of manifest destiny that pervades the poetry of Walt Whitman owes much to the fusion of providential and personal forces that govern the writing of seventeenth-century Puritans like Edward Taylor. The historical determinism of Reformation Calvinism reappears in the dramatic narratives of William Faulkner, and the eschatological figures of biblical typology are adapted in the synecdoches of Robert Frost. Even the antimillennial visions of Norman Mailer are indebted to the Puritan imagination and its pervasive influence in American writing, because the fulfillment of the early American dream has been a persistent force in the development of American literature from the "errand into the wilderness" to the present. Other writers, like Robert Lowell in *The Mills of the Kavanaughs*, illustrate the continuing Puritan strain less metaphorically, but with a similar extension of the New England Puritan influence beyond the parameters of the historical movement. When Frederick Jackson Turner focused attention on the enormous importance of westward expansion in the cultural development of the United States, he established a tension between eastern and western alternatives in the fulfillment of the American dream. Even this prominent critique, however, was unable to address the significant prophetic modes of expression that persist from the early seventeenth century into modern times. Though it is certainly not peculiarly American to envision one's destiny as that of an "elect nation" and though many of the doctrinal positions adopted by Americans owe their origins to English Puritanism and to the continental Reformation, it is clear that in American literature a prophetic strain has evolved and been transformed by succeeding generations of writers. The language of Canaan, a complex form of expression that has governed the development of American self-awareness from Winthrop to Whitman, has only recently lost the prominence it once enjoyed as a prophetic mode of writing that each rising generation would learn to use. Hemingway and Fitzgerald were well aware of this unusual language through their reading of Melville and Hawthorne, and the *Zeitgeist* originally generated by the biblical interpreters of the New England Way was perhaps best expressed by F. Scott Fitzgerald when he wrote, in a letter to his daughter, "You and all the generations of Americans since the Civil War have believed that you are about to inherit the earth." Inheritance, indeed, forms an important link between past and future, and the language of Canaan was perhaps the most crucial legacy of New England Puritanism to modern America. Influences like the work-ethic and the impulse to make the world safe for democracy have value at particular historical moments, but the language in which these impulses are expressed changes gradually to meet the needs of prophetic expression, though the tensions between conservative tradition and contemporary application operate throughout generational adaptation. The language of Canaan — from the sermons of John Cotton to the prophetic symbols of *Walden* — is based on structural and metaphorical principles articulated by the writers of the Bible, whose guiding vision of eternal purpose pervaded every image and type and gave eschatological meaning to each historical episode. It is, then, a biblical impulse that defines America's purpose, not only in the prominent errand theme but also in the application of language to the expression of that theme, and it has been the objective of this study to examine that impulse in history, literature, and the language of theology. The secular transformations of the eighteenth and nineteenth centuries have given new meaning to terms like "type" and "fulfillment," but the original organizing principle of the language of Canaan remains clear. America's deepest rhetorical impulse has always been the expression of future promise, an articulation of imminent fulfillment that will no doubt characterize the literature throughout the centuries to come.

Notes, Index

NOTES

INTRODUCTION

1. Everett H. Emerson, *Puritanism in America: 1620-1750* (Boston: Twayne Publishers, 1977), p. i.

2. Charles Feidelson, *Symbolism in American Literature* (Chicago: University of Chicago Press, 1959), pp. 18-19.

3. Perry Miller, Introduction for Jonathan Edwards' *Images or Shadows of Divine Things* (New Haven: Yale University Press, 1948), p. 4.

4. Ibid., p. 4.

5. Ibid., pp. 6-7.

1. MEDIEVAL AND REFORMATION BACKGROUNDS

1. Samuel Parker, *A Discourse of Ecclesiastical Polity* (London, 1670), pp. 75-76.

2. William Sherlock, *A Discourse Concerning the Knowledge of Jesus Christ* (London, 1674), p. 114.

3. Symon Patrick, *A Continuation of the Friendly Debate between a Conformist and a Nonconformist* (London, 1669), p. 2.

4. Samuel Butler, *Hudibras,* ed. John Wilders (1967), p. 238 [III, ii.ll.151-152].

5. William Shakespeare, *Twelfth Night,* ed. Sylvan Barnet (New York: Signet Publications, 1962), p. 43.

6. "The Mad Zealot," in *Rump,* i.239. Cf. Johann Buxtorf, "The Epistle Dedicatory," A4, in *A Short Introduction to the Hebrew Tongue,* trans. John Davis (1656).

7. Patrick, *A Continuation of the Friendly Debate,* p. 1. Cf. "The Godly Man's Legacy to the Saints upon Earth" (London, 1680), p. 5. This document is a satirical biography of the nonconformist Stephen Marshall.

8. Ben Jonson, *The Alchemist* (London, 1610), III.i.ll.5-6.

9. Patrick, *A Continuation of the Friendly Debate,* pp. 89-90. Cf. "The Holy Sisters," in *Rump,* ii.158.

10. Richard Baxter, *The Saint's Everlasting Rest* (London, 1662), p. 639.

11. See Sacvan Bercovitch, *Typology and Early American Literature* (Amherst: University of Massachusetts Press, 1972), and *The Puritan Origins of the American Self* (New Haven: Yale University Press, 1975), William G. Madsen, *From Shadowy Types to Truth* (New Haven: Yale University Press, 1968), and Barbara Lewalski, *Donne's Anniversaries and the Poetry of Praise* (Princeton: Princeton University Press, 1973).

12. See Barbara Lewalski, *Protestant Poetics and the Seventeenth-Century Religious Lyric* (Princeton: Princeton University Press, 1979), p. 6, where the following appears: "Augustine's *De Doctrina Christiana* is the *locus classicus* for this topic: Augustine cites examples of all three levels of style and of various rhetorical excellences in Scripture, but he affirms that the eloquence of the Scripture writers is not chiefly a matter of their conformity to the rules of rhetoric but rather of their inspired wisdom and truth."

13. Harry Caplan, "The Four Senses of Scriptural Interpretation and the Mediaeval Theory of Preaching," *Speculum*, 4 (1929), 283. For thorough discussions of the patristic and medieval backgrounds to Puritan exegesis, see Thomas M. Davis, "The Traditions of Puritan Typology," in Sacvan Bercovitch, ed., *Typology and Early American Literature*, pp. 11-47; John M. Steadman, *The Lamb and the Elephant: Ideal Imitation and the Context of Renaissance Allegory* (San Marino: The Huntington Library, 1974), pp. vii-lvi; and Robert Hollander, "Typology and Secular Literature: Some Medieval Problems and Examples," Karlfried Froehlich, " 'Always to Keep the Literal Sense in Holy Scripture Means to Kill One's Soul,' " both in Earl Miner, ed., *Literary Uses of Typology from the Late Middle Ages to the Present* (Princeton: Princeton University Press, 1977), pp. 3-20 and 21-49.

14. Dante Aligheri, "Epistola X, Letter to Can Grande della Scala, *Epistolae: The Letters of Dante*, ed. Paget Toynbee (Oxford: Oxford University Press, 1966), pp. 199-200, as quoted by Lewalski, *Protestant Poetics*, p. 8.

15. Lewalski, *Poetics*, pp. 27-28. As Barbara Lewalski has shown, "It is necessary to approach Augustinian poetics not in medieval but in Reformation terms. The important new factor introduced into this poetics by the Reformation is the new, indeed overwhelming, emphasis on the written word as the embodiment of Divine Truth. The Christian writer, or poet, is accordingly led to relate his work not to ineffable and intuited Divine revelation, but rather to its written formulation in Scripture, and that affords him a literary model which he can imitate."

16. St. Augustine, *The City of God*, XV, 27, trans. Marius Dods (New York, 1950), as quoted by Jesper Rosenmeier, "The Image of Christ," Ph.D. diss., Harvard University, 1965, p. 27.

17. Ibid., p. 27.

18. Eric Auerbach, *Scenes from the Drama of European Literature* (New York: Meridian Books, 1959), p. 42.

19. See the discussion of Augustine's distinctions between typology and allegory in Auerbach, *Scenes*, pp. 37-49. Noah's Ark is *praefiguratio ecclesiae* (a "prefiguration of the church"; *De Civitate Dei*, 15, 27); in several different ways, Moses is a *figura Christi* (e.g., *De Civitate Dei*, 10, 8 or 18, 11); Aaron's *sacerdotium*

is *umbra et figura aeterni sacerdotii* ("shadow and figure of the eternal priesthood"; *De Civ.,* 17, 6); Hagar, the slave woman, is a *figura* of the Old Testament, of the *terrena Jerusalem* ("earthly Jerusalem"), and Sara of the New Testament, of the *superna Jerusalem civitas Dei* ("the heavenly Jerusalem, the City of God"; *De Civ.,* 16, 31; 17, 3); Jacob and Esau *figuram praebuerunt durum populorum in Christianis et Judeis* ("prefigured the two peoples of Jews and Christians"; *De Civ.,* 16, 42); the kings of Judaea *Christi figuram prophetica unctione gestabant* ("by being anointed by the prophets bore a prefiguration of Christ"; *De Civ.,* 17, 4).

20. The early history of scriptural exegesis indicates a sharp division between commentators who would support the reading of Scripture for its literal as well as its spiritual value, and interpreters who read in Scripture *only* an allegorical significance. The former group were commonly regarded as followers of Tertullian and the Antioch school of exegesis, while the allegorists were related to Philo and Origen and the school of Alexandria. The most crucial distinction between these two major exegetical schools was the difference between their respective methods of interpreting the Old Testament in its relation to the New. Although both schools sought to give meaning to the Greek word *tupos,* "type," the allegorizers of Alexandria provided a very different exegesis from the typologists of Antioch. This *tupos,* which appears in the New Testament and refers to the Old Testament figures, is central to any system of typology, and it will be useful to establish a working definition of the term. "The Greek word for 'type,' *tupos,* occurs fourteen times in the New Testament. Although it has several meanings, the word has only two basic ideas: (1) pattern, (2) that which is produced from the pattern, i.e., a product. *Tupos* is used of the mark (or pattern) of the nails (John 20:25). It is also used of that which is formed, an *image* or *statue* (Acts 7:43). The word *tupos* describes a pattern of teaching (Rom. 6:17). It is also used to stand for the *content* or *text* of a letter (Acts 23:25). It is used technically of an *archetype, model,* or *pattern* both by Stephen and by the writer of Hebrews (Acts 7:44) (Heb. 8:5). It is most frequently used of an *example* or *pattern* in the moral life, (Phil. 3:17; I Thess. 1:7; II Thess. 3:9; I Tim. 4:12; Tit. 2:7; I Pet. 5:3). Finally, it is used of *types* given by God as an indication of the future, in the form of persons or things (Rom. 5:14; I Cor. 10:6). Adam was the type of the one who was about to be, namely Jesus Christ, the head of the new humanity (Rom. 5:12). Certain evil actions of the children of Israel and what resulted are typical warnings of what will befall Christians if they follow a similar course (I Cor. 10:6, 11). The episodes happened and are recorded in the Old Testament so that Christians will not desire what is forbidden, or become idolaters, or practice immorality, or tempt the Lord, or murmur (I Cor. 10:6-11). The Greek adjective *antitupos* (anti-type) has the meaning 'corresponding to something that has gone before.'" From A. Berkeley Mickelsen, *Interpreting the Bible* (Grand Rapids, 1963), p. 239. Mickelsen's emphasis on the moral value of the Old Testament types is not universally shared by critics of typological exegesis. See also the definitions provided by William F. Arndt and F. Wilbur Gingrich, *A Greek-English Lexicon of the New Testament and Other Early Christian Literature* (Chicago, 1957), pp. 837-838, and the discussions of typology in exegesis by G. H. W. Lampe and K. J. Woolcombe, *Essays on Typology* (Naperville, 1957). See also Henri de LuBac, "Typologie et Allégorisme," *Recherches de Science Religieuse* (1947), pp. 180-226.

21. William G. Madsen, "From Shadowy Types to Truth," in *The Lyric and Dramatic Milton,* ed. Joseph Summers (New York: Columbia University Press, 1965), pp. 99-100.

22. K. J. Woolcombe, "The Biblical Origins and Patristic Development of Typology," in *Essays on Typology,* p. 65.

23. Auerbach, *Scenes,* p. 30. This judgment is corroborated by Helen Frances Dunbar, *Symbolism in Medieval Thought and Its Consummation in the Divine Comedy* (New Haven: Yale University Press, 1929), p. 267: "Unlike Origen, Tertullian argued that interpretation of Scripture by the so-called allegorical method was permissible only when the symbol was true in its literal sense . . . He points out that the use of resurrection to symbolize a moral change rests on the premise that the prophets speak in figures of speech. There can, however, be no figure without verity. If your face is not here, you cannot see it in the mirror." Auerbach has analyzed how clearly Tertullian saw the distinctions between typology and allegory: "Tertullian expressly denied that the literal and historical validity of the Old Testament was diminished by the figural interpretation. He was definitely hostile to spiritualism and refused to consider the Old Testament as mere allegory; according to him, it had real, literal meaning throughout, and even where there was figural prophecy, the figure had just as much historical validity as what it prophesied. The prophetic figure, he believed, is a concrete historical fact, and it is fulfilled by concrete historical facts."

24. Auerbach, *Scenes,* pp. 53-54.

25. *The Holy Bible,* Authorized Version (Cambridge: Cambridge University Press, n.d.), p. 788. Hereafter, only textual references will be given.

26. Justin Martyr, c. *Trypho,* 100, quoted by Gilbert Cope, *Symbolism and the Bible in the Church* (New York: Philosophical Library, 1959), p. 89.

27. Irenaeus, *adv. Haer.,* III, xxii, 4, quoted by Cope, *Symbolism and the Bible in the Church,* p. 89.

28. G. W. H. Lampe, "The Reasonableness of Typology," in *Essays on Typology* (Naperville, 1957), p. 33.

29. Ibid., pp. 33-34. "This kind of typology tends, like allegory, to disregard historical verisimilitude, the original context of history, and the intention of the ancient authors. To this sort of typology belongs the supposed correspondence which was popular in the Church of the Fathers between the scarlet cord of Rahab at Jericho, which served as a token of Salvation, and the blood of Christ, the sign of the salvation of Mankind. Here, the parallel between the type and its supposed fulfillment is plainly unreal and artificial. Historically, the only connection lies in the fact that in both cases there is immunity from destruction, guaranteed by a sign; but this kind of destruction, of immunity, and of signs is different in each case, while the fact that both the thread of Rahab and the blood of Christ were red is of no significance outside the mind of the over-ingenious typologist."

30. S. P. Bromyard, s.v., "Accidia," ms. Camb. Univ. Libr. II, iii, 8, fol. 145 (Thos. Wimbledon? fl. 1388), quoted by G. R. Owst, *Literature and the Pulpit in Medieval England* (Cambridge: Cambridge University Press, 1961), p. 75.

31. Perry Miller, Introduction to Jonathan Edwards' *Images or Shadows of Divine Things* (New Haven: Yale University Press, 1948), p. 9.

32. Martin Luther, *Works,* ed. Jaroslav Pelikan and Herman T. Lerhman (St. Louis: Concordia Publishing House, 1958), XXXVII, 254-255.

33. Ibid., p. 258. Jesper Rosenmeier's commentary on the distinctions between Luther and Calvin is particularly helpful. See "Image of Christ," pp. 41-52.

34. Rosenmeier, "The Image of Christ," p. 46.

35. John Calvin, *Commentaries,* ed. J. Haroutunian (Philadelphia: The Westminster Press, 1958), p. 107.

36. Herman Melville, *White-Jacket* (New York, 1959), p. 189, as quoted by Rosenmeier, "Image," p. 54.

2. The Puritan Figural Imagination and the Language of Canaan

1. William Perkins, *The Arte of Prophesying* (London, 1609), pp. 30-31. Hereafter, references to this document will be provided in the text.

2. William Perkins, *A Cloud of Faithfull Witnesses: Leading to the Heavenly Canaan, or, A Commentarie Upon the Eleventh Chapter to the Hebrewes* (London, 1631), p. 74.

3. William Perkins, *A Reformed Catholike* (London, 1608), in *Works of William Perkins* (London, 1608), I, 580.

4. Henry Ainsworth, *Annotations upon the Five Bookes of Moses* (London, 1627), p. 39.

5. Richard Reinitz, "Symbolism and Freedom: the Use of Biblical Typology as an Argument for Religious Toleration in Seventeenth-Century England and America," Ph.D. diss., University of Rochester, 1967, p. 118.

6. Sacvan Bercovitch, "Annotated Bibliography," *Typology and Early American Literature* (Amherst: University of Massachusetts Press, 1972), p. 251.

7. Ibid.

8. William Guild, *Moses Unvailed, or those Figures which Served Unto the Patterne and shaddow of Heavenly Things, Pointing Out the Messiah Christ Jesus, Briefly Explained* (London, 1626), Sig. A3.

9. Thomas Taylor, *Christ Revealed* (London, 1635), p. 4.

10. William Ames, *A Fresh Suit Against Human Ceremonies, in God's Worship* (Rotterdam, 1633), I, 4.

11. Ibid., I, 35-36.

12. Ibid., II, 273.

13. William Ames, *Medulla Sacrae Theologiae* (London, 1629), translated as *The Marrow of Theology,* by John Eusden (Philadelphia: Pilgrim Press, 1968). References to this document will be provided hereafter in the text by chapter number.

3. The Canticles Tradition

1. John Cotton, *The Keys of the Kingdom of Heaven,* in Larzer Ziff, ed., *John Cotton on the Churches of New England* (Cambridge: Harvard University Press, 1972), p. 89.

2. John Cotton, *Some Treasure Fetched Out of Rubbish: . . . concerning the Imposition and Use of Significant Ceremonies in the Worship of God* (London, 1650), p. 27.

3. John Cotton, "Letter to Thomas Shepard," *Massachusetts State Archives,*

Hutchinson Papers, I, 103-106, as edited by Lawrance Thompson, "The Letters of John Cotton," master's thesis, Columbia University, 1934, p. 185. It is subscribed in Hutchinson's handwriting, "Much about the Sabbath, 1646."

4. Ibid., p. 180.

5. Theodore Beza, *Master Beza's Sermons upon the Three First Chapters of the Canticles of Canticles,* trans. from French by John Harmon, (Oxford, 1587), p. v.

6. William Gouge, *An Exposition of the Song of Solomon* (London, 1615), p. 18.

7. Henry Ainsworth, *Solomon's Song of Songs in English Metre, with Annotations and References to Other Scriptures* (London, 1623).

8. Joseph Hall, *Salomon's Diving Art of Ethickes, Politickes, Oeconomicks* (London, 1609), from the "Epistle Dedicatory."

9. William Guild, *Love's Entercours between the Lamb & His Bride, Christ and His Church* (London, 1658), p. 6.

10. Arthur Hildersham, *The Canticles, or Song of Solomon, Paraphrased* (London, 1672).

11. Symon Patrick, *A Paraphrase upon the Book of Ecclesiastes and the Song of Solomon, with Arguments . . .* (London, 1735).

12. Christopher Jellinger, *The Excellency of Christ, or, The Rose of Sharon* (London, 1641), pp. 2-5.

13. George Gyfford, *Fifteene Sermons upon the Song of Songs of Solomon* (London, 1598), Epistle Dedicatory.

14. Ibid.

15. Nathanael Homes, *A Commentary Literal or Historical, and Mystical or Spiritual, on the Book of Canticles* (London, n.d.), p. 14.

16. Ibid., p. 17.

17. Henoch Clapham, *Three Partes of Salomon, His Song of Songs Expounded* (London, 1603), p. 1.

18. Arthur Jackson, *Annotations upon Jobe and the Song of Solomon* (London, 1658), p. 119.

19. Ibid., p. 120.

20. John Robotham, *An Exposition of the Whole Book of Solomon's Song* (London, 1651), p. 9.

21. John Gill, *An Exposition of the Book of Solomon's Song, Commonly Called Canticles,* 3rd ed. (London, 1768), p. 17. See also Thomas Wilcox, *An Exposition upon the Whole Book of Canticles* (London, 1585).

22. Thomas Draxe, *The Lambe's Spouse, or, the Heavenly Bride* (London, 1608), Sig. B. 4.

23. John Owen, preface, in *Clavis Cantici* (London, 1669), Sig. B.

24. James Durham, *Clavis Cantici, or, An Exposition of the Song of Solomon* (London, 1669), p. 6. See Karen Rowe, "Sacred or Profane? Edward Taylor's Meditations on *Canticles,*" *Modern Philology,* 20 (1974), 123-138, where the relationship of Durham's *Clavis* to the Canticles tradition is discussed fully.

25. See John Cotton, *An Exposition upon the Thirteenth Chapter of the Revelation* (London, 1656), pp. 93ff.

26. See Jesper Rosenmeier, "The Image of Christ: The Typology of John Cotton," Ph.D. diss., Harvard University, 1965.

27. John Cotton, *A Brief Exposition of the Whole Book of Canticles* (London, 1642).

28. Ibid., preface.

29. Anthony Tuckney, preface to John Cotton, *A Brief Exposition of the Whole Book of Canticles* (London, 1655).

30. John Cotton, *A Brief Exposition of the Whole Book of Canticles,* p. 37.

31. See Karen Rowe, "Sacred or Profane? Edward Taylor's Meditations on *Canticles.*"

32. *Edward Taylor's Christographia,* ed. Norman Grabo (New Haven: Yale University Press, 1966), p. 287.

4. Samuel Mather: Figures, Types, and Allegories

1. Samuel Danforth, *A Briefe Recognition of New England's Errand into the Wilderness* (Boston, 1670), p. 5. All subsequent references will be provided parenthetically in the text.

2. J. Paul Hunter, *The Reluctant Pilgrim: Defoe's Emblematic Method and Quest for Form in Robinson Crusoe* (Baltimore: Johns Hopkins University Press, 1966), pp. 100-101.

3. Ibid., p. 101.

4. William Bradford, *Of Plimouth Plantation,* ed. Samuel Eliot Morison (New York, 1967), p. 58.

5. John T. Albro, "Introduction to *Theses Sabbaticae,*" in *Works of Thomas Shepard,* 3 vols. (London, 1850), I, xcv.

6. Ibid., p. xcvi.

7. Perry Miller, *The New England Mind: The Seventeenth Century* (Cambridge: Harvard University Press, 1954), p. 229.

8. Ibid., p. 229.

9. John Flavel, *Husbandry Spiritualized* (Boston, 1709), p. 157. All subsequent references will be provided parenthetically in the text.

10. John Flavel, "The Proem," *Husbandry Spiritualized,* sig. A4v.

11. Ibid., sig. B4v.

12. Flavel, *Husbandry Spiritualized,* p. 15.

13. John Davenport, *The Knowledge of Christ* (New Haven, 1652), p. 13. All subsequent references will be cited parenthetically in the text.

14. Samuel Mather, *A Testimony from the Scripture against Idolatry and Superstition* (Cambridge? 1672?), pp. 30-31. Hereafter, all citations to this document will appear in the text.

15. See Samuel Mather, *The Figures or Types of the Old Testament* (Dublin, 1683), pp. 75-76. The Puritan attack on Anglican ritual and symbol was incorporated into their own internal disagreements, e.g., the long-standing strife between Increase Mather and Solomon Stoddard over the Lord's Supper. See Everett Emerson and Mason Lowance, "Increase Mather's Confutation of Solomon Stoddard's Observations Concerning the Lord's Supper," in *Proceedings of the American Antiquarian Society* 83 (October 1973), 29-65.

16. Samuel Mather, *Testimony from Scripture,* p. 35. The Ceremonies examined include: (1) The Surplice, (2) The Sign of the Cross in Baptism, (3)

Kneeling at the Lord's Supper, (4) Bowing to the Altar, (5) Bowing at the Name of Jesus, (6) Popish Holy Days, (7) The Holiness of Places, (8) Organs, or Cathedral Music, (9) The Book of Common Prayer, (10) The Prelacy, or Church Government of Bishops.

17. See Thomas Shepard, *Theses Sabbaticae* (London, 1651). A full examination of this document in its relation to millennial eschatology appears in Chapter 6 of this book.

18. Cotton Mather, *Magnalia Christi Americana,* 2 vols. (Hartford, 1855), II, 47.

19. Samuel Mather, *The Figures or Types of the Old Testament,* 2nd ed. (London, 1705), p. 55. Hereafter, references to this edition will be cited in the text.

20. See Samuel Mather, *Figures or Types of the Old Testament* (London, 1705), ed. Mason Lowance, Jr. (New York: Johnson Reprint Corporation, 1969).

21. Benjamin Keach, *Tropologia: or, A Key to Open Scripture Metaphors . . . Together with Types of the Old Testament* (London, 1681), pp. iii-iv.

5. TAYLOR'S MEDITATIONS AND SERMONS AND THE PERSONALIZING OF THE BIBLICAL FIGURES

1. Norman Grabo, ed., *Edward Taylor's Christographia* (New Haven: Yale University Press, 1962), p. 287.

2. For a glimpse into the earlier controversy over Taylor's classification as a "metaphysical" or "Puritan," see Austin Warren, "Edward Taylor's Poetry: Colonial Baroque," *Kenyon Review,* 3 (1941), 355-371; Wallace G. Brown, "Edward Taylor: An American Metaphysical," *American Literature,* 14 (1944), 186-197; Herbert Blau, "Heaven's Sugar Cake: Theology and Imagery in the Poetry of Edward Taylor," *New England Quarterly,* 26 (1953), 337-360; Roy Harvey Pearce, "The Poet as Puritan," *New England Quarterly,* 23 (1950), 31-46. More recent studies include Charles Mignon, "Edward Taylor's Preparatory Meditations: A Decorum of Imperfection," *Publications of the Modern Language Association,* 83 (1968), 1423-28; Alan B. Howard, "The World as Emblem," *American Literature,* 44 (1972), 359-384; Donald Stanford, "Edward Taylor," in *Major Writers of Early American Literature,* ed. Everett Emerson (Madison: University of Wisconsin Press, 1972); and three longer studies: Norman Grabo, *Edward Taylor* (New York: Twayne, 1961); Karl Keller, *The Example of Edward Taylor* (Amherst: University of Massachusetts Press, 1975); and William Scheick, *The Will and the Word* (Athens: University of Georgia Press, 1976). In addition, Barbara Lewalski has included a splendid chapter on Taylor's aesthetics in her book, *Protestant Poetics and the Seventeenth-Century Religious Lyric* (Princeton: Princeton University Press, 1979); Karen Rowe has thoroughly described the structural divisions of Taylor's use of typology and allegory in "Puritan Typology and Allegory as Metaphor and Conceit in Edward Taylor's *Preparatory Meditations,*" Ph.D. diss., Indiana University, 1971; Ursula Brumm devoted a chapter to Edward Taylor in her pioneering study, *American Thought and Religious Typology* (New Brunswick: Rutgers University Press, 1970).

3. Barbara Lewalski, *Protestant Poetics,* p. 417.

4. Ursula Brumm, *American Thought and Religious Typology,* p. 9.

5. Ibid., pp. 83-93. As Taylor himself stated in the ninth sermon of the

Christographia, "Sometimes she setts him /Christ/ out in orientall Colours and in most Allegorical accomplishments, as Cant. 5. 10-16" (*Christographia,* p. 287).

6. In an article called "Sacred or Prophane: Edward Taylor's Meditations on *Canticles,*" *Modern Philology,* 20 (1974), 123-138, Karen Rowe divides Taylor's treatment of the Canticles Meditations in the following way: "Meditations II.115-128 consecutively analyze the figures relating to Christ's bodily and spiritual beauties from the *Song of Solomon,* 5:10-6:1. The titles usually specify the dominating similitude . . . Particularly in Meditations II.134-144, and 147-153, Taylor explicates those metaphors from *Canticles* 6:4-10 and 6:13-7:6, which 'Speake out the Spouses spirituall Beauty Cleare' (II.151.50). The Spouse whose 'hair is like a flock of Goats that graze on mount Gilliad' (II.137) whose 'Navill is a round Goblet' and 'belly is a heap of Wheate set about with Lillies' (II.149), and whose 'two breasts are like two young Roes that are twins' (II.150), is 'beautiful as Tirzah . . . Comely as Jerusalem' (II.134). Taylor's recognition of the figurative nature of *Canticles* confirms his fundamental agreement with an orthodox Puritan approach to the Song" (p. 14).

7. Barbara Lewalski, *Protestant Poetics,* p. 297.

8. Norman Grabo, *Edward Taylor* (New York: Twayne Publishers, 1961), p. 141.

9. Lewalski, *Protestant Poetics,* p. 420. "Taylor's meditations on *Canticles* texts invite consideration as a group; they comprise sixty-six poems, in all, almost one third of his production in this kind. Moreover, as the first and last few poems in Taylor's total *oeuvre* are based on *Canticles,* and the longest unified sequence (II.115-153) is on consecutive verses from *Canticles* 5:10 to 7:6, that biblical work may fairly be said to encompass and dominate Taylor's poems. The metaphors and images of *Canticles* — the spousal relationship of Bridegroom and Bride, the physical beauty of the spouses, the gardens of nuts and spices, the luxuriant feasts, the jewels, perfumes, flowers, colors, and textures — are the very substance of these poems. This pervasive imagery, together with the medieval explication of *Canticles* as an allegory of mystical experience and love-union with Christ, has led several critics to postulate a strong strain of mysticism and ecstatic religious experience in Taylor."

10. Edward Taylor, ms. sermon to accompany *Preparatory Meditations,* Second Series, 1. I am grateful to Charles Mignon of the Department of English, University of Nebraska for permission to quote from this recently discovered manuscript of Edward Taylor's sermons corresponding to the thirty-six meditations of the Second Series. See his article in *Early American Literature* (XII, 1978), where the following outline is presented in greater detail.

[1]	28 3m 1693	Col. 2.17	1-15
[2]	20 6m 1693	Collos. 1.15	15-34
[3]	15 8m 1693	Rom. 5.14	35-60
[4]	24 10m 1693	Gal. 4.24	61-76
	[21 11m 1693	second sermon of the "Treatise Concerning the Lord's Supper"]	
	[12m 1693/4	fourth sermon of the "Treatise"]	
[5]	4 1m 1693/4	Gal. 3.16	77-93
	[17 1m 1694	fifth sermon of the "Treatise"]	
	[1 2m 1694	sixth sermon of the "Treatise"]	

	[5 2m 1694	seventh sermon of the "Treatise"]	
	[12 2m 1694	eighth sermon of the "Treatise"]	
[6]	20 3m 1694	Isai. 49.3	93-108
[7]	5 5m 1694	Psa. 105	108-127
	[10m 1694	third sermon of the "Treatise"]	
[9]	[undated]	Deut. 18.15	127-164
[10]	10 12m 1694/5	Act. 7.45	164-198
[11]	19 3m 1695	Jud. 13.3.5	199-219
[12]	7 5m 1695	Ezek. 37.34	200-241
[13]	1 7m 1695	Ps. 72	241-258
[ ]	9 2m 1699	Matth. 12.39.40	[259-280] unnumbered
[14]	3 9m 1695	Collos. 2.3	283-316
[15]	12 1[1?] 1694/5	Matt. 2.23	315-333
[16]	9 1m 1695/6	Lu. 1.33	333-358
[17]	16 6m 1696	Ephe. 5.1	358-392
[18]	18 8m 1696	Heb. 13.10	392-426
[20]	7 12m 1696	Heb. 9.11	461-492
[21]	16 3m 1697	Col. 2.16.17	493-508
[22]	4 4m 1697	1 Cor. 5.7	509-533
[ ]	[undated]	Act. 2.1.4	534-540
[25]	6 1[?]m 1697	Numb. 28.4	[541-564] unnumbered
[23]	17 8m 1697	1 Joh. 2.2	565 [-590]
[24]	26 10m 1697	Collos. 2.16.17	591 [-] 613
[26]	26 4m 1698	Heb. 9.13.14	637 [-656]
[27]	4 7m 1698	Heb. 9.13.14	[656-] 689
[ ]	11 10m 1698	Collos. 2.17	689 [-708]
[29]	5 12m 1698	1 Pet. 3.21	709 [-730]

The *Christographia* sermons intervene here, dating from October 26, 1701, to October 10, 1703. In the Grabo edition, these sermons correspond to *Meditations* 42-56 and form a cohesive unit that is briefly examined at the end of this chapter. The recently discovered sermons do not conclude a sequence like *Christographia,* nor are they all concerned with figural language and typology. The sequence continues thus:

[*Christographia* sermons from 31 August 1701 to 10 October 1703]

[58]	5 10m 1703	Matth. 2.15	731 [-762]
[59]	6 12m 1703	1 Cori. 10.2	763 [-786]

[60A]	16 2m 1704	Joh. 6.51	787 [-810]
[60B]	30 5m 1704	1 Cor. 10.4	811 [-834]
[61]	17 7m 1704	John. 3.14.15	835 [-858]
[ ]	25 9[?]m 1706	Collos. 2.11.12	859 [-882]
[71]	20 8m 1706	1 Cor. 5.8	883 [-] 906

From Charles Mignon, "The Nebraska Edward Taylor Manuscript, 'Upon the Types of the Old Testament,' " *Early American Literature,* 12 (Winter 1977/78), 296-301.

11. "Edward Taylor on the Day of Judgment," in Thomas M. Davis and Virginia L. Davis, eds., *American Literature* 43 (1972), 535.

12. Edward Taylor, *Meditation* One, Second Series, in *The Poetry of Edward Taylor,* ed. Donald Stanford (New Haven: Yale University Press, 1960), p. 127.

13. Samuel Mather, *The Figures or Types of the Old Testament* (London, 1705), p. 52.

14. Thomas Taylor, *Christ Revealed* (London, 1635), p. 2.

15. See Karen Rowe, "Sacred or Prophane: Edward Taylor's *Meditations* on *Canticles,*" *Modern Philology,* 20 (1974), 123-138.

16. Kathleen Blake, "Edward Taylor's Protestant Poetic: Nontransubstantiating Metaphor," *American Literature* 42 (1971), 7.

17. See Barbara Lewalski, *Protestant Poetics,* pp. 420-426.

6. THE SHAPING OF THE FUTURE

1. For a discussion of millennial typology as an exegetical system, see G. W. H. Lampe, and K. J. Woolcombe, *Essays on Typology,* Studies in Biblical Theology Series (Naperville, Ill., n.d.); Thomas M. Davis, "The Traditions of Puritan Typology," in Sacvan Bercovitch, ed., *Typology and Early American Literature* (Amherst: University of Massachusetts Press, 1972), pp. 11-47; and Mason I. Lowance, "Samuel Mather and New England Typology," introduction for Samuel Mather, *The Figures or Types of the Old Testament* (London, 1705; New York: Johnson Reprint Corporation, 1969), pp. v-xxvi. See also John Seelye, *Prophetic Waters* (New York: Oxford University Press, 1977).

2. See *Hastings Encyclopedia of Religion and Ethics* (New York, 1926), III, 383-391.

3. The tradition of exegesis in which the authority of Scripture governs the movement of typology from premillennial historical prophecy to static metaphor would include John Cotton, Thomas Shepard, Samuel, Increase, and Cotton Mather (though Cotton less than his predecessors), Thomas Bray, and the nineteenth-century adventist leader named William Miller. See also Robert E. Shalhope, "Toward a Republican Synthesis: The Emergence of an Understanding of Republicanism in American Historiography," *William and Mary Quarterly* (January 1972), and Sacvan Bercovitch, *The Puritan Origins of the American Self* (New Haven: Yale University Press, 1976).

4. *The New Schaff-Herzog Religious Encyclopedia* (New York, 1947), p. 374.

5. Among modern studies occupied with the themes of wilderness and pastoral, usually without reference to scriptural foundations, we may include Perry Miller, *Errand into the Wilderness* (Cambridge: Harvard University Press, 1956); R. W. B. Lewis, *The American Adam: Innocence and Tradition in the Nineteenth*

Century (Chicago: University of Chicago Press, 1955); Henry Nash Smith, *The Virgin Land: The American West as Symbol and Myth* (Cambridge: Harvard University Press, 1950); and John Seelye, *Prophetic Waters* (New York: Oxford University Press, 1976).

6. Samuel Sherwood, *The Church's Flight into the Wilderness* (New York, 1776), pp. 22-46.

7. In 1794, David Austin brought together under one cover several millennial documents that argued the perfection of society as a sign of the coming millennium. He included Jonathan Edwards' *The Millennium, or, The Thousand Years of Prosperity, promised to the Church of God in the Old Testament and in the New, shortly to commence and to be Carried to Perfection under the Auspices of Him, who, in the Vision, was Presented to St. John;* and Joseph Bellamy, *Prophecy of the Millennium,* which had originally been published in Boston in 1758. See Austin, *The Millennium* (Elizabethtown, N.J., 1794).

8. Hillel Schwartz, "The End of the Beginning: Millenarian Studies, 1969-1975," in *Religious Studies Review,* 2.3 (July 1976), 5. This essay is an excellent review of recent millenarian scholarship and complements the survey of "Millenarian Scholarship in America" prepared by David E. Smith (*American Quarterly,* Fall 1965, pp. 534-549). See also Nathan Hatch, *The Sacred Course of Liberty: Republican Thought and the Millennium in Revolutionary New England* (New Haven: Yale University Press, 1977).

9. See "Johann Heinrich Alsted and English Millennialism," in Robert G. Clouse, *Harvard Theological Review,* 62 (1969), 189-207.

10. Thomas Brightman, *A Most Comfortable Exposition of the Last and Most Difficult Part of the Prophecie of Daniel* (London, 1635), p. 94.

11. Thomas Brightman, *A Revelation of the Revelation* (Amsterdam, 1615), as quoted by Peter Toon, *Puritans, the Millennium, and the Future of Israel: Puritan Eschatology from 1600-1660* (Cambridge: James Clarke, 1970).

12. Thomas Parker, *The Visions and Prophecies of Daniel, Expounded: Wherein the Mistakes of Former Interpreters are Modestly Discovered, and the True Meaning of the Text Made Plain . . .* (London, 1646), p. 46.

13. Joseph Mede, *Clavis Apocalyptica,* trans. as *The Key to Revelation* (1650), I, 1.

14. For a full discussion of Mede's contributions to millennial thought, see Robert G. Clouse, "Johann Heinrich Alsted and English Millennialism," *Harvard Theological Review,* 62 (1969), 189-207; Joseph Hall, *The Works of Joseph Hall,* 12 vols. (Oxford: D. A. Talboys, 1838), VIII, 507-560; R. G. Clouse, "The Rebirth of Millenarianism," in Peter Toon, ed., *Puritans, the Millennium, and the Future of Israel,* pp. 42-66.

15. Joseph Mede, *Treatise on Psalm 50.14,* in *The Works of the Pious and Profoundly Learned Joseph Mede* (London, 1677), LI, 285.

16. Ibid.

17. Stephen Marshall, *God's Masterpiece, a Sermon Tending to Manifest God's glorious appearing in the Building up of Zion* (London, 1645), pp. 6-7.

18. Ibid., p. 7.

19. See Sacvan Bercovitch, "Typology in Puritan New England: The Williams-Cotton Controversy Reassessed," *American Quarterly,* 19 (1967),

166-191; Richard Reinitz, "The Separatist Background of Roger Williams' Argument for Religious Toleration," in Bercovitch, ed., *Typology and Early American Literature*, pp. 107-139; and Jesper Rosenmeier, "The Teacher and the Witness: John Cotton and Roger Williams," *William and Mary Quarterly*, 3rd series, 25 (1968), 403-431; and "New England's Perfection: The Image of Adam and the Image of Christ in the Antinomian Crisis, 1634-1638," *William and Mary Quarterly*, 3rd series, 27 (1970), 435-459.

20. John Cotton, *Some Treasure Fetched Out of Rubbish* (London, 1660), p. 16. For discussions of typology among the first-generation writers see Jesper Rosenmeier, "With My Owne Eyes: William Bradford's *Of Plimouth Plantation*," and Richard Reinitz, "The Separatist Background of Roger Williams' Argument for Religious Toleration," both in Bercovitch, ed., *Typology and Early American Literature.* See also essays relating to the Cotton-Williams controversy: Sacvan Bercovitch, "Typology in Puritan New England: The Williams-Cotton Controversy Reassessed," *American Quarterly* 19 (1967), 166-191; Jesper Rosenmeier, "The Image of Christ: The Typology of John Cotton," Ph.D. diss., Harvard University, 1965, and "The Teacher and the Witness: John Cotton and Roger Williams," *William and Mary Quarterly*, 3rd series, 25 (1968), 403-431; and "New England's Perfection: The Image of Adam and the Image of Christ in the Antinomian Crisis, 1634-1638," *William and Mary Quarterly*, 3rd series, 27 (1970), 435-459; and Bercovitch, *The Puritan Origins of the American Self* (New Haven: Yale University Press, 1976), ch. 5, "The Myth of America."

21. John Cotton, *The Bloudy Tenent Washed and Made White With the Bloude of the Lamb* (London, 1647), pp. 54-55.

22. Ibid., p. 68.

23. Perry Miller, *Roger Williams* (Indianapolis: Bobbs-Merrill, 1953), p. 37. Jesper Rosenmeier said, "In the sermons preached in New England after 1630 there is a growing shift of emphasis, evident especially after 1638, from Christ's *redeeming* the world to His having *already redeemed* it. Satisfied that the Church was the model for the millennium, the Puritans, while still anticipating Christ's return, no longer felt the intense need to believe that the history of redemption was a dynamic process. Between the time of their establishing the Congregational model and Christ's descent to His Zion, no further fulfillment of the promises was foreseen; the major remaining task was to exhort the saints, about to be translated into eternal blessedness, to be the very images of eternal love. As a consequence of this shift of emphasis toward the 'perpetuall,' the Old Testament types became spiritualized, but even more significant was the resort to nature as the primary source of spiritual edification. If Christ's incarnation was most important for its spiritual, eternal virtues, where could they be found more clearly revealed than in the Logos, God's eternal law of nature? And if nature contained all the emblems and lessons necessary for spiritual sustenance, was there any need for a man, in his own life, to imitate the *history* of Christ's crucifixion and resurrection?" Rosenmeier, "The Teacher and the Witness," p. 424.

24. John Cotton, *The Churches Resurrection* (London, 1642), pp. 7-8.

25. Larzer Ziff, *John Cotton on the Churches of New England* (Cambridge: Harvard University Press, 1968), p. 27.

26. John Cotton, *The Keys of the Kingdom of Heaven*, in Ziff, ed., *John Cotton*

on the Churches of New England, p. 89.

27. Perry Miller, *The New England Mind: From Colony to Province* (Cambridge, Mass.: Harvard University Press, 1967), pp. 185-188.

28. Sacvan Bercovitch, "Images of Myself: Cotton Mather in His Writings 1683-1700," in Everett Emerson, ed., *Major Writers of Early American Literature* (Madison: University of Wisconsin Press, 1972), pp. 93-151, and "From Horologicals to Chronometricals: The Rhetoric of the Jeremiad," *Literary Monographs,* 3 (Madison: University of Wisconsin Press, 1970).

29. Emory Elliott, *Power and the Pulpit in Puritan New England* (Princeton: Princeton University Press, 1975), p. 167.

30. Increase Mather, *Meditations on the Glory of Our Lord Jesus Christ* (Boston, 1705), and *The Mystery of Israel's Salvation* (Boston, 1669).

31. Increase Mather, *The Mystery of Israel's Salvation,* p. ix. Elliott shows how Mather, when not treating the millennium but when developing frightening images of the judgment, relied less on typology and used Scripture for metaphorical examples: "Although [Increase Mather] still went to the Old Testament for types of the situation in New England, he no longer pressed an obvious relationship between these types and the second generation. In *Returning to God,* he presented these figures only as scriptural examples, as 'lessons', not prophecies for New England. He said that calamities that fell upon the Hebrews need not fall upon the colonists, if they would show their willingness to return to God." (Elliott, *Power and the Pulpit,* p. 127).

32. Cotton Mather, *Wonders of the Invisible World* (Boston, 1692), as quoted by Bercovitch, "Images of Myself," in *Major Writers of Early American Literature,* p. 109.

33. Thomas Hooker, *The Application of Redemption,* pp. 5-7.

34. Elliott, p. 186. Another obvious source of this chiliastic emphasis in the late seventeenth and early eighteenth centuries was Samuel Sewall's *Phaenomena quaedam Apocalyptica . . . or, Some Few Lines Towards a Description of the New Heaven, as it Makes to Those who Stand Upon the New Earth* (Boston, 1697). In his opening argument, Sewall declares: "The New Jerusalem will not straiten, and enfeeble; but wonderfully dilate, and invigorate Christianity in the several Quarters of the World, in Asia, in Africa, in Europe, and in America." The geographical argument was a prominent proof of America's destiny as the site for the earthly kingdom.

35. Thomas Shepard, *Theses Sabbaticae,* ed. Thomas Albro, 2 vols. (Hartford, 1850), I, 163-164.

36. Shepard, I, 169-170.

37. The obligations of the Massachusetts Bay theocracy were then explained wholly in moral terms: "Now this law, thus revived and reprinted, is the decalogue, because most natural and suitable to human nature, when it was made most perfect; therefore, it is universal and perpetual; the substance also of this law being love to God and man, holiness towards God, and righteousness toward man . . . Hence also this law must needs be moral, universal, and perpetual . . . the things commanded in this law are therefore commanded because they are good, and are therefore moral, unless any shall think that it is not good in itself to love God or man, to be holy or righteous" (Shepard, *Theses,* I,

151-153). See Samuel Mather, *The Figures or Types of the Old Testament* (London, 1705), pp. 444-445.

38. "In 1665 he wrote his first book about the millennium (*The Mystery of Israel's Salvation*). The occasion that impelled him to the topic was the excitement in 1665 caused by Sabbatai Sevi, that strange Levantine Jew who came out of Gaza proclaiming himself the Messiah. For a brief moment, it seemed to Jews around the world that the Messiah had come. The news—it reached Boston from London in the early winter of 1666—plunged Mather into an intense study of the role of the Jews in the working out of Christian history, particularly their conversion and return to their homeland as a harbinger of the thousand-year reign of the saints and the angels on earth." William L. Joyce and Michael G. Hall, "Three Manuscripts of Increase Mather," *Proceedings of the American Antiquarian Society*, vol. 86, pt. 1 (April 1976), pp. 120-121.

39. Robert Middlekauff, *The Mathers: Three Generations of Puritan Intellectuals, 1596-1728* (New York: Oxford University Press, 1971), p. 181. It is not central to the thesis of this chapter to develop in detail the numerological scheme employed by the Mathers for predicting the date of the millennium's beginning. However, both father and son relied heavily on William Whiston's *Essay on Revelation,* first published in 1706. In *A Sermon Shewing that the Present Dispensations of Providence Declare that Wonderful Revolutions in the World are Near at Hand* (Edinburgh, 1710), Increase Mather argues that the year 1716 will see the commencement of millennial peace: "So that in the Year 456, there were Ten distinct Kingdoms in the *Roman* Empire; consequently from that Year we are to date the Commencement of Antichrist's Reign: Which is to continue from first to last but 1260 Years, which added to 456, brings us to the year 1716" (p. 23). Whiston's chronology also appears in Cotton Mather's commentary on Revelation in the manuscript "Biblia Americana." Whiston's view was that the primitive church had remained in a state of relative purity until the year 456, when Antichrist (in the form of the Roman Empire, which was immediately followed by the Roman church) rivaled Christianity throughout the Western world. When 1260 years are added to this date, the result is 1716. The 1260 years are provided in Scripture as the time of Antichrist's reign, so all prophetic signs pointed to this time for the beginning of the end.

40. See Joyce and Hall, "Three Manuscripts of Increase Mather," pp. 113-123. This manuscript is in the hand of Cotton Mather, who often was the amanuensis for his father. In "The Morning Star" (see pp. 64-84 in Mather, *The Excellency of a Publick Spirit* [Boston, 1702]), Mather notes the exegetical difficulty confronting reformed commentators who examined Revelation: "There are many dark and difficult places in the *Scripture,* that formerly could not be understood, which of late have been opened with great clearness. And especially in this Book of *Revelations.* The first Reformers did very few of them search into it; and these few that did saw but a little. *Calvin,* though I believe he was the greatest interpreter that ever wrote on the Bible, yet he would not muddle with the Book of Revelations." Increase Mather was less reticent, and he manages well a thorny exegetical problem in both the *Mystery of Israel's Salvation* and the *Dissertation.* Most exegetes stumbled over the problem of two resurrections but only one judgment day in Revelation. This problem lent credence to those who said

the first resurrection was either at the crucifixion when the graves opened, or whenever grace came to the individual. Then the second resurrection was the general resurrection at the judgment day. Mather solves this problem by making the judgment day 1000 years long (thus tying into the tradition of sabbatism). The elect are resurrected in the morning; the damned rise in the afternoon and are judged by both Christ and the saints. This is significant because it avoids a static millennium; time, an essential adjunct of human experience, lasts through the millennium only ending with glorification in the third heaven. I am indebted to David Watters for this suggestion, and for a close reading of the manuscript of this chapter.

41. Miller, *The New England Mind,* p. 188.

42. Joyce and Hall, "Three Manuscripts," pp. 122-123.

43. Bercovitch, *The Puritan Origins of the American Self,* p. 3.

44. Middlekauff, *The Mathers,* p. 211.

45. Ibid., p. 105.

46. See Middlekauff, pp. 107-108. "In Increase's hand, typology became more than a technique for penetrating the puzzle of Scripture: it became a method for understanding the history of his own time . . . Intended to solve so much, typology created an ambiguity that always resisted Mather's best efforts at resolution. Good typologist that he was, Increase insisted that two Israels were referred to in Scripture, and by an extension of thought easy to make, he was led almost unknowingly to think of two New Englands. By two Israels, Mather meant first historical Israel, or as he sometimes called it, "carnal" or "natural" Israel. This was the Israel of Jacob, national Israel, the covenanted people whose literal history was told in the Old Testament. But there was another Israel as well. This was spiritual Israel. Like most Puritan divines, Increase believed that the term sometimes served as a kind of shorthand for those chosen for salvation by God. The Scriptures worked back and forth between these two meanings and so, naturally, did he. In the same manner, he sometimes thought of New England as the entire people in covenant with God, and as that small body of saints who had been chosen for salvation." See also my *Increase Mather* (New York: Twayne Publishers, 1975), ch. 2.

47. Bercovitch, *The Puritan Origins of the American Self,* p. 171.

48. "Traditionally, in both its pagan and its Christian contexts, the *translatio studii* stems from the cyclical-providential view of history; it offers an explanation for mankind's 'sad Vicissitude,' the 'fatal Circle' that circumscribes the course of empire. Religion stands ready to pass to the American strand, wrote George Herbert, but there, too, sin and darkness will dog her progress." Bercovitch, p. 146.

49. See also Pierre Jurieu, *The Accomplishment of the Scripture Prophecies, or, the Approaching Deliverance of the Church* (London, 1687). Jurieu was the first to lay out in great detail these historical, scientific, and scriptural proofs of an American location of the millennium. Jurieu was well known both in England and America because of his leadership of the French Protestants during the persecution and uprising of the Camisards. He also had the good fortune to prophesy the date of the Glorious Revolution in England, almost to the day.

50. Cotton Mather, *Perswasions from the Terror of the Lord* (Boston, 1711), p. 5.

51. For a comparison of the two Mather views, juxtapose *India Christiana* (Cotton Mather) and Increase Mather, *The Mystery of Israel's Salvation,* e.g., p. 150: "Furthermore, it is evident, that there is a peculiar excellency in these truths, because the right knowledge of them maketh one blessed," or pp. 153-154, "The truth is, that whilst a man is dwelling upon these meditations, he is as it were in heaven upon earth, he hath fellowship with the Angels in heaven . . . When men of God in former times have had their minds taken up with divine Visions, Angels of God have been with them; verily so it is with the servants of God at this day, though the Ministry of the holy Angels be more secret, spiritual and invisible, than sometimes formerly." Mather argues, pp. 154-155, that those who have no grace in their hearts cannot find God's truth when meditating on those texts that describe the conversion of the Jews. He then notes, "But as for those whose understandings God hath opened to *conceive* and *receive* these truths they see a glory in them above the world, that eye hath not seen, nor tongue can express" (p. 155). He then goes right into the signs of the times, for it is the literal event through which the regenerate sees God's work, not the metaphorical event in the language of the Bible as Cotton Mather would have it.

52. Bercovitch, *The Puritan Origins of the American Self,* p. 113. "The image required confirmation through what we would now call symbolic interpretation. The New England colonist not only had a private vision to convey, he had to convey it in metaphors that overturned the conventions from which those metaphors arose. He had to prove the Old World a *Second* Babylon; otherwise, his readers might consider it (along with America) to be part of the universal spiritual Babylon. He had to *convince* them of the supernatural quality of the Atlantic. How else could they surmise the baptismal efficacy of the ocean-crossing? Most important, he had to demonstrate the eschatological import of the New World, to create his distinctive desert-garden *allegoria* from the details of his landscape. And the demonstration could only persuade symbolically — not through the sure atemporal significances of allegory . . . but through a highly personal inference drawn from secular experience."

53. "Cotton Mather never gave up the belief that his America had much to teach Europe, but he did not envisage the new society serving as a blueprint for the old. Its corruption, which drew relentless afflictions from the Lord, rendered any such suggestion simple arrogance. As for New England standing as a type for the New Jerusalem, for anyone who took seriously the catalogue of sins presented in the jeremiads, that notion was better left unexamined . . . If Cotton made his father's hopes his own, he did so in his own way, imparting his own flavor to the conventional versions of the Puritan mission to America." Middlekauff, *The Mathers,* pp. 210-211.

7. Cotton Mather's *Magnalia Christi Americana,*
"Biblia Americana," and the Metaphors of Biblical History

1. Cotton Mather, *Magnalia Christi Americana* (Hartford, 1853), I, 25.
2. Cotton Mather, *A Pillar of Gratitude* (Boston, 1700), p. 3.
3. Ibid., p. 5.
4. Cotton Mather, *Work Upon the Ark* (Boston, 1689), pp. 1-2.
5. Ibid., p. 2.

6. Mather, *Magnalia Christi Americana,* 2 vols. (Hartford, 1820), I, 104.

7. Ibid., 109-110.

8. Poem by Benjamin Woodbridge, from "Life of John Cotton," in *Magnalia,* I, 259. See also Sacvan Bercovitch, "New England Epic: Cotton Mather's *Magnalia Christi Americana,*" *ELH,* 33 (1966), 337-351.

9. *Magnalia,* I, 48.

10. "Introduction," Mather, *Parentator, Memoirs of Remarkables in the Life and the Death of the Ever-Memorable Dr. Increase Mather* (Boston, 1724), p. ii.

11. *Magnalia,* I, 152.

12. Ibid., II, 426.

13. Ibid., 228.

14. Ibid., 163-164.

15. Ibid., I, 23, 32. The second part of this quotation describes Mather's technique in the "Biblia Americana," which is discussed in the General Introduction to the *Magnalia* as a way of making "all learning . . . glorious and subservient unto the *illustration* of the *sacred Scripture.*"

16. Thomas J. Holmes, *Cotton Mather: A Bibliography of His Works,* 3 vols. (Cambridge, Mass.: Harvard University Press, 1940), II, 734. As the *Magnalia* advertisement for the "Biblia Americana" makes clear, Mather had been working for a number of years to prepare the Bible commentary for publication.

17. *A New Offer to the Lovers of Religion and Learning* (n.p., n.d. [Boston, 1714?]), p. 12. From Holmes, III, 731.

18. "Biblia Americana," ms. (6 vols., in Massachusetts Historical Society, n.d.), II, n.p. I should like to thank Stephen T. Riley, former director of the Massachusetts Historical Society of Boston, for his kind permission to publish excerpts from Cotton Mather's manuscript of the "Biblia Americana," which is housed in the Historical Society.

19. "Biblia," II, n.p.

20. "The Harmony of the Gospels," in "Biblia," III, n.p.

21. "Biblia," II, n.p.; see Chapter 6 of this study.

22. Ibid., I, n.p., hereafter, citations to "Biblia Americana" will appear parenthetically in the text.

23. "Commentary on Genesis," in "Biblia," I, n.p.

24. Ibid. See also Samuel Mather, *Figures or Types of the Old Testament* (London, 1705), ed. Mason I. Lowance, Jr. (New York: Johnson Reprint Corporation, 1969), p. 84.

25. *Ark,* p. 4.

26. "Commentary Upon Genesis 8," in "Biblia," I, n.p.

27. Ibid.

8. Jonathan Edwards and the Great Awakening

1. Alan Heimert, *Religion and the American Mind from the Great Awakening to the Revolution* (Cambridge: Harvard University Press, 1968), pp. 62-63. Heimert notes that "Edwards' achievement in placing the millennium on this side of the apocalypse was to provide Calvinism with a formula in which the good society would and could be attained solely through natural causes. But the aspect of

creation involved in the Work of Redemption was, for Edwards, the super-natural realm, — that portion of the universe which was above and beyond nature, consisting in man's union and communion with God, or divine com-munications and influences of God's spirit. The earthly kingdom of the Calvinist Messiah was not of the natural, material world, but within men. It consisted not in things external, but in happiness and the dominion of virtue in the minds and hearts of mankind. The Work of Redemption was one with the regeneration of humanity; it depended on no awful display of Divine power, no shattering of the physical creation, but on the gradual restoration of the influences of the Holy Spirit which had been withdrawn at the Fall." Obviously, the restoration of typology was one of these "influences."

2. Sacvan Bercovitch, *The Puritan Origins of the American Self* (New Haven: Yale University Press, 1975).

3. See Emory Elliott, *Power and the Pulpit in Puritan New England* (Princeton: Princeton University Press, 1974); Sacvan Bercovitch, *From Horologicals to Chronometricals* (Madison: University of Wisconsin Press, 1970); Robert Pope, *The Half-Way Covenant* (Princeton: Princeton University Press, 1968), and Sac-van Bercovitch, *The American Jeremiad* (Madison: University of Wisconsin Press, 1978).

4. Bercovitch, *Horologicals to Chronometricals*, p. 33. This excellent study has been revised and expanded, see Bercovitch, *The American Jeremiad*.

5. Sydney E. Ahlstrom, *A Religious History of the American People* (New Haven: Yale University Press, 1972), p. 281.

6. Jesper Rosenmeier, ms., n.p., n.d.

7. Perry Miller, "From Edwards to Emerson," *The New England Quarterly*, 13 (December 1940), 589-617.

8. John Seelye, *Prophetic Waters: The River in Early American Life and Literature*, (New York: Oxford University Press, 1977), p. xix.

9. See Sacvan Bercovitch, "The Image of America: from Hermeneutics to Symbolism," *Bucknell Review*, 20 (Fall 1972).

10. David Austin, *The Millennium* (Elizabethtown, N.J., 1794).

11. Isaac Backus, *The Testimony of the Two Witnesses, Explained and Improved* (Providence, 1786), pp. 42-43. Other writers concerned about an identification of the American Revolution with the fulfillment of Scripture promises would in-clude: Thomas Bray, *A Dissertation on the Sixth Vial* (Hartford, 1780); Timothy Dwight, *A Sermon Preached at Stamford, Connecticut, Upon the General Thanksgiving, December 18, 1777* (Hartford, 1778); and Dwight, *Discourses on Some Events of the Last Century* (New Haven, 1801); Ezra Stiles, *The United States Elevated to Glory and Honor* (New Haven, 1783); Joel Barlow, *The Vision of Columbus* (Hartford, 1787); Jeremy Belknap, *A Discourse on the Discovery of America* (Boston, 1792); Samuel Hopkins, *A Treatise on the Millennium* (Boston, 1793); Elhanan Winchester, *Three Woe Trumpets* (London, 1793, and Boston, 1794), and Abraham Cummings, *A Dissertation on the Introduction and Glory of the Millennium to which is Prefixed, A Discourse on the Two Witnesses* (Boston, 1797).

12. Samuel Sherwood, *The Church's Flight into the Wilderness* (New York, 1776), p. 19.

13. Modern treatments of millennialism would include B. S. Capp, *The Fifth Monarchy Men: A Study in Seventeenth-Century Millennarianism* (London: Faber

& Faber, 1972); Ernest Sandeen, *The Roots of Fundamentalism: British and American Millenarianism, 1800-1930* (Chicago: University of Chicago Press, 1970); and Ernest Tuveson, *Millennialism and Utopia* and *Redeemer Nation* (Chicago: University of Chicago Press, 1971). Peter Toon's *Puritans, The Millennium, and the Future of Israel: Puritan Eschatology 1600 to 1660* (Cambridge, Eng.: James Clarke, 1970) is another useful volume. The best article is James Davidson's "Searching for the Millennium: Problems for the 1790's and 1970's," *New England Quarterly,* 5 (1972). See also James W. Davidson, *The Logic of Millennial Thought: Eighteenth-Century New England* (New Haven: Yale University Press, 1977), and Nathan Hatch, *The Sacred Course of Liberty: Republican Thought and the Millennium in Revolutionary New England* (New Haven: Yale University Press, 1977).

14. See Marie Ahearn, ms. on Massachusetts Artillery sermon tradition, n. 48. For strains of millenarianism see the sermons of 1674, 1678, 1691, 1705, 1710, 1728, 1747, 1758, 1772. Cotton Mather's 1691 sermon is a pastoral idyll of the peace and plenty that will prevail in the latter days, which are imminent. This sermon, however, ought to be yoked with his sermons to the Charlestown Artillery, "Military Duties," 1687, and "Souldiers Counselled," 1689, addressed to an expedition against the Indians. For two other sermons that develop the peace that will eventually reign in a postmillennial manner, see Thomas Barnard's 1758 sermon. An interesting presentation of the postmillennial view accommodated to the occasion of an Artillery sermon, Barnard paints a futuristic picture of peace and plenty; in his picture, a pious people will have a soldiery infused with the spirit of religion. "We are to reflect on the present state of mankind respecting war, as part of a plan or connected series of Administrations of God, tending gradually to a perfection worthy of its author" (p. 17). In addition, he goes on to assure his auditors that there is a "Tendency in Religion to Success in Wars" (p. 19). See also Nathaniel Robbins, 1772, pp. 16-17. Robbins avows that Jerusalem, that is, God's People, is tending toward peace, and he declares that peace can be understood as temporary prosperity in general. But if Jerusalem is threatened, then even peaceful men will go to war, and he addressed the Artillery in these words.

15. For correlative typology, see Barbara Kiefer Lewalski, *Donne's Anniversaries and the Poetry of Praise* (Princeton: Princeton University Press, 1973), pp. 160-163; "Samson Agonistes and the Tragedy of the Apocalypse," *PMLA,* 85 (1970), 1050-61; "Typology and Poetry: A Consideration of Herbert, Vaughan, and Marvell," in *Illustrious Evidence,* ed. Earl Miner (Berkeley: University of California Press, 1975), pp. 41-69. Also, Steven N. Swicker, *Dryden's Political Poetry: The Typology of King and Nation* (Providence: Brown University Press, 1972), esp. ch. 1, "Metaphorical History"; Sacvan Bercovitch, *The Puritan Origins of the American Self,* pp. 35-39. See also Thomas Taylor, *Moses and Aaron, or the Types and Shadows of our Saviour in the Old Testament Opened and Explained* (London: John Williams, 1653); Benjamin Keach, *Tropologia: A Key to Open Scripture Metaphors . . . Together with Types of the Old Testament* (London, 1681).

16. Philip Freneau and Hugh Henry Brackenridge, *The Rising Glory of America,* in *Poems Written and Published during the American Revolutionary War,* by Philip Freneau (Philadelphia, 1809), I, 77-78.

17. Emory Elliott, Jr., "Generations in Crisis: The Imaginative Power of

Puritan Writing, 1660-1700," dissertation, University of Illinois, 1972 Dissertation Abstracts, 33, p. 5675-A, p. 106, *Power and the Pulpit*, p. 74; Robert Scholes, *Structuralism in Literature* (New Haven: Yale University Press, 1973), esp. ch. 1, "Structuralism as a Method," and ch. 4, "The Mythographers: Propp and Levi-Strauss."

18. Jonathan Edwards, letter to William McCullock, March 1743, quoted by Douglas Ellwood, *The Philosophical Theology of Jonathan Edwards* (New York: Columbia University Press, 1960), p. 78.

19. Joseph Bellamy, *Sermons on Several Subjects: The Millennium* (Boston, 1758), pp. 48-49.

20. Joseph Bellamy was by no means the only eighteenth-century millennial commentator to give prominence to the role of typology. Aaron Burr, president of Princeton, argued that the regenerate only could understand the types, and that the elect, eventually, "shall clearly see how the *Glorious Grace of the Gospel* was revealed under all the *Types and Shadows of the Law.* Meanwhile, however, when God converses with his people, he retains a veil of mystery, 'for the internal Glories of his Ministration which were delivered in *Types and Figures of Good Things to Come* were rendered obscure and dark,' by the carnal perceptions of fallen men, 'by the *blindness and Prejudices of their Carnal Hearts.*' " Aaron Burr, *A Sermon Preached before the Synod of New York* (New York, 1756), pp. 8-11. See also George Duffield, *A Sermon, Preached in the Third Presbyterian Church in the City of Philadelphia,* Thursday, December 11, 1783 (Philadelphia, 1784); Isaac Backus, *The Testimony of the Two Witnesses, Explained and Improved* (Providence, 1786), pp. 42-43; and Samuel Hopkins, *A Treatise on the Millennium* (Boston, 1793).

21. Alan Heimert, *Religion and the American Mind*, p. 114.

22. Abraham Cummings, *A Dissertation on the Introduction and Glory of the Millennium* (Boston, 1797), p. 31.

23. Thomas Frink, *A King Reigning in Righteousness* (Boston, 1758), p. 6. See A. W. Plumstead, *The Wall and the Garden: Massachusetts Election Sermons from 1670 to 1775* (Minneapolis: University of Minnesota Press, 1968), introduction. Plumstead has not included Frink's sermon in this collection because he does not consider it to be as significant as others artistically, but he does view its importance as a philosophical statement of typology's importance to New England.

24. Though the Millerites were a radical group of advent enthusiasts during the 1830s and 1840s, the role given to typology in proving Miller's argument was in fact more significant than that accorded Scripture prophecy. The prophecies were treated in *Evidence from Scripture History of the Second Coming of Christ, about the Year 1843, exhibited in a Course of Lectures* (Troy, N.Y., 1836), but Miller's own numerological proof was deduced from his commitment to the typology of the sabbath in *A Lecture on the Typical Sabbaths and Great Jubilee* (Boston: Joshua Himes, 1842).

25. A treatment of Edwards' epistemology and reading of the book of nature is covered in Chapter 10 of this study. For some discussion, see Roland Delattre, *Beauty and Sensibility in the Thought of Jonathan Edwards: An Essay in Aesthetics and Theological Ethics* (New Haven: Yale University Press, 1968); and my own essay, "The *Images or Shadows of Divine Things* in the Thought of Jonathan Edwards," in Bercovitch, ed., *Typology and Early American Literature*, pp. 209-249.

26. Alan Heimert, *Religion and the American Mind,* p. 68.

27. Jonathan Edwards, "Miscellany Number 638," as quoted by Perry Miller, *Images or Shadows of Divine Things* (New Haven: Yale University Press, 1948), pp. 52-53n.

28. I am indebted to Thomas Shafer of the McCormick Theological Seminary, Chicago, for allowing me to use his personal transcriptions of these miscellaneous entries, which will appear in his edition of *Edwards' Miscellaneous Notebooks* for the Yale collection of the *Works of Jonathan Edwards.*

29. This observation Edwards made in his manuscript "Notebook on the Types," a small gathering of observations about typology that contains some of his most succinct statements of theory. It is largely unknown but is being edited for the Yale Edwards collection by Wallace Anderson of the Ohio State University and should be published soon as part of the volume on Edwards' prophetic miscellanies, called *The Typological Writings,* eds., Wallace Anderson, Mason I. Lowance, Jr., and David Watters (New Haven: Yale University Press) [forthcoming]. The manuscript of "Types" is part of the Andover collection, which has never been published.

30. "Types," ms., p. 4.

31. Ibid., p. 8.

32. Ibid., p. 10.

33. Jonathan Edwards, "Paradise in America," ed. Michael McGiffert, *Puritanism and the American Experience* (Reading, Mass.: Addison-Wesley, 1969), pp. 160-163.

34. Jonathan Edwards, *Personal Narrative,* in *Selections from Jonathan Edwards,* ed. Clarence H. Faust and Thomas H. Johnson (New York: Hill and Wang, 1962), p. 68.

35. Jonathan Edwards, *The Works of Jonathan Edwards* (Worcester, Mass., 1820), I, 569-570. See also C. C. Goen, "Jonathan Edwards: A New Departure in Eschatology," *Church History,* 27 (March 1959), 32.

36. Of Edwards' work on the *Harmony,* Jesper Rosenmeier remarks: "Had Edwards lived to complete the Harmony, he would have made the most exhaustive compendium of Biblical metaphors yet undertaken in America. His purpose, however, went far beyond working out the precise meanings and correspondences between Old Testament prefigurations and their New Testament fulfillments. Rather, Edwards was interested in the harmony and beauty of the relationships, for he was convinced that it would continue to grow in the future, and that whoever understood the present divine communications might gain a view of the harmony that would be manifest in the New Jerusalem. So dynamic did Edwards consider the process of redemption to be that he perceived not only the Bible but Nature as a prophetic part of the gyre of salvation." (unpubl. mss., 1971, p. 23). See also Stephen Stein, "Providence and the Apocalypse in the Early Writings of Jonathan Edwards," *Early American Literature,* 12 (1978/9), 250-267.

37. I am indebted to Christopher Jedrey for a close comparison of Lowman's *Paraphrase* and Edwards' *Redemption,* which he prepared as a course paper in 1972. Although Lowman's study is not concerned with typological figuralism, it is concerned with the interpretation of symbols and figures that appear in the book of Revelation as they apply to literal events of the future. See Moses Lowman, *A Paraphrase and Notes of the Revelation of St. John,* 2nd ed. (Lon-

don, 1745).

38. Jonathan Edwards, *A History of the Work of Redemption,* in *Works,* ed. Sereno Dwight (Hartford, 1820), III, 227.

39. Ibid., III, 233.

40. Ibid., III, 417.

41. Jonathan Edwards, Miscellany 262, as quoted by Douglas Ellwood, *The Philosophical Writings of Jonathan Edwards* (New York: Columbia University Press, 1960), p. 74.

42. Jonathan Edwards' *Miscellaneous Notebooks.* Again, I am grateful to Thomas Shafer for the use of these entries that treat typology.

43. Jonathan Edwards, Miscellanies 146 and 147, as quoted by Douglas Ellwood, *The Philosophical Theology of Jonathan Edwards* (New York: Columbia University Press, 1960), pp. 160-161.

44. Timothy Dwight, *A Dissertation on the History, Eloquence, and Poetry of the Bible* (New Haven, 1772).

45. "The rising glory myth may be seen as a blend of three components, all notions prevalent in Western culture before the 18th century. The first of these is the idea of progress, the belief in inevitable improvement which received its fullest expression in the Enlightenment faith in reason. The idea that society continually advances toward a golden age is of course ancient, prominent in the classical literature revived by the Renaissance and especially fashionable in the 18th century. In Augustan England it was closely associated with the rise of the New Science of Newton and Locke and with the commercial and technological expansion that seemed to betoken an earthly paradise for citizens of the triumphant empire. In France during the Enlightenment emphasis in the idea of progress was on the development of democracy, social equality, and individual education. Progress continued to attract believers, reaching another high point in Victorian England, which subscribed to the notion that improvement was inevitable and that each year would bring further evidence that perfection was nearer at hand.

"Allied to the idea of progress is a second component of the rising glory theme: millennialism. Prediction of Christ's thousand-year reign on earth may even be considered a theological version of the idea of progress, since both looked toward the achievement of earthly perfection; one difference is that proponents of progress hesitated to equate the achievement of perfection with the end of the world, preferring instead less precise answers to when and how mankind would know perfection had arrived than millennialists who gladly cited the date and time when the world would end. Although alike in their fundamental perception of the promise of future improvement, the idea of progress and millennialism must be considered separately as sources for the theme of the rising glory of America since millennial thought appeared mostly in Puritan writings and the idea of progress in secular ones.

"Most directly influential in the development of the rising glory theme were two classical motifs, the *translatio studii* and *translatio imperii.* These depicted, respectively, the inevitable westward movement of the arts and sciences and of empire. Expressions of these ideas abound in antique, medieval, and Renaissance literature. They were especially appealing to American colonists because they added to the idea of progress and millennialism a strong geographical orientation. Whereas no specific site for the end of the world was predicted in millennial thought, and progress was believed possible—indeed, unavoidable—everywhere, the *translatio* explained the achievement of earthly perfection in strict geographic terms: civilization moved westward, carried by muses like Science, Art, Liberty, and Commerce from Greece to Rome to Western Europe to England—and, as colonials added, necessarily onward to America. The advantage to Americans of the *translatio* motif was that it predicted concretely that civilization, folding wings across the Atlantic, would inevitably appear on American soil." From William Andrews, "The Rising Glory of America: Early Sources of a National Myth," ms. (1972).

46. Timothy Dwight, *A Discourse on Some Events of the Last Century* (New Haven, 1801), pp. 41-42. Indeed, millennial enthusiasm is muted in *The Conquest of Canaan*. William L. Hedges contends that "the kind of Puritanism represented by *The Conquest of Canaan* keeps promising an earthly reward for righteousness, a pure society, an Eden, a millennium, while insisting at the same time on man's basic incapacity for peace on earth. History, theoretically the working out of God's plan, reduces—and the poem insists on this—to a series of wars and revolutions in which the occasional triumphs of virtue are always promptly undermined by vice." "Towards a Theory of American Literature, 1765-1800," *Early American Literature,* 4, no. 1 (Spring 1969), 11.

47. Timothy Dwight, *A Sermon Preached at Stamford, in Connecticut, upon the General Thanksgiving, December 18th, 1777* (Hartford: Watson and Goodwin, 1778), p. 14.

48. Timothy Dwight, *Greenfield Hill* (New York, 1794), p. 153, l. 113.

9. JOEL BARLOW AND THE RISING GLORY OF AMERICA

1. See William Andrews, "The Rising Glory of America: Early Sources of a National Myth," Ph.D. diss., University of Pennsylvania, 1972, pp. 142-146. See also Emory Elliott, "Economics, Religion, and Rhetoric in Revolutionary America," ms., (1976) p. 9-10. "The spirit of piety which swept the colonies in the 1730s and 1740s made a deep and lasting impact upon those who were reaching adulthood in the two decades before the revolution. After years of moderation in religious education, this generation experienced a sudden resurgence of stern discipline in religious training and a return of strict authority in households. Ministers like Jonathan Edwards called for firmer control in the home to assure the lasting effects of the revivals. The high proportion of adult males converted during the Awakening indicates that families witnessed a reassertion of paternal authority over moral and spiritual life . . . Thus, while the Great Awakening revealed divisions in doctrine among the clergy, it served on an emotional level to unite vast numbers of the colonists of different regions." The emotional unity provided by the Awakening was only a foreshadowing of the political and social synthesis that would result from the psychology of rebellion generated during the 1760s and 1770s.

2. Theodore Frelinghuysen, *A Sermon Preached on Occasion of the Late Treaty Held in Albany* (New York, 1754), p. ii, as quoted by William Andrews in "The Rising Glory of America: Early Sources of a National Myth," pp. 114-115.

3. Andrews shows that during the very early years of the eighteenth century, from roughly 1710-30, just before the Great Awakening, the millennial im-

pulse was muted in the literature and sermons. This is partially correct. Increase Mather had predicted 1716 to be the date of the commencing of the millennium, but Cotton Mather had dropped the subject altogether by this time and had turned to an investigation of the natural world, which he attempted to reconcile to revelation in Scripture, an achievement which Jonathan Edwards would have to conclude. But Andrews is right to isolate the pre-Awakening decades of the eighteenth century when he asserts, "A fundamental belief in it (the millennium) can be seen in some of the jeremiads, in the emphasis on New England as a chosen place, and in the works that try to explain and predict the millennium, or interpret the ways of God in earthquakes and storms. But for about twenty years it was largely below the surface of New England writing, occasionally rising to the level of explicit expression when external events called forth the rhetoric of the jeremiad, but seldom invoked as strongly as it had been one hundred, or even fifty years earlier—and never in as open a way as it was to be voiced in the last third of the century. With occasional exceptions, the public writing of New England during the first thirty years of the eighteenth-century showed its inhabitants to be, as Neal simply put it in the conclusions of his history, 'a Dutiful and Loyal People.' " (Andrews, "The Rising Glory of America," p. 76.)

4. Emory Elliott, "The Literary Calling in the New Republic," paper delivered at Williamsburg, Virginia, December 8, 1976, pp. 3-4.

5. Sacvan Bercovitch, "How the Puritans Won the American Revolution," *The Massachusetts Review,* 17, no. 4 (Fall 1976), 604.

6. Ibid., p. 606.

7. *The American Crisis, Number II,* in *The Political Works of Thomas Paine,* (Springfield, 1826), pp. 223-224.

8. *The American Crisis, Number V,* in *The Political Works of Thomas Paine* (Springfield, 1826), pp. 290-291.

9. William L. Hedges, "Towards a Theory of American Literature, 1765-1800," *Early American Literature,* 4, no. 1 (Spring 1969), 9.

10. Nathaniel Evans, "Ode on the Prospect of Peace," 1761, in *An Exercise, Containing a Dialogue and Ode on Peace* (Philadelphia, 1763), p. 3. Cf. Andrews, pp. 140-156.

11. David Humphreys, *A Poem on the Happiness of America* (London, 1786; reprinted, Portsmouth, N.H., 1790), p. 27.

12. David Humphreys, *A Poem Addressed to the Armies of the United States of America* (New Haven, 1780), pp. 5-6. See Andrews, pp. 150-160.

13. James Davidson, "Searching for the Millennium: Problems for the 1790's and the 1970's," *New England Quarterly,* 45, no. 2 (June 1972), 260. See also Andrews' excellent chapters on Humphreys and the "Rising Glory" tradition.

14. Joel Barlow, *The Columbiad* (Philadelphia, 1807), IX, 348-349.

15. Joel Barlow, *The Prospect of Peace, A Poetical Composition Delivered in Yale-College, at the Public Examination, of the Candidates for the Degree of Bachelor of Arts, July 23, 1788* (New Haven, 1788), p. 5. Hereafter, only page references will be cited.

16. Barlow's use of the "morning star" imagery is conventional in Christian doctrine. The analogy of Christ to the morning star, which brings the light of a new day, is clearly stated by Increase Mather in his 1702 sermon, *The Morning Star: Revelations XXI,* 16, in *The Excellency of a Publick Spirit* (Boston, 1702), p. 75, where he says: "This may be a special reason why Christ here in this Book of

Revelation is represented as the *Morning Star,* because in this book he does bring glad Tidings into the World; he brings Tidings of his own Coming, as in the context before us, *Behold, I come Quickly.* In the Morning Sun if you see this star, you may conclude that the Sun will quickly arise upon the world. So Christ does in the conclusion of this Book bring Tidings of a glorious day approaching unto the Church, that the Church shall one day be Triumphant not only in Heaven to all Eternity, but here on Earth, too, when *New Jerusalem* shall come down from Heaven, when the Saints in glory shall come down from Heaven and be reunited to their Bodies, and reside here on earth, during the glorious dispensation of Judgment, then comes the New Jerusalem down from Heaven. And Christ brings to the Church glad tidings of such a day." This conventional imagery is also found in Milton's "Nativity Ode," where the birth of Christ is associated with the dawning of a new day, and where the imperfect shadows of Christ's presence that had foreshadowed his arrival are now abrogated by the flesh. Barlow utilizes such conventional tropes to illustrate, through a similar analogical process, the coming of America's commercial and millennial fulfillment.

17. Joel Barlow, *Two Letters to the Citizens of the United States, and One to General Washington* (New Haven, 1806), p. 29.

18. James Woodress, *A Yankee's Odyssey: The Life of Joel Barlow* (Philadelphia: Lippincott Publishing, 1958), p. 124.

19. Barlow, *Two Letters to the Citizens of the United States,* pp. 46-47.

20. Ibid., pp. 24-25.

21. Joel Barlow, *An Oration Delivered at Washington on July 4th, 1809* (Washington, 1809), p. 6.

22. Joel Barlow, *Prospectus of a National Institution* (Washington, D.C., 1806), p. 5. Barlow was not, of course, unique or original in his claim that education and its improvement would ultimately benefit America and establish the westward course of empire. He argued that an ideal society could be established without the assistance of grace; nevertheless he followed convention and tradition in citing America as the locus of the new learning. As early as 1733, John Hubbard wrote a poem on the subject called *The Benefactors of Yale College.* As in Barlow's writing, science is given prominence: "When first to visit western *India's* Land/Minerva gave the *Sciences* command"; the poem goes on to celebrate the founding of Yale College as the latest advance in this westward movement:

> What learned *Greeks* and polish'd *Romans* were
> Will then appear in a *New-English* Air;
> Their beauties mingled with our native fire,
> Adorn'd with what a Christ'an's thoughts inspire
> May *Cicero* unite with *Paul* divine,
> To offer incense at the *Gospel* shrine.

The obvious conflation here of classical and Christian allusions is structured around the typological, recapitulative cycle, whereby the analogy established between the classical model and the New England experience is a revolution in the spiraling historical process. Thus New England's learning regenerates the system originally appearing in the classical past.

23. Barlow, *Oration delivered at Washington on the Fourth of July, 1809.*

24. Leon Howard, *The Vision of Joel Barlow* (Los Angeles: University of California Press, 1937), p. 21.

25. Joel Barlow, *An Oration Delivered at the North Church in Hartford, July 4th, 1787* (Hartford, Conn., 1787), p. 20.

26. Ibid., p. 21.

27. Joel Barlow, *The Vision of Columbus: A Poem in Nine-Books* (Hartford: Printed by Hudson and Goodwin, for the author, 1787), p. xxi.

28. Barlow, *Vision,* 1787, I, ll.29-30.

29. Ibid., pp. 77-78.

30. Robert Richardson, "The Enlightenment View of Myth and Joel Barlow's 'Vision of Columbus,' " ms., p. 6.

31. Thomas Paine, *The Age of Reason,* reprinted in *Thomas Paine,* ed. H. H. Clark (New York, 1943), p. 241. Robert Richardson corroborated this view in his lecture at Colonial Williamsburg, December 7, 1976, "The Enlightenment View of Myth and Joel Barlow's 'Vision of Columbus,' " when he stated that "various epics and parts of epics in late eighteenth-century American literature can be related to the rising tide of interest in myth. Trumbull's *M'Fingal* counts on its audience knowing Ossian, Richard Alsop's fragmentary *Conquest of Scandinavia* depends on the new Nordic myths which the English-speaking world down to Bulfinch got from Thomas Percy's *Northern Antiquities* (1770). Timothy Dwight's *Conquest of Canaan* pursues religious and national purposes through Biblical and neo-Biblical mythology. Most interesting of all, in this respect, is Joel Barlow's 1787 *Vision of Columbus,* the first major self-conscious effort to write a national epic rooted in native American myth." I would dispute this final claim, since Cotton Mather's *Magnalia Christi Americana* develops a national myth out of the more universal "errand into the wilderness" and the traditions of biblical typology and makes a metaphorical use of the biblical figures in a way that anticipates Barlow's association of classical and Christian symbols.

32. Richardson, "The Enlightenment View of Myth," pp. 10-11.

33. Barlow, *Vision,* 1787, I, ll. 229-233.

34. Barlow, *Vision,* 1787, I, 33-34.

35. Barlow, *Vision,* 1787, I, 253-254.

36. Barlow, *Vision,* 1787, I, 252-253.

37. Woodress, *A Yankee's Odyssey: The Life of Joel Barlow,* p. 247.

38. Ibid., p. 245.

39. As quoted by Leon Howard, "Citizen Joel Barlow," ch. 9 of *The Connecticut Wits* (Chicago: University of Chicago Press, 1943), p. 323.

40. Andrews, "The Rising Glory of America," p. 189.

41. Howard, *The Connecticut Wits,* p. 313.

42. Barlow, *The Columbiad,* p. xiii.

43. "When Barlow reaches Books VI and VII, he expands his account of the American Revolution into three books. His aim is to make the heroes of the war more heroic, the action more epic, and the subject matter more detailed. These books, the most successful of the poem, have a genuine epic quality about them. The British are now sinister tyrants, and Washington strides across the continent like Milton's Michael leading the cohorts of heaven against Satan." (Woodress, *A*

Yankee's Odyssey: The Life of Joel Barlow, p. 249). The ninth Book contains some of Barlow's most meaningful and important prophetic verse, and the metaphorical associations he drew there — recasting the language of Canaan to suit a new end — have been anticipated throughout the earlier books in the modified patterns of language.

44. Barlow, *Vision,* 1787, IX, 255-256.

45. (a) Barlow, *The Columbiad,* 1807, X, 378, ll.546-556.

(b) Barlow, *The Columbiad,* 1809, II; X, 164, ll.546-556.

46. Barlow, *Vision,* 1787, p. 216.

47. Barlow, *The Vision of Columbus: A Poem in Nine Books,* 5th ed., corrected (Paris: English Press, 1793), p. 230. See John Seelye, *Prophetic Waters,* for an excellent discussion of neoclassical imagery in American writing of the Colonial and Federal periods.

48. Barlow, *The Columbiad,* 1807, IX, 318-319.

49. Barlow, *The Columbiad,* 1807, IX, 438n.

50. Ibid.

51. (a) Barlow, *Vision* (Hartford, 1787), IX, 241-244.

(b) Barlow, *Vision* (Paris, 1793), note to Book IX, p. 256n.

52. (a) Barlow, *Vision* (Hartford, 1787), IX, 241-244.

(b) Barlow, *Vision* (Paris, 1793), note to Book IX, p. 258.

53. Barlow, *Vision* (Hartford, 1787), VIII, 216-217.

54. Barlow, *Vision* (Hartford, 1787),VIII, 217.

55. Barlow, *Vision* (Paris, 1793), VIII, 231.

56. Barlow, *Vision* (Paris, 1793), VIII, 244n.

57. Barlow, *Vision,* (Paris, 1793), Note to Book IX, pp. 258-259.

58. Barlow, *The Columbiad,* 1807, Note to Book IX, pp. 438-439.

59. Howard, *The Connecticut Wits,* p. 315.

60. Barlow, *The Columbiad,* Preface, p. vii.

61. Howard, *The Connecticut Wits,* p. 317.

62. Joel Barlow, note for Preface to *The Columbiad,* as quoted by Howard, *The Connecticut Wits,* p. 320. See also John Griffin, "*The Columbiad* and *Greenfield Hill,*" in *Early American Literature,* 10 (1975/76), 235-250.

10. JONATHAN EDWARDS AND THE KNOWLEDGE OF GOD

1. Samuel Mather, *Figures or Types of the Old Testament,* 2nd ed. (London, 1705), p. 52, reprinted in *Series in American Studies* (New York: Johnson Reprint, 1969), with introduction and notes by Mason Lowance, Jr.

2. *A History of the Work of Redemption,* reprinted from the Worcester edition (New York, 1845), p. 299.

3. Ibid., pp. 299-300.

4. Ibid., p. 306.

5. Ibid., pp. 275 and 191.

6. *Jonathan Edwards: A History of the Work of Redemption* (New York: American Tract Society, 1841), pp. 85-86.

7. Edwards' "Miscellany 1069" exists in manuscript in the Beinecke Library of Yale University. It is being edited by David Watters and Mason Lowance as part of the Miscellaneous Notebooks of Jonathan Edwards for the Yale Edition of Edwards' Collected Works. An adequate edition of this particular

entry may be found under the title, "Types of the Messiah," in Vol. IX (Supplement) of the London edition of Edwards' *Works* (London: Hamilton, Adams, 1847).

8. I am indebted to Thomas A. Shafer of the McCormick Theological Seminary, Chicago, for indicating these entries, and for sharing his typescript of them with me.

9. Jonathan Edwards, "Types of the Messiah," or Miscellany 1069, *The Works of President Edwards* (Edinburgh: Ogle, Oliver and Boyd, 1847), IX, 401.

10. Ibid., p. 404.

11. Ibid., p. 408.

12. Ibid., p. 419.

13. Ibid., p. 494.

14. Perry Miller, Introduction to Jonathan Edwards, *Images or Shadows of Divine Things,* (New Haven: Yale University Press, 1948), p. 9.

15. Cotton Mather, *Agricola, or the Religious Husbandman* (Boston, 1726).

16. Miller, Introduction to *Images or Shadows*. All subsequent references to this document will be cited parenthetically in the text.

17. "Miscellany No. 362," housed in Beinecke Library, Yale University. This manuscript of Edwards' Miscellanies is being edited as part of the Yale edition of Edwards' *Works* by Thomas Shafer.

18. Edwards, *Images or Shadows of Divine Things,* p. 44. All subsequent references to this document will be cited in the narrative.

19. Jonathan Edwards, "Miscellany No. 638," quoted by Miller, *Images or Shadows,* pp. 52-53n.

20. *Images or Shadows,* pp. 69-70.

21. Quoted by Miller, *Images or Shadows,* pp. 69-70.

22. *Major Writers of America* (New York: Harcourt Brace, 1962), I, 136.

23. *Magnalia Christi Americana* (Hartford, 1853), II, 366.

24. Ibid.

25. Ibid., p. 367.

26. "Personal Narrative," *MWA,* I, 137-138.

27. Ibid.

28. Jonathan Edwards, *A Treatise Concerning Religious Affections,* ed. John E. Smith (New Haven: Yale University Press), pp. 270-271. For a discussion of Edwards' idea of beauty and the philosophical foundations for his psychology, see Roland Delattre, *Beauty and Sensibility in the Thought of Jonathan Edwards* (New Haven: Yale University Press, 1968).

29. Ibid., p. 271.

30. Ibid., p. 274.

31. Ibid., pp. 272-273.

11. From Edwards to Emerson and Thoreau: A Revaluation

1. Perry Miller, *Errand into The Wilderness* (New York: Harper and Row, 1962), p. 184.

2. Ibid., p. 185.

3. Clarence Faust and Thomas H. Johnson, eds. (New York: Hill and Wang, 1959), p. 102.

4. Faust and Johnson, pp. 103-104.

5. See Roland Delattre, *Beauty and Sensibility in the Thought of Jonathan Edwards* (New Haven: Yale University Press, 1968), and John E. Smith, Introduction, *A Treatise Concerning Religious Affections* (New Haven: Yale University Press, 1959).

6. Ralph Waldo Emerson, *Nature,* in *Major Writers of America,* ed. Perry Miller (New York: Harcourt Brace, 1964) I, 493.

7. Ibid., p. 495.

8. Henry David Thoreau, *Journal,* VIII, 306-307, entry for July 16, 1851.

9. Sacvan Bercovitch, "The Image of America: From Hermeneutics to Symbolism," an address delivered to the New England American Studies Association, April 5, 1972, and published in *The Bucknell Review,* 20 (fall 1972).

10. Ibid., p. 9.

11. Ralph Waldo Emerson, from "Nature" in *Selections from Ralph Waldo Emerson,* ed. Stephen Whicher (Cambridge: Houghton Mifflin, 1960), p. 39.

12. *Emerson,* p. 41.

13. *Emerson,* p. 168; see also Frederick Lorch, "Thoreau and the Organic Principle in Poetry," *PMLA,* 63 (1938), 286-302; Joseph J. Moldenhauer, "Images of Circularity in Thoreau's Prose," *Texas Studies in Language and Literature* (Spring 1959), pp. 249-263.

14. Henry David Thoreau, "Walking" in *Excursions* (New York: Meridan Books, 1962), p. 162.

15. Ibid., p. 175.

16. Ibid., p. 207.

17. Henry David Thoreau, *Walden* (New York: Twayne, 1962), p. 25.

18. Henry David Thoreau, *Excursions,* p. 110.

19. For a thorough discussion of Thoreau's use of this archetypal symbol, see: Joseph J. Moldenhauer, "Images of Circularity in Thoreau's Prose," in *Texas Studies in Literature and Language* (Spring 1959), pp. 249-263.

20. Henry David Thoreau, *A Week on the Concord and Merrimack Rivers* (Cambridge, 1867), p. 15.

21. J. Lyndon Shanley, *The Making of Walden* (Chicago: University of Chicago Press, 1957).

22. Sherman Paul, *The Shores of America* (Urbana: University of Illinois Press, 1958), p. 183.

23. Shanley, *The Making of Walden,* p. 60.

24. Ibid., p. 67.

25. William Drake, "Walden" in *Thoreau,* ed. Sherman Paul (Englewood Cliffs, N.J., 1962), p. 90.

INDEX

Most works are indexed under their authors, and short titles are frequently used.